THE POWER OF INTERNAL MARTIAL ARTS

THE POWER OF INTERNAL MARTIAL ARTS

Combat Secrets of Ba Gua, Tai Chi, and Hsing-I

BRUCE KUMAR FRANTZIS

North Atlantic Books
Berkeley, California

A Clarity Press Book

The Power of Internal Martial Arts:
Combat Secrets of Ba Gua, Tai Chi, and Hsing-I

For information contact:
B. K. Frantzis Energy Arts®
P. O. Box 99
Fairfax, CA 94978-0099, U. S. A.

First Clarity Press Printing, 1998

Distributed by
North Atlantic Books
P. O. Box 12327
Berkeley, California 94712

The Power of Internal Martial Arts is sponsored by the Society for the study of Native Arts and Sciences, a nonprofit educational corporation whose goals are to develop an educational and crosscultural perspective linking various scientific, social, and artistic fields; to nurture a holistic view of arts, sciences, humanities, and healing; and to publish and distribute literature on the relationship of mind, body, and nature.

Library of Congress Cataloging-in-Publication Data

Frantzis, Bruce Kumar
    The power of internal martial arts : combat secrets of ba gua, tai chi, and hsing-i / Bruce Kumar Frantzis.
       p.   cn
    ISBN 1-55643-253-4
       1. Martial arts--Psychological aspects.   I. Title.
    GV1102.7.p75F73   1998
       796.8--dc21   97-21285
                                                                         CIP

1 2 3 4 5 6 7 8 9 10

Printed in the United States of America

Dedication

I dedicate this book to the martial arts practitioners of all methods, whose honest effort is helping to preserve and nourish the living traditions of the martial arts for future generations.

Note to the Reader

All **boldface terms** in this book that appear in the general text and the feature boxes are defined in the main alphabetized glossary located in the back of the book. For the reader's convenience, there is also—in the general text only—a sidebar glossary that defines boldface terms in the margin of the page on which they first occur. This sidebar glossary gives brief definitions that often are expanded in the main glossary.

The practice of martial movements and the meditative arts may carry risks. Individuals with medical, mental, or emotional difficulties should consult their healthcare provider before doing these practices.

About the Author

Bruce Kumar Frantzis has spent more than 35 years studying Oriental healing practices, martial arts, and meditation. A lineage disciple in the Taoist arts, Mr. Frantzis teaches the internal martial arts, primarily in North America and Europe. He also instructs in those Taoist techniques that heal, increase vitality, and enhance spiritual growth. He is one of two disciples of the late Taoist Sage Liu Hung Chieh. Liu formally passed on his lineage to Mr. Frantzis, empowering him to teach this ancient body of knowledge to the Western world. In addition to Liu Hung Chieh, B. K. Frantzis studied with a number of other renowned Oriental internal martial arts adepts whose knowledge he combined and demystified for all those interested in this intriguing area of the martial arts. Mr. Frantzis is the author of *Opening the Energy Gates of Your Body* (North Atlantic Books, Berkeley, California, 1993).

CONTENTS

3 SIMILARITIES AND DIFFERENCES

4 TAI CHI

5   HSING-I

A PERSONAL ODYSSEY
THROUGH THE MARTIAL ARTS

Northern Shaolin 255

8 USING ENERGY TO HEAL

A PERSONAL ODYSSEY
THROUGH THE MARTIAL ARTS

**Martial Artists and
Aging** 288

APPENDICES

AUTHOR'S ACKNOWLEDGEMENT

Many people in the martial arts graciously gave their time and effort to this book as it developed. I would like to thank the following reviewers for their feedback and advice:

FRANK ALLEN
Director and Chief Instructor
Wu Tang Physical Culture Association
New York, New York

BERNARD LANGAN
Senior Instructor
Taoist Internal Arts Studio
Berkeley, California

HAL LEHRMAN
Head Instructor
Aikido of Park Slope
Brooklyn, New York

CLARENCE LU
Assistant Director
Wu Tang Physical Culture Association
Creator of Mandarin for the Martial Arts
Language Program
New York, New York

ALAN PEATFIELD
Tai Chi Instructor
Thirty-year Practitioner of Asian Martial Arts
Dublin, Ireland

ERIC PETERS
Tai Chi and Chi Gung Instructor
Martha's Vineyard, Massachusetts

RACHEL ROBINSON
Third Degree Black Belt, Kempo Karate
Haverhill, Massachusetts

BILL RYAN
Director
with Senior Staff
Brookline Tai Chi
Brookline, Massachusetts

ERIC SCHNEIDER
Founder and Chief Instructor
Northeastern Tai Chi Chuan Association
New York, New York

MICHAEL A. WIECK
Hsing-I (I Chuan) Instructor
San Francisco/Los Angeles, California

Special appreciation goes to Stuart Kenter for his invaluable editing and for his work in presenting complex ancient Oriental knowledge in a way that makes it clear and accessible to modern readers.

Credits

DEVELOPMENTAL EDITOR/COPY EDITOR
Stuart Kenter

EDITORIAL INPUT
Caroline Frantzis

COVER PHOTOS
Mark Thayer

INTERIOR AND COVER DESIGN
Janet Bollow

PREFACE

Carrying preconceived notions into mortal combat is a limited reality that might well get you killed.

Giving up, at any given moment, what we hold to be the truth is the most difficult task for the warrior, but surrender is not an option when in a life-and-death situation. Everyday civil life is not a stream of life-and-death events, but it is a challenge to yielding and to investigating that which is before us.

The wielding of power is a definite part of the warrior's undertaking, and power is the ability to act in the interest of making change. Preconceived notions limit our ability to change, and the inability to adapt through change hinders our growth. Growth is a process of surrendering, without quitting, that which we have built ourselves upon. It means coming out of our personal armaments and reconnoitering the impinging peripheries of possible new ideas.

Fortunately, most martial art practice does not entail the actuality of killing. Therefore, there is space and time to lessen one's guard and drop one's perceptions to allow a different belief to enter into our personal world of experience. If we hear the land outside our own is different and unimportant, do we accept this belief as our reality or do we visit the terrain and see for ourselves?

The soldier's battle training emphasizes the aggressive animal instinct that goes beyond ordinary rage. The soldier is taught to "allow no doubt to enter the mind." The fact of the matter is that there is no doubt life will surprise us regardless of how hard we cling to beliefs about the world and ourselves. The tighter we grip life to impose the unyielding hardness of our thinking, the more life's events will try to shake us loose of limited perceptions. Guaranteed, we will be shaken to the very roots of the foundations we conceive and perceive as our "identity" in this mundane world. Everyday, if we are truly on a path of martial growth, we will be openly challenged by our own degree of openness to the unknown, the personally untested. The inability to have an inquiring mind will not allow us to observe the true nature of the battlefield. The ultimate battle lies in the plane of our internal existence. Do we blindly accept? Do we blindly reject? Do we blindly know all there is? Our eyes must be opened wide to begin to comprehend the vastness within ourselves and the world's makeup.

As warriors, we have an obligation to surrender to the fact that we could be limited in all we know and have programmed ourselves to be. We must recognize our limits in daily civil existence, be they positions of unyielding power due to fear, positions of absolute authority based on partial knowledge, or positions of everyday social interaction based on what we seek to present to the world. All these lives are the sum reality of our internal operations. If we cannot move out of who and what we believe life to be, we are ordinary soldiers following marching orders of the ego.

The good fight is having to recognize the mechanics of our inner need to be right and the egotistical rebellions we project on the unknown and the feared. Recognizing this inner personal functioning as a limit to the ideas of life and death allows us the experiences of humility and the warrior's understanding of duty to unlimited growth. We must make room in our belief strategies to survive the wars we create.

In my personal experience of everything war can be, I carried from the battlefields to civil life the epitome of unyielding hardness and battle rage. I carried this aspect of life into the dojo and my training. I was so physically taut and mentally hardened, conditions that served me well in mortal combat, that I became ill. Training with Bruce Kumar Frantzis demonstrated to me that hardness and mind-set in the martial arts was limited. In my thirty years of study in the martial arts, I have never met another man with the completeness of knowledge Bruce Frantzis demonstrates. His is authentic. Not only can he demonstrate with great skill the internal power possible in fighting, he is a great teacher of the healing capacities of chi. His ability to transmit the Taoist meditative practices has brought great and comfortable change to my life without my having to give up the ability to deliver the goods when combat becomes mortal.

The knowledge in this book is an elixir containing all things possible within the internal martial arts. I strongly recommend Bruce's training to anyone who seeks a complete system of fighting, healing, and meditation in the internal martial arts.

Lee Burkins
U. S. Army Special Forces Combat Veteran
Montrose, Colorado

Many Chinese and Japanese names of prominent martial artists recur throughout this book. Given the unfamiliarity of Oriental names to Western readers, a who's who is provided here for easy reference. Chinese names are usually written with the surname (family name) first and Japanese names with the surname last. Here, all names are listed with the surname first. Alternate transliterations sometimes follow in parentheses. Many of the people on this list are direct lineage students of others on the list, as well as descendants of others who hold a family martial art lineage.

Please note that, although many of the teachers encountered in this book may be considered masters or even grandmasters of their respective martial art, such titles are not being used in front of their names in this work.

Bai Hua (Peh Hua) A student of Liu Hung Chieh in hsing-i, ba gua, and a student of Lin Du Ying in the Old Yang style of tai chi. Bai Hua is a Taoist who has specialized in internal alchemy. One of the author's principal internal martial arts teachers.

Chang Chao-Tung (also known as Chang Chang K'uei, Zhang Zhan Kui) Wang Shu Jin's primary teacher. A major figure in the hsing-i lineage and a ba gua student of Tung Hai Chuan and Cheng Ting Hua.

Chang Chun-Feng The person who brought the 64-posture method of the post-birth ba gua system of Gao Yisheng from Mainland China to Taiwan. Teacher of Hung I Hsiang and his brother, Hung I Min.

Chang I Chung The author's first tai chi teacher in Tokyo. One of Wang Shu Jin's senior students who served as assistant teacher when Wang was in Japan.

Chang San Fen According to one legend, the Taoist Immortal who created tai chi chuan from watching a fight between a snake and a crane.

Chen Fa Ke (Ch'en Fa K'e) The first major Chen style tai chi teacher of the twentieth century to leave his ancestral village and come to Beijing to teach.

Chen I Ren An important hsing-i teacher in Hong Kong, and one of the two people who brought the internal martial art of liu he ba fa to Hong Kong.

Chen Man-ching (Zheng Manqing) Teacher who first introduced the author to tai chi chuan. One of the first high-level tai chi masters from China to teach in the earliest days of tai chi's introduction into America, in New York City.

Chen Pan Ling (Ch'en P'an Ling) An important figure in pre-World War II internal martial arts in Mainland China and afterwards also in Taiwan. Tai chi teacher to both Wang Shu Jin and Hung I Hsiang.

Chen Wang Ting (Ch'en Wang T'ing) Creator of tai chi chuan, according to one theory of the origin of this art.

Cheng Ting Hua (Ch'eng T'ing Hua) One of the principal students of Tung Hai Chuan, the founder of the martial art of ba gua chang. His line is a widespread school of ba gua.

Cheng You Long (Ch'eng You Lung) Cheng Ting Hua's son. Liu Hung Chieh's first ba gua teacher, who formally initiated Liu into the ba gua lineage.

Chi Chi Guang A famous ancient Chinese general whose training manual of military techniques formed the basis of 29 of the 32 physical movements of the original Chen style of tai chi.

Chuan You (Ch'uan You, Quan You) Yang Lu Chan's best nonfamily student. Co-founder of the Wu style of tai chi along with his son, Wu Jien Chuan. His line is one of the three main branches of the Wu style.

Confucius (usually called kong zi or k'ong tzu but also kongfuzi/k'ong futzi)   The ancient philosopher upon whose thought the foundation of China's traditional secular culture is built. His concepts strongly influenced social interactions, etiquette, customs, and the hierarchical nature of most of the martial arts of China and Japan.

Dai Long Bang (Tai Lung Pang)   The teacher of Li Luo Neng, the modern father of hsing-i, whose students and their students spread hsing-i throughout China in the nineteenth and twentieth centuries.

Feng Zhi Qiang (Feng Zhiqiang)   The author's Chen style tai chi teacher in Beijing. The last serious student of Chen Fa Ke in Push Hands. Feng is renowned throughout China for his abilities in Push Hands, and has created a well-respected Chen style short form.

Fu Chen Sung (Fu Zhen Sung)   One of the five martial art tigers of Southern China who was a ba gua and tai chi specialist. He created the combination Fu style tai chi form.

Gao Yisheng (Gao I Sheng) Teacher of the 64-technique post-birth method of ba gua that passed from his student, Chang Chun-Feng, to Hung I Hsiang and Hung I Min.

Goto   Senior student of Kenichi Sawai of Taiki-Ken, the I Chuan school of hsing-i.

Gu I Jai (Ku Yu Cheung) One of the five martial art tigers of Southern China who was a hsing-i specialist. He is known in the West through the picture of him breaking a waist-high stack of bricks with a single iron palm strike.

Guo Yun Shen (Kuo Yun Shen)   Student of Li Luo Neng, Guo is one of the most important figures in hsing-i. Two of his students formed major branches of hsing-i—Sun Lu Tang (the synthesized method) and Wang Hsiang Zai (I Chuan)

Han Hsing Yuan   The author's I Chuan teacher in Hong Kong. One of Wang Hsiang Zai's four main disciples.

Hao Wei Zhen (Hau Wei-Chen)   Person from whom the name of the small frame tai chi style derives its name. The tai chi teacher of Sun Lu Tang, who created the Sun style combination tai chi style.

Huang Hsi I   One of the author's principal teachers in internal martial arts, as well as chi gung tui na. One of Hung I Hsiang's top hsing-i students, who subsequently became one of the finest chi healers of his generation in Taiwan.

Hung I Hsiang   One of the author's main teachers in internal martial arts. A principal teacher of ba gua and hsing-i in Taiwan from the 1950s to the 1980s. Student of Chang Chun Feng and Chen Pan Ling.

Hung I Min   Senior student of Chang Chun Feng along with his brother, Hung I Hsiang.

Jiang Fa   A mysterious fugitive who, according to one theory, originally brought tai chi to the Chen village.

Ju Wen Bao   Ba gua teacher of Liu Hung Chieh. The first person to teach Liu Tung Hai Chuan's methods of Taoist meditation.

Kanazawa, H.   An important master of Japanese Shotokan karate known for his exceptional technique, his fighting spirit, and for winning the All-Japan Karate Championships with a broken arm in the 1950s.

Kawashima   Senior student of Chang I Chung in Tokyo.

Kung Pao Tien (Gong Bao Tian)   Ba gua student of Yin Fu.

Kuo Lien Ying (Guo Lien Ying)   One of the first high-level tai chi masters to teach in the earliest days of tai chi's introduction into America, in San Francisco. Creator of the Kuan Ping combination tai chi style.

Lee, Bruce   A famous martial arts film star in the 1960s and 1970s. Creator of the Jeet Kune Do style of martial arts. Student of Yip Man.

Li Luo Neng (also known as Li Neng Jan or Li Nengran) A seminal figure of modern hsing-i whose line of students spread hsing-i throughout China in the nineteenth and twentieth centuries.

Li Tsung I (Li T'sung I, Li Cunyi) Important figure in the hsing-i lineage. His collaboration with ba gua's Cheng Ting Hua resulted in a commingling of these two important internal martial arts systems.

Liang Jr Pang (Liang Chih P'ang) An important hsing-i teacher in Hong Kong, and one of the two teachers who originally brought the internal martial art of liu he ba fa to Hong Kong.

Liang Tung Ts'ai (also known as T. T. Liang) The author's teacher of the New Yang style of tai chi. Cheng Man-ching's student and a seminal teacher of tai chi in America.

Lin Du Ying Bai Hua's teacher of the Old Yang style of tai chi, as well as the author's teacher in Xiamen (Amoy) in China's Fujian (Fukien) province. A student of Yang Pan Hou's most important disciples, Tien Chau Ling and Wu Hui Chuan.

Ling Shan Yang Lu Chan's best student in the soft energy phase of tai chi chuan.

Liu Hung Chieh Tai chi student of Wu Jien Chuan and member of the original Beijing ba gua school. Also a Taoist meditation master. The author's last and principal teacher of the internal martial arts and Taoist meditation.

Lo Te Hsiu Hung I Hsiang's best student of Gao I Sheng's linear 64-hands method of post-birth ba gua. One the finest ba gua adepts of his generation in Taiwan.

Ma Gui (also known as Ma Shr Ching or Ma Shi Ching) One of the "Big Four" students of ba gua founder Tung Hai Chuan. An important teacher of Liu Hung Chieh.

Pao, Jack A ba gua instructor and training partner of the author in Hong Kong.

Sawai, Kenichi Author's hsing-i teacher in Tokyo. A student of I Chuan's founder, Wang Hsiang Zai, in China for 10 years. Sawaii called his hsing-i system "Taiki-Ken."

Shr Liu (Shi Liu) One of the main ba gua students of Tung Hai Chuan. Specialized in the Single Palm Change.

Sun Hsi Kun (Sun Xikun) Student of Cheng You Lung. Sun wrote an important book on ba gua in Chinese and taught in Hong Kong and Taiwan after the Chinese civil war.

Sun Lu Tang A significant figure in the history of all three internal martial arts. Sun Lu Tang wrote the first book on the internal arts in Chinese. The primary student of hsing-i's Guo Yun Shen and an important student of Cheng Ting Hua. Founder of the Sun style of tai chi chuan.

Sung Shr Rong (Sung Shirong) An accomplished adept in both the hsing-i and ba gua lineages.

Tan Hsiu Fa Shr A patriarch of the Tien Tai (Tian Tai) school of Chinese Mahayana Buddhism. Liu Hung Chieh's principal Buddhist meditation master.

Tien Chau Ling (Tian Zhaoling) Principal student of Yang Pan Hou and the Old Yang style. One of the top tai chi fighters of his generation. Teacher of Lin Du Ying.

Tu Hsin Wu (Du Xinwu) Renowned for his kicking abilities, Du was an important figure in the martial arts of Northern China in the early part of the twentieth century. A practitioner of Natural Gate Boxing, he was Wan Lai Sheng's principal teacher. Tu also briefly taught Liu Hung Chieh.

Tung Hai Chuan (Dong Haichuan) The modern founder of the martial art of ba gua chang, who taught during the latter half of the nineteenth century.

Tung Hu Ling Tung Ying Chieh's son Hu Ling was one of the first high-level tai chi masters from China to teach in Hawaii during the earliest days of tai chi's introduction into America.

Tung Ying Chieh (Dong Yingjie)   Principal student of tai chi's Yang Chen Fu. Tung and his family descendants were instrumental in spreading the New Yang style of tai chi throughout Southeast Asia and the United States.

Ueshiba, Morihei   Author's teacher of aikido. Known in Japanese as O-Sensei, or Great Teacher, Ueshiba is the founder of the modern Japanese internal energy-based martial art of aikido.

Wan Lai Sheng   One of the five martial art tigers of Southern China, who practiced Natural Gate Boxing. Tu Hsin Wu's main student, and colleague of Liu Hung Chieh.

Wang Chun   Yang Lu Chan's best student of tai chi's hard energy.

Wang Shu Jin (Wang Shu Chin)   One of the author's principal internal martial arts teachers and one of the most important practitioners who brought hsing-i and ba gua to Taiwan from Mainland China. Student of Chang Chao Tung in hsing-i and ba gua, Wang Xiang Zhai in I Chuan, and Chen Pan Ling in tai chi.

Wang Tsung Yueh (Wang Zongyue)   According to one theory, the Taoist who originally brought tai chi to the Chen village, creating modern tai chi chuan. Said to be the principal author of the Tai Chi Classics.

Wang Xiang Zhai (Wang Hsiang Chai)   Last student of hsing-i's Guo Yun Shen and founder of the I Chuan school of hsing-i. Teacher of the author's three I Chuan instructors: Wang Shu Jin, Kenichi Sawai, and Han Hsing Yuan.

Wei Shao Tang   Taught the author and T. T. Liang the Half-Step Praying Mantis Method in Taiwan.

Weng Hsien Ming   One of Hung I Hsiang's senior students who won the all-Taiwan full-contact competitions three times in a row.

Wu Hui Chuan   Main student of Yang Pan Hou and the Old Yang style. One of the top tai chi fighters of his generation. Teacher of Lin Du Ying.

Wu Gong I and **Wu Gong Zao**   Sons of Wu Jien Chuan. These brothers created another branch of the Wu style of tai chi.

Wu Jien Chuan (Wu Chien Ch'uan, Wu Jianquan)   Chuan You's son, also commonly known as the co-founder of Wu style tai chi, along with his father. His teaching line accounts for the majority of Wu style practitioners. Liu Hung Chieh's principal tai chi teacher.

Wu Yu Hsiang (Wu Yuxiang)   Student of Yang Lu Chan, who returned to the Chen village and created an important small-frame style of tai chi. A significant figure in the literary tradition of tai chi.

THE YANG FAMILY

Yang Lu Chan (Yang Lu Ch'an)   "Yang the Invincible" was the founder of Yang style tai chi. Most renowned for his formidable tai chi fighting skills. This is the Yang who brought tai chi out of the secrecy of the Chen village into China's awareness and from there to the rest of the world.

Yang Pan Hou (Yang Ban Hou)   Yan Lu Chan's son, the second generation of the Yang family tai chi teaching tradition. The most important tai chi teaching figure of his generation and, along with Wu's father, the primary teacher of Wu Jien Chuan.

Yang Shao Hou   A third-generation Yang known for his superb fighting skills and bad temper. He died young.

Yang Cheng Fu (Yang Ch'eng Fu)   A third-generation Yang, the source of the New Yang style. The form he created, with its multitude of variations, is the basic tai chi form done by the vast majority of the world's Yang style tai chi practitioners.

Yang Shou Jung (also known as Yang Shou-chung or Yang Shouzhong) A fourth-generation Yang, and Yang Chen Fu's oldest son. He was based in Hong Kong and taught the author there.

Yin Fu One of the principal students of Tung Hai Chuan, the founder of the martial art of ba gua chang. His line represents a school of ba gua that is widely practiced.

Yip Man Main teacher of the Hong Kong branch of the martial art of Wing Chun, the other school being centered in Fatshan, Canton province. Teacher of Bruce Lee.

Yue Fei (Yueh Fei) The renowned ancient Chinese general whom legend credits as the founder of hsing-i chuan.

SCHOOLS OF THE INTERNAL MARTIAL ARTS MENTIONED IN THIS BOOK

Tai Chi
Original Chen style
Yang style
   Old Yang style
   New Yang style
Hao style
Wu style
Combination styles
   Sun Lu Tang
   Chen Pan Ling
   Kuan Ping
   Fu style
Family, Secret, and Lost Lineages

Hsing-I
Shansi style
Hebei style
I Chuan (also known as Da Cheng Chuan, Da Cheng Quan, or Ta Cheng Ch'uan)
Honan style also known as the Muslim style

Ba Gua
Cheng Ting Hua—Dragon style
Yin Fu—Willow Leaf Palm style
Shr Liu
Sung Shr Rong
Gao Yisheng—64 technique post-birth method

INTRODUCTION

As a boy, I was fairly awkward physically until, in 1961, I began training in **judo** at the age of twelve and **karate** soon thereafter. Eventually, through consistent practice in a variety of martial arts, coordination came to me, more through a striving for martial effectiveness than from an explicit desire to move gracefully. I held a classic samurai battlefield feeling about technique: Did a martial application work in actual fighting? How well? In what way and under what dangerous conditions would it save me from injury?

While maintaining a peripheral interest in the health and meditative aspects of martial arts throughout my youth, I shunned its aesthetics. Who cared whether the movements were beautiful or ugly? Beautiful movements may or may not be martially functional. Martially workable techniques may or may not look good. Consequently, as a young man, my competitive urges were reserved for winning sparring matches. Form contests meant nothing. It was the deep desire for combat competence that drove me to train long hours daily in multiple martial arts for decades. Initially, this passion brought black belts in judo, karate, **jujitsu,** and **aikido** before I was nineteen. Then, in a personal odyssey to discover the very roots of martial arts, I traveled to Japan for intense training in karate, judo, and aikido for several years at the black-belt level, and studied full time in China for another ten years to deepen the process. It was the exposure to the internal martial arts of China that changed me irrevocably.

In 1968, after completing a year of grueling karate training with the team that won the All-Japan University Championships, I went on vacation to Taiwan. There, I began to study the internal martial art of **ba gua** with Wang Shu Jin. Shortly thereafter, I studied **hsing-i** in Tokyo with Kenichi Sawai and tai chi with Wang's student, Chang I Chung.

JUDO
A Japanese external martial art based on wrestling, joint-locks, submission holds, and chokes.

KARATE
The Japanese external martial art based primarily on kicks, punches, hand strikes, foot sweeps, and a few throws.

JUJITSU
The unarmed-combat external martial art of the samurai; based primarily on throws, joint-locks, submission holds, and chokes.

AIKIDO
A Japanese internal energy-based martial art.

BA GUA
One of China's three main internal martial arts.

HSING-I
A Chinese internal martial art that uses the mind to create its fighting movements.

1

SHORIN RYU
A major Okinawan hard style of karate.

WHITE CRANE
A martial art that mimics the actions of the bird called the white crane.

WING CHUN
A southern Chinese martial art based on hand strikes.

MONKEY BOXING
A martial art system that mimics the movements of a monkey.

CHINESE WRESTLING
China's traditional martial art of throws.

NORTHERN PRAYING MANTIS
An animal-form Shaolin method that mimics the actions of the praying mantis insect.

EIGHT DRUNKEN IMMORTALS
A martial art whose practitioners mimic the lurching movements of a drunk.

NORTHERN SHAOLIN
A fighting style emphasizing extended body movements.

TAI CHI
One of the three internal martial arts of China; known for its emphasis on softness, slow-motion movement, and sophisticated chi gung methodology.

GUNG FU (KUNG FU)
A generic term normally used for all the external or external/internal Chinese martial arts.

My karate training had run full circle. After **Shorin Ryu** special black-belt karate training in Okinawa in the spring of 1970, my commitment to excel in the punch, kick, and strike martial arts had clearly shifted toward the Chinese styles. At this point, the only real no-nonsense fighting Chinese martial arts I had been introduced to and seriously practiced since that vacation time on Taiwan were internal systems. The journey through internal martial arts during the ensuing decade led me into some side roads of the Chinese external/internal martial arts. Along those ways, I studied **White Crane, Wing Chun, Monkey Boxing, Chinese Wrestling, Northern Praying Mantis, Eight Drunken Immortals,** and **Northern Shaolin.** Two reasons motivated me to put in the supplemental hard work to throw these external/internal martial methods into the mix when my main goal was to master ba gua, **tai chi**, and hsing-i. First, it is wise to know what any potential opposition might try on you, and how to counter it. What you remain ignorant about martially can defeat you. Second, from the viewpoint of attack, cross-research into other styles can provide knowledge of gross techniques that help to develop the next (and more refined) levels of the internal martial arts. I operated on the principle of "assume nothing." The information gained from cross-training gave insights into how to recognize gaps that could be exploited in both external martial arts and the internal systems.

Excellent teachers in wide-ranging Chinese martial disciplines were almost always available at certain urban centers in the Orient, a situation not then existing in the West. Taking advantage of this unique opportunity, I began to understand how the fighting applications of the internal and external systems were both similar and different. I also wanted to grasp the complete potential of my prior love, karate, to determine how far it was capable of going. The **gung fu** arts satisfied my need to engage in sparring, especially when there were no internal martial arts practitioners available with whom to play and trade blows and throws.

It was personally fulfilling to learn and use new martial techniques and perspectives while simultaneously analyzing their various physical, emotional, and strategic strong and weak points within different tactical situations. This comparative exercise freed me from the emotional need to have the all-too-common fixed partisan belief that "my style is the best," without knowing the cold realities of what else is out there. My interest was in growing and being effective, not in protecting an emotional investment in the superiority of any martial art system. After all, it is ultimately the person who fights, not the martial art system.

Learning different external/internal methods provided the context to raise useful questions about comparative fighting applications. Such inquiries led to a serious deepening of my primary ongoing training and focus on the internal martial arts. If asked politely, internal fighting masters will often answer questions pertaining to comparative techniques.

However, if not asked, they just as often remain silent on this point and about how they would unravel the methodology of a system not their own. If you show them what another approach entails, chances are they will say something on the order of, "Well, we don't do that," and then will explain why, or, "We do that, but differently," and then go on to demonstrate the whys, wherefores, and cautions involved in the technique.

I became fascinated with the philosophical question of what, at the core, "martial arts" are as a whole. This inquiry ultimately ended in a realization that martial arts are more than just a mere collection of multi-faceted moves and techniques for vanquishing an opponent. This aware-ness occurred during the final round of my martial studies in Beijing with the extraordinary **Taoist** adept, Liu Hung Chieh, whom I met in 1981, and who, over the ensuing several years, showed me how healing, spirituality, and the martial arts converged into a unified whole. At that time, when I was in my early thirties, my attention became concentrated completely on the internal arts.

This book meets an obligation I have felt for a long time toward the martial arts community and will, I hope, incline readers, especially younger readers, toward the more spiritual side of the internal martial arts. Here, I would like to acknowledge and profoundly thank all my teachers who so kindly shared themselves and their valuable information with me. Without their willingness to reveal knowledge, this book would never exist.

TAO/TAOISM
The Way. The practical mystic religion of China whose concepts include the yin-yang play of opposites, spiritual natu-ralness, spontaneity, Chinese medicine, and the art of strategy and war.

The author performs a movement of Dragon and Tiger chi gung, which is a Shaolin Temple method that was influenced by Taoism. This motion is done for health to benefit the heart and for fighting to produce tremendous striking power.

ANIMAL, HUMAN, AND SPIRITUAL

1

Three Approaches to Martial Arts

The range of martial arts practiced across the globe is fairly wide. When you look behind the differences, though, at the roots of the practices themselves, three distinct approaches emerge: fighting like an animal, fighting as a human being, and fighting as a way to become an evolved spiritual being. Consistent martial arts training of any kind can either reinforce some animal aspects of human nature or help human beings realize their spiritual potential. The attitudes of practitioners, along with the specifics of how they train, will naturally incline them in one direction or the other.

As humans, we may have inherited from our remote primate ancestors a deeply ingrained need to engage in behaviors of domination and submission. Such displays occur often in society, individually on both physical and psychological levels—as within competitive groups from sports to business—and in the political arena, where disputes and wars have been a constant in human history. By its very nature, the field of martial arts deals directly with this area of human existence, not by sublimating our natural violent tendencies, but by delving into them. Ideally, the practice of martial arts initially gives individuals a visceral understanding of the core causes of our inclination toward violence and, ultimately, allows them to transcend this force.

In martial arts, the door is always open, inviting adherents deeper down into their own animalistic impulses and/or up along a continuum into their higher spiritual possibilities. More humanizing practices in martial arts can and do train people to rely on reason, to move beyond the instinctual flaring of violence-causing emotions. This capability is especially valuable now when we need all the help we can get to handle the intensifying stress stemming from the extremely rapid pace of our supertechnological world.

SAMURAI
The warrior knights of ancient Japan characterized by the top-knot hair style, and the wearing of two swords, which they were expert at using.

BUJITSU
Japanese martial arts whose sole goal is the development of efficient fighting and killing techniques.

BUDO
Japanese martial arts whose goal is to simultaneously cultivate martial technique, character, and spirituality.

From one perspective, it could be argued that all martial arts have, at the level of pragmatic fighting, been systematically diminished by the advent and development of firearms, from the single-shot musket to fully automatic weapons. Regardless, the martial arts can and do provide powerful tools for refining both the character and spirituality of human beings, just as they did after the Meiji Restoration in Japan in the latter half of the nineteenth-century. Then, the **samurai** were legally barred from wearing swords and engaging in fights to the death. The Japanese martial arts that focused purely on the no-nonsense science of efficiently killing enemies were called **bujitsu** or "martial technique." The original Chinese word *tao* (of the Taoist spiritual tradition of Lao Tse and the *I Ching*) is pronounced *do* in Japanese. Thus, Japanese martial schools that concentrated on teaching efficient technique *as well as* on developing the spiritual character of the participants were called **budo,** or "martial way."

All martial arts applied in battle are only as good as the person using them. Martial arts are more than just fighting an opponent; they can become a way to defeat the enemies of life—poor health, low self-esteem, stress, and the lack of a spiritual center. In these respects, those martial arts that worked well in the agricultural and early industrialized eras, when people earned their bread from their labor, may not be as useful in the current high-tech world, where it is our nerves and brain cells that are being stressed, not our muscles. Today, it is wise to look at the animal, human, and spiritual aspects of martial arts for what they are able to do for us on the battlefield of contemporary life.

THE ANIMAL APPROACH

Obviously, the subject of animal behavior is huge. Considerable scientific knowledge, both experimental and observational (as well as anecdotal), has been collected to date, and research continues. With all this effort, we probably have discovered only a fraction of what there is to know. Theories abound, some attempting to link animal fighting behavior specifically with the violence that emerges from human beings. Let it be very clear that the discussion here does not hold or suggest that violence is a purely animalistic act. Rather, the approach described is restricted to the particular situation where a single animal is challenged by another individual animal or a pack of animals for whatever reasons, and exhibits one or another of the classic behavioral responses of fight, flight, or freeze. There are wide-ranging sociobiological and philosophical debates on the question of how the violence of animals relates to the violence of humans, especially in such areas as territorial disputes, sexual rivalry, gain and loss, and perhaps ritualistic behaviors. This chapter has nothing to do with this debate. The concern here is only what happens to animals and humans at the instant they are engaged in actual physical combat.

In the main, the image of the fighting martial arts presented to the general public through various media conveys the idea of controlled violence—gnashing of teeth, tensing of muscles, projected anger. In films and stills of American, European, Japanese, and Hong Kong martial arts heroes (and all too often in real life), we are treated to the spectacle of a fighter making animal-like sounds, with twisted facial expressions and body muscles coiled. All these effects clearly try to evoke the frenzy of a dangerous and cornered animal. After all this drama, the fighter then frequently exhibits a peaceful demeanor. This basic, animal-kingdom, glandular-based display serves to motivate many martial artists. It represents a strong energetic force. In fact, throughout human history, invoking this animal response has been one of the easier ways to stir people to physical violence.

In primitive times, when a saber-toothed tiger arrived at the campfire, the human glandular system was immediately activated for fighting or fleeing. This reaction was a pure survival mechanism that probably predated human intellect. We now call it the "fight or flight (run away)" reflex. Such encounters left an imprint deep within the human psyche. The presence of that imprint is there to help us survive, yet many civilized people have a psychological resistance to the idea that it is permissible to physically hurt another in order to preserve one's own personal security. (The experience of fighting another human being face-to-face is a far cry from the safety of pushing a button to kill someone in a video game.)

Many martial arts utilize the "animal" adrenal response to activate and develop a practitioner's motion and physical strength. When an individual directly confronts the fear that violence normally provokes, the greatest obstacle to using any learned self-defense techniques is inhibition and paralysis. By practicing at length to bring the adrenals "on line," a martial artist prepares for acting under pressure, predominantly by turning into the strongest, nastiest animal around. In any arena where the physical attributes of strength, speed, and endurance are paramount, this approach is reasonable. However, in our modern electronic age, where the opponent is unprecedented stress and the illnesses that accompany it, the animal approach may be counterproductive.

If you continuously practice setting your glands on fire to motivate yourself in fight-or-flight situations, you risk carrying this pattern into other areas of your life. Sometimes this transference is useful, as when doing manual labor, for instance. In this situation, your whole body is involved, and when the physical action is over, it's over. This is a natural closure. The operating principles of external martial arts generally draw on this approach.

The Early Emphasis on Karate and Aikido

 I did not, as a boy of twelve, begin the study of judo and karate for sport, for self-confidence, or for spiritual reasons, but purely to gain an ability to protect myself from the real possibility of harm from New York City's violent element. My interests soon widened to include jujitsu, where I was first introduced to healing and meditation through the practice of **shiatsu massage** and **Zen.** (My first two-week sitting Zen retreat took place in my early teens.) Around this time, a neighbor who was a black-belt holder in judo mentioned a "new" martial art called aikido, which I started learning at once and continued to study, ultimately going on to train with its founder. Having the internal **chi** or **ki** energy propel and motivate body movement was a totally new and fascinating idea to me. I can still vividly remember my first experiences with extending chi from my belly through my torso and out of my fingertips onto the mat during aikido practice. I played with the energetic force emanating from my fingers in nonmartial contexts, using it, for example, to pull my whole body forward to walk faster down the streets of Manhattan when I was a part-time delivery boy.

During high school, I practiced both the **Tomeki** and the **Hombu** styles of aikido, but my commitment to the martial art of karate remained strong. After my Okinawan Shorin Ryu karate instructor left New York City, I continued to train throughout high school both in the Japanese **Goju** and **Shotokan** styles. Passion for karate led me to intensify its study at an advanced level. In fact, the fierce yearning for deeper knowledge of karate, judo, and aikido was why, after graduation, I opted to enroll at Sophia University, Tokyo, rather than continue my education in the West.

SHIATSU
A Japanese massage method in which the fingers press acupuncture points for therapeutic effect.

ZEN
A Buddhist spiritual discipline created by a fusion of Taoist and Buddhist methods.

CHI/KI
The life-force energy upon which acupuncture is based.

TOMEKI
A style of aikido that is an amalgamation of judo and aikido.

HOMBU
The original style of aikido; translates as "headquarters."

GOJU
A karate style that has strong Fukien province Southern Shaolin roots. It has both Okinawan and Japanese branches.

SHOTOKAN
A hard Japanese karate style that emphasizes low stances and long, extended movements.

Much of the time, though, the glands-on-fire method is not so helpful, especially in white collar and skilled technical blue collar occupations. In this case, the situation is really different. Events happen very quickly. The tiger can return to your desk many times in an hour as you perceive a crisis emerging: the deal is falling through, the project must be completed before the deadline, you must cover your back, a major error must be corrected, someone in a critical position is going to judge you, the computer has crashed, and so on. Stress is unrelenting throughout our days. If, through animal-style martial arts training, your glands develop an overt or subliminal habit of firing up every time you want to turn on to maximum performance, you are likely to become overly stressed.

When the fight-or-flight glandular animal reaction is aroused, the blood goes to the outer muscles of the body (which is what you need to fight the tiger) and is therefore taken away from the internal organs and brain. Over time, such continuous activity may damage the digestive system, central nervous system, and the heart and brain functions, since critical blood is not going where it is needed. It's a safe bet to assume that tigers did not visit a Neanderthal cave anywhere near as many times as they metaphorically prowl modern worksites. To avoid being ripped apart by a ferocious beast may be worth having your digestion interrupted once or twice a month, but how many of the rather severe and sometimes deadly stress-related illnesses are worth it? This consideration is especially important for workaholics and for teenagers with raging hormones.

Bear in mind that martial artists of *all* schools, be they internal or external, may functionally end up using the animal approach. Although the "glandular" response lessens with age, older martial artists of any school may still maintain the habit of animalistic explosions. While "setting the glands on fire" is most often associated with the external martial arts, that response is not even always the same there. Ideally, while internal martial artists are not supposed to fire up their glands, what happens is that many do so when they are pressured in combat or even in sparring or set, two-person training exercises.

The next level of martial arts teaches trained fighters to be effective *without* engaging in animal-like behaviors. It does so by tapping into our human potential instead.

THE HUMAN APPROACH

This is the animal way of martial arts: A potentially violent situation arouses animal instinct, which leads to fear, which activates the glands, which raises the heart rate, which engages the body, and it fights. This is the human way of martial arts: A potentially violent situation instantly arouses the human ability to detect how to best handle the situation, without stressful anger, then the mind/body becomes tranquil and highly alert, which allows the focused mind immediately and consciously to activate the chi, which causes the body to engage with speed and power, but without the glands becoming activated or the heartbeat rising or anger being generated. At the human stage of martial arts, it is the intellect that masters the actions of the body, calmly and dispassionately; that is, the decision of how to act is made by your mind, not by your glandular system. (The human approach presumes, of course, that the individual in question wants to rise above his or her animal instincts.)

Although tensing the body/mind to the greatest extent possible may be useful for an animal before it fights for its life, keeping this behavior up all the time drains the joy from modern human life. A cat can relax after a kill; most human beings cannot. Gradually, this sustained animal tension makes the body grow rigid, and, as mentioned, the stress coming from this rigidity can become the dominant context within which a person lives.

The internal martial arts of China deliberately do something else. They work to create, through a highly focused fusion of the intellect and subtle energy of the body, a human form of efficient fighting accomplished without involving glandular instinct. This road is more difficult to follow because the animal way is genetically wired in. In the internal martial arts, it takes time, a lot of frustration, failures, and considerable effort to fuse the consciousness into the body, which is what is required for the human element to overcome the animal instinct and make peace with it. Mastering the internal martial arts necessitates transforming the normal human central nervous system into one that can effectively handle a physically violent confrontation (and/or move into any high-performance mode) instantly, with the capacity to neutralize the effects of repetitive stress. In our modern information age, the ability to remain relaxed under pressure could easily become the best defense against the life-threatening consequences of stress.

A method for transforming the central nervous system into one that can cope with extreme pressures while simultaneously avoiding the disrupting glandular input is the 16-part chi development process (see p. 62) of Taoism. These **nei gung** practices can transform the ordinarily tense human central nervous system into a very fluid one in which there is virtually no time lag between conscious will and the body moving swiftly or delivering power. Ultimately, a great deal of the fighting prowess of internal martial arts derives from the absence of central nervous system lag time. With reaction time virtually nonexistent, the internal martial artist is able to change fighting techniques faster than an opponent can, and is able also to combine the normally separated areas of body power into one integrated, unified, and powerful whole.

NEI GUNG
Internal power. The original chi cultivation (chi gung) system in China invented by the Taoists.

What Is the "Art" of Internal Martial Arts?

Fighting technique evolves into creative art when art involves our putting the imaginative or higher aspects of ourselves into some material or mental form. The creativity to make art must be drawn out of the depths of the human heart and soul through some kind of medium, including fighting. The artistry of internal martial art forms is manifested in several ways. First, there are the dancelike elements, in which one sees the refinement, effortlessness, and perfection of the human body moving through space with authority, grace, and precision. Second, there is the development and expression of chi and internal power (both subtle and gross) in the internal martial forms, elements that people cannot ordinarily access. Third, there is the creation of elevated states of mind that are reached during form movements and sparring interaction. These states ultimately allow the soul to express its energies through the body.

The martial artist committed to the human approach considers the artistic perfection and interconnection of fighting technique as a goal in itself, thus expressing the same higher artistic impulses through fighting form that a painter expresses through brush strokes or a novelist through words. In fact, the humanist martial artist experiences the shades of power as well as the usefulness and efficiency of fighting technique in much the same way a painter sees shades of color. Different types of both subtle and gross fighting techniques (punches, kicks, throws, joint-locks, etc.) can be like different styles of painting in different mediums.

This kind of creativity is usually not the initial experience of beginners going to a "self-defense class." They have much more limited goals. Once beginners feel they have learned to "take care of themselves," they will usually stop studying martial arts and will move on to something else. Such, however, is not the case with martial artists who, decades later, find their artistic passion for a particular martial art or the martial arts in general continuing to grow long after they have reasonably "learned to fight" for effective self-defense. Martial craftspeople will stop when they feel their product is completed. Martial artists will continue to keep learning and growing because the creative artistic expression of their martial art is their goal. They do it because they love it.

Classically, the ancient Orientals held the view that the creative act manifests itself in martial arts in the same way that it does in painting, music, and other artistic endeavors that can be traced to the human spirit.

THE SPIRITUAL APPROACH

The spiritual approach to martial arts consists of two levels. The first is a preparatory phase that requires great soul-searching and struggle to free oneself of many emotional and spiritual blockages. The second concerns specific meditation practices that can directly lead an individual to experience higher and more refined states of consciousness.

The most initially challenging spiritual task is to free oneself from the emotional and psychic conditioning of one's past to become a mature human being, that is, someone who can take inner and outer responsibility for his or her thoughts and actions. Another spiritual challenge involves locating the balance between responsibility and personal power. To find this balance, individuals must develop a capacity for feeling genuine remorse for unnecessary damage they have caused, both on and off the training floor, and be willing to correct their moral shortcomings.

In order to stabilize themselves spiritually, practitioners of martial arts will need to balance both their animal and human passions. Individuals at the human stage of martial arts can practice without animalistically firing up their glands, yet at the same time be vicious, greedy, spiteful, full of loathing and hatred, arrogant, or self-deluded—in short, far from spiritual. To be able to go beyond spiritual blockages, practitioners must either be natural saints or undergo a moral purification process in which they develop and internalize a genuine, heartfelt sense of morality. During this purification, one's morality, in all its aspects, is constantly developed and tested, both in seated meditation and physical sparring. Without morality, the true process of spiritual martial arts cannot begin.

Although the morality of the internal martial arts of ba gua and tai chi obviously comes from Taoism, the study of martial arts does not require students to change their religious beliefs. A personal morality system could be drawn from any of the world's great lasting religions, Eastern or Western, or could simply come from an internalization process, such as serious introspection or soul-searching.

Whether derived from a religious source or through secular inner reflection, morality in the spiritual martial arts is explored, developed, and tested down to its deepest roots, until it becomes permanently woven into the moral fiber of an individual's being. Sparring acts like a mirror that often magnifies awareness of a person's spiritual strong points (courage, kindness, generosity, forgiveness, compassion, understanding, balance, and insight, for example) as well as the blocked spiritual weak points inherent in the human condition.

Humans through internal martial arts training also have the capacity to rise to awareness of a universal consciousness. Whether martial artists remain stuck in their lower natures or rise to their spiritual potentials is to a great degree determined by their willingness to consciously delve inside themselves and do battle with their "spiritual opponents" (the human dysfunctionalities within everyone: hatred of self and others, negativity, deceit, jealousy, anger, inflated ego, the need to subjugate others, etc.).

This spiritual war is waged until victory is found in the clear space where positive energy and a genuine spiritual center resides.

In two-person fighting exercises, your awareness of what is happening to inner mental, emotional, or psychic states is at least as important as whether a technique works martially. You train to become aware of how every aspect of your inner being is reacting to external stimuli. As your partner "fights" with you, you learn about your clarity of mind—how it is being undone by possible anger, fear, anxiety, paralysis, or failure to rise to the challenge. As you spar, those places within you that lack spiritual cultivation emerge. The task is then to conquer your spiritual weak points and cultivate inner spiritual strength, while you simultaneously develop your martial technique. In time, you learn that sparring does not have to involve conflict. This realization slowly but surely establishes the spiritual base on which you begin the second level of spiritual practice.

The second level of the spiritual approach centers on specific meditation methods geared to bringing a martial artist into that higher realm of consciousness where the sense of self is supplanted by a greater awareness of the **Universal Consciousness** or energy that pervades everything. The prime goal of the practitioner who reaches this point is to become a living bridge between the ordinary human world and the spiritual universe. In order to achieve this spiritual work through martial arts, it is necessary to deal with inner energy blockages and personal mental "enemies." The weapons the martial artist uses in this battle are awareness, solo practice forms, two-person fighting practices, and seated meditation. The path winds through the thicket of your struggle with the internal contradictions of your own animal and human nature and leads to that place where you accept all your human limitations. Finally, the path leads to a transformation of the soul that, in turn, opens the gate to genuine spiritual awakening.

UNIVERSAL CONSCIOUSNESS
The underlying something, which cannot be defined, of which the whole universe is composed. Called the Tao in ancient China.

Taming the so-called lower emotions (hate, greed, rage, ignorance, and so on) requires that an individual develop a reverence and respect for all life and creation. The meditative work seeks to foster balance, harmony, and compassion, and to develop the wisdom to know when to act and when to be still. This is the aim of the spiritual martial arts. Of all the martial arts approaches, the Taoist practices of ba gua and tai chi are unique, not only in their incorporation of spirituality as a core value, but also in fully integrating the entire Taoist spiritual tradition and the methodologies used to implement them.

Techniques to begin the process of spiritualization are done in the solo form postures. There are both specific and general ways to practice so that the energy channels of the body are first opened, then purged of negativity, then established at higher levels of harmony where love, compassion, balance, discrimination, and wisdom are fostered. From here, the practi-

EMPTINESS
A profound state of spiritual, mental, and psychic equilibrium that is a major goal of all Asian meditation practices.

MEDITATIVE STILLNESS
A level of accomplishment in meditation where the practitioner's mind becomes exceptionally quiet and rests relaxed and centered within itself.

WU STYLE TAI CHI
A style of tai chi chuan especially known for its healing and meditation components. A small-frame fighting style that developed from the Yang style.

tioner learns to unify the whole body/mind and establish stillness. That point at which the body is moving and the mind is still is the point at which it can be said that the process of moving meditation has begun. Here, the emphasis for the practitioner shifts into learning how to consciously manifest the different gradations of what the Taoists call **"emptiness,"** or advanced stages of **meditative stillness** that exist along the road to understanding Universal Consciousness.

The Taoist solo sitting and moving transformational practices are used to dissolve or transform whatever spiritual blockages have become apparent during the physical sparring practices. As mentioned, two-person sparring gives you a way to confront what is inside yourself, which amounts to a strong spiritual reality check that vanquishes complacency and self-delusion.

The sitting meditation practices used in the ba gua and **Wu style tai chi** taught to the author by Liu Hung Chieh (see p. 241) originated from Taoist meditation's alchemical tradition, which does not require martial art activity. However, historically, in some lineages, Taoist sitting meditation tradition has been integrated and specifically adapted to help resolve any spiritual blockages that naturally arise from martial art solo and two-person fighting practices. Conversely, whatever arises during your meditation can be adapted and tested in your sparring and solo forms. Thus, meditation, solo forms, and two-person sparring complement and naturally reinforce one another.

For example, in sparring you may find that in certain situations there arises within you a clear sense of paralysis, rage, insecurity, fear, and so on, that makes no sense tactically, emotionally, or rationally. At the end of sparring, you can sit and meditate and begin to focus on the energy of that paralysis, anger, insecurity, or fear. As you peel away the layers of unconsciousness, you may discover prior patterns of unperceived paralysis, anger, insecurity, or fear that have plagued you for your whole life. Such inner spiritual blockages can be resolved during seated meditation; they may also, using specific meditation methods, be cleared from your body when you practice solo martial art forms. Minute changes in your movement can increase your awareness of the internal mechanisms behind the paralysis you may experience when engaged in activity. Your reactions to the pressures of two-person sparring will reveal whether you have actually gone past the blockages or need to work on them more. One set of resolved blockages sets the stage for the next spiritual gap to show itself, and each time this happens, the meditative work should begin again.

The difference between animal, human, and spiritual martial arts has nothing to do with the physical attack and defense techniques used. Rather, it has everything to do with the type of person that emerges, and with the nature of the practices themselves. The kind of self-awareness the martial art focuses on, its morality, and the essence of its meditation and mind training are critical to the spiritualization process. In brief, the words of the Chinese masters apply: "What you practice, you become."

Aikido and the art of hsing-i chuan are involved with the spiritual approach in a different way. They both embrace a spiritual base, though neither incorporate in solo form movements nor in two-person sparring exercises specific Taoist or other transformational meditation techniques (see p. 76). While both of these arts do have sitting practices, these are primarily used to develop the chi of the central nervous system for physical and psychic power, and are not for transforming inner consciousness and awareness. Aikido, for example, places great emphasis *philosophically* on resolving conflict through relaxation, love, and harmony.

People who use the human approach to martial arts can and do accrue certain psychospiritual powers to a certain extent (the ability to project energy, for instance), yet without an authentic spiritual base of some sort, these enhanced abilities can be a danger. They can lead any individual to a false sense of power and to unhappiness, because the egoistic drive for power may usurp the joy and balances of life itself. In the spiritual approach to martial arts, separate meditation or meditation-like techniques are absolutely required. These may well be acquired independently of fighting methods—as with Zen in Japan, for example, or Tantra in Tibet—but, ideally, are seamlessly integrated into them.

Train Sensibly

Whatever your martial ability or ambitions, training for fighting should be done in ways that never bring harm to your body. This guideline is a very different one from that of Western boxing, for example, where practices can often result in significant injuries. It is hard to argue the case that the continuous taking of punches to the head (as are delivered in Western boxing) is good for your health. Head-pounding is, in fact, potentially extremely dangerous, and boxers commonly suffer from accumulated training or fighting injuries in old age. Nonetheless, many professional athletes, such as professional football players, will continue to play to win even though they know they may be permanently crippled when their careers are over. Most martial artists accept that, if you want to become a really good fighter, you must guard against destroying your body in the process.

The Taoist perspective is that health and performance excellence must be balanced. To cripple your body with permanent injuries while learning to defend yourself is a contradiction. In this case, the only thing being defended would be your ego and its need to win.

Wang Shu Jin—Incredible Chi

Photo by author

were playing saxophones. I was absorbed in this surreal scene, pondering the meeting of ancient China with the twentieth century, when a massive man in white pajamas came waddling down the street carrying two bird cages. It was Wang Shu Jin, a rotund senior citizen supporting 250 to 300 pounds on his 5-foot, 8-inch frame.

I was nineteen then, a recognized young karate champion, and had brought with me a traditional gift of respect for Wang: a substantial amount of high-quality ginseng. At our initial meeting, Wang did not hesitate to express his low regard for karate, telling me in no uncertain terms that, "karate is only fit for fighting old women and children." As karate had been a large part of my life and my passion at the time, this off-hand remark insulted me to the core. I was forced to swallow my indignation, though. In our ensuing sparring, Wang defeated me thoroughly on every occasion, tapping me lightly at will all over my body to demonstrate his easy circumvention of my defenses. Despite my best efforts and despite Wang's enormous girth, his ba gua chang enabled him to effortlessly evade all my blows and end up behind me at will.

To graphically show me there was much to learn, he allowed me, after several days of study with him, to strike him with full power anywhere on his body. I put all the force at my command into these strikes, but they might as well have been the blows of a three-year-old. I kicked him in the knees and groin without effect, hit him in the neck and elbowed his ribs. Like many ba gua masters, he had the ability to absorb blows without injury. When I kicked him in the shin, my foot hurt long afterward.

In the summer of 1968, I traveled to Taiwan from Japan in search of the internal arts ba gua master Wang Shu Jin, who was widely considered to be one of the best empty-hand fighters in Asia. I tracked down Wang's class, which met at the amphitheater shell in the park in Taichung at five-thirty in the morning. There were many people in the park at that hour, doing all sorts of things, including **Shaolin gung fu,** karate, tai chi, and badminton. Some individuals hung from branches of trees, stretching themselves, some just strolled, others

Wang Shu Jin—Incredible Chi, continued

When I drove my fist into his belly, it felt as if the blow had broken my wrist. Wang would often tap me on the head during sparring just to demonstrate how easy it would have been for him to demolish me. One time, in fact, he tapped me lightly on the head, dropping me to the ground instantly. I sat there in utter surprise, feeling as if I had just been jolted by a high-voltage electrical current.

After a while, I could tell he was getting bored with my low level of skill and my inability to hurt him. Sometimes, he would grab me with his arms and bounce me three or four times back and forth off his stomach like a yo-yo, my feet flying in the air. Then Wang would snap me back. I later heard that, as a young man in challenge matches on the Mainland, Wang had actually broken opponents' spines in this manner. Years later, I learned from another teacher that the only defense against this technique was to turn sideways so your hip bone and not your stomach made contact with his formidable belly. Otherwise, you were finished.

Following my enlightening, if disconcerting, initial exposure to Wang's abilities, I wanted nothing more than to study his ba gua, which he himself had learned from Chang Chao-Tung, who was known as a student of Tung Hai Chuan, the man credited with making ba gua chang public in the late nineteenth century. Wang decided to test my sincerity before he accepted me as a student. He gruffly ordered me to assume the ba gua chang posture called Wild Goose Leaves the Flock and maintain it until further notice. This static posture calls for one leg to be raised to waist height as the torso is coiled

to one side, and both arms are extended. As instructed, I assumed the posture. Holding it minute after minute, I collapsed several times, and each time Wang's assistant immediately drenched me with a bucket of cold water and ordered me to resume the posture. After two hours of this trial, a smiling Wang agreed to accept me as his student. What was Wang testing? Was it my commitment, ability to endure hardship, sincerity, or craziness (that is, passion for the martial arts)? Perhaps it was all of these.

Wang's fighting skills were astounding. Notwithstanding his age and his weight, Wang was unbelievably agile, lightning fast, in excellent health, and had incredible physical power. In the West, we assume that, if people are fat, they cannot be fit, must be clumsy and slow, and must be uncomfortable with their image. Wang certainly showed this stereotype to be inaccurate. He was perfectly at ease with himself. Wang commonly took on full-contact, no-holds-barred challenges from the best fighters in Japan and Southeast Asia, and always won. When into his eighties, he could beat the toughest young men. On cold practice days, his students would stand around him to warm their hands, as if he were a stove—a testament to his amazing level of chi development. It was from Wang that I first learned how to use chi to create a high level of health and vitality. He also showed me how to use chi to generate power for fighting.

Wang was a deep believer in chi. At our first meeting, he said to me, "I can eat more than you, I can have more sex than you, and I can fight better than you, but you call yourself healthy. Well, young man, there is a lot more to being healthy than being young, and it all

Wang Shu Jin—Incredible Chi, continued

comes down to how much chi you have." His words affected my nineteen-year-old mind sufficiently to cause a significant shift in my Western way of thinking about the reality of the body and how it works. Wang, it turned out, was also experienced in Taoist meditation, and was an active and knowledgeable master of Taoist sexual energy practices. He taught these subjects to only a select few.

His students were formidable fighters themselves. The level of skill of his students revealed perhaps more about the effectiveness of the internal arts than Wang's abilities. They illustrated that Wang was not superhuman, but had a superior combination of talent, dedication, and ability to provide quality instruction. When I started studying with Wang, several of his students, from fifteen to seventy years of age, beat the stuffing out me. I could not believe it! Men and women both were able to hit me with no pulling of my punches. For a proud nineteen-year-old karate champion to be given a hard time in a fight with an old woman was a bitter pill to swallow. Some of the older people had been with Wang for just a few years. They trounced me so much that first day, I felt like quitting. I remember distinctly thinking, what are they going to do next, bring out a small child to beat me up?

Many of Wang's students started late in life. In fact, one of Wang's specialties was taking on people in their fifties and sixties who had all sorts of physical problems and making them healthy and strong. At that time in Taiwan, elderly people had little to fear from random violence since the police were particularly rough on anyone who victimized them. Accordingly, Wang's elderly students did not initially

come to him to learn self-defense. Nonetheless, even though these older students started studying with Wang purely for health reasons, they still became good fighters because that training was part of Wang's programs.

In Taiwan, I talked with some of Wang's students who were in their fifties and had only recently begun to study ba gua with no previous martial arts experience. They came to Wang because they had started to become impotent or were suffering from chronic diseases. After practicing ba gua, their impotence was reversed and their health, reflexes, and clarity of mind improved markedly. Their chronic illnesses either vanished completely or lessened.

Wang's students constantly tried to find their own chi, thereby opening up the energy channels of their bodies. They would try to replicate the feeling of the chi of a blow Wang delivered to them in a watered-down but still shocking manner. Wang was expert at projecting chi. He could issue enormous power that you could feel and be hurt by even when his hand began moving from only slightly away from your body. He could also place his fingers lightly on your chest, and if he decided to project a little chi, he could throw you effortlessly against a wall or put you in such pain that you thought you were going to die, *even though his hand did not move more than a fraction of an inch.* This ability to bring all of one's power to a single point instantaneously is one of the techniques that the art of ba gua develops. When this methodology is explained, it sounds very clinical, but when the theory is applied to your body, things can be tremendously exhilarating or frightening. Absorbing such chi power can feel like a pleasant gust of wind or a thunderbolt.

Wang Shu Jin—Incredible Chi, continued

When I first started doing **Rou Shou** (the ba gua two-person equivalent of **Push Hands** in tai chi) with Wang in 1968, he would touch me and I would go flying. Ten years later, the last time I saw Wang in Taichung, I was again given the privilege of doing Rou Shou with him. From the methodologies I had learned from Wang himself and from what I had learned in the intervening years from other masters, I was now just barely able to evade Wang's power. Wang could not "get me" as he had done so easily before. This fact made me ecstatic. It was like graduating to a higher level of the art form. I was finally able to do those things dreamed about for ten long years, which was what fueled the Big Mistake. At one point, I wanted to see if I could now match Wang's power, bearing in mind his advanced age of eighty plus. My body language challenged him. In response, he sent a burst of energy into my torso that lodged in the muscles between my shoulder blades. It took three months of intensive bodywork and acupuncture to clear it out and make the pain go away. This was not a pulled muscle but a ball of energy Wang had buried deep inside my body. Clearly, there were yet more advanced levels for me to learn. On one hand, that was an exciting prospect and, on the other, a good reminder never to get too swelled a head.

Wang would mostly teach by showing a movement that students would watch and copy as best they could. He emphasized deep, relaxed breathing and a powerful belly. He would also physically position a student's body to correct faults in body posture and internal alignments. His chi and internal power were so obvious and strong that one could get a tangible physical sense of the type of chi he was transmitting. As mentioned, he would demonstrate what the chi of the technique was like by physically hitting the student, using just enough force for the student to be in no doubt as to what had occurred. Alternatively, he would use **fa jin** (see p. 110) to project the type of power into your body that he wanted you to feel, so that you could tell what his chi was like. This action of projecting chi into a student was typical of all the genuine fighting internal martial art masters I personally met in China. They believed that merely teaching technique visually was insufficient. It was their position that, if they were genuinely going to teach someone, they had to let the student feel the subtle and gross realities of what different types of internal power were like. They believed this necessary for the student to be capable of re-creating the techniques for self-defense. Wang's students would try to replicate his chi with as much creativity as they could.

Wang's teaching was mostly by example and relatively nonspecific. His main concern was whether or not you could manifest power, or chi. This teaching method gave few precise details about exactly how one was to accomplish this replication. Wang's basic advice was to practice. He would recommend repetitively practicing certain moves, such as the **Single Palm Change** (see p. 217) or the first movement of hsing-i called "Splitting" (see p.187) for hours and hours on end. "Practice," he would say, "and skill will come naturally." I took him at his word.

An archival photo of B. K. Frantzis at age fifteen doing a karate flying side kick.
The study of karate and judo was the beginning of his journey from the external
to the internal martial arts.

A CONTINUUM

The External and Internal Martial Arts of China

2

THERE ARE MANY KINDS OF MARTIAL ARTS

In China, as in the rest of the world, people have physically fought each other for all sorts of reasons, both wise and foolish, just and unjust. War, crime, corrupt governments, competition for resources, and the human propensity toward violence have always been with us. In Asia (and China in particular), generation after generation created systematic organized martial forms for efficiently fighting the "enemy." People have fought with their bodies and, in pre-gunpowder times, with weapons such as knives, swords, staffs, spears, whips, and chains. The same pattern occurred in the Western world where practical fighting techniques, such as boxing, wrestling, and fencing developed into art forms.

The word *martial* comes from Mars, the ancient Roman god of war and physical competition. It is to be expected, then, that much of the training involved in martial arts can also enhance both high-performance competitive sports and ordinary recreational exercise. In martial arts, just as in all cutting-edge amateur and professional sports, the limits of human mind/body capacities are continuously tested, analyzed, and surpassed. The martial arts of China are among the most sophisticated in the world. However, the difficulty of the Chinese language and China's inclination (until recently) to limit or avoid interaction with foreign nations have kept the West essentially uninformed about many aspects of ancient Chinese mind/body culture, including martial arts.

There are many and varying colorful legends in China concerning the origin of their martial arts. All that can reliably be said is that martial arts in various forms have existed in China for three thousand years.* There are between fifty and sixty major branches of martial arts in China, including over four hundred distinct schools with specific names and coherent philosophies. The majority of the physical techniques that schools impart are superficially similar.** However, each school has its own way of executing the same techniques, as well as countless variations on the physical motion and the type of power employed. Each school also has particular techniques in which it specializes. Furthermore, each school has its own philosophy or theories, which are then applied practically in combat. Some schools have clear military, religious, secret society, underworld, or family overtones.

The names of many of the schools are derived from animals (bear, horse, tiger, monkey, leopard), birds (white crane, swallow, hawk), insects and arachnids (praying mantis, scorpion), and mythological beasts (dragon, phoenix, unicorn). Some take their names from famous male or female martial artists (Wing Chun and Wu Mei) or martial arts families (Chen family, Yang family, or Wu family tai chi chuan or Hung, Choi, or Li family Southern Shaolin) who originally created the forms or made them public. Some schools have poetic names, others are named after lofty Chinese philosophical ideas (hsing-i chuan, or "Mind/Form Boxing") or religious principles and images drawn from Confucian (Upright Boxing), Buddhist (Lohan or Jin Gang Temple Guardians Boxing) or Taoist origins (tai chi, ba gua, yin-yang, and Eight Drunken Immortals Boxing).

To the uninitiated, all these names can be confusing. It must be borne in mind, however, that China's population has exceeded that of Europe for most of its history. China's 3000 years of continuous traditions have produced numerous creative geniuses. Many of these have specialized in using the martial arts to unleash the latent capacities of the body/mind.

---

*The most common if historically inaccurate legend is that the great Buddhist meditation master from India, Bodhidharma or Damo, began martial arts at the Shaolin monastery in 526 A.D. He allegedly undertook this task in order to strengthen the bodies of the monks so that they could withstand prolonged daily meditation without physical deterioration. This is usually cited as the origin of the Shaolin school of martial arts. That Bodhidharma brought what became Zen/Chan Buddhism to China is a certainty. Martial arts, though, existed in China long before his arrival. He may have brought some martial arts with him, but we have no way to verify this.

**In all the martial arts of China, there is no way to calculate the exact number of arm, foot, throwing, and locking techniques. How is such a calculation to be made? Is the same strike done at close, middle, or long range, or at high, middle, or low height six different strikes, or simply variations of one single technique? Should the same technique done with the left or right side of the body be counted as one or two? Is the same movement done standing upright, crouched down in a low stance, lying on the floor, jumping up in the air, or rolling on the ground one technique or five? With all this taken into consideration, Chinese martial arts can be said to have a basic arsenal of 300 to 500 finger, knuckle, palm, palm edge, back of the hand, wrist, forearm, elbow, shoulder, and head striking techniques. There are also approximately 50 to 100 kicks and knee butts, 100 throws, and 100 joint-locking techniques.

China invented gunpowder over 1000 years ago, but the Chinese chose to ignore the technology of firearms and develop martial arts instead. The ancient Chinese held the interesting belief that if one human being killed others without looking at them, without personally feeling the reality of creating death, by using gunpowder's "death at a distance" people would become subhuman and engage in remorseless mass killing. Firearms to them were potentially immensely effective, but completely dehumanizing. One need only look at the destruction of entire cities through conventional and nuclear bombs or the senseless random drive-by shootings of today to see that the ancient Chinese had a point.

Martial arts require years of constant training to reach a high level of competence. During that long process, a practitioner has plenty of time to seriously consider what life, death, pain, frivolous violence, conscience, and remorse really mean. It seems as if there should be more moral weight felt by the aggressor (that is, more feeling involved) when violence is inflicted directly in a highly conscious way than that experienced by someone inflicting violence remotely by pushing a button or pulling a trigger. The martial arts of China that are derived from a religious or philosophical framework commonly address the issue of the ramifications of violence. This consideration occurs in order to make individuals aware of the pragmatic, psychological, and moral implications of violence within themselves and within society.

Over time, all the diverse martial arts spread throughout the Far East. The martial arts of China appear to have been the technical source or at least the original inspiration for the martial arts in the nations of Japan, Korea, Okinawa, Burma, and Thailand. In Malaysia and Indonesia, there is more of a mix of martial techniques from both India and China, with clear echoes of Chinese fighting ways at the physical, mental, and strategic levels.

Although China has hundreds of different martial art schools, all boil down to one of three basic styles: external, internal, or some kind of amalgamation. In this chapter, we will examine these three basic styles in terms of how they work with the building blocks of fighting, including physical power, strength, speed, endurance, and reflexes.

Bowing, Belts, and Uniforms

For the public in the Western world, the term *martial arts* conjures images of rigid discipline. Such images may include barefoot people wearing white pajama-like garments with various colored belts around their waists (a black belt indicating that a person is an "expert") and constant formalized bowing. Although such elements may be characteristic of most Japanese and Korean martial arts (karate, **tae kwon do**, judo, and so on), they simply do not represent most of the other martial arts in the world.

TAE KWON DO
Korean karate, an external martial art.

Martial art costumes are usually more of a cultural symbol than something intrinsic to the martial art itself. Designer T-shirts sporting the names of specific martial arts schools or highly stylized symbols, along with fancy uniforms where tops and pants differ in color or design, all fit into the category of fashion statement. The only real requirement for clothing and footwear in the martial arts is that they allow you to move comfortably and well in differing environments. Boxers (Thai and Western) as well as practitioners of Indonesian, Indian, and Chinese martial arts can fight well, yet they may train bare-chested or wearing simple T-shirts or sweatshirts, and any kind of shoes.

Internal martial arts practitioners generally tend to train wearing normal street clothes or commonplace athletic wear. During demonstrations or competitions, however, members of non-Japanese or Korean martial art schools may wear formal national attire (Chinese martial artists may wear silk uniforms, for example) or they may just wear their regular nondescript training clothes. The situation is somewhat analogous to the differences in dress codes of the formal corporate world and the companies of the emerging high-technology cultures. In the former, the quality and cut of a person's clothing conveys status and position in the organization; in the latter, informal clothing is a great equalizer, as corporate counterparts here may wear open-collar shirts, short sleeves, running shoes, even shorts to work.

Visible symbols of rank exist in all cultures to determine who is who in the hierarchy. In martial arts, this issue is reflected in three ways of thinking: (1) the hierarchy should be visibly apparent to its own members and to outsiders; (2) the quality of martial skill should speak for itself without the advertisement of costumes; (3) superlative martial skills should remain hidden. In many martial arts schools, it is fairly easy to determine who is superior in rank and who inferior by observing who is bowing longer or more vigorously or who is barking commands. In other schools, no observable clues to rank are displayed. This situation is especially true for internal martial arts schools. Here, ascertaining who is of what rank usually cannot be done unless the observer has a very skilled eye or just happens to see someone in full action.

The wearing of belts derives from the ancient samurai traditions. For instance, in the Japanese systems, white belts indicate novices and brown belts indicate that the wearer is beginning to learn the ropes. A first-degree black belt, called a *shodan* in Japanese, usually carries the inaccurate designation of "martial arts expert"—for the media and the general public. In Japanese, however, shodan only means "the beginning level," the stage at which individuals are now prepared to learn a martial art, rather than that they already know it. In the Japanese martial culture, a person would have to posses a fourth- or fifth-degree black belt to genuinely merit the designation of "expert." Some schools in China and Indonesia also issue colored sashes or specified fabrics for rank, but the experts may display no visible signs of rank at all.

As a rule of thumb, external schools often have definite symbols that denote a ranking system, as well as military-style discipline. Internal schools, in contrast, often appear to be extremely informal, relaxed, and even sometimes chaotic, all of which can give a misleading impression. In actuality, internal schools strongly emphasize getting the job done without fanfare or ritual, and they concentrate on cultivating inner-directed, rather than outer-directed, discipline.

Is One Martial Art "Better" than Another?

The question frequently raised (usually in provocative tones) by the martial arts media is: "Can this martial art beat that martial art?" The answer is that no one specific martial system is better than another. They are simply different in a multitude of ways. Liu Hung Chieh (see p. 241) would say, "Who wins or loses a fight is not a matter of which martial art style they do, but how much "gung fu" (personal fighting skill) they possess." If we consider the sum total of what it takes for an individual to win in violent combat to be gung fu, or knowledge, then we should reflect on the old Chinese adage: "Some people are born with knowledge, some are given the gift of knowledge from heaven, some gain knowledge through consistent hard work and serious study. Knowledge once acquired, however, is the same."

In terms of martial arts, those "born with knowledge" are naturals. These individuals have an incredible instinct for combat. They tend to learn technique well with only minimal experience, and often beat opponents who are doing everything right when they themselves are doing everything "wrong." Those who have received "gifts of knowledge" may find exceptional speed, power, reflexes, stamina, or the ability to take punishment in the genetic package. Those who "gain knowledge through hard work" are most of us. Applying oneself to the grindstone to learn martial techniques and gather practical fighting experience is traditionally considered to be the ordinary route to acquiring superior fighting abilities. Once a person has achieved fighting gung fu and can consistently fight and win, it doesn't matter how the gung fu was obtained. Once you have it, you have it—"Knowledge once acquired is the same."

That being said, the martial arts of course have many techniques, some more efficient than others. The situation can be considered using the analogy of cars. All cars will get you from point A to point B. Each has its strengths and weaknesses along the continuum of high performance. Speed on different terrains, turning radius, suspension, ease of handling, braking and acceleration, function in differing weather conditions, gas mileage, repair costs—all are part of the mix. Likewise, with all martial arts, you can fight (that is, get from point A to point B in combat). The question is, as with models of cars, which perform best under what conditions? You have to test drive them to find out. The high-performance qualities of a martial art may lie in skills pertaining to kicking, punching, hand strikes, arm or leg locks, restraining holds, chokes, nerve strikes, throws, or soft or hard technique—all are part of the mix. Like cars, each has advantages. Some are best when you are fighting standing upright, others when you are wrestling on your back, crouching, jumping in the air, fighting on solid or slippery ground, with or without weapons, against larger or smaller adversaries, against single or multiple opponents.

Accordingly, whether one martial art is superior or inferior to any other is a question full of considerations—black, white, and gray. If a balanced answer is to be given to the question "Which is better?" it should directly address this concern: Better in what way—where, how, and under what exact conditions? It is natural for long-term practitioners of a given martial art to feel that their style is the best. (If it weren't, why would they be putting in endless hours of hard work and effort practicing it?) Ultimately, every long-term practitioner analyzes martial arts of other styles according to his or her accumulated life experiences and perceptions in the martial art game. At the end of the day, though, it should always be kept in mind that a good driver in a medium car is more likely to win than a bad driver in a good car. It is, as Liu Hung Chieh emphasized, the individual that counts.

What Are Fighting Applications?

Japanese and Korean martial artists practice stylized movements called **kata** and **hyung**; Chinese martial artists practice "forms" or "sets." Why do Oriental martial artists bother to move their hands and feet in the air in set, stylized movements? You do these set motions in order to place your mind into your body and the space around your body (where a hypothetical opponent and/or a physical object might be). As you move your body (using the accumulated combat knowledge of a specific martial art system) against imaginary opponents, you simultaneously invoke specific psychological states, as you clearly envision the visceral feel of a combat interaction. The purpose of doing this activity is to hardwire into your body and mind what in English is called **fighting applications,** (in karate, **bunkai** and in Chinese martial arts, **yung fa,** or "how-to-use" methods). These fighting applications include within them the accumulated ideas of a system's martial technology, field-tested with practical combat experience, and not merely acquired through theories or conjecture. Without these fighting applications clearly being present in martial art kata or form movements, the forms easily become more like dance performances than martial arts. For modern martial art practitioners, learning the com-

KATA OR HYUNG
A form. A set of choreographed martial movements done either solo or with a partner or partners.

FIGHTING APPLICATION
The practical use or range of uses for combat of a specific technique of a martial art.

BUNKAI
The fighting applications of a Japanese martial art move.

plete range of subtle applications for each specific technique makes the forms come alive, and rewards the long hours of practice.

Classically, training for power and speed was always symbiotically tied to the understanding of fighting applications. In martial arts of all kinds, sometimes the promise of teaching the applications themselves was a distant one reserved for the senior or higher-ranked students. This promise was sometimes kept, sometimes not. High-ranking individuals in both external and internal martial arts frequently do not have an in-depth comprehension of the fighting applications embedded in the forms they use. The sad part is that often even senior practitioners do not actually see or learn the applications at all.

In many martial schools, the elements of power and speed of the art are usually kept alive, but the knowledge of the more sophisticated fighting applications is minimized. When asking about the meaning of a form movement, students should be alert to instructors who equivocate instead of providing a clear answer. The truth of the matter is that, if an opponent is superior to you in size, speed, and/or power, it is only skill in fighting applications that will tip the balance. For any martial movement to achieve its potential, it must have usable speed, power, and fighting application. In two-person practices, one should work the fighting applications incessantly until they can be applied with smoothness and authority under any and all conditions. The forms might be compared to computer hardware (the martial art system) whose software (the fighting applications) is what ultimately determines superiority.

Each form movement should carry within it a clear intent, visualization, and feeling of how you fight within a specific situation or general range of conditions. For example, if on a certain kind of terrain, your torso, hands, and feet are in a particular position and your opponent does or intends to do A against you, then you practice one of many specific and effective B responses, depending on the conditions of the situation. These conditions could be simple or complex, and could include myriad variables, all based on what any specific martial arts system believes will work under pressure. Fighting applications should take into consideration:

1. How to fight with one or several opponents of all sizes and builds
2. The specific types of speed and power you want to actualize
3. The optimal angles your hands, feet, and waist should be at when countering an attack, waiting and assessing the situation, or attacking
4. The footwork needed to execute the kinds of fighting techniques your method advocates for effectiveness in unrehearsed and unpredictable sparring
5. How to put your hands on someone's limbs in order to restrain or throw the person, or twist or break the limbs

6. How to kick, punch, or strike an opponent in order to use your arms and legs to target strategically vulnerable parts of your opponent's body

7. What to do when your opponent is at a close-, medium-, or long-range distance from you, with and without weapons

8. What to do if you are up in the air, hugging the ground, standing upright, crouching, on solid ground, on slippery or moving surfaces, or in blinding winds or other adverse weather conditions

9. How to defend yourself in a darkened area, in a small, confined space, or with your back against a wall or on the edge of a cliff, and so on

The Ingenuity of Form Movements Containing Fighting Applications

In all martial arts, even tai chi, movements are practiced singly and in combined forms. In solo practice, single techniques are usually repetitively done while standing on one spot or moving forward, either in straight lines or at various angles. Forms, on the other hand, include combining different single movements together, transition techniques between movements, and simulating moving out of one situation into another. Forms provide practice for developing the mental flexibility that will allow you to be able to change smoothly from one tactical situation to another, without your mind freezing up or getting stuck by inertia. Form work saturated with fighting applications is a fundamental and time-efficient tool for learning enough options to deal with multiple attackers.

Often, even trained individuals introduced into new fighting situations will freeze up despite their martial knowledge, because they do not have the mental flexibility to bridge the gap to novel conditions. Forms force you to think about and develop trained responses for situations you normally would not consider merely by practicing straight-line or repetitive single-technique drills. Forms give the body/mind a way to see how to adapt favorite and well-practiced techniques to varied circumstances. You might not use the exact same hand and foot techniques of a form in a real confrontation, but you may well apply one or more variations of the principles they imparted, which in and of itself increases your chances of surviving a fight.

Thus, forms greatly widen the repertoire of techniques of any given martial art. For example, in hsing-i, you practice lines of punches as much as you would in karate or Shaolin. By definition, lines focus on hitting something in front of you. It is difficult to get lethal power in a punch while stepping backward. However, hsing-i has worked out how to do it, but *through its forms*, not its forward-moving practice lines.

Many existing martial moves, including martial techniques embedded in forms, have been created in response to an environmental stimulus. A technique in a form may have been invented to counter the nastiest methods of other styles, such as throws or chokes in judo. If that technique is transferred to another geographical environment where judo never existed, the usage could be lost due to neglect. Or, if there were no high kickers, for instance, a form technique that at one time had been designed to counter high kicks might be kept due to tradition. Yet nobody would know why it was there, and implausible stories about its martial meanings might well be invented.

Traditionally, martial arts styles were confined to small geographical regions. In this day and age, the incessant international movement of people and tremendous explosion of communication technology have sent every known martial art technique all over the world. Consequently, if you are a dedicated martial artist, it is probably a good idea for you to learn what is done in other styles, as you may well have to deal with their techniques sooner or later. Such exposure was not possible historically as the basic techniques and strategies of most martial art styles were closely guarded secrets, and woe to the stranger who tried to ferret them out. If you visited a rival martial art school and were not introduced and accepted as a friend, you could face overt challenges that would probably require a blood response.

With the greater open-mindedness of contemporary martial arts instructors, it is now possible to do cross-research in various areas of martial arts without being treated as if you are an enemy spy. This freer atmosphere helps many talented students to go beyond their frustrations and see the positive aspects of what their own teacher really has to offer. Students can now have the means to assess their shortfalls and strengths through comparative exposure that can aid them in reaching their full potential. All you have to do is get rid of the "us versus them" mentality, and overcome limiting ideas of "status" within your own organization. Instead, focus on the passion and joy of learning.

Good Martial Art Forms Were Created by Professionals

The founders of the martial arts became famous as combat adepts not because they wore impressive uniforms, had great public relations, yelled loudly, had beautiful training halls, or could tell stories about the fighting prowess of their martial art ancestors. They achieved fame for fighting and winning against the best of their generation's most highly trained professionals, not by beating enthusiastic but unskilled amateurs or their own students. These men would only practice what they thought really worked. In eras past, people took martial arts very seriously. Bad practitioners could die young. At one point in China, if you had a school, or a bodyguard or security service, and someone came along and beat you in a fight, that person had the absolute and culturally accepted right to take over all your business. Just as in professional boxing, fame and fortune were gained by victories won through authentic martial skill, not merely talk.

However, being an extremely talented fighter does not necessarily mean that one could train another to the same standard. To do so, there had to be a clearly defined systematic training methodology in place. This requirement insured that any young practitioner who was equally motivated and willing to train hard could unambiguously understand how to go through the same process, and recreate the same abilities as the instructor, more or less. How could the technology of martial knowledge be transferred? How could one pass on the trade secrets concerning what was most important when you engaged in hitting, kicking, throwing, joint-locking, ripping, choking, falling, and so on? How could one pass along what tactics to use, what strategies to consider, how to change from one tactic or technique to another, and what martial attitudes to appropriately apply in differing situations? These trade secrets were communicated through forms, which were completely interlinked and integrated with all kinds of two-person practices.

Living and Dead Forms

The purpose of the forms was to catalog the martial applications in one place. The more real and alive the forms are, the more realistic are the fighting applications they contain, and the more techniques they utilize during two-person practices and unrehearsed sparring. The masters of living, functional martial arts systems repeatedly maintained and proved the high functional vitality of these systems across several generations. Masters considered movement forms with their fighting applications intact to be essential for preserving martial legacies. Without such forms, they believed martial systems could easily degenerate into minimally functional or dead traditions.

In forms that are genuinely alive, a single movement can be likened, along the dimension of providing information, to a chapter in a book (a small technique, for instance, contains numerous martial principles, each with variations on a theme); in semi-alive forms, to paragraphs or sentences; and in dead forms, merely to simple phrases or single words. High-level martial art forms with *living traditions* are like whole libraries of extremely useful information. Using exactly the same physical form movements, high-level martial art masters can, if they are willing, teach you how to read, chapter by chapter, book by book, the gross and subtle fighting application information encoded within each tiny piece of each movement. If all the information is completely given, it is the student's obligation to act on it. In dead traditions of all martial styles, the physical movements are present, but lack most of the fighting applications. Dead forms have watered down their inherent fighting applications to satisfying commands, such as those given in karate to be faster, stronger, fiercer, or in tai chi to be softer, relaxed, lower, more calm, and so on. Although these commands may be good in and of themselves, if they are only used alone, without the knowledge of the complete, applied fighting technique embedded in the movement being conveyed, the student will undoubtedly miss most of the point of the movement.

If an instructor did not share many "books" with a student, odds are that student will be practicing a dead form. If that person then goes on to teach, a dead tradition will be perpetuated. Unfortunately, this sad situation is all too common. It is the bane of the classical martial arts community that many previously noble and exceedingly effective martial art forms have been reduced to posing and posturing with "sounds of fury, signifying nothing."

Anyone who wishes to learn martial arts that "work" must either find a living tradition to become involved with or mix and match whatever knowledge is available and create one's own,* which can produce results varying from excellent to extremely poor. Any living tradition, however, may be more or less complete, depending on how many volumes of fighting application have been lost or how much access to those remaining is available. The often-heard refrain from people who learned from dead traditions, when they encounter a live one is, "Why didn't I learn that from my teacher?"

Practitioners of dead traditions normally do not know how to effectively use the techniques of their system's forms or katas in actual combat. These martial arts have hundreds of form movements, but when it comes down to real fighting, the practitioners usually use only a few, with the rest serving only to develop physical coordination. If this is the case, it indicates that the fighting application information in their forms has been lost. This kind of loss can occur in an entire martial arts system or any of its designated branches or even within a single school.

In the living internal martial art traditions, every genuine **Circle-Walking** ba gua technique (both **pre-birth** and **post-birth**—see p. 210— passed down from Tung Hai Chuan, the modern founder of ba gua), every slow-motion tai chi movement that appears innocuous, and every standing posture or moving punch movement of hsing-i does have clear, multiple practical applications for fighting. With the living internal martial art traditions, the way in which practitioners move in a form is more or less the way the movements are applied in combat. If your form movements lack this reality, you are not learning a fully alive tradition. In the internal martial arts practiced today, dead or incomplete martial traditions are

CIRCLE-WALKING
The primary training method of the internal martial art of ba gua.

PRE-BIRTH
That which happened to a human between conception and the time of birth.

POST-BIRTH
That which happens to a person after leaving the womb. Talents, skills, or accomplishments not inherent, but acquired after birth.

---

*This happens frequently. The hybrid Jeet Kune Do created by the famous martial arts film star Bruce Lee is a well-known example.

most common in tai chi and least common in hsing-i, with ba gua falling somewhere in the middle.

In the traditional internal schools, the fighting applications within form movements are first taught to enable individuals to acquire an inventory of specific techniques to respond to specific defenses or attacks. Then, basic power training is taught both within the forms and with separate chi gung methods. Next, the applications and the power training are fused together within the forms. In the end, the forms are primarily performed to make the body/mind of individual practitioners more agile and adaptable to martial change, and to create the "still" mind and advanced chi methods that will supercharge the fighting applications.

Dead Forms and Facing Reality In addition to forms and chi training (the source of internal power), long hours of realistic partner or multiple-person training are necessary to master the physical fighting techniques of ba gua, tai chi, and hsing-i. Many people want to believe that doing external or internal martial arts movement forms alone will turn them into supernaturally superior fighters. To borrow a phrase from the George Gershwin song, "It ain't necessarily so." Forms should train your intention and power, and if these two elements are missing from your forms (and from your two-person sparring training, for that matter), the odds are you will not fare well in a genuine confrontation.*

Fighting is an act of performance and competence. Your physical survival or well-being could depend on it. Fighting requires energy, intuition, and know-how. If any external or internal martial arts master, teacher, or friend cannot realistically demonstrate how a technique is used in fighting, then this is the wrong person from whom to learn this technique. Learn only from someone who can demonstrably apply the fighting technique being taught.

Some who train in internal martial arts primarily for health, longevity, and meditation also wish to practice for fighting. If one of your goals is to feel secure from physical aggression by learning self-defense, or if you want to become a competent internal martial arts fighter, learn ba gua, tai chi, and hsing-i only from people who can use these arts in a fight and can clearly teach them to others. (Some teachers know only empty-hand fighting, some only fighting with weapons, and some both, to one degree or

---

*This position was clearly articulated in the 1970s by Bruce Lee, who stated that classical martial arts were dead. This feeling was commonplace in China among both young and old fighting masters of the more vibrant schools. I heard this sentiment expressed in China by many fine fighting masters, who said things on the order of "that's a very interesting form movement but *do you know how to use it?*" This drive toward functionality in form work is epitomized by the phrase that hsing-i practitioners and others like to use to describe their form movements: *Bu hao kan, hen hao yung,* which translates as "the movements do not look pretty, but they work exceptionally well."

The Value of Cross-Research in Martial Arts

There are a great many crossover areas in external, external/internal, and internal martial arts. My own experience was that, whereas the external arts delivered much in the way of fighting applications and some in the way of chi development, it was the internal arts that fulfilled the complete range of my expectations. The large techniques of the external/internal martial arts usually operate from gross movements, each one of which comprises a single martial idea. These same ideas and fighting techniques usually exist in the internal systems with more variety, subtlety, and with smaller movements. While in the more external arts one martial idea is usually expressed as one large movement, in an internal martial art, the same idea is usually expressed in a much smaller and subtle movement, perhaps, for instance, as only tiny physical circles or even at the invisible level of pure intent about how energy is manifesting. The internal arts can achieve such aims because they are able to bring greater flexible power, sensitivity, speed, and awareness to that critical juncture in combat where the ability to manifest internal power within a microsecond can decide victory or defeat.

The internal martial arts were able to absorb and integrate into their forms and fighting applications all the combat elements of the external/internal arts I learned. I also found that the internal systems could go to subtle places that Shaolin could not, predominantly because the internal arts had methods to handle the internal power gaps between the end of one technique and the beginning of another, gaps that are built into most external martial systems.

As many of my internal teachers pointed out, external martial arts can teach the one, two, three sequences of external motion in fighting, but it is the internal martial arts that teach the internal power that allows the seeds of external martial arts to grow into strong trees. After more than a decade of cross-research, my focus returned completely to the internal martial arts. I wanted effectiveness in combat *without aggression*, and I found that internal martial arts could give both *and* make me healthy, as well as serve as a genuine vehicle for the practice of meditation.

another.) If you want to improve, train with people who have both the enthusiasm and willingness to fight. Do not confuse sensitivity training or martial play with genuine combat training. It takes a certain kind of courage, grit (often called "heart"), and willingness not to be afraid of either being hit or thrown or hitting or throwing a fellow human being. It also takes emotional maturity, compassion, and spiritual awareness not to have your ego explode when you experience a newfound sense of "power," which may or may not be real.

It will only be after you can keep a calm, stable mind when being scared, hit, or frustrated that you will be able to use the superior fighting application techniques of the internal martial arts in a down-to-earth way.

THE FOCUS OF EXTERNAL MARTIAL ARTS

A fundamental concern in all martial arts focuses on how the body/mind connection is perceived. Does the practitioner conceive of the body as a separate external object to be trained to produce certain desired fighting abilities? Or does the practitioner let the mind enter the body (that is, feel the mind in the body), thereby creating a mind/body fusion to produce skills for fighting? When martial artists deliver blows, do they imagine their bodies moving like combatants in a Nintendo game (external approach), or do they literally feel everything that is happening inside their bodies and ultimately their minds (internal approach)?

External martial artists focus on the same sense of physicality as do participants in modern sports. Emphasis here is on developing the bones, muscles, tendons, ligaments, and efficient use of oxygen. Externally oriented martial artists, much in the manner of modern competitive athletes or dancers, often fall into the trap of being excessively mechanical in training. They may be concerned solely with the goals of wanting the body to go faster, be stronger, last longer. Applying this approach, many are unaware of how they can possibly damage both body and emotional well-being. Moreover, athletes as well as fighters following the external path can become addicted to the "high" produced by the adrenal secretion stimulated by intense competition or by punching someone.

The more that external practitioners engage in touch-oriented practices, the more aware they tend to become of the feelings inside their own bodies. Two-person practices, where both participants are touching each other (for example, in wrestling, "sticky hands," Push-Hands, or joint-lock practice), are geared to develop the ability in one person to feel the body of the other. It then becomes natural for individuals to explore the feelings inside their own physical selves.

Often, purely external hit-and-kick martial artists do not possess a linkage to internal sensitivity. In fact, this lack of internal body/mind awareness often shortens their competitive years, as it does with top athletes. Pushing the body beyond its limits without internal sensitivity can also lead to damaging short- and long-term health consequences. Learning to "feel" your limbs and exercise reasonable restraint can yield positive, lifelong benefits and extend competitive athletic careers that are often cut short due to injuries from practicing a sport (such as gymnastics, baseball, basketball, football) or from excessive training in that sport.

Power and Strength

The power and strength needed for a blow, kick, or throw would be acquired in the old days by various means. Most of these are still being done nowadays. They include:

1. Weightlifting with crude devices such as stones, heavy blocks, and tubs of water. External martial artists were famous throughout China's history for being able to lift and move objects that weighed hundreds of pounds. Modern training simply substitutes contemporary weightlifting techniques.

2. Moving heavy free weights, such as blocks of stone, in the air while doing empty-hand martial arts forms; also practicing martial art forms that use extra-heavy weapons. The prime example of this latter activity may be seen in the external martial schools of southern China, where students practice both standing still and moving across a floor, wielding a thirty- to forty-pound metal weapon with a curved blade called a *guan dao*. This weapon was actually only used by fighters on horseback. It was totally impractical as a ground-fighting weapon, but was excellent, however, when used in practicing on the ground for developing physical strength.

3. Throwing heavy objects in the air and then catching them (bags of beans or rice, concrete blocks, chunks of metal); pulling the bark off trees with bare hands; twisting ropes and pieces of wood for hours on end. All such training was for the purpose of developing the strength of one's grip for effective grabbing.

4. Using pulleys to lift heavy weights or bags of sand, hundreds or even thousands of times per practice session to simulate throwing techniques.

5. Hitting objects for developing power strikes or kicks. Heavy bags, metal, stone, compacted dirt, bales of agricultural produce, logs, wooden dummies, trees, and water were all hit, punched, and kicked.

6. Jabbing the fingers into sand, beans, marbles, iron filings, and dirt hundreds or even thousands of times a day to develop finger-hitting strength. (Even if protective Chinese medicines were externally applied during

this practice, it was not unusual for the practitioner to end up with health problems, such as arthritis, in old age.)

7. Banging the arms and legs repeatedly with all sorts of hard objects to harden the bones. Partners would continuously bang each other's arms and legs to see who was stronger or who more intimidated. Wooden dummies would also be smashed for the same purpose. As well as making the bones hard, many of these practices have traditionally been linked to health problems down the road, including the damage resulting from cumulative shock to the body and the acupuncture meridian lines.

8. Doing push-ups, sit-ups, gymnastic exercises, dynamic-tension breathing, and muscle-tensing exercises for overall body fitness.

CHI GUNG
Internal energy work/power. The ancient Chinese art and science of developing and cultivating chi by one's own effort.

All these methods for building strength and power had a common denominator: They emphasized alternately relaxing and then tensing the muscles of the body. They all strove for results that would be physically obvious rather than concentrating on practices that would build chi (subtle body energy). The **chi gung** (energy work) practices were sometimes done by external martial artists as a completely separate undertaking, and were virtually never integrated into the main training regimen. (This was especially true of chi gung practices done to withstand blows.)

Speed

Speed capability was and still is normally developed by:

1. Repetition of movements done continuously faster and faster, either alone, in time with a teacher's command, or by beating some imaginary clock (or, today, using electronic timers); these movements could be done repetitively as single motions, pre-set combinations, or incorporated in forms.

2. Training with weights on the arms, legs, and waist to slow the body down so that when the impeding weights were taken away, the body would move faster.

3. Sparring practices, which demand that reaction and attack times be continuously increased for survival.

Endurance

The capacity to endure was, and in many cases still is, achieved through:

1. Countless repetitions of various exercises and forms of a given martial art. Since external practices are generally quite aerobic, repetitive motions were often all that was done. Forms or single-training moves were

often done to a point beyond human endurance. The no pain/no gain, do-one-hundred-and-fifty-percent percent philosophy was in full force.

2. Staying frozen for long periods in difficult low stances or with one leg extended in midair to the height of the throat or head.

3. Jumping up and down for a long time while executing various martial arts movements.

4. Running up hills or climbing large numbers of stairs, sometimes thousands, to reach a training place. (This last was a common endurance-training scenario in many monasteries in the mountainous areas.)

5. Wrestling or sparring continuously without rest for hours on end until a practitioner was physically incapable of continuing. If this method were used regularly, medicinal herbs were usually ingested to protect the internal organs from long-term damage. In contemporary circuit training, an individual goes from one form of exercise to another in regular patterns to develop maximum strength, speed, and stamina. External martial arts in China had their own versions of this training technique. They might, for example, move from doing a form at slow speed, to doing fast squats, to perhaps jumps or kicks, to heavy weight training, to holding a posture for a long time (such as a leg in the air), to doing a series of forms extremely fast.

Reflexes

Reflexes are to a great degree determined by the intrinsic talent of the individual practitioner. By definition, genetic makeup normally is an ultimate limiting factor where reflexes are concerned. Even if individuals trained night and day for years on end, if they lacked innate central nervous system speed, they could easily be beaten by a beginner with minimum training who was naturally fast. Usually, reflexes slow down after middle age, and most aging external martial artists succumb to this natural process unless they incorporate internal practices. The slowing of reflexes is a major factor precluding old people from successfully learning external martial arts, along with the diminishing ability of an older body to absorb shock without impairing function. In China, it is in the area of internal martial arts where age is overcome as a factor in learning fighting skills. External martial arts do, however, employ a number of techniques to help create new reflexes. Among these are:

1. Cadences to accompany specific movements, singly or in combination, where the timing and speed of the movements are changed at regular intervals. The speed and timing of the beats could, as in drumming, be altered to create fast reflexes in the person, where moves are synchronized to the beat. This practice tends to remove hesitation from one's movements, which is a key component of fast reflexes.

2. Specific fast/slow timing sequences embedded in the external martial arts forms themselves. These sequences become more subtle in the forms requiring more coordination as the student advances.

3. Custom-designed sparring exercises. These are performed repeatedly, ultimately in a completely automatic, unconscious way to develop the exact reflex desired.

4. Use of spontaneous environmental forces to sharpen the reflexes. These are used in a variety of situations. Some examples: attempting to catch an erratically running chicken (this develops foot reflexes as well as hand-eye coordination); trying to hit a leaf three times while it is being randomly blown about in the air, especially in crosswinds; grabbing a darting fish with bare hands; attempting to catch a specific insect or bird from among a rapidly dispersing group; snaring a mosquito in flight with a pair of chopsticks.

The important point to remember about developing the reflexes in the external martial arts is that the focus of attention is always *outside* the practitioner. Usually, effective techniques are based on muscular tension. The body is prepped to react like a robot on command. Push the button and the body blocks, kicks, hits, throws, or applies joint-locks. If the body goes faster, that is considered to be good; if not, more practice is needed. There is usually little awareness on the part of the practitioner as to what is happening internally to the central nervous system, emotions, or mind as a technique is being executed. This can leave little room for the external martial arts practices to move into the area of emotional or spiritual well-being, which is based on these internal awarenesses.

The External Martial Arts Inside and Outside China

The most familiar of the non-Chinese external martial arts include boxing, wrestling, **savate,** fencing, judo, jujitsu, karate (virtually all styles), tae kwon do (virtually all styles), **Thai boxing, bando, penchat, silat,** and **kuntao.** Within China, the more widely known external martial arts (generically known as "kung fu" in the West) can more or less be divided into those that come from the north or the south of that vast country. Even the martial arts of western or central China carry the flavors of the northern or southern versions. This north/south division refers to martial arts stemming from the Shaolin temple, which is one of the legendary birthplaces of Chinese martial arts. Working together in the Shaolin temple, both the monks and the political refugees residing there were protected by the ancient religious right of sanctuary. They practiced and cross-fertilized martial art techniques. The word *Shaolin* is synonymous in China with the external martial arts.

SAVATE
A French martial art that combines kicking and Western boxing.

THAI BOXING
The traditional external martial art of Thailand.

BANDO
Burmese style of martial art.

PENCHAT/SILAT
Indonesian martial arts having a wide variety of specific styles, that are mostly external or external/internal.

KUNTAO
An Indonesian martial art strongly influenced by Chinese martial arts.

(Text continues on page 41.)

The Bridge from the External to the Internal

 As a third-degree black belt in karate, having trained daily for nearly nine years, I went to study in Okinawa, the birthplace of modern karate and tae kwon do. Both because I met the minimum ranking requirements and because of a lucky personal connection, I was admitted to a select special research student program in karate via the Shorin Ryu karate system, called in Japanese **kenkyusei.** Here, the innermost secrets of karate are introduced to future teachers. Weapons training, night fighting, and special breathing and martial techniques not taught to most black belts were essential parts of the course.

After a few months, it became obvious that many of the most "secret" techniques were ones I had already learned in my first two years of basic training in the internal martial arts of tai chi, hsing-i, and ba gua. Many karate people had to wait five to twenty years before being taught the same material in Shorin Ryu karate. This kenkyusei situation was quite similar to what was happening at the time with other karate styles in Okinawa and Japan. My instructor in Okinawa was the senior black belt after the elderly master of the style. I asked him how it was possible for me to have learned these things from Chinese masters in Japan and Taiwan that he himself had not learned?

Besides being an exceptional karate man, this instructor was also a jazz musician. He was much more open-minded than the average Japanese or Okinawan karate master. He answered more frankly than one in his position normally would have to a foreigner. He said I was right. He had sparred with martial art experts from Taiwan and he had been both confused and beaten by them. He also acknowledged that the Chinese martial arts knew how to efficiently combine traditional Oriental medical principles with martial arts training in ways that were mostly absent in karate. The Chinese martial arts, he admitted, also had a better medical knowledge of the body than was present in karate. He further said that the martial art material in Taiwan was of a higher level, although the Okinawans did have powerful and useful techniques that worked extremely well, which was true.

I then asked him why he didn't go to Taiwan, which was next door to Okinawa, and learn more. It was obvious that he loved karate and martial arts in general, and his jazz background had given him a fondness for experiments that would expand his abilities. His answer was typical of the

The Bridge from the External to the Internal, continued

ongoing Asian battle between orthodox conservatism and new frontiers of knowledge. He said he knew that the martial arts in Taiwan were better than what he did. (This was quite a statement considering this man was about as good as karate people got.) He then emphasized that he was an Okinawan and, as such, would never consider learning from the Chinese because this would cause his style of Okinawan karate to lose face. It was a matter of national pride. Most importantly, however, it was a matter of "face." Years later, my teacher in Beijing, Liu Hung Chieh, would comment many times about life in a Confucian society, "You can go for one of two things in life, to be happy or to save face. It is your choice."

This sense of competitive face has plagued the martial arts of Asia for hundreds, if not thousands, of years.* This attitude causes people to invest incredible status and pride in the specific martial art they do, rather than investigate how to expand their already existing body of knowledge by seeking new possibilities. Consequently, existing knowledge of martial arts stagnates and tends to be lost because of misplaced secrecy and pride. This situation is fortunately changing in the West. There, practitioners of karate and other martial arts take advantage of an open society in which they can freely adapt what is useful from other styles without experiencing a sense of betrayal to their own.

This experience in Okinawa caused me to take a much more open point of view regarding martial arts than many of my colleagues at that time. (From the 1950s to the 1970s, the idea of borrowing from a martial art that was not one's own was unheard of.) It also firmly moved me in the direction of the internal side of martial arts, which I admittedly favor. I've observed that, if one wishes an investment to pay off in the long term, it is wise to be open to other proven, higher yielding investments, even if your feelings of possessiveness and previous accomplishment must temporarily be put aside.

I returned to Tokyo from Okinawa in the spring of 1970 and took stock of how to proceed to the next stage of my martial arts journey, quietly reflecting on the words of my Okinawan master. I was just twenty then, full of raging hormones and crazy for the back and forth intensity of

*The Chinese term for this is *men hu jr jien*, which, freely translated, means that anyone outside our gate (that is, martial art style) is to be considered an enemy and therefore disliked, ignored, and denigrated.

The Bridge from the External to the Internal, continued

"mixing it up" with hands, feet, throws, and joint-locks. Although I continued to spar with high-ranking karate people, it was clear that I was not going to seriously train in karate anymore. It also was obvious that my knees were not going to be able to continue to withstand high-level judo, as they had already given out on one occasion. I had no desire to become a partial cripple. Painful knee difficulties had felled a number of my friends, who had ignored warning signs of impending knee damage.

Morihei Ueshiba (see p. 118), the founder of aikido with whom I had been studying, had passed away the year before and, although I continued training at the aikido headquarters, it did not feel the same after O-Sensei died. I concentrated on continuing training in tai chi, but was still working with Push Hands and had not yet reached the free sparring phase. One bright spot during that time of sadness was training in hsing-i with Kenichi Sawai.* I did a lot of **standing chi gung** together with his other students, along with a fair amount of intense and varied sparring.

STANDING CHI GUNG
Chi gung that is done standing still, either with the practioner's arms resting at the sides of the body or else held in the air in a static posture.

---

* See *Taiki-Ken* by Kenichi Sawai (Tokyo: Japan Publications, 1976).

Southern Shaolin styles are known for (a) short range in-close hand techniques; (b) short, wide, and low stances; where "short" refers to the distance between feet when one foot is ahead or behind the other; (c) power blocks; (d) minimal footwork appropriate for a person fighting in a confined space, such as the deck of a small boat; and (e) emphasis on hand techniques rather than kicks. Generically, Southern Shaolin styles are called **nan chuan** or Southern Boxing.

Northern Shaolin is known for (a) long-range extended hand techniques; (b) long, extended stances; (c) deflection and evasion tactics rather than power blocks; (d) extensive footwork and jumping techniques for fighting in large, open spaces; and (e) strong emphasis on kicking techniques as well as hand strikes. The classic Chinese martial arts phrases are "Southern hands" and "Northern feet." Generically, Northern external martial arts are called **chang chuan** (Long Boxing) or *Bei Shaolin* (Northern Shaolin). Mostly, the Northern external styles formed the basis for the internal martial arts of tai chi chuan, ba gua chang, and hsing-i.

Some martial art styles had Northern and Southern branches, such as Praying Mantis, White Crane, Monkey, Tiger, and Hung boxing. Typical

NAN CHUAN
Southern Fist. All the Southern schools of Chinese martial arts.

CHANG CHUAN
The basic method of Northern Shaolin Chinese external martial arts.

CHOI LI FUT
A Southern Shaolin fighting style from Canton province.

MOK GAR
A Southern Shaolin fighting style from Canton province.

WU MEI
An external/internal Southern Shaolin martial art.

FIVE ANCESTORS
A Fukien province Southern Shaolin style, that is a primary source for all Southern short-hand systems.

LOHAN
Temple Guardian Boxing. A Northern Shaolin style.

LOST TRACK BOXING
An external Northern Shaolin fighting system.

KENDO
The Japanese art of swordsmanship practiced with a bamboo sword.

IAIDO
The Japanese art of swordsmanship practiced with a metal samurai sword.

Southern styles practiced in the West include **Choi Li Fut, Mok Gar,** Wing Chun, **Wu Mei,** and **Five Ancestors.** Most of the purely Northern styles have not yet reached the West, with the exception of Chinese wrestling, chang chuan, Northern Shaolin, **Lohan,** and **Lost Track Boxing.** In general, martial arts activity was most intense in northern China, an area that consistently produced the strongest military fighters and professional bodyguards. Historically, the Western world was exposed mainly to the Southern styles because China's seaports were located in the southern region. Recently, however, now that immigration from the north of China has become possible, more and more immigrants and visiting students are bringing their martial arts to the West.

As martial arts enthusiasts move along a continuum to the mixed styles of the external/internal martial arts and to the yet more subtle internal arts, they find that many of the same physical practice methods (hits, throws, etc.) may continue to be used. The major differences do not center on physical technique, but evolve around the issues of (a) muscles versus chi; (b) mind over physicality; (c) the systematic training of the unconscious mind; (d) whether physical tension is advocated or proscribed; (e) whether the coordination between different parts of the body is minimally, partially, or totally integrated.

External Martial Arts Mixed with Some Internal Work

In China, higher levels of most external work evolve after many years to encompass some level of using chi (or subtle life-force energy). Usually, the internal work is begun with the teaching of breathing techniques rather than with methods of developing chi. Over time, the work with breath leads to an awareness of subtle energy. Often, a given external martial art will graft onto its system a chi gung (energy work) technique. Such adaptations are usually held to be the "big secrets" to be given only to the most worthy of students. In general, the Chinese conceive of higher-level martial art skills in terms of meditation and internal chi development work, not in terms of raw physical abilities. This paradigm is very different from the way Westerners normally perceive their martial arts of boxing, wrestling, and fencing.

Sometimes a chi gung system will be practiced separately by someone who is also doing an external martial art based on muscular tension. In such instances, the chi gung will not change the way the external practices are done. Rather, it has the effect of a higher octane fuel that adds power and efficiency without influencing the design of the car's engine. An external martial artist may also practice Zen Buddhism, which may create a calmer mind but not significantly change the technical muscular tension structure of the martial art. Zen Buddhist meditation is commonly incorporated into Japanese external martial arts, such as karate, and sword arts, such as **kendo** and **iaido.**

THE FOCUS OF EXTERNAL AND
INTERNAL MARTIAL ARTS COMBINED

In external/internal martial arts, the development of chi is at least equal to, if not more important than, the development of raw physical power. Muscular tension is still employed, but not nearly to the same extent nor with the same ferocity as it is in the purely external martial arts. In this amalgamated form, relaxation becomes significantly more emphasized than tension in all fighting technique and training procedures.

In the continuum of external/internal martial arts, each individual martial art usually has a clear bias toward either external or internal techniques. External practices are those that are based on (a) muscular tension; (b) aerobic activity rather than cultivation of chi; and (c) tendencies to separate the body training into segmented parts; for instance, arm training, leg training, waist training, etc. Internal martial arts are those that are completely based on (a) muscular and mental relaxation; (b) whole body integration; (c) obvious or subtle circularity in all physical motions; (d) the mind directly linking to the central nervous system to create speed and reflexes; and (e) awareness and conscious use of the internal, nonmuscular components under the skin, such as spine, blood vessels, internal organs, glands, joints, brain, all the energy centers, channels, and points inside the body, and the external aura.

There are various progressive stages in the middle ground of martial arts that bridge internal and external arts.

1. The first stage utilizes chi practices to relax the central nervous system and muscles *before* the practitioner explodes into power strikes using muscular tension. At this stage, the practice is more external/internal. This relaxing of the chi of the mind and the central nervous system is critical to any internal practice. The external martial arts also relax the body and mind before exerting power, but they do not specifically practice to gain control of the chi, which stabilizes the relaxation process.

2. The next stage involves learning how to feel the breath tangibly enter every part of the body. For example, when you are executing a fighting technique, your breathing would cause the concrete feeling of pressure in the part of your body being employed—in your hand if hitting or grabbing, in your leg if kicking or throwing, or in your elbow or forearm if blocking or striking. The more external the practice, the more the feeling of breath will be localized; the more internal the practice, the more the whole body will be aware of the breath. This feeling of breath will add power and subtlety to your techniques at all levels.

3. Various breathing methods will be coordinated with techniques done both moving and standing still. Among these breathing methods are (a) vibrating the breath, with and without explosions at the end (as in

Fukien White Crane); (b) machine gun-like, continuous, short exhalations common to Southern Shaolin short-hand styles; (c) animal-like roaring/vibrating breaths. These function to make the internal nerve impulses accelerate like an excited animal and produce extreme explosiveness, anger, and speed. This power is then projected at the opponent; (d) rhythmic breaths that use both regular and broken patterns; (e) slow, deep breathing done both internally and to breathe chi in and out of single or multiple body parts at will.

4. A basic maxim of chi gung practices is that the chi moves the blood. Over time, the objective is for you to consciously feel how your chi is moving your blood. This feeling enables you to get a clear sense of whether or not your chi is going where it is directed. When blood is moved quickly by the chi, it feels warm, even if the body is not externally moving. In the beginning, for most people, the sensation of blood feels heavier and more tangible than chi, so it is easier to use as a reality check in the early stages of chi development. The next stage involves feeling the chi as a separate entity from the breath as the chi moves inside your body while you do some martial art technique. Sometimes visualizations will be used to induce the concrete feeling of chi moving up and down and in every direction through your body. Chi gung, rather than being a separate technique, is now partially or completely fused into all your martial arts techniques. As this process increases, your practice becomes more internal.

5. With progress, you will become aware of and feel how first the breath and later the chi are directly moving through the nerves of your body. This sensation is remarkably light and incorporeal. It is this stage of practice that allows you to gain control of your autonomic nervous system. With such mastery, it becomes possible to gain highly unusual control of body functions, an activity for which the Indian and Tibetan yogis and Chinese chi gung practitioners are famous.

6. This stage employs all sorts of self-hypnosis and visualization techniques to increase performance capacities. These include visualizing and simultaneously feeling yourself going through repetitions of movements or seeing yourself going through sparring maneuvers with untold variations. Such practices can pattern the nervous system so that you can gain the nerve reflexes to do a given skill without having to put in as much physical practice time. These techniques are applied both while doing forms and in seated meditation sessions. Trance states are also used to make the body more rooted, faster, more agile, or stronger than would be possible through ordinary physical exercise. Music is sometimes used to deepen the trance states during training, a practice that is especially prevalent in the martial arts of Africa, India, and Indonesia. Common techniques focus on the ability to explode instantaneously with great ferocity and to become amazingly sensitive and

reactive to a perceived danger. These mental patterning techniques must be carefully monitored for any potential negative side effects on your central nervous system or personality. Mental agitation, depression, paranoid tendencies, and explosive mood swings can be increased or created in the practitioner.* A balanced approach between mental well-being and physical performance capacities is the best defense against negative patterning of the central nervous system. Historically however, many internal/external masters only focused on battlefield fighting competence and were unconcerned with balanced mental health. Sensitivity on the part of the teacher as to the subtle realities of how post-traumatic shock can be created or forestalled is an important issue if you wish to have a more human or spiritual approach to martial arts.

7. There is a stage at which both the use of the body and the integration of the body becomes finer than is possible in external martial arts. The coordination of the six combinations of the body (hands/feet, knees/elbows, shoulders/hips) becomes a major focal point. Most good external martial arts try to use the centrifugal horizontal turning force of the waist to move the arms and legs with force and speed. The internal systems go further by trying to connect up all the vertical body points that can move simultaneously with horizontal movement. For example, the elbow and knee must move in precise coordinated synchronization rather than only vaguely together. Internal joint movement will be connected and coordinated, so that when an elbow joint bends or extends x degrees, the knee joint will bend or extend the same x degrees. The more internal the practice, the finer the coordination between the body parts will be, and vice versa. It is especially common in the Southern Chinese schools to release power sequentially, one joint at a time, moving up the body with a whiplike effect that unleashes a rapid series of strikes. It is also common to use the power of only one, isolated, single joint or a specific combination of joints. Hitting an opponent using separate components of the six combinations is less common in Northern Chinese schools. There, all the six combinations will be applied simultaneously, although with nowhere near the detail, refinement, and cohesion of the Taoist internal martial arts of tai chi, ba gua, or hsing-i.

---

*When I practiced Fukien White Crane in the 1960s and early 1970s, I saw and heard about many White Crane masters who were obviously suffering from some of these problems. Later, after years of research, it became apparent that these sorts of difficulties can appear throughout all of the external/internal martial art visualization and self-hypnosis practices. Many masters whom I interviewed were greatly concerned (and went into great detail about) how to prevent these problems and how to reverse them, if possible, in either their early or later stages.

TUN TU
The Shaolin martial art term for sucking in and spitting out, which is not the same as, but which on the gross level bears similarities to, the internal arts practice of open/close.

WHITE EYEBROW
A Southern short-hand external/internal Shaolin fighting style.

COTTON BOXING
An external/internal martial art of North China.

BA JI CHUAN
An external/internal martial art of North China that focuses on hand techniques.

8. The storing and then releasing of chi becomes the major way all techniques are performed. Generally, in the Shaolin systems, this process is called swallowing and spitting or, in Chinese, **tun tu.** Here, the object is not only to relax and explode out (which is also done in external martial arts) but also to store energy and release it with the whole body instantaneously. This release of energy can be done in two basic ways. The first is through a single, continuous power strike. The second is through one big burst of energy that includes a series of regularly spaced, multiple jackhammer, whipping, vibrating, or wavelike strikes or slaps.

9. An advanced stage involves manipulating the chi outside the body in the external aura. This chi gung technique is done for two purposes: first, to strengthen and balance the practitioner's chi; second, to teach how to manipulate, control, or disrupt the chi in the external aura of your opponents, to weaken them, set them up for an attack, or generally to confuse their senses.

Some of the better-known external/internal martial arts in the West include Southern systems, such as White Crane, Southern Praying Mantis, **White Eyebrow**, Snake, Wu Mei, and Northern systems, such as **Cotton Boxing, Ba Ji Chuan,** and Eight Drunken Immortals. There are many more styles in China, most of which have never come to the West. These systems tend to use various combinations of Taoist, Buddhist, Shaolin, and Kunlun types of chi gung. Indonesia also has a variety of external/internal styles on its many islands.

THE FOCUS OF INTERNAL MARTIAL ARTS

In the purely internal martial arts, a shift begins to happen—the issue of long-term health and therapeutic healing of the body also becomes a major consideration. In both the external and the external/internal martial arts, health is normally considered in terms of fitness. The healing of body malfunctions is not usually included in the skills of the external or amalgamated forms, nor is it even within their priorities. The driving force in each is found in the creating or refining of useful fighting techniques.

The primary Taoist internal martial arts of ba gua chang, tai chi chuan, and hsing-i chuan are derived from the nei gung tradition (see p. 62) of Taoist meditation. This system formed the underlying basis for traditional Chinese medicine. Taoist meditators were primarily concerned with health and mental well-being, not with warfare or self-defense. They often lived in inaccessible locations where there was no one around to attack them. Their chi technology was incorporated into Taoist martial arts

(*Text continues on page 49.*)

White Crane

 I revisited Wang Shu Jin in a park in Taichung in the summer of 1969 for some additional training, which was excellent. Afterwards, I spent a few days in Taipei with a friend of mine. In the hotel where we stayed, my friend introduced me to a "young master" of Yang style tai chi. This master was very soft, good at Push Hands and able to take full-body elbow blows effortlessly. Most importantly, he could do the fa jin uprooting technique of tai chi chuan very well. Both Wang Shu Jin and Kenichi Sawai, with whom I studied hsing-i in Tokyo, could do fa jin, but at this point had not yet specifically taught the technique to me. I trained for a while with the young master and returned to Japan.

The next summer, I worked with Wang some more and then, returning to Taipei, looked up the young master again. We got to know each other somewhat and I visited his family in the central Taiwan village of Hsilo, home of many of the Taiwanese martial arts, including White Crane. This young master offered me a deal: He would teach me the "secrets" of fa jin (see p. 110), if I would take him to Tokyo and sponsor him there.

Like many naive youths eager for a shortcut to knowledge and success, I jumped at the chance, thinking I could get around the conservatism of the old masters. He came to live in my small Japanese apartment in the winter of 1970. He was not easy to have in my life but, after a while, he showed me the "secret." He taught me to vibrate the breath and body rather fiercely and loudly like a growling lion, stretch the tendons, turn the waist like the motions of a food mixer, hit my own body, and then flap my hands in the air. He then returned to Taiwan.

My temporary perspective at the time was that all this was great. I trained very hard at these "secrets." They worked. I began to get very soft, fast, and sensitive, and started accruing some fa jin, although of a shocking nature, rather than the smooth kind that can come from tai chi. It was intriguing to discover that mere slaps with the wrists, open hands, and fingers could dislocate and even break the thicker bones of the body. The practice definitely helped my sparring. The drawback was that it made my energy jumpy, piercing, and explosive.

I returned to New York the next year and did a lot of Push Hands practice at Cheng Man-ching's school while he was away in Taiwan. The vibrating "tai chi" method worked well. However, the members of Cheng's school judged it effective but "hard." Back in the Orient, I was to find out

White Crane, continued

that what the young master had really taught me was an indigenous martial art of Taiwan, Fukien White Crane,* specifically, *Tsung He* or the vibrating crane branch of that method. This art specialized in sinking chi to the lower tantien and making the root very heavy. It emphasized Push Hands sensitivity training, especially the folding of the joints. This way of pushing hands has many similarities to the Push Hands of tai chi, although without the smoothness or variability of tai chi technique. Practicing it, I could always get a good workout with highly motivated individuals while still improving many of the primary skills of tai chi. I often did this method in the mornings in many Taiwan parks, which were always filled with willing participants.

On my second trip to Taiwan, it was exciting to find one of the sources of Goju karate (which comes from Fukien province), a form I had practiced when younger. Fukien White Crane's primary stance, for example, is also the Three-War **San Chin** stance.** White Crane also used many of the inside arm touch techniques of Goju, albeit with a much larger repertoire and degree of sophistication than I had previously seen either in Japan or Okinawa. A trademark quality of this Southern style is a focus on sophisticated power breathing techniques to develop the capacity to absorb and effortlessly withstand body blows. For example, one female White Crane practitioner, who demonstrated this art in Taiwan tournaments, used to allow powerful men to hit her full bore without experiencing any obvious discomfort or fear. Years later, in Beijing, Liu Hung Chieh told me that, in the 1928 China full-contact National Fighting Championships, he saw the Fukien White Crane people regularly take killer blows from the Shaolin people without effect, but that the hsing-i people with their powerful "internal" blows were able to make Fukien White Crane contestants drop.

SAN CHIN
A pigeon-toed martial arts stance commonly used in conjunction with power breathing techniques.

---

*All forms of White Crane originate from the Shaolin Temple. Besides Fukien White Crane, the other two major schools are Cantonese and Northern White Crane. Each school has several branches and subgroups. Cantonese White White Crane is often called *Lama Pai*, and is supposed to have originated in Tibet. It is known for its long Northern Shaolin style, having long strikes and short, rapid steps. Northern Crane is known for its emphasis on the long, languid, smooth, flapping extended strikes of the bird, and/or of Cotton Palm (see p. 97), rather than for vibrating strikes.

**Tai Tzu, which also uses a variation of the Three-War stance, is another Southern Shaolin style from Fukien province, and is also the source of the Okinawan Uechi Ryu karate.

White Crane, continued

Acquiring a background in the folding and vibrating techniques of White Crane was valuable as preparation for learning to utilize in combat the folding and elbow and shoulder techniques in the internal martial arts. Learning White Crane helped with my understanding of the bird techniques in hsing-i and ba gua, and the elbow and shoulder techniques in tai chi. In my experience with the pure internal arts, I found that, although the broad principles were similar to White Crane practice, the details were much finer, smoother, more comprehensive, and more calming to the spirit.

as an exceedingly effective power source, to be used in the secular world. Health, healing, therapeutic diagnosis, and developing clear meditative states of mind were essential concerns of Taoist martial arts. Fighting was viewed mostly as a useful by-product.

The prime directive of the Taoist internal martial arts is aimed at developing your chi and calming your mind. According to the Taoist way, if a practice is harming your body or mind, no matter how effective it makes your fighting ability, it must not be followed. To damage your body or mind in learning to defend yourself is, to the Taoists, a foolish long-term health and wellness strategy. Millions of people in China practice the internal martial arts purely for preventive health maintenance, healing injuries and illness, and as a form of meditation and stress management. It is the nature of the health practices that they can be done in a follow-the-leader fashion, like aerobics, once the internal principles have been learned.

The internal martial art masters who emphasize the practical side of fighting are considered to be the best fighters in China. Internal martial arts are held to be the most subtle, complex, and sophisticated in the Chinese martial arts world. In the internal arts, circularity of motion becomes more important than linear action. To become a genuinely effective internal martial artist requires hard work, intelligence, and perseverance. It also requires that individuals be self-directed and able to practice by themselves. Externally motivated people who need the physical presence of leaders to follow in order to practice movements ordinarily are not able to easily adjust to the higher levels of internal practice.

Discovering the Inside of My Body and Chi—Learning to Stand

 Experiencing the amazing chi of Wang Shu Jin in the summer of 1968 was the definite turning point that motivated me to commit fully to learning the Chinese way of developing chi for martial arts. Although I wanted to remain in Taiwan indefinitely to study with Wang, obligations to continue at the university in Tokyo prevented it. Back in Japan, I explored the internal martial arts scene there frequently. As fate would have it, this search lead me to a primary route for developing chi and an awareness of how it worked inside the body. I found Chang I Chung and the practice of standing.

Three days a week, Chang I Chung (one of Wang's main students) taught tai chi in a large cement-floored storage room above the Botan coffee shop in Tokyo's Shibuya district. The class began with standing, a chi gung warm-up series, and then progressed to doing the **Chen Pan Ling** combination form (see p. 304), a cane form, Push Hands, and two-person fighting sets (bare-handed and with a cane). For the first few months, I did the warm-ups,* and then the form, putting hours a day into practicing the form on my own, as well as attending other Japanese martial arts classes.

CHEN PAN LING
A combination form of tai chi chuan.

After a few months I asked the teacher, "If I really want to improve my tai chi, what should I do?" A week later, he answered: "If you really want to learn tai chi, first seriously focus on standing and only afterwards on the basic exercises. Then you will be ready to learn the tai chi form." He then said, "This has been told to many of the students here wishing to learn tai chi as a martial art, but rarely do they listen. Will you?"

Shortly thereafter, I received this same advice from three other martial artists I highly respected. The first was a man named Kawashima, a serious karate practitioner and graduate student who was one of Chang's better proteges. Kawashima had followed the advice to stand, and

---

* Later I learned that these warm-ups were part of an ancient Taoist chi gung series, although they lacked the last component of a spine stretch. Although I first learned the external aspects of these exercises from Chang, it took eighteen years of difficult cross-research to actually understand all the internal work of this 3000-year-old Taoist methodology. I learned the most important interior components from Liu Hung Chieh in Beijing. Without Liu's teaching, I could never have discovered how to complete the work begun with Chang. (*Editor's note:* For more information on this chi gung series, see B. K. Frantzis, *Opening The Energy Gates of Your Body,* North Atlantic Books, Berkeley, California, 1993.)

Discovering the Inside of My Body and Chi, continued

explained that Chang was very generous in telling me the no-frills truth. The second was Kenichi Sawai, leader of the I Chuan school (see p. 180) in Japan, and third was his immensely powerful student, Goto. Each told me that the standing practice would lead to real internal power. (In my view, they all obviously had it.) I took all this advice to heart, and concluded that it was serious business. Since I had traveled half-way around the world to learn "the real stuff" of martial arts, I undertook a rigorous standing practice. Besides learning the tai chi form, I reached a point over the next few years where I was capable of holding the standing-posture only,* or standing and doing the whole set of basic internal power development exercises for six hours continuously, without breaks.

Religiously following Chang's original advice to stand, I was eventually, after two years, able to surpass most of his advanced students, even some who had over a decade of experience in tai chi. Throughout the next twenty years in all parts of China, I was to hear this high regard for standing chi gung expressed across a wide spectrum of top tai chi and hsing-i masters, each of whom had more or less parallel procedures for holding tai chi and hsing-i postures. In Beijing, Chen style tai chi stylists also advised that, after being able to do the movements reasonably well, one should practice standing, arms in the air as if hugging a tree, for a long time. This practice, they said, is a requirement for obtaining authentic internal "gung fu"; that is, power and skill. The consensus of the many internal masters I met in China was "It is necessary to stand and do basic exercises (called *ji ben gung*—see p. 84), if you want your movements to have power and not be empty."

---

*Years later, this same static process was suggested to me by teachers for San Ti (see p. 190) in hsing-i and for various postures in tai chi. Although I did not do the tai chi postures continuously for several hours, the practice of holding them for up to an hour at a time clearly was one of the reasons for my eventual success in being able to sink my chi.

Internal martial arts have both internal and external aspects. The goal is to seamlessly fuse the two into one integrated whole. Internal martial artists consider the physical movements of fighting techniques to be external. Accordingly, they may use any of the fighting techniques from the external or external/internal repertoires, though usually in a more sophisticated, circular, and internally coordinated whole-body way. In essence, internal artists feel that fighting techniques deal with the other person, not the internal practitioner's own body, mind, and spirit. The basics of the internal components of the internal martial arts concentrate on the intention, chi, and consciousness. The effectiveness of internal arts fighting techniques is based on the judicious use of internal power, not upon external body movements and technique, which internal martial artists also do exceedingly well. The mind is clearly given primacy over physical technique.

Speed, reflexes, power, and endurance are accomplished by increasing your reservoir of chi, by making your central nervous system more efficient, by transmuting the physical tissues of your body (especially the nerves), and by developing a high level of unattached centeredness and mental clarity through subtly changing and supercharging your internal structures. You become able to manifest external performance abilities such as athletic and fighting skills. Among the critical considerations of the internal martial arts are:

1. Complete use of the 16 basic components of the Taoist nei gung system (see p. 62), including precise body alignments to prevent the flow of chi from being blocked or dissipated. Practicing these principles brings exceptionally effective biomechanical alignments.

2. The conversion of every form of chi into functionally powerful and useful fighting, healing, or meditation techniques.

3. A totally expanded and functional use of the six-combination body integration principle (see p. 61). The object is to make the whole physical body, chi, and mind move like one totally integrated cell, with no separate moving parts. Two highly significant phrases in the tai chi classics illustrate this point. They are: "From posture to posture the internal power remains unbroken," and "When one part moves, all parts move and when one part stops, all parts stop."

4. Exact methods of how to use the intention and the deepest levels of the human mind (conceptualized as the "heart/mind" in Chinese and Japanese) to move chi to affect an individual's emotions and consciousness. How to fuse Taoist meditation techniques of stillness and higher states of consciousness into standing, moving, sitting, and lying down chi practices and martial art forms.

To fully understand what the internal martial arts are from a fighting perspective, it is necessary to realize that they incorporate virtually all the fighting techniques of the external arts, while simultaneously superimposing their own internal qualities onto them. They add unique methodologies and fighting strategies based on yin/yang theory and the *I Ching*. Historically, people who have wanted to upgrade their fighting capacity in external and external/internal martial arts have used the chi gung of the purely internal martial arts to increase their already existing abilities.

Each of the separate internal systems has subdivisions that specialize in certain aspects of fighting, and all share an emphasis on health and wellness. Some styles and subdivisions are rare, some popular. The popularity of a given system does not indicate its martial superiority or inferiority. The styles one is likely to encounter in the West are tai chi chuan with the **Yang,** Wu, **Chen, Hao, Sun,** and **Combination Form** styles; ba gua chang with the **Yin Fu** and **Cheng Ting Hua** styles; hsing-i chuan with the **Hebei, Shansi, Muslim, Hsin I, I Chuan,** or **Da Cheng Chuan** styles, as well as **Liu He Ba Fa.** All incorporate the basic concept of chi.

Chi and the Reality of Self-Defense

In the beginning phase of internal martial arts training, students usually do not have much chi. The initial ba gua practices, for example, involve developing good body mechanics and coordination while learning to lengthen and spiral the body. The body mechanics of the internal martial arts are significantly more sophisticated than those of the external martial arts. They are based upon internally and externally connected body movement and spirals, which use the opening and closing, compression and expansion of the fluids inside the body to release power. As students become more advanced, even if they are very strong, they start to rely less on strength and more on the chi flowing through the system. The chi then gives them power and moves their bodies. It is like moving from a 1950s computer, whose hardware took up a whole room but had little power, to a modern laptop computer, whose hardware fits in a small briefcase, but has many times the power of the 1950s model.

Beginners often have the mistaken idea that their chi alone is going to be enough to defeat an opponent without any need to master the skills of hitting, kicking, throwing, and joint-locks. This is like putting the cart before the horse.

The ultimate object in ba gua, for one example, is to use pure chi as the power to defeat an opponent. To do this requires internal power, called **nei jin** in Chinese. This is realized when the chi of your body is tuned to a specific frequency that unifies the body and allows you to project a tremendous amount of internal power. However, you must be at a very high level to do this. In the beginning, training is much more physical, and it takes years before it becomes nonphysical. Not only must you increase

YANG TAI CHI
The most popular form of tai chi today.

CHEN TAI CHI
The original form of tai chi.

HAO TAI CHI
A rare style based on small-frame internal movements.

SUN TAI CHI
Mixes the Hao style with hsing-i and ba gua.

COMBINATION FORM TAI CHI
Mixes several styles of tai chi, hsing-i, and ba gua together.

YIN FU BA GUA
Uses the Willow Leaf Palm.

CHENG TING HUA BA GUA
Uses the Dragon Palm.

HEIBEI HSING-I
Commingles hsing-i and ba gua.

SHANSI HSING-I
Original form of hsing-i.

MUSLIM HSING-I
A particular style of hsing-i.

HSIN-I HSING-I
Heart-mind boxing.

I CHUAN HSING-I
A style based on eight standing postures.

DA CHENG CHUAN
Another name for I Chuan.

LIU HE BA FA
A combination internal martial art that is not tai chi.

NEI JIN
Internal power that unifies the chi of the whole body.

your chi, you must also learn the physical techniques. This requires at least as much physical coordination as is required in the external martial arts.

The Reason for the Emphasis on Ba Gua in this Book

Although this book is about all the Chinese internal martial arts, an emphasis is placed on ba gua. Why should this be, considering that the art of tai chi is much more popular and far more widely practiced? There are several valid reasons. First, ba gua is most likely the only purely Taoist martial art.* As such, it contains a great deal of original martial information that has not been changed or adulterated by time. Second, ba gua is considered by highly respected internal masters to be the most technically sophisticated and effective of the internal martial arts. Third, ba gua includes all the internal and external circling and spiraling techniques completely or partially absent in the linear martial arts. Fourth, ba gua is one of the clear antecedents of aikido, the major internal martial art of Japan, and includes the overt health and energy practices usually missing in aikido. Fifth, ba gua has the grace and beauty of the other internal arts, but its movements are done at normal and/or fast aerobic speeds, rather than in the slow motion of tai chi, which many martial artists shun. Sixth, ba gua includes the complete spiritual tradition of martial arts, which is found much less often in tai chi and hsing-i. Seventh, ba gua fulfills many of the reasons people do tai chi, but with heightened internal awareness and in a much more dynamic form of relaxation.

Iron Shirt Chi Gung

As you and a practice partner work on internal two-person fighting applications of martial arts through sparring and joined-hand exercises, including Rou Shou (see p. 235), what started out as light taps may evolve into strong blows, either by accident or by mutually agreed-upon escalation of force. Going beyond a certain level of escalation can be dangerous.

IRON SHIRT CHI GUNG
Technique that gives the ability to take heavy physical blows without pain or injury, as though you were wearing a protective shirt of iron.

PAI DA
A Shaolin method of developing the ability to take blows with impunity.

At this point, you might want to start learning **Iron Shirt** techniques, which give you the ability to absorb powerful blows without danger or distress. Some ba gua people, such as Wang Shu Jin (see p. 16), are famous for just standing still and allowing their opponents to hit them, knowing all along that the blows will have no effect. Shaolin Iron Shirt techniques, called **pai da,** involve hitting your body in systematic patterns with tiny sticks, iron rods, or socks full of hard objects, such as stones or marbles. Ba gua Iron Shirt does not use any external objects to hit the body in order to develop the ability to absorb energy. Rather, internal

---

*Although the founder of modern ba gua, Tung Hai Chuan, studied Lohan Boxing *before* he learned ba gua, his ba gua itself is purely Taoist in all its internal aspects.

energy practices done both within the form and as separate nei gung sets are sufficient for this purpose. In ba gua, you can train by using your arms to hit your body, or by manipulating your internal organs to alter your internal pressures, bringing chi to specific areas of the body for protection.

It is not a good idea for martial artists to learn Iron Shirt early in their training because it may hinder sensitivity development. As you may imagine, if practitioners can absorb powerful blows without harm, they will hardly tend to pay attention to sensitivity and movement. This attitude could prove tremendously disadvantageous when sharp cutting weapons come into play. Neglect of sensitivity can also eventually reduce "aliveness" inside your body. Internal practitioners consider the quality of being alive, being responsive to your environment, to be significant. It would be a big mistake to allow your ego to deny this sensitivity to you simply so you could feel proud of being able to "take an opponent's best shot."

Weapons Training

The traditional weapons of the internal martial arts are the same four main weapons that are used in all Chinese martial arts: the **straight double-edged sword,** the **broadsword/knife,** the **staff,** and the spear. The internal art of ba gua makes no distinction between the practices of the straight sword and the broadsword, which is somewhat strange in the martial arts world. This lack of distinction is an effect of the toe-in, toe-out, spinning footwork, and spherical movements unique to the ba gua practice of Circle-Walking. When the movements of ba gua (in its post-birth methodology—see p. 212) are done with footwork more like that found in tai chi or hsing-I, the distinctly different methods for practicing each weapon *are* clearly differentiated. However, in the pre-birth methods of ba gua, due to the arc-like eddies that create the weapon's spherical motions—stabbing, bludgeoning, cutting, blocking, and deflecting— actions tend to flow in and out of themselves without allowing identification of distinct shapes or usage, which normally the natural functioning of each specific weapon appears to demand. Tai chi specializes in the straight sword, which requires more skill and precision. Tai chi clearly differentiates between straight and broadsword technique. The broadsword is considered a hacking weapon, where strength and power count, and is ideally suited for combat with several people. The straight sword requires more sensitivity and circular movements. It is clearly superior in duels, but is not as good for fighting numerous opponents, such as soldiers on a battlefield or a group of bandits. The art of hsing-i avoids the straight sword and specializes in a type of broadsword that is like the long Japanese samurai sword known as a **katana.**

Hsing-i also specializes in the spear, and to a lesser extent, the staff. Tai chi works mostly with spears, and does numerous Push Hands exer-

STRAIGHT DOUBLE-EDGED SWORD
The basic sword used for one-on-one combat in the Chinese martial arts. This sword can cut equally with both edges and has a pointed tip that can pierce flesh.

BROADSWORD/KNIFE
The primary curved-blade weapon used in Chinese martial arts for fighting multiple opponents.

STAFF/POLE
A primary noncutting weapon of Chinese martial arts that is usually made of wood, but can be made of metal.

KATANA
A Japanese curved samurai sword.

cises with them. The nature of the turning and twisting of ba gua Circle-Walking reduces the difference between the spear and the pole, and both are practiced in essentially the same manner.

The spear, "the king of long weapons" in traditional Chinese martial arts (the spear is about nine feet long) and the pole (about six feet long) share many of the same techniques and some different ones that relate to the difference in their arcing motions. In general, spears are used to cut or stab, and poles to stab and bludgeon. The best spears are fashioned from a special wood called *bai la gan* that grows in Shandong province. Spears made of this wood are thick and flexible and can whip flexibly in an arc of up to three feet if blocked, which is enough room to break someone's leg or head (if a spearhead is attached, its slicing action can cause mortal wounds). Given the flexibility of the wood, the head of a spear can spin its tip faster than any snake can strike. Bai la gan wood, being extremely flexible, can usually bend to the full blow of a sword without damage.

Although the primary weapons training always centers on the four main weapons, each of the internal martial arts has its own secondary weapons. Chen style tai chi, for instance, has a bewildering assortment of long and short traditional weapons. Although these are preserved in the Chen village, virtually no one practices using them today outside the village itself. In hsing-i, on the other hand, people often practice with daggers, which are obviously still relevant. Ba gua has other weapons, such as needles fitted on a ring, whips, and deer horn knives that look like two curved blades put together facing opposite directions with a space in the middle where the weapon is held. These were convenient weapons that could be carried in a belt. Their use fits well with ba gua's spiraling movements. These ancient weapons are excellent for training the mind and body, and they add flavor and variability to modern martial arts practice. Although they were state-of-the-art in their day, their practical value diminishes significantly in modern times in the face of the firepower available from concealed guns.

The energies that a martial artist generates when using open-hand practices are not the same as those produced when metal weapons are used. In general, when you study the weapons form of Chinese martial arts today, you are told that the purpose of such training is to teach you to be able to send your chi through the weapon.* Some members of the ba gua school would consider this statement to be only partially true. They believe that when a fighter uses a metal weapon, such use changes the frequencies of what the Taoists have identified as the eight primary energetic levels in humans (see p. 76). Consequently, how these energetic levels interact within the body is changed. In ba gua, weapons practices are done purely to develop **sha chi,** or the energy of killing, be it the killing of

---

*This statement is more or less correct for the use of wooden weapons, but not for weapons made of metal.

another person, an animal or of an internal mental demon. Sha chi metal weapons practice makes one physically very strong, not only because a free-weight heavy weapon is used during physical exercise, but also through an alchemical reaction between the metal of the weapon and the energy of the person wielding it.

As a practical matter, if you can work well with empty-hand techniques, it is not all that difficult to work with weapons. One line of thought is that, if you are seeking health and spiritual benefits, there is no need for practicing weapons. However, if you wish to be a complete martial artist, then these traditional weapons should be studied. Tai chi people traditionally worked out with extra-heavy swords in order to develop their chi to handle weapons that require significant physical strength with softness, relaxation, and adroitness, as well as training with wooden swords to develop exceptional lightness and sensitivity. Hsing-i people used an extremely heavy hacking broadsword for strength training. Ba gua people commonly work with oversized or especially heavy weapons weighing between four and twenty pounds to develop their chi to the maximum. In battle, practitioners of all internal arts used medium-weight swords with a personally adjusted center of balance to strike the best medium between speed, strength of metal, and sensitivity of handling.

Cheng Man-ching—Slow Motion and Fast

Courtesy of Ken Van Sickle

One of the people at the aikido school I attended in New York after high school hours was a judo teacher named Lou Klinesmith. Knowing of my passion for the fighting arts, Lou asked me one day if I had any interest in finding out about a new kind of "soft" punch. Curiosity aroused, I said, "Sure, why not?" He then put his hand about an inch from my body and, in a completely relaxed way, gave me a light tap. Initially, it felt as if he had not hit me at all, then in about half a second, my insides exploded. The pain doubled me in half. After Lou rubbed my body for a few seconds, I recovered completely. He then started telling me about tai chi chuan and his teacher, a sixty-year-old master named Cheng Man-ching. He suggested I look into his work.

At that time—the mid sixties— Cheng Man-ching was teaching at the Chinese Cultural Center on Manhattan's Upper East Side. As this location was only about half a mile from where I lived, it was relatively easy to check out. The Center had large bay windows through which you could see the class from the outside. The slow-motion movement of tai chi looked very weird to me, and I walked past the place a few times before finally entering.

Cheng introduced me to the tai chi form but did not push me or do anything to "sell" me on the martial value of tai chi as Lou had, and I was too shy to ask about it. Cheng was obviously a very skilled martial artist, as were other masters in New York at the time. However, Cheng was apparently not teaching practical punch, kick, throw, and joint-lock fighting techniques. My own goal was simple. I was an active, healthy teenager who had never known the impact of illness in my life and wanted only to learn fighting. To me, Cheng was not teaching anything that had to do with martial technique, so I left his school after two weeks, going back to my "old stuff," the Japanese fighting arts (karate, judo, aikido, and iaido, or samurai sword). Being a short-sighted teenager, I was incapable of grasping the valuable potential of tai chi for health, self-defense, or general well-being until I was much older and in college.

Being exposed to Cheng for those two weeks, however, was exceptionally valuable. As I studied Cheng Man-ching doing his movements, my attention was always drawn to the slow-motion lotus kick at the end of his short Yang style tai chi form. One time in class, Cheng demonstrated the lotus kick by doing it exceedingly fast. I perked up. I then focused intently on how he executed the lotus kick, experimenting with it and other slow-

Cheng Man-ching—Slow Motion and Fast, continued

motion kicks at home. Four things became immediately obvious to me about doing slow-motion kicks. First, they developed balance. Second, they stretched out my small muscles much more than fast kicks did. Third, they coordinated the body and increased my awareness of every tiny fault and flaw in my kick, knowledge that you really need if you desire to improve. Fourth, if you started doing high kicks in slow motion, they were much harder to execute than fast ones were.

I began to adapt the slow-motion method to the high side kicks of karate. (No one was doing these karate kicks in slow motion during the mid 1960s in New York.) After leaving Cheng, I got to a point over the next two years where I could do ten controlled slow-motion high side kicks in a row, without putting my foot down. This slow motion method was a critical ingredient in developing my best competitive karate fighting technique—a high side kick—that was responsible for my winning many competitions. I completely credit Cheng Man-ching's teaching and inspiration for this approach. There is no way I would have ever figured it out on my own.

All internal martial arts have punching techniques. Hsing-i uses them
the most, ba gua the least, with tai chi somewhere in the middle.
Unique to ba gua is the spiraling omnidirectional punching and cutting
fist method. Here, Liu Hung Chieh refines the author's technique.

SIMILARITIES AND DIFFERENCES

The Internal Martial Arts of Tai Chi, Hsing-I, and Ba Gua

FIVE CHARACTERISTICS OF INTERNAL MARTIAL ARTS

There are five important elements in the practice of ba gua, tai chi, and other nei gung (see p. 62) arts that make them unique in the martial arts world.

1. All motions have a spiraling or twisting energy that involves all parts of the body, including the abdominal cavity, the internal organs, bone marrow, tendons, ligaments, muscles, and the deepest layers of fascia. Sometimes these twisting actions are externally more obvious and sometimes very subtle, and some occur deep within the body with minimal visual clues.

2. All internal martial arts emphasize **liu he,** or the six combinations of the body. Physically, this refers to the three external combinations: the elbow with the knee, the hand with the foot, and the shoulder with the hip. It implies that the outer limbs must coordinate with one another through the center of the body. In the three internal combinations, or **nei san he,** the intention, the energy, and consciousness must coordinate with one another as well as with the external body.

3. Movements emphasize and use all the body systems connected to the spine. This process maximizes the strength and flexibility of the spinal column, can help heal spinal injuries, and develops the sensitivity, strength, and stamina of the central nervous system. The internal arts move the vertebrae of the spine continuously, powerfully pumping cerebrospinal fluid through the system.

4. All are concerned with the specifics of **opening and closing** joints and body cavities, which includes the expansion and compression of the **synovial fluid** within the joints. External martial arts, such as judo, karate, boxing, and gung fu, are for the most part not concerned with

LIU HE
Six combinations of body parts (shoulders-hips, elbows-knees, hands-feet) that must be finely coordinated to maximize physical power in the internal martial arts.

NEI SAN HE
The three internal components of the mind in Taoist theory: the "I" (intention), chi (energy), and shen (spirit or consciousness).

OPEN/CLOSE
The Chinese yin/yang paired opposites concept of growing/shrinking, expanding/contracting, and lengthening/shortening, etc. This universal pulsing occurs at the subatomic, cellular, and cosmological levels.

SYNOVIAL FLUID
A bodily fluid that is present inside the space between the joints of the body.

CENTRAL CHANNEL

The main energy channel located in the exact center of the human body between the perineum and the crown of the head.

LEFT CHANNEL

One of the three primary energy lines in the body; on the left side.

RIGHT CHANNEL

One of the three primary energy lines of the body; on the right side.

YIN AND YANG MERIDIANS

The twelve major vertical subtle energy channels of the body used in acupuncture.

JING LUO COLLATERAL MERIDIANS

The acupuncture meridians that wrap around the body horizontally and connect its vertical acupunture lines.

EIGHT EXTRAORDINARY OR SPECIAL MERIDIANS

The eight acupuncture meridians that have special uses in acupuncture over and above those of the normal vertical and horizontal meridans.

these methods, except perhaps in the most general of ways. In contrast, the internal arts are much more subtle and consequently more powerful, especially for stress release, body therapy, and slowing the aging process. Ba gua differs from hsing-i and tai chi in that the practices of these latter two arts prohibit you from crossing the center line of the body. In other words, they do not allow the left hand to go to the right side of the spine or the right hand to go to the left side. In ba gua, this crossing over happens all the time, without any of the internal energy channels within the body being short-circuited or nullified. Consequently, ba gua works with more aspects of the body's chi than does tai chi or hsing-i.

5. The opening of the major energy channels of the body is an important goal of ba gua and tai chi. The opening of the physical body (joints, cavities) helps to free up the energy flows within the body. There are many energy channels in the body. The three most important are the **central channel,** the **left channel,** and the **right channel.** (See Appendix C, p. 317.) Others are the **yin and yang meridians** of the body. The yin meridians run along the inside of the arms and legs and down the front of the body. The yang meridians run along the outside of the legs, up the back, and on the outside of the arms. There are also the meridians that circle your body in the manner of connective belts (these are called the **jing luo**) and also meridians referred to as the **eight special** or **extraordinary meridians.**

All these channels are opened and joined through the initial ba gua practice of Walking the Circle and, later, through standing and sitting practices. Walking the Circle with the body properly aligned helps to develop the spiraling energy that characterizes ba gua. Furthermore, in the more advanced levels of ba gua, sitting nei gung practices are extremely important for the process of opening all the energy channels of the body, of which several thousand are functionally useful.

DEVELOPING MARTIAL POWER WITH CHI

The 16-Part Nei Gung Internal Power System

The primary Taoist internal martial arts of ba gua chang, tai chi chuan, and hsing-i chuan are derived from the nei gung tradition of Taoist meditation.*

Editor's note: The author has in the past tried to teach these internal nei gung components simultaneously with the external movements of tai chi, hsing-i, and ba gua, but has found over the years that the complexity of the physical movements inhibits attention to the internal energies. Students in the beginning can usually focus on one or the other, but not both. Accordingly, he now teaches these energetic practices in a separate six-part chi gung program. These particular chi gung practices have been passed down unchanged for thousands of years. They have withstood the test of time, and continue to work extremely well. (See p. 344 for information on the B. K. Frantzis Energy Arts® program.)

The Taoist nei gung system seems to be the root from which all the other chi gung systems in China have obtained some or the bulk of their information and capacities.* It is also the root of the essential chi work and the internal power of the internal martial arts of ba gua, tai chi, and hsing-i, of chi therapy and bodywork, and of Taoist meditation. The sequence of learning the 16 components is not cast in concrete. Where you start is determined by what your goal is—for example, increasing capability for high performance, personal health, learning martial arts, learning to heal others, or advancing in meditation. The 16 basic components of Taoist nei gung include:

1. Breathing methods, from the simple to the more complex.
2. Feeling, moving, transforming, and transmuting internal energies along both the descending, ascending, and connecting energy channels of the body.
3. Precise body alignments to prevent the flow of chi from being blocked or dissipated—practicing these principles brings exceptionally effective biomechanical alignments.
4. Dissolving blockages of the physical, emotional, and spiritual aspects of ourselves.
5. Moving energy through the main and secondary meridian channels of the body, including the energy gates.
6. Bending and stretching the body from the inside out and from the outside in along the direction of the yin and yang acupuncture meridian lines.
7. Opening and closing all parts of the body's tissues (joints, muscles, soft tissues, internal organs, glands, blood vessels, cerebrospinal system, and brain), as well as all the body's subtle energy anatomy.
8. Manipulating the energy of the external aura outside the body.
9. Making circles and spirals of energy inside the body, controlling the spiraling energy currents of the body, and moving chi to any part of the body at will, especially to the glands, brain, and internal organs.
10. Absorbing energy into, and projecting energy away from, any part of the body.
11. Controlling all the energies of the spine.
12. Gaining control of the left and right energy channels of the body.
13. Gaining control of the central energy channel of the body.
14. Learning to develop the capabilities and all the uses of the body's lower **tantien** (hara or elixir/cinnabar field).

TANTIEN
Three primary centers in the human body where chi collects, disperses, and recirculates. The tantiens govern the energetic anatomy of a person.

---

*The other main chi gung systems in China are Buddhist, Martial Arts, Medical, and Confucian. In general, there is common sharing of techniques among them. However, there are also differing specializations, goals, and philosophical tenets from one to the next.

15. Learning to develop the capabilities and all the uses of the body's upper and middle tantiens.

16. Connecting every part of the physical body into one unified energy.

The Chinese have an expression, *ba gua shen fa*, which roughly translates into "what ba gua does for your body." The internal effects of ba gua are part of what the Chinese call **nei jia,** or internal development, which encompasses all chi or meditation work. Nei jia chuan, or internal martial arts, differs appreciably from **wai jia chuan,** or external martial arts, which, as indicated, are based on muscular fitness, endurance, and reflexes. In many ways, the nei jia martial arts with their medical benefits, stress reduction, and emphasis on meditation could easily become the martial arts of choice for the twenty-first century.

In the internal martial arts, all movement begins from deep inside the body and works outwards towards the skin. The object is to completely fuse the inside and outside. External martial arts work the outside of the body (that is, the muscles and reflexes), but eventually they can work their way to the inside if they incorporate chi gung. As a rule of thumb, the internal arts of China work with a person's general internal awareness to gain concrete feelings of the deepest subsystems in the body. External martial arts are essentially concerned with moving the muscles and the outer frame of the body.

Even if an external art has a movement that is exactly the same as one found in an internal art, the external will normally never penetrate below the outer layers of the body. To the trained eye, a tai chi master and a ballerina doing the exact same movement would not look even remotely similar. A layman, however, commonly would not detect much of a difference. *How* the movements are done internally is the critical issue. The nei gung system is the key.

How Internal Chi Power in Martial Arts is Created by the 16-Part Taoist Nei Gung System

The sophisticated nei gung discovered and developed by the Taoists thousands of years ago ultimately became the source of chi power in the internal martial arts of ba gua, tai chi, and hsing-i. The Taoists discovered this energy system long before the external martial arts are supposed to have begun in the Shaolin temple. In fact, many of the Shaolin martial arts, in their secret internal power techniques, borrowed heavily from it, adapting the "soft" nei gung energy techniques to a "hard " philosophical approach.

The Taoists originally discovered these powerful nei gung energy techniques as they delved deeply inside their own minds and bodies through meditation. They meditated primarily in order to uncover, personally

NEI JIA
A term used to describe all the internal martial arts or Taoist chi practices as one family.

WAI JIA CHUAN
External martial arts such as gung fu, karate, and judo.

experience, and immerse themselves in the underlying spiritual realities of the universe. They did not consider meditation to be a subdivision of learning how to fight better. Taoists also used the nei gung system to maintain superior health, heal illness, and continuously upgrade their own internal energies for the purpose of experientially realizing the secrets of profound inner stillness and spirituality.

Training for developing high performance in martial arts or competitive sports is, in the nei gung internal power method, accomplished in two clear stages. The easiest first stage addresses the specific goals of increasing health and healing overt or hidden injuries. (See Chapter 8.) Training in nei gung for health is a necessary preparatory stage for achieving high performance in athletics or martial arts. In any training method that will create real physical power and speed, a weak or ill body will not suffice. The health phase of nei gung training clears up any injuries or other problems that can make arduous training impossible and seriously diminish a student's eventual chance of achieving superior performance. As the body becomes healthier and more vibrant, it naturally can move better, faster, with more strength, and maintain stamina more easily.

The second stage of training is geared to provide high performance. This stage uses all the same internal techniques; however, they are utilized with a significantly more serious level of commitment. The difference lies not in *what* you train (that is, which component of the 16-part nei gung system you are working with), but in *how* you train. Using exactly the same techniques you did for developing health, you must work harder, spend more time training, use different training methodologies, and significantly raise your minimal acceptable standards of achievement. This requires your willingness to put in the necessary added effort needed for the next level, where you not only achieve great health, but also exceptional strength.

The Relationship of Chi Gung to Martial Arts Form Training

Within internal martial arts, internal power is taught through two primary methods. In the first, you learn internal power by first studying nei gung/chi gung as a separate art. This study accomplishes several purposes: The health of your body is upgraded, you acquire a clear awareness of chi, and, to some real extent, you have absorbed into your body an understanding of the nature of the internal work you need to develop for the specific martial art you are attempting to master. All this internal work occurs without you being burdened by an initial need to learn the complex physical coordination necessary to do martial movement well. In the early phases of starting something new, learning one challenging skill at a time is not only easier but is often a more productive long-term strategy for doing mind/body work. Learning two challenging skills simultaneously is more difficult and time consuming. Tackling one skill at a time is best for those with limited free time to study.

Next, you learn the movement and fighting applications of your specific internal martial arts style, incorporating the newly acquired nei gung components into all your physical movements. After your body has more or less absorbed a basic ability to fuse the internal energy work within your physical movements, you can focus on amplifying your internal power to the maximum. This intensification can be done with progressively more advanced stages of training, both within your developmental solo martial art form work and in combat training with opponents.

In the second method of imparting internal power, you will learn how to put the nei gung work into your physical martial art form movements *as you are simultaneously learning the forms.* When you reach an intermediate or advanced stage of form practice, you next intensely practice separate chi gung sets (which you learned in the beginning of the first method). The purpose of this stage is to dramatically shift your emphasis, to get you to rely on chi for power, rather than on the habit of relying on physicality for power. After this stage has stabilized, the practitioner finally begins to learn the most advanced chi work of the internal martial arts within the martial movements themselves, and not within separate chi gung sets.

The discussion has thus far concentrated on those learning internal martial arts. If you practice aikido or external martial arts, such as karate or tae kwon do or such external/internal martial arts as silat or many kinds of gung fu, learning chi gung can greatly upgrade your internal power base. If an internal martial arts master is willing and is sufficiently mentally flexible, you can be taught how to adapt the chi gung material to your specific martial art. After all, tai chi chuan was originally created by fusing regular external martial arts with nei gung. In the same way, nei gung could be added to karate or any other not fully internal martial art. Aikido practitioners, who are already seriously interested in ki work (*ki* is Japanese for Chinese word *chi*), would especially benefit from the upgrades of nei gung/chi gung's highly systematic internal energy chi training, especially in the area of health. Nei gung can extend the physical prowess of external martial artists, possibly for decades, spark their creativity, and compensate for any boredom they might be experiencing with their style.

Three Basic Suggestions for Realistically Obtaining Internal Power

Knowing about the existence of any precious thing is a far cry from actually acquiring it. Nei gung has benefitted humans for millennia. In presenting this information coherently, the hope is that it will help raise the awareness level of internal arts across the board. There are many highly motivated, creative, and intelligent people who, once they comprehend the implications of this information concerning nei gung, will be given valuable tools with which to help future generations. In order to genuinely comprehend, rather than only have partial information about, nei gung, follow these three suggestions:

1. Understand what is involved in the material itself. Knowing of its existence, begin to look for the 16 components within yourself and within your teacher. If you can see that your teacher has embodied any of the 16 nei gung elements, politely ask that each one he or she uses be taught to you. This may require some persistence on your part, as many teachers will not give over the information easily; some, however, will generously teach if you simply ask in a respectful manner.

2. Next, you must try to ascertain if your teacher has learned the whole system, large parts of the system, or only a few parts of it. It is not easy to ascertain if a teacher has encompassed nei gung in whole or in part. Anyone can say the right words, but having the actual knowledge is another matter. The untrained student could easily be given Shaolin concepts and training procedures that could appear to be the same as those of Taoist nei gung. For example, the Shaolin technique of tun tu or "sucking in and spitting out" could be confused with the nei gung process of **kai-he**, which is a more refined method of energy control than the Shaolin-derived squeezing and releasing of the muscles.

KAI-HE
Opening and closing.

3. The most critical requirement for learning nei gung is to actively seek out a teacher who knows it. Only a teacher who unequivocally knows the nei gung system can recognize the optimum time when it is or is not useful for you as a student to learn any specific part of the system. The teacher has to be able to recognize when and how the student is processing the nei gung imparted, and has to be able to gauge when the student is ready for more. In short, with nei gung, the teacher must carefully guide the student's growth. In this respect, the teacher is like the proverbial gardener who tends the student's growth, weeding out what is unnecessary, pruning and replanting when required, and nourishing with new information.

The Process of Learning Nei Gung

After you have learned the easier nei gung health practices, you retrain in each of the 16 elements to bring out maximum internal power. Your long-term practice will go through phases wherein you manifest within yourself three alternating distinctly different energetic qualities whose proportions depend on which one of the three internal martial arts that you are studying. (Remember that what is being discussed here is the invisible energy within your body, not the physical qualities of your muscles or other tissues, which do not tense and which ideally should maintain superior tone and relaxation.) One quality makes your internal energy and energy channels immensely yin—soft, amorphous, and relaxed—which over time will allow you to manifest speed and effortless, coordinated fluid movement. The second quality will make the energy inside your body immensely yang—compressed, defined, and hard—which over time will increase both your overt and subtle ability to project power. The hard and soft are the opposite sides of the same power. The third quality is the ability to instantaneously change or remain in flux between the hardness and the softness.

The hard and soft attributes can be manifested as an overall quality of an entire martial art or chi gung method or as an element within any specific single nei gung or martial art technique. The comment of the Taoist adept Liu Hung Chieh (see p. 241), about practicing tai chi chuan, which is relatively soft and also ba gua chang, which is relatively hard, is indicative of this whole situation. Liu said, "For more than forty years, when I felt my chi was getting too hard and strong and I was no longer completely comfortable practicing ba gua chang, I would emphasize doing tai chi more. And over time, emphasizing tai chi, when I no longer felt completely comfortable with being too relaxed and empty and wanted my chi to feel more solid and strong, I would again emphasize practicing ba gua more."

Sequential Order of The Learning Process   Here is a suggested sequence for learning nei gung:

1. Learn a physical movement, either within a chi gung program, a static martial arts posture, or a martial arts form.
2. Learn it gently for health and to prepare your body and central nervous system for the more advanced training.
3. Next, put a nei gung component into each and every part of the movement, focusing on its hard aspect. This practice should make the internal energy in your body like steel and, over time, manifest itself as clearly defined external power.
4. Now work on the nei gung component in a soft way until the hardness is integrated into your central nervous system in an effortless, comfortable, and relaxed way.
5. Finally, practice extensively until you can deliberately switch your energy from hard to soft, both gradually and instantaneously, with little and then no effort.

This process of focusing on hard, soft, then integration of both repeats ad infinitum. The more energetic hardness you can achieve in the current round, the greater your ability to achieve energetic softness in the next round, which gives you the ability to become harder the next round than you could have become if you had not integrated with softness first. The cycle keeps repeating itself.

The Nei Gung Process Is Like Forging a Samurai Sword This entire process of developing nei gung's internal power can be compared to the manufacture of the blade of a samurai sword. The classic samurai sword, which incorporates strength, flexibility, and sharpness of edge, was arguably forged of the finest steel in the world.

A samurai sword blade is made by seamlessly folding multiple layers of steel together. Each layer of steel, separately forged by a master swordmaker and those assisting him, is combined with previous layers to achieve strength and durability.

Each one of the 16 separate nei gung components is like the layers of a samurai sword. Like the forging of the layers of steel that comprise the core metal of the sword, learning each nei gung component requires training in each of its many separate layers, day after day, in a continuous stream of practice. Nei gung practitioners work the qualities of hardness, softness, and integration of the two into every step of learning each separate nei gung component, as well as when combining several nei gung components. Eventually, this procedure enables the internal martial artist to seamlessly fuse hard and soft together. Then, as if working the dimmer switch of an electric light, expert practitioners can instantaneously control how much and what kind of power they are manifesting. This ability is as useful for competitive athletes as it is for martial artists.

SPOTLIGHT ON A NEI GUNG ELEMENT: THE DISSOLVING PROCESS

The Outer-Dissolving Process

Through concentrated but relaxed use of both the mind's intent and the heart/mind (see p. 74), a person can learn to break up and release energy blockages with a meditation technique called the **outer-dissolving process.*** These blockages, which may have physical, mental, emotional, or psychic origins, can exist anywhere inside the body or outside the body in its surrounding **aura**, or bioelectrical field. Such energetic blockages may be dissipated or dissolved by mental effort, and their energy ejected outward. For martial artists, the clearing of the energetic field surrounding the body is important because it enables them to be extremely sensitive to the energetic gap between themselves and their opponents *before* the fight-

OUTER-DISSOLVING PROCESS
A basic Taoist chi (nei gung) practice for releasing blocked internal energy and projecting it outside the physical body. Used primarily to heal and strengthen the energies related to the physical body.

AURA
The energetic or bioelectric field that surrounds the living human body.

---

*Editor's note: Explicit instructions concerning how to do the outer-dissolving process may be found in *Opening the Energy Gates of the Body* by B. K. Frantzis (North Atlantic Books, Berkeley, California, 1993). The simultaneous inner-and-outer dissolving technique will be discussed in forthcoming works by Mr. Frantzis.

SAN TI
The primary internal power development technique of hsing-i.

ers' bodies touch. Dissolving your outer aura makes you as a martial artist less susceptible to being overpowered by your opponent's mind. (If your aura is completely dissolved, it cannot be influenced.) Outer dissolving is especially critical to all standing practices, **San Ti** (see p. 190), and holding postures in tai chi.

The outer-dissolving practice allows you to release (and outwardly expel) tension from deep inside your body, which increases the speed of your nerve reflexes and reaction time. This increase, in turn, enables you to move faster while executing a single technique or while changing from one technique to another. The dissolving practices (both the inner and outer versions) increase your timing.

The outer-dissolving process can be used extensively to release those energy blockages that prevent coordination between body parts that should be usefully interconnected. It will also clear blockages in the energy channels, allowing power to explode from the body and permitting the nerves to operate at maximum capacity, bringing superior speed, reflexes, sensitivity, and stamina. The healing of minor or major injuries with the outer-dissolving process is important to the continuous progress and ultimate success of both athletes and martial artists.

In practicing outer dissolving, your mind scans your body for blocked or uncomfortable places. Such blockages may be encountered at a specific point, a part (shoulder, thigh, etc.), an entire section (legs, belly, back, torso, etc.) or an internal body part (liver, joint, blood vessel, ligament, etc). At its location, an energy blockage may render the body incapable of being comfortable or relaxed. The outer-dissolving process is a meditative tool to make comfort and relaxation possible; it is applied until eventually the whole body can relax. Regular relaxation alone will not necessarily release the energy blockages that impede the clear circulation of chi in the body, nor will it necessarily cure illness. The outer-dissolving process, which clears the body's aura, has been used for millennia in China and can heal. In terms of the needs of tai chi/ba gua purely for health/high performance, the outer-dissolving process is sufficient.

The Inner-Dissolving Process

INNER-DISSOLVING PROCESS
A basic Taoist chi (nei gung) practice for releasing energy blocked *anywhere* within a person.

The **inner-dissolving process** also uses the mind to dissolve blocked energy, but in this process, the dissipated negative energy is moved inward, deep into internal space, rather than outward, away from the body. This inner space can be experienced as being as large as the external universe. Ultimately, the emotional, mental, or psychic energy content of the block is released into the recesses of the consciousness, into a spiritual place the Taoists call "emptiness." Inner-dissolving is most easily learned sitting in meditation.

The inner-dissolving is the major meditation access point for resolving emotional difficulties, such as unworkable attitudes, dysfunction, temporary or lifelong negative patterns, or lack of perseverance when confronted with situations that are hard to handle emotionally.* Problems like these often prevent even the most talented of individuals from actualizing their full potential. A well-balanced, adjusted, or at least realistic emotional base is necessary for performing well at anything over time. The inner-dissolving process is critical to the emotional stability required for high performance and is definitely useful for counterbalancing the egomania that often accompanies "star" performers. Moreover, this process is a key for undoing energetic blocks in the way of intellectual accomplishment. Practiced properly, this dissolving technique can lead to intense spiritual development. Incorporated into the structures of the internal martial arts, the nei gung inner-dissolving will allow the full array of physical and psychic powers of these arts to come forth.

Dissolving into Inner and Outer Space Simultaneously

Advanced dissolving work allows for dispersing the bound energy in the body in both directions at once—that is, outside the body and deep into the interior of consciousness. It takes a long devotion to the practice of Taoist meditation to gain this skill. Generally speaking, it can be said that the dissolving techniques form the bridge between chi gung, martial arts, and meditation.

THE STAGES OF FEELING: "I," "CHI," AND "HSIN"

The four levels of chi development present in ba gua chang are similar to, but not exactly the same as, the arts of tai chi chuan, chi gung, and aikido.

In all chi development arts, the standard phrase is "the mind leads, the chi follows the mind, the blood follows the chi, and the strength follows the blood." Mind produces chi, chi moves the blood, and blood produces strength. As can be seen from this axiom, the source of accomplishment of all chi arts originates in the mind. The mind, however, has two distinct dimensions (which could be said to be the real demarcation between beginning and advanced internal work). These two dimensions of the mind are what the Chinese call the **"I"** (pronounced "yee"), the projecting, thinking, and analyzing mind, and the **"hsin,"** or the heart/mind, from which thought originates and where the essence of a human resides

"I"
Will, intent, intention, mind, and projecting mind.

HSIN
Heart/mind. The ultimate source of a person's being, which is both subtle and nonphysical and is located near the physical heart.

---

*The dissolving process is not meant to, nor can it, replace professional psychological or psychotherapeutic work. Anyone with serious emotional or mental problems should consult a trained professional before practicing any of the dissolving processes.

before the stirrings of the intellect. Chinese philosophy believes that the hsin is located at the core of your being, in your heart center (the middle tantien).

The Nature of the "I" or Intention

Human beings have the innate ability to think and imagine and feel. The part of your mind that projects thoughts is known in Chinese as the "I" (pronounced "yee"), the mind of intention. Through imagination, the thinking mind can activate the body far beyond what is considered normal. There are many theories about how the mind/body linkage is accomplished. However, the reality is that, if your eyes are closed, one way you can open them is by changing the sensation in your body that is linked to the chi of your eyelids and eyeballs. Your mind, which is linked to the chi, then feels how the chi is connecting to your body. Through this feeling, the mind thinks the eyes open.

If your awareness of your own body is nonexistent, you will not feel your eyes; they will just physically open and close. If your mind has some body awareness, you will feel the muscles and tissues of your eyes stir and move as your eyes open and close. If your mind gains intense body awareness, you can feel the chi that activates the physical tissue that causes your eyes to open. The "I", chi, and hsin methods discussed in the following sections are based on the approach of ba gua. Tai chi and hsing-i also have approaches—some similar, some different—to accomplish the same goals.

Level 1: Feeling Your Body and Chi To some degree, either your physical nerves or psychic nerves (that is, your subtle energy channels) must open up and become sensitive before you can feel anything. However, just like the person whose eyes are open but whose mind cannot feel that they are, your chi can be moving, but you cannot feel it. At this initial level of practice, it is highly unlikely that you will feel chi flow in your body. To learn to feel chi directly, you must first concentrate on gaining the ability to feel the individual parts of your body separately (shoulder blades, spine, joints, inside the belly, etc.). Then you must work on feeling the whole-body physical motions of ba gua, or whichever chi art you practice.

Level 2: Transition Movements—Further Developing the "I" After the goals of Level 1 are accomplished, your "I" (mental intention, will, or projection) has begun to move your chi through your arms and legs. However, movement from your lower tantien through your torso to your neck and head is also important. Here, there must be a strong focus on the transition movements, which connect one static ba gua arm posture to another static ba gua arm posture. (See Chapter 6, p. 216) The "I" will make the chi move.

Existing outside the human body (usually starting at the outer boundary of your skin and extending to between a fist distance to five or six feet away) is the body's first layer of external energy. It is this layer of chi that transfers the energy coming from the cosmos to the human body. Commonly called the **etheric body** (chi body) or aura, this outer layer of energy directly stimulates and regulates the energy inside the human body. At the same time, the energy inside the human body creates the etheric body. It is a chicken-and-egg situation, in which the interconnection is so tight that to affect one is to affect the other. It is largely for this reason that the hands in all nei gung postures, including tai chi, ba gua, and hsing-i, do not come closer to the body than the width of one fist's distance. If they come too close, they can short-circuit or diminish the energy circulating between the physical body and etheric energy field.

Somewhere between this fist distance and a few feet from the body will be the range at which your stimulation of the etheric body by your hands will be at its weakest or strongest. Where it is strongest, this feeling will be the most tangible to you and, where weakest, the least tangible.

Continuing in a natural progression of Level 1 practices, in order to facilitate moving chi through specific energy channels in your torso, your teacher will guide your hand movements in specific ways in order to enable you to project chi from your palms or fingertips. These specific ways will usually be taught in the many different transition moves from one static posture to another. In the beginning you will make the transition move a number of times to stabilize your feeling of the energy channel. Then, over time, through holding the specific static posture the opening of that energy line will become stable. At this point you will feel the chi in that circuit as it settles in your hand position.

These chi projections will usually open up your energy flow and will happen in three progressive stages: (1) through the **middle burner** located between the **lower** and **middle tantien,** which is located between the pubic area and the solar plexus; (2) then through the lower tantien to the arms and the head; (3) and, finally, from the head to the feet and the feet to the head, moving first on the surface of the body (including the spine and back) and then deeper into the internal organs and bones. Eventually, in the third stage, your chi moves through the central channel and bone marrow. The mental projection and visualization method that moves the chi is called **I chu dzuo,** or "the intention moves the chi." This is the easiest way to access chi in the body, but not the most powerful level of chi in the body. It is, however, sufficient for health, healing, and self-defense purposes.

Level 3: Specific Energy Channel Work At this level of attainment, you begin to move your chi effortlessly through your body using conscious thought only. For your ba gua, you now need to know the correspondence between

ETHERIC/CHI BODY
The bioelectric field that extends anywhere from a few inches to a few hundred feet from a person's body. Commonly called the aura in the West.

LOWER TANTIEN
Located below the navel in the center of the body, this energetic center is primarily responsible for the health of the physical body.

MIDDLE BURNER
Located in the torso between the solar plexus and the lower tantien.

MIDDLE TANTIEN
One of the three major energy centers in the body. Two separate places are considered to be the middle tantien: the point located at the solar plexus just below the sternum and the point located near the heart on the central channel.

I CHU DZUO
A basic chi cultivation method where one uses "I" to create a mental picture (visualization), that then indirectly moves chi through the human body.

a particular body movement and its relation to chi flow in your energy channels. This material is usually taught in one of three ways, depending on the type and level of knowledge of your teacher. Of the three, the self-defense mode seems to be the easiest for most to learn. Bear in mind that, even if you request explicit information, an underqualified teacher may not be able to honor it and a master may not be willing, for whatever reason, to accede to your request. The three approaches are:

1. To teach how to move the chi from point to point in order to develop power. This approach is usually linked to self-defense applications and is probably the most simple for the student to learn because the fighting applications are fairly graphic and relatively easy to remember. Even if you are terrified of violence (or abhor it), the most rudimentary knowledge of a ba gua (or tai chi) defense technique for a particular movement (which usually will require much more in-depth training for practical self-defense) will give you a practical and reliable method of mentally activating your chi pathways. This basic chi practice is also a very practical reason for learning the elementary self-defense applications of tai chi, ba gua, and other internal arts even if you have no interest in practical fighting.

2. To teach the functioning of chi flows either in terms of practical medical effects and benefits for yourself personally, or how energy from a movement is applied in chi gung therapy or bodywork. In normal Western thinking, opposites are usually perceived as being antagonistic. From the point of view of the *I Ching* and Taoism, opposites are complementary, with blending qualities. Accordingly, the same basic energy practices can be used to cure or harm (either yourself or another) depending on your intent and application.

3. Movement and how the chi moves are taught by linking this to a story or allegory, which is used for purposes of meditation. Here, the energy moving through certain chi lines induces a specific state of mind and/or emotion. While the story is being told, the teacher monitors and adjusts the story to most strongly stimulate the chi flows in the listener.

One result of practicing these three ways of moving chi around in your body will be that you will begin to develop the ability to store and stabilize energy in your lower tantien, as if it were a battery or reservoir. As a battery can store energy, so it can release energy. After you have some chi stored in your lower tantien, you now work on the next progression: consciously absorbing or discharging chi from any point in your body instantly.

Level 4: Hsin or Heart/Mind The I chu dzuo method can only take you so far. The amount of mental energy employed to this point is considerable. However, the chi is still only superficially following your conscious thoughts. Levels 1, 2, and 3 identified here prepare you for the nei gung phase of tai chi and ba gua chi energy work which is based not so much on "I" but hsin and the **chi chu dzuo** principle.

In the "I" level of practice, your mind needs to think and, through great physical and mental effort (that is, visualization), move chi through your body. Now, however, you must go beyond your conscious mind and draw upon the deepest essence of your being, your unconscious heart/mind, in order to come into direct contact with your chi. The "I" method still includes a dichotomy between your "I" and chi, that is, conscious thought *influences* your chi to move, but it is not yet one and the same with it.

Direct and Indirect Movement of the Chi

The rational, analyzing, calculating human brain/mind is usually insufficient to allow people to be completely at ease with themselves. Thought and imagination can certainly generate sufficient chi to make your body reasonably healthy, and yet not let you be at peace with yourself or have harmonious relationships with others. You have to delve deeper into the root of your conscious mind to change its fundamental character and inner reality. The "I" intention can enable you to get things done, but it will not change the inner fabric of your being. The heart/mind, or hsin, can.

In the West, we call the hsin the subconscious mind or the intuitive mind. To the Chinese, it is the source from where thoughts arise. Let your "I" (intention) flow to an external object. Next, to whatever extent you can, go beyond the form of that object, that is, its shape, color, size—whatever its physical attributes happen to be. Get beyond identifying words, names, or *any* ideas connected with the object. Now, from the depths of your being, see if you can genuinely comprehend what this object is in its entirety, *without your cognitive mind interfering in the direct relationship between the object and the essence of your being.* Although you are aware of conscious thought (mind), you are now operating from the hsin/heart core of your being.

The Chinese believe the true mind of a person is located in the subtle energy of the heart—the center of one's being. This is where you get the higher mental capacity to perform the actions of ba gua.

When you have practiced the "I" techniques sufficiently up to and including the third level, a reservoir of chi will, as mentioned, gather in your lower tantien. This accumulation is in no way an idea or an abstraction of chi but is actual chi itself, which can be felt. At this point, you can begin to slowly nurture the hsin until it can contact and merge with the central unifying chi of your body—**jeng chi**—which is residing in your lower tantien. You should now have a direct, deep contact with the chi of your body at its deepest levels and can thus begin to use all the Taoist nei gung practices useful to ba gua and tai chi. Moreover, you should now also be able to focus your chi not only on your essential body processes

CHI CHU DZUO
The method of moving a felt bodily sensation of chi as a live force from the lower tantien into whichever energy channels the practitioner consciously directs it.

JENG CHI
Unifying chi. The one chi that unifies all the chi of the body, which the practice of all the Taoist internal arts seeks to cultivate.

EIGHT ENERGETIC BODIES
Eight clear vibratory frequencies of energy that comprise a human body.

(organs, glands, brain, joints, cerebrospinal system, soft tissue, and bones) but on the different aspects of all of what the Taoists call your **eight energy bodies** (physical, chi/etheric, emotional, mental, psychic, causal, individuality, and the Tao).

Through this flowering, your potential being is realized in stages as your conscious awareness of hsin grows. You are able bit by bit to be aware not only of your own personal chi but the Universal Chi from which all manifested form and nonmanifested essence derive. This focus on the hsin as the most essential element in all the Chinese Buddhist and Taoist practices eventually leads to "direct movement of your chi" or chi chu dzuo. To perform the chi chu dzuo, the hsin must be developed. It could be said that the "I" method is a more external chi gung practice manipulating the outside chi to go in the body, whereas the hsin chi chu dzuo is a more internal nei gung method, where from the depth of the mind and center of one's internal chi, energy is made to circulate. The hsin nei gung method alone is responsible for the **nei dan** inner cosmic pill/egg advanced chi practices of Taoist internal **alchemy,** which forms the foundation of higher Taoist meditation practices. With the I chu dzuo, there is always an infinitesimal gap between your mind thinking and your chi moving. In the chi chu dzuo method, your mind and chi become one.

NEI DAN
Literally, inner cosmic pill/egg. A term for the internal alchemy methods of Taoism.

ALCHEMY
The process of changing one substance into another, externally in the environment or internally in the body.

In Taoist nei gung practices, including ba gua and tai chi, sooner or later the practitioner not only develops the hsin (the ultimate foundation of meditation), but also simultaneously directly controls the chi of the body, necessary for organic change at the cellular level. The chi chu dzuo method is in large part responsible for the immense strength and vibrancy of many eighty- to ninety-year-old ba gua and tai chi practitioners in China.

The I chu dzuo is like knowing the shadow of your chi/mind connection, where chi chu dzuo gives you direct experience of it. The chi chu dzuo method based on hsin is probably the highest level of Taoist chi work, whereas the I chu dzuo method is more easily used by the average person. The chi chu dzuo method, based upon Taoist nei gung, is best learned by studying personally with a genuine adept. Most people can eventually attain the hsin/chi chu dzuo capacity as long as they relax and persevere, which is how individuals attain genuine internal gung fu, or skill regardless of what they study.

TAI CHI, HSING-I, AND BA GUA— WHAT'S THE SAME, WHAT'S DIFFERENT?

Each of these three internal martial arts have similar chi cultivation and fighting techniques. They just practice them very differently. Their specific types of practices also produce a very different type of body, encourage different types of strategies for thinking, and have different philosophical approaches for accomplishing goals. Each has its strengths and weaknesses.

Of the three, hsing-i has the simplest internal structure, tai chi is in the middle, and ba gua is the most complex. Physically and mentally, the slow, rhythmic motions of tai chi are the easiest for the general public to learn, especially the sick or injured, whereas the moves of ba gua are the most complicated to learn. Hsing-i tends to have the greatest appeal for young people, tai chi for old people, and ba gua appears to appeal equally to people of all ages. At whatever age, a powerful synergy seems to be created in the body by combining the extreme softness of tai chi's yin energy with the strength that ba gua's yang energy develops.

In the beginning, hsing-i is the easiest and most practical way to learn to fight, tai chi is the most perplexing, and ba gua ultimately the most complete and effective. Some schools of ba gua and the Wu style of tai chi have more of a meditation orientation than hsing-i or other styles of tai chi have.

Philosophical Perspectives: Hard, Soft, and Change

Each art differs psychologically and philosophically. Hsing-i focuses on the direct approach, on being aggressive. Characteristics of the hsing-i mentality include tackling problems head on, overcoming whatever obstacles appear, having an exceptionally strong self-confidence that refuses to accept failure, and a "go for it" attitude in attaining goals. Mentally, hsing-i practitioners never retreat. They simply view stepping backwards as a temporary tactical situation to allow them to get on with their main business of attack and conquer. The two phrases that characterize hsing-i are: "My will be done" and "Never retreat." These are banner cries as a hsing-i fighter advances and aggressively defeats an opponent. This hard, militaristic mentality is quite useful in developing a success-oriented competitive spirit and self-discipline, and in restoring a positive self-image to someone who exhibits a weak or damaged ego.

Tai chi emphasizes softness, attaining goals in an indirect, non-obvious fashion, subtlety, and flowing around obstacles rather than confronting them. Deception, not giving someone a solid place to attack, being subtle and circumspect, and all sorts of counterattack strategies form the core of tai chi's psychological profile. A tai chi orientation will offer minimal or no resistance to an obstacle, person, or situation. Tai chi practitioners yield to an oncoming force, and while appearing to be weak, draw that force into themselves, move around it like water going around a rock, and then counterattack at the most unexpected moment.

The operative phrases in tai chi are: "Forget yourself and follow the other" and, "Thy will be done," so that opponents get whatever they want, but not in the way they expected it. In the process of giving the opponent what they want through yielding, tai chi fighters move from a weak position to an advantageous one.

Tai chi's major principle is to absorb any incoming force or resistance and use that force's energy to defeat it. Tai chi, unlike hsing-i, does not like to attack, but if a tai chi fighter is attacked, the energy of the attack will be used to defeat the attacker. Although both tai chi and hsing-i both use only internal principles, their strategies for how to deal with problems or difficult situations are exactly opposite. Tai chi is defensive whereas hsing-i is aggressive. Within the soft velvety glove of tai chi, however, lies a fist of steel.

The tai chi philosophy is exceptionally useful for stressed personalities who have great difficulty relaxing under perceived pressure. Such individuals can benefit from learning to let go, relax, and yield to the inevitable, in the many situations where there is no way to exert control. Tai chi is the most popular stress reduction program used by the successful business and professional class in the booming economies of northeast Asia. While the hsing-i approach is very hard, linear, and masculine in nature, tai chi is soft, round, and feminine in approach. Both are equally powerful and functional. Tai chi would be psychologically valuable for any individual who wants to be able to successfully join together the yin elements of receptivity and sensitivity with the yang elements of strength and the capacity to accomplish goals.

Psychologically, ba gua is based on the idea of being able to smoothly and appropriately change from one situation to another. Awareness and adaptability to the natural flux of situations is its basic guideline. Unlike tai chi and hsing-i, the art of ba gua does not have a hard or soft philosophy, although it uses the strategies of both when useful. Change and the seeking of naturalness in all its actions is its prime directive. Ba gua uses all sixty-four psychological and spiritual paradigms of the **64 hexagrams** of the *I Ching* without becoming fixated on any one of them. As such, ba gua is more challenging than either tai chi or hsing-i.

In ba gua, there is little concern either for self or opponent. Instead, the concern is that "the event is occurring" at this moment in time. There is attention given not only to your own energy and that of the opponent, but also to the energy of the surrounding environment, including that of the earth, the stars, the sky, the trees, and all the natural forces of energy surrounding you. In order that your movement and projection of force will harmonize with the matrix of energy of all of these environmental energies coming together, you must leave behind your sense of self and any agenda. The potent self-defense applications of ba gua should be considered as by-products of this interaction, and not as ends in themselves. In fact, many people in China practice ba gua chang without any martial consideration, concentrating instead on its health and/or meditative benefits, as well as on the pure joy of blending with the forces of nature.

Ba gua also shares commonality with tai chi chuan's basic principles of softness and yielding. In fact, ba gua follows many of the principles of the tai chi classics, including: (1) not breaking the flow of internal energy from posture to posture; (2) realizing that the body has five bows; (3) seeking the straight from the curved; (4) listening to energy; (5) interpreting

64 HEXAGRAMS
Sixty-four basic energetic changes of the *I Ching*.

energy accurately; (6) counterattacking by beginning after the opponent has begun but arriving before his attack has finished.

The Way the Three Move

Several analogies are commonly used to describe the types of movement and feeling particular to the three internal arts. Tai chi is fluid, like water, but rooted, like the earth. Hsing-i is like a mountain, a solid immovable force, with light and agile footwork. Ba gua is like a tornado, or a tumble-weed that moves freely with the wind. In like manner, there are similes for the type of body that is developed through their practice: Tai chi is like a rubber ball; hsing-i is like an iron pole; ba gua is like flexible steel. The body trained by ba gua practice is exceptionally springy and strong. It is also quite relaxed, but not with the kind of extreme relaxation that is associated with tai chi. Whereas the ba gua body is not as relaxed as the tai chi body, it is generally considered to be the stronger of the two.

All three internal arts have the ability to absorb and project tremendous power. As a martial art, ba gua differs from the others because, in addition to its own distinct qualities, it encompasses those of both tai chi and hsing-i. Hsing-i has a powerful and aggressive penetrating energy that can go through the arm/hand defenses of an opponent like a hot knife through butter. Some ba gua practitioners develop so much power that they do not even need to circle. Their feet do not appear to move. Just by turning the waist they can blast right through you. This methodology is similar to hsing-i. On the other hand, ba gua also embodies tai chi's ability to yield and get out of the way, especially when **dai** is used, or leading techniques (upon which aikido is based). While hsing-i is considered hard and tai chi soft, ba gua is neither. It has the ability to be hard and the ability to be soft, but its true essence is change. It therefore occupies middle ground between hard and soft. A ba gua adept can change positions or motion to adapt instantaneously to the needs and circumstances of the moment.

DAI
Ba gua's energetic technique for leading an opponent where one's energy and that of the opponent blend into one nonseparate stream.

The Emphasis on Footwork, Waist, and Hands

Whatever your level of ba gua, you must never stand in one place for more than a fraction of a second. Tai chi people will assume a position and hold it, move at the waist, and counterattack. Hsing-i people will move right into the opponent or stand their ground and slug it out. In contrast, a ba gua player's first and foremost objective is to move. All motion, whether offensive or defensive, originates in the feet. In ba gua, a hand never moves by itself. For a hand to move, a foot must move either in space or at least by changing pressure against the ground.

This approach is different from both hsing-i, in which the hands lead all movement and the waist and foot follow, and tai chi, in which the waist initiates everything and the hand and foot follow. In ba gua, the foot moves, and the whole body moves with it. This difference holds true for all ba gua schools. If the waist or hand leads the action, this usually means that the ba gua techniques have been mixed with the methodology of hsing-i or tai chi. Such mixing is common in the West, where the practice of any of the three arts often exhibit mixed characteristics of the others.

In ba gua, whether standing still or moving, one's root must be maintained at all times, whatever the speed or direction of movement. There is no vertical up and down hopping from step to step. Motion consists of a smooth continuum from one position to the next. Although in combat a step may last only a tenth of a second, during that instant the root must be strong. That instant should be enough time to take care of the opponent. If not, practitioners should keep moving until an advantageous position is gained.

Common Denominators

In each of the three internal martial arts, all the movements have the capacity to produce internal power that can be directed externally through physical techniques to control or harm an opponent. Fighters of each art focus all their creativity and intelligence on practicing how to bring this power out of their bodies. All the chi work will be devoted to producing maximum power, speed, usable flexibility, and the capacity to rapidly change techniques. This training will involve much harder concentrated physical effort than that required for health and longevity, which the fighter gets in any case as a by-product of Taoist internal power training. Due to immoderate enthusiasm, most beginners in the internal martial arts overtrain at times, which can result in injury and exhaustion. In order to avoid this, students should learn the difficult lesson of limiting their training to about 70 percent of what the human body can withstand. (The limit should be at an even lower percentage if a physical handicap or injury exists.)

Weak Points

Internal martial artists must constantly test their power against superior opponents to gauge the validity of their training. This experience tests the progress of strength, mastery of style, and familiarity with a range of techniques. Most importantly though, it exposes weak points so that practitioners may analyze defects in their fighting ability and seek ways to realistically correct them. Genuine martial art masters will always point out weaknesses to a sincere student—by words, physical lesson, or obvious example. If the student is capable of recognizing valid criticism and taking it to heart, the master's advice will be followed. This path is historically considered the fastest proven way to progress. Criticism can come in the form of words from a teacher or defeat in combat.

The Need to Seek and Test Reality

Traditionally, students of fighting internal martial arts adopt the attitude that they will be locked in a real physical life-and-death struggle at some time. If they are wise, they will take their lumps up front and have their ego bruised during training, rather than have their egos *and bodies* destroyed in actual combat.

In training, every movement in the solo forms is done by the practitioner while visualizing and feeling an imaginary opponent. Students must then constantly practice to make the techniques work against live attackers, first with people within their own school and later with others who are not their friends and who know other methods of fighting. In combat with live opponents, the ba gua practitioner seeks to concentrate on increasing power, sensitivity of touch, speed, waist turning, and the ability to change from technique to technique fluidly. The practitioner also focuses on getting body and feet out of the attacker's way, to use deception, to dominate the opponent, and to disappear and reappear like a ghost. These same conditions exist with tai chi chuan except that, in tai chi, greater emphasis is focused on yielding, extreme softness, less active foot work and rooting the feet for longer periods of time in one place.

Going Beyond Intimidation and Fear

Most fighters seek to intimidate an opponent much as one big animal scares another. Most external martial arts instructors spend a lot of time teaching their students how to intimidate or "psych out" an opponent, without themselves being intimidated. If you can be made to fear, you will freeze up under pressure and not be able to use whatever superior fighting skills you possess, allowing an opponent with inferior skills to beat you. The screaming in karate, the boxer who says, "Take your best shot for all the good it will do," the person with the eyes of a homicidal maniac, the individual whose mind alone can induce psychic terror, the threat of the knife, broken bottle, or gun, all these are the mental weapons the effective fighter uses to paralyze the opponent's heart with fear. This impact is like the headlights in the dark that freeze the rabbit on the road from fifty yards away. The rabbit has plenty of time to run, but it gets killed anyway because intimidation has induced paralysis.

This fear (which is ultimately the fear of death and the unknown that for many cannot be completely controlled) also causes the massive ego dominance and submission so common in animal groups and military actions. When a human being can overcome this fear—which each and

A PERSONAL ODYSSEY THROUGH THE MARTIAL ARTS

Fighting with Balanced Emotions

 Weng Hsien Ming, a senior student at Hung I Hsiang's school (see p. 203), had won the Taiwan full-contact championship three times. One day, Weng and I had a rigorous sparring session that lasted for some time. It took place on the cement basketball court where Hung I Hsiang taught his evening classes. We both lightly hit and scored on each other once in a while and, while fun, it was also a battle royal. At some point, by accident, I hit him in the eye, knocking out his contact lens. Normally, a blow to the eyes would incur rage and extremely primal responses. None of that happened. We stopped sparring while a group of Hung's students and I helped Weng search for the contact lens on the cement. We found it, and Weng put it back in place after the obligatory cleaning.

If this incident had occurred in any external martial arts school in the Far East (or in the West, for that matter), it is possible that an extremely violent confrontation could have taken place, either from a fear reaction or the ego's need to save face. Weng knew that it had been an accident (we'd both hit each other many times and neither one of us had been bothered by it), and we continued to spar full bore without fear, revenge, or pride coming into it. This was not weakness on Weng's part but showed, rather, great stability of mind. From this introduction, we became good friends. Sometime later, I roomed with him.

Weng was capable of causing great bodily harm in a short period of time in a real fighting situation, either in formal competition or a challenge match. However, he could not be intimidated, nor did he try to intimidate his opponents. He focused instead on keeping his mind clear and his techniques powerful, practical, efficient, and without any wasted motion. His example is a good one to emulate, if you wish to become a superb fighter with well-balanced emotions.

every internal ba gua, tai chi, and hsing-i martial artist must do—then the severe violence of many human fighting confrontations can be tamed.

Efficiency and the Risk-Reward Ratio

Fighters must focus on how to use their internal power to greatest practical effect. In every possible specific circumstance, they must prepare themselves to understand the nature of their opponent's force and discover the most efficient way to counter it. What does it mean to move too much or too little in combat? To use too much or too little power in a microsecond of time? When to move or to stand still? When to use power, what kind of power, and for how long? These questions must be tested over and over again. What are the odds of succeeding with a hit, a throw, a joint-lock, or a kick? What are the odds that if you use this technique you will be countered, and with what kind of counter? Over and over again, you must train until you know the risk-reward ratio, until it becomes second nature to you. In real combat, the most important decisions requiring action or waiting happen instinctively, before your mind has time to formulate a thought. Hundreds, thousands, or tens of thousands of hours of solo and two-person training are what give you the ability to act calmly and spontaneously in a flash when under life-and-death pressure.

Studying Ba Gua, Tai Chi, or Hsing-I for Fighting

You get what you pay for, so spend your money (that is, your chi and effort) wisely.

For using internal martial arts to fight (or indeed for using any martial art), it may be helpful to remember these points:

1. Doing things poorly is easy. To succeed, it is mandatory to practice seriously and faithfully.
2. To quote Wang Shu Jin, "It is better to be able to do one or two techniques well than to do 10,000 poorly."
3. It is not so easy to do a few things well.
4. It is extremely difficult to do many things well.
5. It is virtually impossible to do all the techniques of ba gua or tai chi well. Even Tung Hai Chuan, Wu Jien Chuan, Yang Cheng Fu, and the Chen family members did some moves much better than others.

When internal martial arts instructors teach, it is their responsibility to present the lineage fighting techniques as clearly and as accurately as possible. The responsibility of students is to practice solo and with partners until they can manifest the fighting skills as well as or better than the instructor. Students must choose for themselves which techniques they want to master, and then do the work. The Chinese have a classic phrase *shr fu jing men* (the master takes you into the gate), *lien dzai ge shin* (the practice is your own and its fruition develops from the effort of your own individual heart/mind).

When your teacher demonstrates something for you, you are obligated to practice it, or else you may invoke the following consequences of your own free will: (1) Your teacher may not correct you because your actions have shown that you really did not want to learn the skill; (2) you will not achieve the skill; (3) if you learn the next stage of the skill, it will be weak because it has no foundation; (4) your skill will not rise to a high level until your attitude changes.

In the process of practicing and competing, martial artists and athletes inevitably experience physical injuries, from both the movement alone and from the physical contact of their endeavors. It is possible to keep on practicing with an injury, but you should avoid re-injuring yourself through overstraining. If you injure your arm, for example, only practice your chi gung or your ba gua walking until your arm heals. If you hurt your leg, practice upper body techniques. Continue your training, but not in such a way as to put any strain whatsoever on your injury. Re-injuring yourself merely postpones the time you can start training fully again. Be sensible. Do not let small or medium-sized injuries become long-term chronic injuries, which ultimately can curtail your ability to be effective.

Health and Martial Arts Competence

If practitioners were studying ba gua for their health, they were taught the specifics of how to make their bodies extremely healthy and strong. If they were learning ba gua for fighting or meditation, their instruction was focused on those particular areas. The Taoist belief is that the training procedures of a martial art first and foremost must nourish your body and cultivate your mental and emotional well-being. Only when your body and character have become strong can you truly learn how to use the art for fighting. Fighting ability always remains a secondary, though very important, consideration. Ba gua people believe that martial artists must be heroes not cowards, and that this heroism must come from genuine internal centeredness, confidence, and skill, not from bravado, raw physical talent, a violent mind, or a mere intellectual conjecture of the art.

Basic Power Training

JI BEN GUNG
The basic power training through which all the Chinese martial arts develop the specific types of power they specialize in.

The traditional internal practice of basic power training called **ji ben gung** generally works from the inside of the body to the outside. Ji ben gung develops the internal energy or "juice" that is needed for internal martial arts. With this practice, for example, ba gua people feel, along with most traditional internal schools in China and Japan, that it is better to do one simple technique. This technique in ba gua could be the pre-birth, Circle-Walking Single Palm Change, or in hsing-i and tai chi, standing practice, San Ti, or a chi gung method with only a few movements. It is best to do a simple practice with your chi full and body connected to your energy, mind, and essential nature, than to do many techniques feebly, none of which develops your body or mind fully for effective fighting.

The alternate method was to learn *hou tien*, or post-birth ba gua. This method works from the outside of the body to the inside, and involves learning a tremendous number of outer movement forms or hsing, each with a few specific fighting applications. After years of this practice when students were proficient at the outer forms, they would learn the internal power training.

Three postures from Ten Heavenly Stems, a moving post-birth ba gua school basic power training method, done by ba gua adept Lo Te Hsiu of Taipei, Taiwan.

Courtesy of Catherine Helms

In the final analysis, whatever allows you to be victorious with the fewest injuries, or at the very least leaves you intact so that you can run away, is the primary objective of the fighting aspect of ba gua, tai chi, hsing-i, and all other internal martial arts.

The Importance of Standing Practice for the Long-Term Development of Internal Power

In standing practice, the critical issues are learning to:

1. Become aware of the interior landscape of your body.
2. Release the tension of your body from the inside, without strain.
3. Let the sense of physical strength go, which causes the body to soften while maintaining excellent muscle tone.
4. Sink your chi and develop root.
5. Become able to feel the six combinations of your body and link up their corresponding chi pathways in your body.
6. During martial art movements, maintain the ability to feel the inside of your body clearly, thereby gaining self-awareness of both the inside and the outside of your body simultaneously. This eventually allows you to not get distracted by your chi during movement. This ability is critical in high-speed movement, especially in ba gua with its fast spins and turns, where people tend to disconnect from their insides in order to maintain awareness of their external physical movement in space.
7. Become sensitive to the chi in the space around your body.

Standing builds the foundation for successfully learning all the other advanced methods of chi gung. Further along in training (in the moving, sitting, lying down, and sexual Taoist practices), standing creates the context to move chi at will. Similarly, all the advanced chi practices done for health and/or internal power can also be done standing. In general, the internal standing methods of tai chi, hsing-i, and ba gua are mostly absent in the normal course of training in the West. For example, when the author taught the standing practice in the early 1970s* in New York City, there was apparently no one else doing it. In the 1980s more people began teaching standing, with the trend strongly increasing worldwide by the 1990s.

---

*The rare exception to this in America was Kuo Lien-Ying, who regularly taught the Universal Post standing posture at this time to his students in San Francisco.

Photo by author

Standing method of basic power training, done by the late Wang Shu Jin.

BA GUA'S EIGHT STAGES OF PRACTICE FOR DEVELOPING FIGHTING SKILLS

Transcendence from Form to Formlessness: The Goal of High-Level Internal Martial Arts

In any field of knowledge, beginners need a structure, a form, to initially learn the basics. This is especially true for the internal martial arts. After the basics and the technical requirements have been mastered, though, true excellence lies in going beyond the form and arriving at the essence of what you originally tried to learn. At this point, you can move into that creative space where "that which cannot be taught" naturally and spontaneously flows from your very soul. It is here that you transcend form, leave the "how-and-what-to-do" level, and operate on the plane of the formless.

In the internal arts, you learn form in order to master a technique, then you forget the form, and eventually arrive at a state the Chinese call **wu wei** or "doing without doing." This formlessness is the ultimate goal of all the internal martial arts.

WU WEI
Doing without doing. The fundamental Taoist concept of having action arise from an empty mind without preconception or agenda. Action that operates by simply following the natural course of universal energy as it manifests without strain or ego involvement.

Mastering internal martial arts can be likened to becoming a topflight jazz pianist. When these musicians first learn the technique or "form" of playing the piano, they may spend hours a day practicing the scales (physical technique—punches, kicks, throws, joint-locks, balance, speed, footwork, and so on). Then they may practice the chords (differing kinds of internal power, fluidity, internal energy work, mastering subtle movements, making the mind still, and so on). The pianists begin with simple standard pieces (fighting one opponent at a time) and progress to increasingly complex riffs (fighting multiple opponents).

The pianists may know the technical side of their craft and perform well, even flawlessly, but something is missing. In jazz, it's often called the magic side of improvisation, where musicians play from a place beyond internal restrictions, beyond form or technique. Here, they don't just play the music right, they jam splendidly, with sound that grips the soul. They have leapt beyond technical virtuosity, and are being fueled by inspiration, sheer creativity, and the act of letting go.

In time, diligent internal martial artists also master all the technical matters of their craft and, indeed, become fearless. But to move into that sublime and wondrous space where the freely improvising jazz musician ignites requires abandoning a reliance on technical proficiency, requires flying far beyond it—to where normally perceived expectations of time and space are suspended. The ability to take this journey in the internal arts necessitates a profound stilling of the mind and an expansion of consciousness more akin to meditation than what is ordinarily thought of as martial arts. This is the nature of the path that must be traveled to move from the fifth to the eighth stage of fighting in ba gua. At the first stage, though, things are relatively simple.

Stage I

Solo: Here, you are learning basic physical coordination. You will need to be able to visualize and physically experience some kind of fighting application for each part of every technique.

Two-Person Exercises: Consist of applications to make the visualization of each solo movement real to you, so that you can do the solo movements with intent.

Stage II

Solo: Opening and closing the joints and activating the spinal pump are emphasized for developing power. You learn to clearly differentiate absorbing and discharging power.

Two-Person Exercises: Emphasize the spinal and joint pumps so they can open and close without experiencing glitches or freezing, which is the case with most beginners; also emphasize hitting and kicking techniques.

Stage III

Solo: Begins to concentrate on smooth and rapid openings and closings, speed walking, and rapid palm changes in solo movements.

Two-Person Exercises: After you have learned to fall safely, the focus is placed on throwing techniques and vertical up and down applications. These emphasize double and triple strikes by rapid openings and closings.

Stage IV

Solo: Emphasizes the twisting of body tissue (arms, legs, and waist), horizontal turning power and extremely rapid changes. Goes beyond the fixed formal movements; the intent is now to begin training to create physical movement out of thought. When you think, your body should mold to your thought. This state is the beginning of creating a mind/body fusion. Very complex footwork emerges.

Two-Person Exercises: Emphasize applications based on storing an opponent's energy as you twist one way and release the stored energy back to the opponent instantaneously by reversing the twist. Here, with the reversal principles in play, joint-locks and throws come into their own. At this stage, speed is emphasized over power.

Up to this stage, the pre-birth and post-birth practices (see p. 212) have similar goals and outcomes. The final four stages, however, result from the pre-birth Circle-Walking practice method only.

Stage V

Solo: Concentration is on following the energies that exist around you: the earth, sky, stars, trees, water, people. You begin to use the natural energies of the environment to catalyze and make both faster and stronger the chi within your body. The qualities of each of the energies of the eight trigrams* become the main point of focus rather than only physical movement.

Two-Person Exercises: Having already mastered a large arsenal of weapons (kicks, hits, joint-locks, throws, and evasion techniques), you now learn how to use and clearly separate each of the eight-trigram energies in

---

*In Taoist thought, each one of the eight trigrams of the *I Ching* embodies one of the basic energies from which the universe was created and all manifestation occurs.

ba gua. You concentrate on how to efficiently blend to best advantage the swirling energies of yourself, your opponent, and the environment at the point of time and space in which you are currently interacting. The energy that is spiraling up and down between heaven and earth is greatly emphasized at this stage.

Stage VI

Solo: You make your body and mind as still and as empty as possible. Yin or very amorphous energy techniques are emphasized, as well as meditation.

Two-Person Exercises: Your techniques must become completely effortless to you. You exert as much force as you would use to scratch your head, yet your technique produces a devastating effect on the opponent. If you have a kind and open heart, then this devastation will have a spiritually profound and ultimately benevolent effect on your opponent. If your heart is self-centered and cruel, it will instill fear, awe, submission, and spiritual contraction in your opponent.

Stage VII

Solo: Your heart will become completely still and be totally at ease. You will lose all sense of doing anything. Your motion and energy will simply move as the earth and sky do. There movement has passed beyond the physical.

Two-Person Exercises: You will begin to manifest physical power that goes beyond leverage, logic, the laws of physics, or anything else you can imagine. For example, Liu Hung Chieh (see p. 241), when eighty years old, could stop the power of a man twice his size with one finger. He could vertically lift such a man up slowly during tai chi Push Hands just like you would lift a bag of potato chips. Liu could also crack a concrete slab under his feet by simply walking on it. He weighed less than 110 pounds and, logically, should not have been physically capable of this feat. At this level of ba gua, the masters tend not to move as much as they did in the earlier stages of their training. They don't need to—their energy does their moving for them.

Stage VIII

This stage transcends our normal conception of reality. It is beyond the power of words to convey. Few in any age, much less the modern era, reach this level. A Master at this level of the game would have no trouble proving his authenticity, should he wish to do so.

INTERNAL FIGHTING TECHNIQUES

Hand and Palm Strikes of the Internal Martial Arts

The internal martial arts possess the same extensive range of hand strikes that is normally found in most external martial arts, such as karate or gung fu: that is, punches as well as both open-and closed-hand strikes. The hand strikes use the wrist, the ridge of the hand (that is, the space between thumb and index finger), the edge and palm of the open hand, and the front, back, inside, and outside of the closed hand. Additionally, though, all three internal styles (ba gua, tai chi, and hsing-i) employ specialized internal strikes, the subject of this section. Each internal style, however, while using the same fighting techniques, differs either slightly or greatly in external form movements and interpretations of two-person fighting applications. The explanation for these differences is found in how each style adapted and expressed the essence of a given technique within its unique philosophical and operational approaches. The ancient internal fighting techniques still surviving today are one reason why the internal martial arts became justifiably famous in modern China.

Ba gua chang, as its name "Eight Trigram Palm" implies, uses the palm more often than the fist. As a general rule, ba gua uses the open hands, forearms, and fingers to great effect. Of the Eight Mother Palms taught in this art, only one is a fist. It should be remembered, however, that most famous technique of Ma Wei Chi (see Appendix B, p. 310) was a spherical punch. Tai chi tends to use an even mix between open-hand and closed-fist techniques. Hsing-i tends mostly toward using closed-fist techniques in its primary Five-Element practices and open hands in its Animal Forms.

There are a number of ways to strike in the internal martial arts. The first is what the beginner who lacks control usually uses: hit the opponent as hard as possible. At the more advanced levels, you must decide whether or not to seriously harm your opponent. If you decide against inflicting injury, you may use the fa jin technique (see p. 110) in which your power passes through the person you hit. Your fa jin will definitely move that person in physical space, but will cause no serious harm.

However, if necessary force is required and your only reasonably viable option is to harm someone, the fa jin can be focused inside the man attacking you so that your power does not leave his body. This causes destruction inside the body through hemorrhaging or other disruptions. The early masters of internal martial arts could hit the outside of a person and not leave a mark on the skin, but that person could subsequently die from damage to the internal organs. This ability to focus force onto very small internal areas is astounding. The technology is similar in application to those tank artillery shells that can kill the enemy tank crew but leave the shell of the enemy tank unharmed. The twisting of the soft tissue, combined with the sudden opening of the body's joints and cavities to discharge chi from a point in the body, are the technical methods by which sudden fa jin release is accomplished.

In China, many consider the internal martial arts to be much more powerful than the external martial arts, and indeed, many people think that there is something supernatural about the striking force of the internal arts. The martial effectiveness of the internal arts is in no way supernatural but relies instead on extremely sophisticated body and chi mechanisms.

Whereas the core of the external martial arts is fighting technique, the core of the internal arts is the development of internal power, or chi. In the beginning of internal martial arts training, the practitioner's external motions appear to be unsubtle. As an internal martial artist becomes more integrated in practice, however, it becomes less and less possible for an observer to externally see what is being done. The feeling that the power displayed is supernatural is just not accurate; one simply cannot see the internal mechanisms being used. However, at the highest levels of chi development, internal martial arts can indeed appear to be a little other-worldly. This phenomenon only occurs when one is not using physical power any longer, but instead is drawing solely on chi. In modern times, very few people have achieved this level.

Presented here are broad movement or energy patterns, rather than any one of hundreds of specific movements or techniques. Each technique can encompass an incredible number of variations and basic movements. These techniques are the ones used for practical hand-to-hand combat and may or may not be used in any of the hand-touching practices—Rou Shou or Push Hands. If any of these techniques appears severe, bear in mind the fact that, today, guns or explosive devices are easily obtained both legally and illegally in most of the world. Also, it takes time to develop these sophisticated internal techniques. During that time, significant training in self-control and moral education concerning the nature of genuine compassion and violence should be taught. This normally prevents the abuses often generated by angry or dsyfunctional people, either with their fists or with a knife or gun.

Types of Strikes and Hand Action

Although tai chi has the greatest number of adherents in China and the West, its full range of fighting techniques is not usually taught. Rather, the primary focus is on forms and Push Hands. While ba gua and hsing-i schools have fewer adherents, many more of their teachers both in the West and China tend to focus on and teach the actual fighting techniques themselves, as well as the forms and Rou Shou/Push Hands training. Since ba gua has the largest repertoire of fighting techniques in the internal martial arts, the following sections on specifics will refer first to ba gua, then to tai chi, and then to hsing-i. Unless otherwise indicated, the names for the form movements of tai chi will be from the Yang style nomenclature, not because of any value judgment concerning superior or inferior standards but because it is the most widespread and has generated the most available literature.

Bear in mind that all the internal martial arts hand techniques described here, and the many more not mentioned here, can be done when opening and issuing energy away from your body, as well as when closing and bringing energy toward your body (see nei gung, p. 62).

The Piercing Strike   The piercing strike usually uses the fingers, the palm, or the edge of the hand. A straight line strike (which actually is the result of an internal spiraling motivating force) is used to (a) penetrate your opponent's body; (b) lift your opponent off the ground as you penetrate his body, limbs, or head; (c) dislocate the joints of your opponent's arms or legs; or (d) knock away your opponent's protecting or attacking arm as you simultaneously spear, hit with your palm, or side-cut him with either edge of your hand. (This last move is one of ba gua's primary strike techniques.) It can also be seen in the tai chi move, White Snake Puts Out Its Tongue and in the hsing-i water-element technique of Drilling Fist.

Upward-Curving Strike   This strike may be executed using palms, fingers, wrist, or elbows. The upward-curving strike is used in safe practice to discharge energy into someone (that is, use fa jin). This technique can lift individuals upward or backward without hurting them. If it is used to injure someone, it can break bone, tear and hemorrhage the internal organs (especially when using the palms and elbows), and tear the muscles of the arms and legs from their insertion points. It can also be seen in tai chi's Commencement (wrist), Fair Lady Weaves the Shuttles (palms), Lifting Hands (fingers), White Crane Spreads Its Wings (elbows), and in the hsing-i fire-element Pounding Fist and the Chicken, Tiger, and Monkey animal forms.

Cutting Actions   Cutting actions are used both to shatter bone, as when chopping an arm or the neck, or most usefully, to cut like a knife. Here the function of the blow is to penetrate deeply into the tissue to the deeper layers of muscle, causing severe damage. Cuts may be executed sideways, upwards, downwards, or diagonally, using the edge or the front ridge of the hand, the knuckles, the back of the wrist, the tip of the elbow, the shoulder, the head, the knees, or the feet. It can also be seen in many of the Roll Back components of tai chi movements, in the transition between the end of White Crane Spreads Its Wings and the beginning of Brush Knee and Twist Step, and in the downward-chopping component of hsing-i's Five Element Splitting Fist, the downward component of Pounding Fist, and the Snake, Eagle, and other bird animal forms.

DIM MAK
Cantonese term for the art of hitting acupuncture points to cause harm or death.

DIAN XUE
Mandarin for dim mak.

Finger Strikes Finger strikes are employed to penetrate flesh. They may use a strong vibration or shaking at the point of impact, a raking or clawing action, a wavelike striking and withdrawing action, or a twisting, boring, drill-like action. One's finger gung fu has to be excellent to strike the head and penetrate without damage to one's own thrusting fingers. This finger training is accomplished by bringing chi to the fingers through the nei gung and Circle-Walking postures of ba gua, and *not* by doing finger push-ups or striking sand or other objects, as is done in Shaolin. Finger strikes are also used to attack specific acupuncture points in specific ways and/or at specific times of day to disrupt an opponent's chi. This can be a deadly form of reverse acupuncture. (These techniques are called **dim mak** in Cantonese and **dian xue** in Mandarin.) The back hand of tai chi's Single Whip and the forward hand of Brush Knee and Twist Step especially work with finger techniques, as do the Monkey, Snake, Tiger, and Dragon Animal Forms of hsing-i.

Knuckle Strikes Knuckle strikes are essentially the same as finger strikes, except when it comes to twisting soft tissue and striking bone. Fingers do finer work at grabbing and twisting an opponent's muscles, tendons, veins, and joints, and ultimately are more effective at striking soft surfaces and soft tissue. However, the knuckles, which use the same physical movements and the same jin (power), are usually safer for the attacker when used against bone. In both tai chi and hsing-i, knuckle strikes are inherent in any punch.

Grabbing Grabbing techniques are employed not only to hold opponents fast as a wrestler would and throw them, but also to rip the skin off the body or twist the arm or leg into a joint-or muscle-lock, causing extreme pain or breakage. These techniques are prevalent throughout Chen style tai chi, Pull Down, and the 131 Split techniques within White Crane Spreads Its Wings, for example. In hsing-i, these techniques are incorporated every time an open hand closes into a fist, especially in the Splitting Fist.

Slaps Slaps can be done with either stiff or loose hands, using either the front or back of the hand. A stiff or loose hand can both be used much like a blackjack to crush whatever it hits, or to send a vibration to damage internal tissue a distance from the strike (for example, a slap to the shoulder may damage the liver, a slap to the top of the head may break the neck, a slap to the stomach may damage the spine.) Soft slaps may be used to break bone (the skull, ribs, sternum, or knees, for instance). Soft slaps, when combined with techniques that use spiraling reversals of motion, are ideal for damaging an opponent's internal organs. In ba gua's Rou Shou, for purposes of safety, power penetration slaps are avoided; whereas in combat, power penetration is used to rupture internal organs.

Slaps to the head are also used, not to break bones, but to rattle the brain against the skull, causing loss of consciousness, internal hemorrhage, or death. These slaps appear in tai chi's Brush Knee and Twist Step, the downward movement in Commencement, Roll Back, the transition between Shoulder Strike and White Crane Spreads Its Wings, and in the Splitting Fist of hsing-i, and in many of the small transition sections of the hsing-i Animal Forms.

Left-Right, Forward-Back, Up-Down Reversals   These reversal techniques are based on the S-shaped movement found in the yin yang tai chi symbol, which incorporates ba gua's spiraling and circling movements. They are clearly found the most in ba gua, next commonly in Chen style tai chi (especially the throws), next commonly in small-frame Yang and Wu tai chi, and least commonly in the large-frame methods of Yang style tai chi.

Reversal Strikes   The first strike employs the first half of the S-shaped movement. This makes your opponent move with a great deal of force in one direction, so that his momentum is clearly going in one direction: up or down, right or left, forward or backward, or along one direction or the other of a diagonal. While your opponent is going one way, your body snakes back and strikes him from the opposite direction. This reversal multiplies the force hitting or throwing the opponent, as it creates the effect of a head-on car collision: your opponent's momentum from the first strike hits your second half of the S-curve power, which is now going in the opposite direction. This head-on collision effect is amplified by the kinetic force of your own weight and energy changing direction. These left-right reversals are commonly used to strike the head, neck, and ribs. The up-down reversals are commonly used to whiplash the opponent's neck and spine and then strike the body on the way up. Your opponent's body is usually so disoriented from the whiplash that an incoming blow cannot be braced against and absorbed, to devasting effect. If the neck and spine are whiplashed, your opponent cannot yield to the blow, which has the same effect as if the body were put up against an unmoving wall while being hit. The forward-backward reversal technique is used to break the neck or back of the opponent, or throw an attacker face first on the ground.

Reversal Throws   Throwing actions follow more or less the same reversal pattern as do the S-curve hand strikes. The vertical drop-to-the-ground technique derived from the tai chi/ba gua Snake Creeps Down posture is a unique aspect of ba gua. It is especially prevalent in the Cheng Ting Hua system of ba gua, which has the most developed throwing techniques. Among these techniques are the following:

1. The vertical downward drop is followed by a left-right or forward-backward reversal, all done in one fast, smooth, coordinated movement.

2. The downward drop of the body (either physically, energetically, or both) is coordinated with a simultaneous upward motion of the arms.

3. When your opponent's body reaches the bottom of your torso, you drop and then reverse direction upwards, causing his feet to fly upwards and his head or body to be propelled toward the ground. This move is further complicated because, in addition to your up and down body/chi motion, your body and/or feet may be moving in any direction. The throws in ba gua are particularly dependent on the rapid opening and closing of the joints and body cavities and the opening and closing, bending, and bowing action of the spine.

Martial artists who have a good repertoire of throws will be able to adapt their techniques relatively easily into Cheng Ting Hua-style ba gua, and will find that ba gua's throwing, hitting, and kicking techniques will be superb complements to each other. Those who are hitting and kicking specialists will find that the ba gua throwing techniques can be integrated relatively easily into a style that focuses on hitting. Throws are important to achieving well-diversified fighting skills. When fighting multiple opponents simultaneously, it is very helpful to throw one opponent into someone else so his body blocks others from closing in on you. This is in effect killing two birds with one stone, especially if an opponent's feet hit the other person in the head or knees.

Along with the turning and footwork patterns of ba gua, the S-curve reversals are greatly responsible for the "now you see it, now you don't" phenomena of ba gua applications. A ba gua person seems to appear and disappear at the most unpredictable times due to the complex footwork, rapid waist turns, and the brief lapse of the opponent's awareness in the middle of a directional reversal.

In tai chi, these S-curve techniques are most prevalent in all branches of the Chen style. They are not nearly as prevalent in large- or medium-frame tai chi as they are in the small-frame tai chi styles. These techniques are the least common in hsing-i, where they are confined mostly to the animal styles, such as Bear and Snake.

DOU JIN
The internal martial art technique of vibrating or shaking the body suddenly and with great force.

Vibrating Strikes Vibration techniques are called **dou jin** in Chinese. In ba gua, with these techniques, the entire chi of the body is made to vibrate, which causes the opening and closing actions of the body to oscillate at high speed. This creates a machine-gun effect in which the opponent is hit with five or six full-power vibrating strikes in the blink of an eye. These shaking techniques are especially useful:

1. From a distance of only one-half inch for shattering bone

2. When fighting at extremely close distances, as when grabbed by a wrestler where there is no distance to generate a strike

3. To free oneself from joint-locks

4. Against fighters who have developed the iron shirt techniques in which they can create a layer of air like a car tire around their bodies, which protects their internal organs

5. Sideways against boxers who can slip around a head punch

In the case of the martial artist who has mastered the Iron Shirt protective technique and the boxer who can dodge, the vulnerable parts of the body are in effect shielded. In using a vibratory technique against such a person, the first or second vibration takes away the opponent's buffer zone and the next vibrating strikes do the damage. The vibrational force originates in the tantien and can flow throughout the whole body at once (likened to a dog shaking water off its body) or focused into any specific body point or points, even the head and hips. Most often seen in the Dragon styles of ba gua, this is an advanced technique, but a very important one. Dou jin is also commonly used in hsing-i (especially the I Chuan branch) as well as in Chen and "old style" Yang tai chi chuan, although not generally in the "new" styles derived from Yang Chen Fu.

Condensation Strikes   In condensation strikes, the power of the strike condenses at a point deep in the target with the feeling of a heavy "thud." With such a strike, one can break, say, the fifth brick in a stack of fifteen. If practicing this technique on a sand bag (which is, however, not usually recommended in ba gua if one wishes to develop one's internal chi to the maximum possible extent), the full power of your blow will concentrate in the center of the sand bag, but the bag itself will not move at all. These strikes can be used to attack internal organs and the brain. This is an earlier level of Cotton Palm, and is often called the internal martial arts equivalent of Shaolin's "Iron Palm." This method exists in all three styles, equally done with open-hands, fists, or forearms.

"Cotton Palm" Strikes   These soft strikes rely on the strength and penetrating power of your internal chi. These strikes should use the same amount of physical force that one would use to stroke a newborn baby's hair. The penetration of the chi, however, can cause the opponent mild discomfort, severe temporary pain with no aftereffect, internal hemorrhaging, or death. This strike requires an extremely high level of expertise and excellent control over one's chi. This technique is equally common to all the advanced levels of all internal martial arts.

Wave-Energy Strikes   Wave-energy strikes appear to be soft or powerless, yet can be tremendously powerful. They depend on sending a shock wave through the opponent. The force of these strikes is similar to the force found below the surface of large ocean waves, which is invisible from the surface. These strikes feel extremely light and weightless. They are included in the advanced levels of all three internal martial arts.

Simultaneous Projection of Energy in Opposite Directions

Energy may be projected from your hands in opposite directions simultaneously so as to destroy joints, break backs, crush internal organs, or penetrate the head. This internal technique is incorporated into many movements in all three styles.

Chin Na

CHIN NA
The branch of Chinese martial arts concerned with using joint-locks to immobilize and capture someone, and dislocate or break arms, leg joints, and vertebrae.

Chin na involves taking an opponent's hand, arm, shoulder, hip and leg joints, or spine, and twisting in a way that causes extreme joint pain or breakage. This activity can include twisting a person's finger to rip out a shoulder or twisting a person's ankle to rip out a knee, hip, or back. In ba gua and most other Chinese martial arts, chin na never accounts for more than 5 or 10 percent of the applications. When opponents are moving very fast and folding their bodies to change their angles, getting hold of any one of their joints can be exceedingly difficult. Having an opportunity to apply a chin na lock can only be called a gift. In the Japanese and Korean arts, where the strikes are usually linear, chin na can be used more often, because the attacker's joint is mostly straightened. However, in the Chinese internal martial arts (and others) where the joints fold and bend and never fully straighten, chin na locks are very difficult to accomplish.

In tai chi, the Chen style has the largest range of chin na techniques and the Yang style the least. Generally speaking, hsing-i has a smaller range of chin na techniques than either ba gua or tai chi.

Throws

SHUAI JIAO
Chinese wrestling.

NINJITSU
A specialized Japanese martial art style historically used exclusively by professional assassins in Japan.

Ba gua has a wide range of throwing techniques. This is especially true of the styles derived from the school of Cheng Ting Hua, who was a **shuai jiao** (Chinese wrestling) expert. Because there are only so many ways to throw a human being, many of the same types of throws in ba gua would be found in judo, jujitsu, aikido, **ninjitsu,** Chinese wrestling, and Northern Shaolin, with their foot sweeps and leg-locks and breaks. Real combat throws in ba gua are usually done to:

1. Damage a person's body by breaking a shoulder, elbow, ankle, knee, hip, or neck
2. Knock the wind out of attackers so they cannot continue to be aggressive
3. Kill the attacker

In ba gua two-person practice, throws are done so no one is intentionally injured. The main point to be emphasized here is not the specific throws found in ba gua (which would take volumes to explain), but the fluidity and interconnectedness between throws, kicks, joint-locks, and arm strikes that is unique to ba gua. Simultaneous joint-lock throws are common in ba gua, as is moving from throwing one person to striking another, or vice versa. Another singular aspect of the art of ba gua is its ability to mix throws, strikes, kicks, and joint-locks fluidly as you move to entirely different angles and different opponents.

In general, the Yang style of tai chi does not strongly focus on throws, although its major variant, the Wu style, does. The Chen style has the most extensive repertoire of tai chi throwing techniques. The throwing techniques of hsing-i are more concentrated in its animal styles than the Five Elements (see p. 186). Overall, of all the internal arts, hsing-i places the least emphasis on throwing techniques.

Kicking Techniques

Ba gua has an extremely well-developed kicking regimen. The kicking techniques of ba gua are part of what is referred to as the *chi shi er tui*, or "seventy-two leg techniques." The vast majority of these seventy-two techniques are concerned with how to use your knees, shins, and feet to attack an opponent while stepping. These include leg-joint locks, throws, and stomps, as well as kicks.

Contrary to what some ba gua books in English contend, ba gua does possess kicks above the waist, although such high kicks are usually kept to a bare minimum. Some Beijing schools do teach ba gua's methods of high-kicking to prospective students who had previously learned high kicks with Northern Shaolin training, which contains high-kicking skills equivalent to tae kwon do, karate, savate, or kickboxing. Such students were taught to convert their previously learned high kicks to high-kicking methods based on internal principles and the specific circularity and spiraling nature of ba gua. The Tianjin ba gua schools usually did not favor kicks above the solar plexus, and many of the ba gua schools of southern China did not like to kick above the waist. Given their choice, Southern ba gua stylists would prefer to not kick above the groin or kidneys. The general principle and preference in all ba gua schools is: "The lower the kick, the more prudent and efficient." All ba gua schools use all sorts of round, back, side, and spinning kicks, most likely derived from Northern Shaolin but with ba gua's distinctly circular and spiraling methodology added.

One of the reasons that many ba gua people avoid high kicking is that standing on one leg to kick exposes genitals, knee, leg, tailbone, and spine to attack as your kicking leg is rising into the air. Most martial artists will focus on blocking a kick and then counterattacking. Ba gua practitioners, rather than doing this, will concentrate on capturing and controlling the kicking leg and, through that control, attack the lower part of the aggressor's body. Because ba gua fighters are aware of how to rip out every joint of the lower body and spine, they have distinctive procedures regarding kicks, especially against multiple foes. As a general rule, all kicking should be preceded by breaking the balance of your opponents, either by your action or theirs. While there are kicks to the head in ba gua, the higher the kick, the more you are exposed. If one is going to kick above the groin or kidneys, it must be done only under specific circumstances, such as:

1. Your hands must be controlling the opponent so that a counter is not possible.

2. If your hands are not controlling opponents, you must be torquing or twisting their bodies so that there still is no way for them to counter.

3 When you have thrown someone who is in midair and thus unable to counter.

The central issue behind the question to kick or not to kick is that, if a person can counter your kick, then you should be able to recognize the counter and stop it, or else abort the kick and change to a different technique. The defensive techniques of all three internal martial arts focus on taking advantage of any opportunities to attack the supporting leg and the spine, if an opponent offers them during a high-kicking attack.

Tai chi has a smaller repertoire of kicking techniques than ba gua. It focuses primarily on front, side, and **lotus** (outside crescent) **kicks**, both high and low, and round kicks to the lower body. Chen style practices jumping kicks, but the Yang and Wu styles do so only within their weapons techniques, especially the broadsword. Hsing-i does not use head kicks, and has only a front and downward stomping kick to the upper torso. It does, however, have the full range of kicks to the lower body, especially the knee.

Kicks in ba gua derive from the following three sources.

A Kick Is a Step and a Step Is A Kick The basic principle of ba gua kicking is that each and every kick is a step, and each and every step is a kick. All the Circle-Walking steps in ba gua can be translated into kicking actions. Ba gua's forward steps create front kicks, backward steps create back kicks, side steps create side kicks, **kou bu** (toe-in) steps create round kicks, and **bai bu** (toe-out) steps create crescent and hook kicks. For example, forward steps can become kicks aimed anywhere from the ankle to the head. These kicks are done right from the ground without raising the knee first before kicking. These kicks are part of the normal walking sequence and usually come up under the opponent's line of vision. Thus, they are relatively invisible to the opponent.

In ba gua, the majority of kicks are not practiced as they are in karate, Northern Shaolin, or savate, in which you stand, raise your knee first and then kick. The majority of the kicks in ba gua are done as you step, where,

LOTUS KICK
A sideways kick in tai chi chuan that begins from the front of the body and moves to the outside of the body, at least as far as the shoulder or even farther.

KOU BU
The toe-in step of ba gua walking.

BAI BU
The toe-out step of ba gua walking.

instead of a step, the leg extends in the form of a kick on a straight trajectory from the floor. These kicking details, hidden in the walking of ba gua, are not well-known.

The same situation exists for tai chi, where the way the foot rests on the ground, is lifted, moved in the air, and set down contains whole hidden repertoires of kicking, blocking, and throwing techniques. To train in these techniques, the speed of the tai chi form must be slowed down dramatically. Slowness is required to develop the exceptional balance, rootedness, and the ability to stick to the opponent's legs for which, in China, tai chi is justifiably famous. Learning these hidden techniques of tai chi and ba gua requires an internal master to explain the subtleties of how you use your mental intention to activate your body. Without such instruction, even a martial art expert might not recognize them. The hsing-i stepping techniques are aimed particularly at stomping or kicking an attacker's lower body.

Form-Derived Kicks and Knee Butts Ba gua form work includes specific moves that lead to front, side, or round kicks, usually involving high kicks to the neck and head, or knee butts to the chest, ribs, and thighs. In these, the knee is usually first raised before the kick is launched. The same applies for the specific kicks in tai chi and hsing-i

Downward-Kicking or Stomping These downward kicks are derived from the sudden dropping of the physical body and sudden sinking of the chi through the leg into the foot. For example, Snake Creeps Down contains a low side kick; a ba gua toe-out step contains a 45-degree stomp to your opponent's knee-shin, ankle, and/or foot; and a downward and sideways back stomp develops from clear downward stepping actions. Stomps to the lower leg or foot are used to throw or break/dislocate an attacker's leg joints or spine. These techniques are especially prevalent in hsing-i.

Whereas ba gua practitioners are specialists in trapping kicking legs and then breaking the attacker's leg and/or spine, they do not themselves throw a kick unless they are sure that the kick is not vulnerable to a counter. These methods include crossing the opponent's arms; controlling the balance of others, usually by grabbing their hands and pulling them off balance; having an opponent's momentum move in such a way that the opponent cannot change directions and grab; or kicking opponents when one or both of their feet are off the ground.

Lack of Matwork

Ba gua has one glaring omission in its martial arsenal—techniques for grappling on the ground. Ba gua considers matwork to be appropriate for one-on-one combat, but strategically unwise against multiple opponents. Ba gua embraces the opinion that, while you are wrestling one opponent on the ground, the opponent's cohorts could converge on you, kick or step on you or do other deadly mischief. Ba gua, however, does execute the chokes and immobilization techniques of groundwork, yet does them in a standing or deeply crouched position. Through its low stances, Circle-Walking, and specific postures in the ba gua form, the art has techniques for ground fighting where your buttocks are only inches from the ground. These postures enable you to go below tall opponents and deal with ground-fighters and wrestlers, as well as to continue to fight eight opponents at once.

Like ba gua, the art of tai chi has extremely low dropping stances (such as Squatting Single Whip, Punch Downward, and extremely low Push Hands practices). Hsing-i has Monkey, Dragon, and Eagle positions for ground fighting.

Generally in the internal arts, a number of techniques may be used when grappling on the ground, such as nerve strikes, grabbing skin to cause severe pain, and delivering damaging blows without any windup. In one-on-one combat, how to fight on your back or belly with an experienced ground-fighting adept who can break your joints or choke you is a very legitimate concern. These training aspects must be considered:

1. Grappling on a mat or on concrete requires a reasonably healthy body because joints and spine are particularly vulnerable to injury during ground fighting. (Those who have chronic bad backs, for instance, should especially avoid being thrown or having their bodies forcefully twisted around from wrestling on the ground.)

2. Grappling is easier to learn when you are younger, although once ground-fighting skills are in your blood, they can be effectively maintained into old age, as a number of top judo and jujitsu people have demonstrated.

SWARI WAZA
The ground-fighting technique of aikido where the practitioner, either stationary or moving across the mat, is upright with one or both knees touching the ground.

3. It is wise to cross-train and learn the value of the grappling methods of judo, jujitsu, and aikido (called **swari waza**), even if you just want to learn how to defend yourself against them. There are, of course, a lot of things you can do on the ground in a real fight that are normally prohibited by the rules of the grappling arts, such as biting, scratching, grabbing the groin, and smashing someone's head into the ground.

4. Once you have achieved expertise in grappling, do not become overconfident and stay on the ground too long. There may, as ba gua cautions, be a real vulnerability if you have to simultaneously deal with multiple attackers.

Striking a balance in terms of how much time you should spend on regular internal arts practice and training in grappling is, like everything else, a matter of weighing the time available against your priorities.

Fighting Angles

In a confrontation, you want to keep from being overpowered, yet at the same time you want to be able to overpower your opponent. The situation may be likened to a mosquito who wants a meal but needs to find a hole in a mosquito net to get it, while you need to have your mosquito net be without holes. Any attack will be most successful if it has a clear line of unimpeded access to its target; that is to say, there is a clear hole in the mosquito net for the mosquito to fly easily through. A martial artist has only a few possible options for opening a clear hole in the net:

1. Your opponent is dazed or in some way incapable of moving at all

2. You can move so fast that your opponent never sees your attack coming or has insufficient time to carry out any useful defense

3. By adjusting the angle of your arms, legs, and/or torso, you can bypass your opponent's strength, and slide unchallenged through any subtle hole that appears in the defense

If your opponent's arms or legs can touch yours, or in some way partially block your clear attack angle, enough power may be siphoned from your attack to render it entirely useless or to reduce its impact to less than the needs of the moment. Punching someone's arms is quite different from having a clear field of fire to the body or head. Defensively, it is the same situation. Effective defensive fighting angles allow the defender to deflect an opponent's force with minimum exertion, making it possible and easier to launch a counterattack. The better the defensive angle, the less of the opponent's power will be absorbed by the defender's body, a major consideration if the attacker is significantly stronger. The more a defender absorbs the force of an attacker head-on, the greater the chance the defender will get stuck temporarily from the shock of the blow, become vulnerable to the next incoming attack, and be unable to counterattack effectively.

Therefore, if your fighting techniques are to be realistically implemented in combat, either in defense or attack, the learning of fighting angles is a basic skill critical to all three internal martial arts. The fighting angle methods of ba gua are arguably the most sophisticated of the three internal martial arts (see p. 231).

Often, in all three internal martial arts, a first phase of teaching the fighting techniques and their basic fighting angles is done through prearranged sets of choreographed attack and defense movements between two people, commonly called *two-person sets*. Two-person sets are useful for developing a fundamental fighting vocabulary in the three internal martial arts. These sets, however, are only an initial departure point for understanding and being able to actualize the potential of the techniques

(Text continues on page. 107.)

A PERSONAL ODYSSEY THROUGH THE MARTIAL ARTS

Wing Chun

At Cheng Man-ching's tai chi school in New York City during the early seventies, no one seemed to be doing free sparring. During this time, I become good friends with the late Clifton Cooke, who was one of the better Push Hands people in the school. We become incessant practice partners of form, Push Hands, sword, and the two-person fighting set both in and outside the school. One day, Cliff told me he was learning a Cantonese Shaolin martial art called Wing Chun. He described it as a linear-based martial method that didn't have much form work or chi gung, but focused instead on a kind of hand-touching sparring called **chi sau.** In chi sau, you can both develop and use the sensitivity of tai chi Push Hands, while you try to punch, strike, and even kick each other's shins and knees. His description sounded great and I began learning Wing Chun alongside him then and when I returned from my next stint in the Orient. Wing Chun appealed to me because its punches and strikes fulfilled a visceral need I had for a sense of realistic sparring using soft technique, which Push Hands didn't offer.

In America and Europe during the 1970s, Wing Chun was about the only martial art available where you could learn or practice arm-touching sensitivity sparring for hours on end with enthusiastic people.* This practice was good because it allowed me to gain experience in the sensitivity necessary for hitting, controlling, and trapping that is required before the "sticking" abilities in any martial art style can really be mastered. In Taiwan, there was never a shortage of willing practice partners and teachers in hand-touching practices in either the internal, external, or amalgamated martial arts. The internal arts practitioners in the West did not as yet do these sparring practices, only Push Hands. Both in the West and in Hong Kong, I learned Wing Chun mostly with members of the Yip Man** school, and did some cross-research in Hong Kong with a member of the Fatshan school.

Wing Chun is based on hand and arm techniques. It also uses kicking techniques, mostly during close-in fighting, where, like the internal martial

CHI SAU
The two-person touch sparring practice of Wing Chun, where both partners attempt to strike, block, and counter each other.

---

*In the 1970s, most of the Shaolin schools of Chinese martial arts were not available in the West. Those that existed were mostly only of Cantonese descent, not because this tradition was most prevalent in China, but rather because few practitioners from the other Chinese provinces had come to the West, either as immigrants or students. This situation began to change somewhat during the late 1980s with the opening of China to the outside world and shifting political conditions in Taiwan.

**Yip Man was the teacher of Bruce Lee.

Wing Chun, continued

arts, it first controls the arms of opponents, and through that control immobilizes them or breaks their balance before the attacking kick, mainly to the lower body, is executed. Its primary techniques are excellent for developing the precision of linear fighting angles in terms of placing your elbows and hands in relationship to the power of your opponent's kicks and punches. Wing Chun develops extremely fast reflexes. It works the linear fighting angles associated with the arms fairly well, but not all those needed in the waist and legs. Like hsing-i, Wing Chun's martial philosophy is a no-nonsense one that values effectiveness above all. In New York City, I found Wing Chun a useful teaching aid in the many women's self-defense courses I taught. I subsequently practiced Wing Chun in my next two extended trips to Hong Kong.

The standard way most martial artists describe Wing Chun is: "It's great if you have to fight in a telephone booth, inside an elevator, or in a similarly confined space, but has problems on other terrain." Especially, I would add, if there is room for you to be thrown. This point was first brought home to me by the late Bill Paul.

Bill was the first person who introduced me to the practical side of Chinese martial arts. In judo circles, Bill's nickname was "the California strong man." He visited my judo class during a trip to New York to compete for a slot in the 1964 Olympic judo trials. A native of San Francisco, he started Chinese martial arts there in the late 1950s, when that city was seemingly the only place in the Western world where a wide variety of Chinese martial arts was available for non-Chinese to learn. Bill sometimes worked as a bouncer, so he had an appreciation for functional martial arts. When the class was over, he stayed and talked for a while. The conversation drifted to the relationship between judo and karate, and Bill began to talk about gung fu, especially choi li fut, **fut gar,** and **hung gar.** Being the only karate person in this judo class, I became his opponent. It was an enlightening experience, as he proceeded to tie me up, trap my hands, and hit me from the front, side, and back in ways I never knew existed. His attacks awakened a lifelong curiosity about gung fu.

Later, during my university days in Japan, Bill and I met again when he came to train at the Kodokan World Judo Headquarters. By this time, I was much more seasoned and we could really trade gung fu techniques, which we did at times, only now Bill was also involved in Cantonese White Crane, Monkey Boxing, and Wing Chun, and I now had a background in internal martial arts and the monkey techniques of hsing-i. We met again a

FUT GAR
An external style of Southern Shaolin from Canton province.

HUNG GAR
An external style of Southern Shaolin from Canton province.

A PERSONAL ODYSSEY THROUGH THE MARTIAL ARTS

Wing Chun, continued

few years later in Berkeley, California, through a new mutual friend. I was on the West Coast to see if the Chinese martial arts training in the Bay Area offered the opportunities to be found in Hong Kong and Taiwan.

That afternoon in Berkeley was a lot of fun. Bill and I started out sparring lightly. Gradually, like two jazz musicians jamming, the heat turned up within each of us, as we used our different Chinese martial arts to attack and counter each other. We were in a fair-sized room, so we had sufficient space to move about. Bill had great elbow techniques, which motivated you to turn your waist to evade them, or else. Recognizing that Bill's grappling was much better than mine, I did not even try to throw him, knowing I would be instantly countered. Both of us were too well trained to allow a successful joint-lock to occur. We were kicking low, as kicking high would be tantamount to asking to be thrown down. The agility to sink and shift weight gained from the internal martial arts served me well. When Bill would go in for a throw, my hand would be in his groin, so after a time he stopped. At different points, we both sent each other flying through the doorway.

After a while, it was decided to do some Wing Chun chi sau, which often flowed into free-form exchanges. At one point, thinking I had the edge in fighting angles, I went in for the kill, strictly using Wing Chun technique. This proved to be a very bad move. Failing to pay attention to all my waist and foot angles as well as my weightings, I found myself flying up in the air in a beautifully timed throw. This experience really drove home the point that, in martial arts, what you do not pay attention to can bury you. For the rest of our sparring, I abandoned this hands-only Wing Chun strategy, and Bill couldn't throw me again. Afterwards, Bill told me where all the good Chinese martial arts schools were in San Francisco, most of which I checked out before deciding to return to the Orient to study.

Throughout the years, I saw this same weakness in Wing Chun against throws again and again, especially in the full-contact tournaments in the Far East, where grapplers would first contact the Wing Chun practitioner's arms and take a hit or grab them, and then proceed to throw them down very hard. I took this insight very seriously in hsing-i, as it too is primarily a hand style. The study of Wing Chun's arm-fighting angles was extremely useful. It helped set the stage for appreciating the more complete range of fighting angles in the internal martial arts (see p. 103), especially in the area of footwork and angle changes of the waist while moving and turning.

themselves and the fighting angles they contain. This potential is usually accomplished by developing the heart/mind, which is developed by joint-hand practices and unrehearsed sparring.

The Meaning of Animal Forms in the Internal Martial Arts

The martial practice of animal forms is common in the external martial arts. The term *animal* used here refers to the whole of the animal kingdom, that is, mammals, fish, birds, reptiles, real or mythological. Chinese martial art adepts keenly watched animals fight, and analyzed what they did that worked effectively. They observed these animals move in particular ways when they fought: monkeys jumped, rolled on the floor, and climbed up animals and trees; bears smothered animals before killing them; birds darted in and out and swooped down; tigers leaped from a crouching position, and mythical animals were assigned all kinds of martial motion. Each animal had its own natural weapon: bears crushed, using their shoulders; tigers clawed; cranes vibrated their wing tips with machine-gun-like rapidity; snakes inflicted precise incisions or squeezed the life out of their prey; monkeys pinched, slapped, ripped with their teeth, and hit with their wrists; and horses smashed with their hoofs.

Over and above physical movements and the natural weapons it is endowed with, each animal displays a specific strategy for how to fight. It will use tactics to implement that strategy: evade and strike, execute a lightning attack, confuse and then strike, move in with overwhelming force, use incredible speed, and so on. The martial animal forms attempt to adapt the various fighting qualities of animals to human combat.

Humans, however, are not animals. We do not have four legs, tails, wings, fangs, or claws. We are not as big or as small as some animals, nor can we fly. But we have a mind, and we can shape our body to do what our mind tells us. In the internal martial arts, the initial stage of teaching animal forms predisposes the practitioner to learn certain specific physical techniques. These may involve crouching, jumping, leaping, skipping, turning, or moving your hands and arms, torso or feet, to mimic the motions of animals. You might form your hands in certain positions to mirror the natural weapons of animals: knuckles could become the hooves of horses, fingers become claws, elbows become horns, palms become paws, backs of the hands become wings, and so forth. For all of that, the physical techniques are not the most important aspect of Animal Forms in the internal martial arts. More significant is that the practitioner becomes the mind of the animal that creates and adjusts its fighting strategies.

Each animal has a quality of mind: for example, bears lumber until they move very suddenly, explosively, and fast; cats, especially tigers, are ferocious; horses are angry; monkeys, excitable and vicious; snakes, slinky and devious; birds, frenetic, and so on. Some animals kill with one clean blow; others depend on multiple attacks to achieve a kill.

The following discussion concerning Animal Forms aplies only to the internal martial arts; it may or my not apply to Shaolin Animal Forms.

Just like the real animal it mimics, each Animal Form of the internal arts has its mind-set of perceiving and responding to the violence or to the threat of it. Each separate Animal Form goes into the intent behind the animal's mind. In practicing, you learn to think like the given animal, perceive situations as it does and rouse your energy as it does. This is not just done as a specific technique, but as a whole way of being and interacting with a situation. This method allows you not merely to mimic a specific physical movement of an animal, but rather to be able to adapt mentally, so you can change from technique to technique just as the animal reacts and changes during an actual violent confrontation. One has to learn to go into the animal's mind, live its anger, viciousness, absolute confidence, ferocity, deviousness, aloofness, ability to stalk, and so on.

All this may sound fascinating, but from another point of view, in becoming an animal you have succeeded only in taking a step down the spiritual evolutionary scale. The next ascending evolutionary step is to retain all the functional martial strategies of the animal but keep a calm, still mind, thereby remaining a human and not becoming an animal. Your mind must learn how to move your body purely by using internal strength and clarity of intent, not by anger or other animalistic emotions, which are all too easily aroused during combat.

As indicated in Chapter 1, clarity of intent replaces the release of violence-producing hormones as the source of your power and motivation to defend yourself, and gets rid of the fight, flight, or freeze response. When this stage progresses far enough, the desire to defeat an attacking man is replaced first with a wish to do him no harm, if possible, then to neutralize the violent intent in him. This neutralizing should occur during the confrontation, and it should also be applied to influencing the attacker's energetic matrix subliminally so his violent disposition is reduced after the fight is over. At this point, the Animal Forms of the internal arts begin to move into the spiritual realm, during both solo forms or fighting applications. In short, specific techniques are imparted that implement the goal of attempting to raise your own consciousness and that of your opponent.

Sparring Practices

Like tai chi and hsing-i, ba gua develops fighting skills through a methodical sequence of solo exercises and practices with partners. As previously discussed, Walking the Circle solo while doing the 16 basic nei gung energy practices is the single most important ba gua exercise for developing martial art power. When combined with holding postures, solo exercises, and palm changes, ba gua can be fully realized as a physical, energetic, and spiritual art.

While doing only these solo practices can possibly lead you to some competence as a fighter, they must be complemented by specific two-person training practices to develop ba gua fully as a fighting art. There is simply no substitute for working with a living human being. The techniques for working two-person applications include: (1) Rou Shou; (2) Walking a Circle with palms joined and engaging in both pre-set and spontaneous attacks and defenses; (3) attacks and defenses executed from close, middle, and long distances (both pre-set and spontaneous); and (4) free sparring.

For the intermediate student of ba gua or tai chi, the key is to keep your techniques rounded so that as you get hit you can continue from one technique to another without pauses caused by inertia, emotional paralysis, or physical tension. This practice develops the ability to keep your head and not freeze up when the pressure is on. Since you must ultimately touch the opponent for a martial technique to work, Rou Shou training introduces you to the process of changes at the point where your body touches the opponent, usually the arms. Rou Shou training then forms the bridge inside the practitioner's body/mind between hesitating and being able to continue on to the next thing, which may be the shock of arms touching and hitting, throwing and joint-locking. The major objectives of the Rou Shou practice are to:

1. Develop sensitivity and aliveness of touch
2. Overcome the tendency towards paralysis or hysteria in combat
3. Develop (as in tai chi Push Hands) the abilities to (a) root; (b) twist the waist, and limbs; (c) fold the arm joints; and (d) activate springiness in the legs for both vertical and horizontal movement
4. Provide a safe, practical way to develop realistic combat techniques short of actual fighting

Rou Shou could prove invaluable to tai chi practitioners, as it forms a natural bridge between Push Hands (see p. 147), which is insufficient for practical self-defense, and sparring. This transition is unfortunately lacking in most modern tai chi schools.

Practice with Your Friends, Fight with Your Enemies

Practicing for a potential self-defense situation or fighting competition is *not the same* as being in an actual, real-life, violent confrontation or a fierce martial arts competition. When the author began judo at the age of twelve, he was always mystified that during normal **randori,** or free practice, the instructor always said that the students were to play judo, but if there were to be a formal competition between two of the students, they

RANDORI
Japanese term for the free sparring used in judo, jujitsu, and aikido.

were to "fight." One moment someone is your friend and playmate and the next your "enemy"? This was confusing. One day when asked, the instructor, a former all-Japan judo champion, explained the situation.

On the mat, the people you practice with are your friends and classmates. The purpose of your practice is to strengthen each other through development of technique. You do not want to hurt each other or you cannot continue to practice. If you lose control of your emotions and do nasty things to your practice partners, they will either make sure to pay you back later or will be unwilling to practice with you. Hurting a practice partner or taking out your emotions on the body of another will pollute the atmosphere, and is considered very bad manners. Etiquette is very important in the martial arts, as are kindness and mutual respect. During practice, winning is not as important as developing your technique. So you play judo, and do not fight in the dojo.

When you engage in a competition the situation is different. The object is not to play but to win. If winning is not your object, do not bother to compete, only practice. This is a martial art, so in a competition your attitude must be to want to fight and win, according to the rules. In a competition you have no friends during the fight, only an enemy to be overcome. Without winning and losing, competition has no meaning. After the fight is over, then you can practice as friends and play judo. Judo for playing and judo for fighting each has its own time and place.

In any martial art, it is important to agree with your practice partner on boundaries and on what level or intensity or use of force you wish to escalate to. You can go gently to full bore, with varying levels of intensity in between.

Fa Jin

Fa means to discharge, release, throw out, or project, and *jin* means power. Depending on the development level of the practitioner, fa jin exists in a continuum, between physical and chi practices. The internal compression and release of the body that result from the openings and closings and twistings of the body facilitate the development of fa jin, or the discharging of energy. For example, discharging of chi is used both in the martial art technique of empty force (see p. 185) and in chi gung tui na (see p. 282).

Whereas most martial arts use physical strength and muscular force, tai chi, hsing-i, and ba gua do not. Achieved in total relaxation and with the absence of muscular tension, fa jin techniques release energy in short, concentrated bursts that create tremendous power. This power can pass through an attacking man's body, bringing him no physical damage or pain, but causing his body to be thrown several feet away as if picked up by a gust of wind. Or, the force of fa jin can be concentrated inside the man's body where the energy released can cause serious harm. The critical issue in fa jin is the storage and sudden release of energy to a specific point in time and space. This ability to release energy suddenly in a concentrated form is not only critical to the martial side of ba gua, but also to the art's skills at clearing out stagnant chi in one's body, healing bodywork, Taoist meditation, and internal alchemy.

Fa jin, especially rising from the feet, is extremely important in ba gua's famous ability to change direction rapidly. The extremely strong openings and closings of the body in a continuous flow allow inertia to be overcome by making everything circular. The sudden release of energy also provides the impetus to reverse the direction of body movements. These principles could be equally applied to a wide range of diverse contact or noncontact sports, such as football, basketball, dance, baseball, soccer, and golf. Inertia never becomes an issue, which is what makes rapid, spontaneous changes possible.

THE MARTIAL QUALITIES OF SMALL-, MEDIUM-, AND LARGE-MOVEMENT METHODS OF TAI CHI, HSING-I, AND BA GUA

Tai chi, hsing-i, and ba gua can all be performed with large-, medium-, or small-frame movements. Both in forms and fighting applications, the term *frame* refers to the size of the area the body moves within, as in the size of a picture frame.

Some styles only have large movements, others only medium-sized ones, and yet others only small style movements at each level of training. However, many styles have large movements at the beginning level, then progress along a continuum to smaller and smaller movements, with the small movements being taught at the most advanced internal level. As the body fully opens up and is able to perform the energetic requirements of a larger frame, it then condenses all its developed abilities and begins to work on the next energetic level, where chi is concentrated and subtle rather than gross and diffuse. In the natural course of training, it normally takes individuals a decade or more of education and practice to refine and integrate all aspects of internal work and advance to each progressively smaller frame of movement.

Usually the progression goes from large to small. In earlier photographs of the Yang style tai chi adept Yang Cheng Fu, you can see that he is clearly doing large-frame movements, yet twenty years later, he clearly had tightened up and progressed to a medium-frame style.*

---

*This progression also appears in the West, where the tai chi of Cheng Man-ching is fairly widespread. Photos from the 1950s show him doing a large-frame style. In his later book (in English), co-authored by R. W. Smith, photos show him doing a medium-frame style. In his seventies, near the end of his life, videotapes clearly show that Cheng's movements had become still smaller and more condensed.

Physical Movement

Visually, large-frame styles display several qualities:

1. Arm and leg postures are very extended, with the hands as far away from the body as the technical requirements of each style will tolerate.

2. Arm movements and stepping actions tend to describe large circles in the air, with the angle between the armpit and the elbow being as large as possible, even in transition movements.

3. The focus during waist-turning movements is on turning as far to either side as is comfortably possible.

4. Stances tend to be long and deep, with an attempt to go as low as possible.

5. Postures are extended, elbows 60 to 90 degrees to the side, and no tiny circle motions are present.

Visually, medium-frame styles have the following qualities:

1. Arm movements will come closer, but not very close to the body, but just for short periods of time before fully extending away from the body again.

2. Stances are of medium height; the buttocks will not descend to be even with or go below the knees.

3. Both arm and leg movements tend to be extended away from the body, but not as far away as they can go.

4. Arm movements and stepping actions tend to use a mix of large and small circular movements, with the bulk of the movements being in the middle.

5. Waist movements will turn 90 degrees to the side, but not more. (Often the waist will only turn 45 degrees, tightening the arc with small movements deep within the belly or lower tantien. These movements are not externally obvious.)

6. Small, wavelike circles will begin to appear in the transitions between obvious postures.

7. The changes within transitions from posture to posture are much more emphasized than they are in the large-frame forms.

8. Elbows tend to face 45 degrees to the side.

9. The circles of the form are smaller than they are in the large style. Some circular movements are fairly obvious; other smaller ones are discernable only if you have an eye trained to detect extremely tiny motion.

Visually, the qualities of small-frame styles are:

1. Arm movements will come very close to the body repeatedly before fully extending away from the body again.

2. Stances will usually be high, often being done with the knees only slightly bent.

3. Both arm and leg movements will tend to be extended from the body less than they could be, often with only a few inches between their extension and retraction.

4. Waist movements often tend to turn only 45 degrees to the side.

5. Circles tend to become exceedingly small, with transition movements often containing not one but several circles, often on multiple planes and angles of movement. Even to the trained eyes of external martial artists and movement specialists, many circular movements that are physically occurring tend to not be externally visible, but if you could look below the skin inside the body, these circular movements would be extremely large and obvious. To do these powerful internal movements requires extremely strong intent and control of chi. In general, the small styles are considered by internal stylists to be the most advanced.

Energy Work

In the internal martial arts and all Taoist chi work, there is a basic saying: "The more on the outside, the less on the inside, and the more on the inside, the less on the outside." In terms of the internal martial arts, this saying means that the more a person moves externally (large frame), the less the body and chi move internally, that is, below the skin, inside the body. Conversely, the less the body moves externally (small frame), the more the body and chi move internally, that is, below the skin, inside the body. The smaller the frame, the more it relies on and develops the internal energetics. The larger the frame, the less it works the energetics, but the more it works and develops the physicality.

Large-frame movements focus more on developing raw energy and power, in a general direction or on a line. Chi movements are simple and as long as possible from point A to B. Energy moves in one clear motion from the beginning of a movement to the end, without other things happening to create secondary energetic movements. For example, a forward vertical energetic movement is only a vertical energetic movement, without a secondary horizontal, diagonal, or backward energetic component.

Medium-frame movements usually have two or three circular energetic movements going on simultaneously, a phenomenon lacking in the large-frame movements. Transition movements have the greatest number of small energetic movements. These create the means for the physical movements to have numerous possibilities that are not obvious on a gross physical level, yet they are clearly manifested energetically, and affect an opponent.

Of the three frames, small-frame movements have the greatest degree of energetic control and the largest range of energetic techniques. They develop the ability to absorb or project power localized at a point. Energetic movements can be minute, even to the degree that they can be centered inside an internal organ or a joint. Small-style movements are often the most useful for healing specific body problems. Energetic movements become smaller and smaller until they can be done at a point or reverse direction at a point. At a high level, small energetic movements progress from being circular to spherical. Small-frame movements are energetically known for circles within circles and spheres within spheres.

Martial Applications

PENG
The Ward Off or rising energy of tai chi.
LU
The absorbing energy of tai chi.
JI
The forward projecting energy of tai chi.
AN
The pushing downward energy of tai chi.

Large-frame styles focus on large power movements where each of the four energies—**peng, lu, ji,** and **an** (see p. 124)—is applied with the power of the whole body. A big action creates a big return: big chops, punches, one-directional kicks and throws or joint-locks. Large-frame styles specialize in long-distance fighting. These are the easiest to learn, but have the least range of tai chi's sophisticated applications. Raw power is emphasized, with long, stretched-out movements, rather than the ability to instantaneously change quickly, fluidly, and within a small distance.

Medium- and small-frame movements can be exceptionally effective the closer you are to your opponent. Whereas large-frame movements can be smothered where there is a minimum distance between you and an opponent, small-frame movements are designed to work within an inch of motion, both defensively and offensively. The smaller the frame, the faster you can change from one martial technique to another, the more combinations you can do in a unit of time, and the smaller is the physical distance required to project or absorb power.

Small-frame movements derive their power not so much from body alignments, as is often the case with large-frame movements, but by moving energy around inside the body. Small-frame self-defense techniques can change the direction of their power, or the body contact point of the power several times a second. Whereas the origination and trajectory of power in a large-style movement can be discerned, in small style movements it cannot. To the viewer, there is no logical sense as to what is causing a particular manifestation of power or even how it could be possible. It is possible because there can be an ability to produce subtle movements of energy within different parts of the body simultaneously. Medium-frame energetic movements mix and match from large- and small-frame applications. To repeat, the larger the frame, the more the raw power; the smaller the frame, the more the subtle power to change and project power to a point.

IMPORTANCE OF MASTER/STUDENT RELATIONSHIPS AND LINEAGE

In ba gua, tai chi, and all the internal martial arts, there were always three levels (classifications) of learning and training:

1. *Students*. These people were only taught the outer forms, exercises, and the most basic applications.

2. *Disciples*. This category was reserved for only very dedicated people and perhaps friends or relatives. In Tung Hai Chuan's original ba gua school, you did not study with Tung or with one of his top students without first becoming an official disciple through a formal ceremony. (This ceremony is called a *bai shr* in Chinese.) Unless you entered into that formal relationship, you would not be taught in comprehensive detail. However, after World War II and the Chinese Civil War, the teachings became less formal. Many ba gua instructors taught students for just a short time without taking them through all the training. Wartime life was too chaotic for complete training, and more was taught incompletely than in Tung's time.

3. *The highest level of training*. This level was reserved for those disciples who were being trained to carry on the lineage. **A lineage disciple** is taught all aspects of the art and is the specific disciple responsible for mastering all of them and for transmitting them to the next generation. In order to be chosen as a lineage disciple, the person must have already demonstrated the ability to communicate effectively. (A nonlineage disciple, in contrast, is not responsible for passing on the entire art to the next generation, only the specific parts of the art he specialized in. He need only be a superb practitioner and representative of the parts of the art that he is taught.) Tung's best original students were all trained as lineage disciples. They were free to choose their own students and disciples.

The term **ba gua men** or ba gua gate refers to those who have reached at least the disciple level and are representative of the system. The traditional Chinese view is that those who do not study with this level of instructor, or do not receive this level of instruction from a qualified person, are not considered to be the real ba gua people. They are, in other words, not "within the gate," or privy to the highest quality instruction. They are also not held responsible for high-quality performance. In China, a disciple is responsible for becoming superlative; otherwise, the teacher loses face. However, a student's poor performance does not reflect on the face of the master. This is classical Chinese tradition. The same situation exists in tai chi chuan and hsing-i chuan, where the terms **tai chi men** and **hsing-i men** refer to the highest complete level of the

LINEAGE DISCIPLE
A formal disciple who is chosen to learn and carry forth to future generations all the knowledge of all that is intact of any specific internal martial arts lineage.

BA GUA MEN
A school of ba gua chang that has the complete martial tradition of ba gua chang intact, usually from a lineage source.

TAI CHI MEN
A school of tai chi chuan that has the complete martial tradition of tai chi chuan intact, usually from a lineage source.

HSING-I MEN
A school of hsing-i chuan that has the complete martial tradition of hsing-i intact, usually from a lineage source.

art and not to the more popularized and watered-down versions that abound.*

All martial arts, including ba gua, if they are to survive and continue the tradition must be creatively passed from one generation to the next with no diminishing of quality. Otherwise, the art will weaken with each generation and will eventually wither away.

Many of the exaggerated stories to be found in the lore of ba gua arise out of the Chinese love of recounting the famous exploits of their ancestors; that is, their lineage. It must be remembered that China has a tradition of ancestor worship, which applies equally to the family of a martial arts or meditation school as to a biological family. The more you can enhance the reputations of your ancestors, the more "face" or status you and your descendants can gather.

Historical accounts in almost all books on ba gua in English and Chinese report that this person studied with that person and that person studied with someone else, and each time they passed on what they knew. More important than such supposed credentials is whether or not a teacher can functionally use ba gua's methods for either self-defense, therapy, or meditation. China contains many ba gua teachers who claim to have received the teaching from a "direct lineage," but who cannot use it pragmatically or effectively. In China, one is always asked, "Who is your teacher? For how long?" and "Who was your teacher's teacher?" in order to determine if a person learned from an authentic source.

There are many situations that parallel the real and false lineage issue: a high-school graduate who cannot read or write, a karate "expert" who is beaten up by an untrained teenager, a health care therapist who does not have positive effects on patients. In such cases, you could very reasonably wonder about the abilities of such people or the credentials of their schools.

Lineage in China carries equal importance in terms of high and low quality learning. A master from a legitimate lineage who was a good student can also be reasonably expected to perform a valuable service for his own students. Poor students break the lineage. Good teachers and lineages tend to produce good students. Legitimate lineage transmitters who are poor teachers weaken or break the lineage by not teaching students well.

Even the best students of weak lineages usually find they never quite reach the potential that would normally result from all their years of applied effort and practice. For the student, a lineage in China means that you are

---

*For example, the original legendary exploits of tai chi players were about practitioners of *tai chi men* only. As the "Gate" has become weakened, each succeeding generation has lost capacities that were actualized by the preceding generation. Accordingly, the vast majority of tai chi "experts" today are not members of *tai chi men* and usually do not have the abilities that made tai chi famous in China. The slow-motion movements of tai chi, however, are so effective that even when done poorly they benefit the health of ordinary people immensely. It seems to be that as ordinary tai chi chuan, especially the simplified varieties increase, *tai chi men* proportionally decreases. (See Appendix A, p. 305.) In many ways, this unfortunate tendency seems to also be happening to ba gua. (See Appendix B, p. 313.)

being exposed to the accumulated experience, knowledge, and quality standards that have made legitimate ba gua or tai chi schools withstand the test of time and become, for good reason, well-respected and justifiably famous.

Legitimate tai chi and ba gua masters are privy to a tremendous amount of critically important information that mediocre or low-level tai chi teachers are totally unaware of. People in the modern era do not usually train the four to eight hours a day for decades that was normal for the masters who invented and developed the Taoist chi cultivation practices. These masters identified what was significant to practice for self-generating progress and ignored the rest.

The important material, when applied correctly, causes the chi to grow inside you and make you become stronger, clearer, and more skilled —well into old age. The window dressing consists of the myriad permutations of a given technique that cause you to have endless internal sensations, but minimal substantial progressive growth. All tai chi and ba gua practices, if you do the movements, will generate various internal feelings and experiences. Each component, either basic or advanced, when it moves to the next logical level of practice, inherently has a whole new set of physical and psychological "wow" experiences.

The nature and specifics of the most valuable components of these arts are such that it would be a billion-to-one chance you would discover on your own the untaught critical components of tai chi, ba gua, or chi gung. It was, however, assumed that good students, once they were taught the next critical level of information, would be able to work out for themselves the permutations inherent in it. Other students, lacking critical information from nonlineage teachers, had a ceiling put on their knowledge so that they stayed more or less at the same level, even if they practiced forever. The only way for them to remove the limitations and get to the next logical level of capacity was to learn new critical components from a more knowledgeable teacher, if they could find a willing one. In China, it was always a big issue whether or not a student was learning "the real stuff" or a watered-down version.

The issue of the quality or legitimacy of a given internal martial arts school or lineage is not purely an academic one. When someone spends time, honest effort, and money to gain the benefits of an education, the quality of the teaching is a significant factor. The more complete the knowledge and the better the teaching skills of your master/teacher, the more therapeutic, self-defense, and meditation capacities you will gain.

If your interest is only in recreation, quality of instruction may not matter to you. As long as you are having a good time, that's enough. However, if you are interested in seriously learning the Taoist energy arts, it does matter. A dedicated internal martial arts student should become very aware of a teacher's background and training. Achievement in the Taoist energy arts depends on both your personal effort and on the quality of your instruction. These are the elements that make the learning meaningful and profound.

Morihei Ueshiba—Where Did He Get His Power?

Courtesy of Virginia Mayhew

I studied with O-Sensei Morihei Ueshiba, the founder of aikido, during my undergraduate days in Japan. My research has indicated that O-Sensei's aikido was in a primary way directly influenced by ba gua chang. My first in-depth, extended experience with a top-level master of internal martial arts was with Ueshiba between 1967 and 1969. Looking back on my training with him, it is obvious to me that much of what Ueshiba's aikido had in terms of the physical techniques came from jujitsu. However, the chi that he manifested when he did aikido appears to have come directly from ba gua, with some partial influence from hsing-i as well.

I saw people in Japan in the late 1960s who were very skilled at the type of **Daito Ryu** aikijitsu, a form of jujitsu, upon which Ueshiba based his aikido. But none of them was able to manipulate chi as subtly or powerfully as Ueshiba or even to articulate the theories of ki (chi) basic to aikido and ba gua. Actually, Ueshiba was far beyond aikijitsu's level of sophistication. His ability to enter, turn, attract, and then play with and lead an opponent's chi and mind was phenomenal. In Japanese history, there was no martial art to compare to it, and no one else in Japan could do anything like it. In his dojo, I often heard that he spent many years in China and only afterwards returned to Japan with this miraculous chi-based aikido ability.

It is my opinion, based upon personal memories of him and my technical analysis of his films twenty-five years after his death, that it is completely reasonable to assume Ueshiba studied ba gua while he was in China. The entering, turning, and leading of one's opponent, as well as the hundreds of subtle energy projections of aikido are fundamental ba gua techniques that existed long before Ueshiba's birth. Because of this, I believe that Ueshiba learned ba gua while he was in Manchuria, China. Before and just after World War II, it would have been extremely politically incorrect and counterproductive for Ueshiba's organization to have credited the Chinese with part of his "new" martial art, given the chauvinistic military and nationalistic bent of Japan in that era.

Ueshiba had great internal power. Internal power is almost incomprehensible to the

Morihei Ueshiba—Where Did He Get His Power?, continued

Western mind, which is conditioned by the overt displays of external power in films and on television. External power is like seeing someone with a wallet stuffed with $100 bills—you automatically assume this is a wealthy person, which may or may not be true. However, an extremely wealthy person can conceal wealth and have a very thin wallet, carrying only one credit card that has a million-dollar credit line (which is the nature of internal power). Things are not always as they seem. In Ueshiba's case, this was very true. When I was with Ueshiba, he was in his eighties and of small stature, yet incredibly strong. When he was old and near the end of his life, his students would carry him into the dojo on a stretcher. He looked extremely weak and frail. However, he would suddenly gather his chi, stand up, and toss exceptionally strong men around like rag dolls. Afterward, he would return to the stretcher and resume being a sick old man.

With Ueshiba, you began to expect the paranormal. I still vividly remember that he could get behind you so quickly it was as if he had disappeared. The same is true of top ba gua people. You could have Ueshiba clearly in your sight, and suddenly he was gone. Then, with equal suddenness, he was back. Ueshiba would then fake a hit and then joint-lock and/or throw you to the ground. In contrast, ba gua

people typically would actually hit you first and then throw you on the ground. This "now you see me, now you don't" is one of the great martial strengths of ba gua adepts. Unlike a boxer or karate person, whose hand you can see coming at you, ba gua people have an incredible power and a strange kind of speed that is so subtle you cannot perceive its origin or destination.

In watching films of the late master, one can see Ueshiba clearly demonstrating many of the chi principles of ba gua. But while these chi principles are referred to in the vaguest of terms in aikido (when they are spoken about at all, which is rare), in ba gua the critical energy principles are articulated in great depth and are specified in a systematic way. This valuable ability to pass on previously accumulated information intact, so the next generation can accurately reproduce the previous generation's skills, is part of the genius of the Taoist internal arts. The Taoist internal martial arts and chi gung also clearly articulate the health, healing, and longevity chi methods that are generally absent in modern aikido. I believe that lovers of aikido will find it both interesting and beneficial to explore ba gua chang and chi gung in order to gain practical insights into what O-Sensei Ueshiba was doing.

Liu Hung Chieh does the Single Whip posture of Wu style tai chi chuan.

TAI CHI $\quad\quad$ **4**

Fighting Considerations and Applications

| TAI CHI CHUAN AS A MARTIAL ART

Over 100 million people do the physical form movements of tai chi every day in China. This number indicates that more people practice tai chi than any other martial art in the world. Tai chi enthusiasts are growing daily throughout the West, South America, Japan, and Southeast Asia. The growth of tai chi is mostly caused by the significant benefits it offers in reducing stress, overcoming illnesses, increasing mental and physical performance, and being a practical and effective tool for aging well, enabling people to bypass many of the more unpleasant situations commonly experienced after the onset of middle age.* As is said in China, "Tai chi can be done by anyone, male and female, young and old, strong and weak, intelligent and slow, healthy or ill." (See Appendix A, p. 297 for a brief history of tai chi.)

Originally, the practitioners of the martial art of tai chi became famous within China not for the health side of the art but for the exceptional fighting ability it imparts. As one tai chi master was fond of saying, "Everybody wants to be healthy, only some people want to learn how to fight." Those who do want to learn how to fight using tai chi should be aware that to be successful demands copious hard work. It also requires the willingness to persevere through frustrations and disappointments, both physical and emotional, just as is required of any successful high achiever in any competitive athletic, business, artistic, or intellectual endeavor. There is a well-known maxim that sums up this situation: "Press

---

*The primary focus of this chapter is on tai chi's martial aspects. If you learn the martial side from a genuine high-level teacher, you will automatically gain the health and energetic benefits. Often, however, obtaining all the health benefits of tai chi from a good teacher does not automatically bring with it an ability to implement tai chi's martial skills.

on. Nothing in the world can take the place of persistence. Talent will not—nothing is more common than unsuccessful men with talent; genius will not—unrewarded genius is almost a proverb. Education will not—the world is full of educated derelicts. Persistence and determination alone are omnipotent."

For those who are interested in martial arts, either physically or intellectually, this chapter can offer some useful insights into what is necessary to actualize tai chi's pragmatic warrior abilities. The fighting ability of tai chi was originally proven again and again in challenge matches with all forms of martial arts in unrestricted combat, both empty-handed and with traditional weapons, such as swords and spears.

The internal martial art of tai chi chuan, usually shortened to "tai chi," is composed of two separate concepts: *tai chi* and *chuan*. (*Tai:* big, a lot of; *chi* or *ji:* superlative, ultimate, best. Note that this *chi* is not the same as the word "chi" often used to denote energy.) Tai chi is the Taoist philosophical term for that place of nonduality from which the specific opposing yin and yang forces of any modality exist in a potential undifferentiated state before they separate into some form of opposite (dual) manifestation: day and night, sun and moon, self and other, attack and defense, this and that. Tai chi, then, refers to a philosophical idea about the nature of existence, but in addition it more pragmatically refers to the chi-based health and internal power aspects of tai chi chuan. It is the tai chi facet that heals and rejuvenates, not the chuan. Chuan means "fist" and, by extension, anything relating to the techniques, philosophies, tactics, or strategies of fighting. As a martial art, tai chi chuan fused these two separate and distinct parts into an integrated whole, originally adapting them to an already existing extensive technical repertoire of the most effective armed and unarmed fighting techniques of seventeenth-century China. Each part contributed something unique to the mix known today as tai chi chuan.

The fighting techniques were derived from the military training manual used by a famous general to train his troops for battlefield success. Tai chi is essentially a hybrid that might be expressed in a word formula such as: Taoist chi gung + Taoist philosophical principles + Shaolin temple gung fu external martial arts techniques = China's newly integrated internal martial art eventually called *tai chi chuan*.

The chi gung added internal power and supercharged the martial art techniques. The Taoist philosophy and fighting strategies generated whole new kinds of fighting applications absent from the movements of the original Shaolin external martial arts. In varying degrees, the whole integration process changed the original fighting moves so they could conform to the sophisticated internal body movement rules of chi gung. For example, gung fu blows delivered with straight arms or legs changed to being executed with bent elbows and knees. This seemingly small change offered several martial advantages. From the perspective of chi gung, it allowed the opening and closing of the joints and spine to generate tremendous internal power; it incorporated the beneficial Taoist axioms of "neither doing too much nor too little" and "to go out is to return and to return is to go out"; and it resulted in an important martial safeguard, as bent arms and legs are significantly less vulnerable to limb-breaking joint-locks than are arms and legs held straight.

Another critical example is the tai chi core emphasis on circularity of physical movement, both within form work and fighting applications. This emphasis did not exist, or at the very least was significantly less, in tai chi's parent Shaolin gung fu techniques. The concept of circularity is at the core of Taoist philosophy and is an essential component of the central operational principles of all Taoist chi gung.

The foundational principles of tai chi were written in a short treatise called the ***Tai Chi Classics.*** These pages were found in a corner of a salt store near the Chen village in China in the nineteenth century. Every tai chi master uses it as a primary teaching tool, referring repeatedly to its short cryptic phrases, each of which has many levels of meaning. Nowhere in the classics, beyond the 13 postures,* are the names of the multitude of tai chi martial techniques, movements, or Push Hands methods mentioned. We are only given generalized Taoist nei gung principles, philosophical concepts, and military strategies and tactics. Even the original 13 postures mentioned in the *Classics* are not presented as explicit how-to instructions; rather, they refer to general internal energy principles. It requires an adept to translate the specific ways to do the physical movements from the material in the *Classics*.

TAI CHI CLASSICS
A nineteenth-century treatise on the foundational principles of tai chi chuan, said to be written by Wang Tsung Yueh.

THE EIGHT BASIC MARTIAL PRINCIPLES OF TAI CHI

Tai chi is based on using the one unified chi energy of the body, called jeng chi in Chinese. However, depending on the function it fulfills, this one chi is called by different names—the chi of this, or the chi of that. There are eight primary body energies used in tai chi. These eight are the foundation of every tai chi form movement and fighting application and are present in single or multiple combinations of every move.

The martial art of tai chi is based on thirteen principles. Five of these relate to the footwork methodology of tai chi, which is responsible for

---

*The term *posture*, which appears throughout this book, is used in both the Chinese external and internal martial arts in general, and especially tai chi chuan, to describe a specific internal or external movement or technique in a form. This idea is also used in the Japanese martial arts. In karate, for example, you have downward and upward blocks (*gedan barai* and *jodan uke*), reverse punches and front kicks (*gyaku zuki* and *mae geri*), or *o soto gari* or *uchimata* throws in judo, or *kokyu nage* in aikido.

moving the feet and body's center smoothly and with stability. These five are called *step forward, step backward, gaze* (that is, focus your intention toward and move) *to the left, gaze to the right,* and *central equilibrium.* The remaining eight principles refer to how energy manifests in the body.

These eight principles regarding internal energy are at the center of what makes tai chi a unique fighting art based on certain tenets of Taoist philosophy (the four sides and four corners). The eight principles concern how energy manifests in tai chi throughout every body part in all the postures and movements of the form, as well as the fighting applications of whatever kind, including Push Hands and sparring. In application, it is assumed that these powers are used first at touch, and later done to the energy of the opponent before you both touch, or when you disengage after touching and before resuming contact.

These eight refer to the nonphysical energies the body can emit. *They do not refer to physical movements.* They are identified by standard Chinese terms and are translated into English as:

1. **Peng** or Ward Off (upward, expansive internal power)
2. **Lu** or Roll Back (backward or absorbing, yielding power)
3. **Ji** or Press Forward (straight ahead, forward power)
4. **An** or Push Downward (downward-moving power)
5. **Tsai** or Pull Down (simultaneously combines the yin energies of lu and an, moving in the same direction)
6. **Lieh** or Split (combines the yang energies of peng and ji moving in opposite directions from an originating point)
7. **Jou** or Elbow Stroke (focuses energy in the elbow)
8. **Kao** or Shoulder Stroke (focuses energy in the shoulder)

The first four refer to the direction energy is moving: *up* with Ward Off, *back* with Roll Back, *straight forward* with Press Forward, and *down* with Push Downward. The next two refer to combining energies: Pull Down simultaneously combines the two yin energies of Roll Back and Push Downward moving in the same direction, and Split combines the two yang energies of Ward Off and Press Forward moving in opposite direction. Each of these first four had a posture named after it in the Yang style of tai chi. However, their real meaning lies in the kind of internal power (called **jin**) that they represent.

JIN
Internal power within the body.

All movements in tai chi are composed of permutations of these eight building blocks, as they continuously combine, separate, and recombine during each individual posture and transitional move. In combat training, tai chi fighters must be able to change from one to the other in a fraction of a second, if they are to win, or at least produce a draw, without getting hurt.

Tai Chi in Tokyo

 In 1968, Chang I Chung's Shibuya school was the tai chi school of choice among Tokyo's black belts. There was an abundance of lower-graded karate black belts at the Shibuya school, as well as several people who held fifth- and sixth-degree black belts from Japanese and Okinawan karate and various other Japanese martial arts. For about a year, I studied the standing practice there with Chang, and had the opportunity to carefully observe the form. Besides the chi development gained from standing, watching the class for hours a week helped me to learn to recognize many of the nuances within tai chi, material that absolutely would have gone by me if I had rushed into learning the physical movements. The ramifications of these nuances continuously motivated me not to give up on the standing process. It became obvious to me that I was going to need and ultimately use all the chi techniques gained from standing to fulfill the potential fighting skills inherent in the tai chi form. The importance of this insight was driven home to me repeatedly over the course of the following fifteen years.

Typically, the first few times that people see any tai chi movement, they miss much of what is actually occurring. Often, it is only after observing a tai chi movement performed hundreds of times that you see it clearly for the first time. This is so whether you are actively learning tai chi movements or passively watching and analyzing them. In my case, comprehending first by observing passively made the later process of actively learning all the material in the forms much easier and more precise; in fact, it saved me from wasting a lot of valuable learning time.

The form class had an interesting structure. This long form was intricate. We practiced it slowly, which meant that it took about forty-five uninterrupted minutes to complete. The whole group (usually a maximum of twenty), would do the form together from the beginning. When someone did not know the next movement, the class stopped. Chang then taught that move to the inquiring student, then demonstrated its basic fighting application, and if a more advanced student queried further, Chang usually elaborated. The beginner would then go to the side and practice solo or be helped by a senior who had arrived late. If no new requests were forthcoming, the class would then continue to the end of the form from where they had stopped, or else cease and repeat the process when the next student needed to learn a movement.

| A PERSONAL ODYSSEY THROUGH THE MARTIAL ARTS

Tai Chi in Tokyo, continued

Both watching the group practice and Chang teach the same movements repeatedly made certain things evident to me over time. The movements of the forms were martially pragmatic: form and function genuinely joined. Form practice developed tremendous balance and built strong legs, especially from the slow motion kicks and the form's low dipping and multiple squatting movements. Tai chi had a lot of intriguing hand strikes that I had not previously seen in Japanese martial arts.

The martial intent of some of the class members was strong. You could almost see them blocking, evading, countering, breaking bones, and putting restraining joint-locks on their imaginary opponents. The slow-motion, relentless, liquid manner of the movements were performed not only to enhance health but also to develop martial precision. The martial efficiency of the movements was beautiful to behold. Slowly, the light dawned that it was realistically possible to fight well without using muscular tension and force.

The slowness and control of the tai chi motions clearly emphasized and developed superior hip- and waist-turning ability, just as every good Japanese martial arts does. Initially, observing the movements was both hypnotic and distracting. However, as I learned to focus, I was able to determine that the overwhelming impressiveness of the form lay in its precision and lack of frivolous motion. This "slow-motion karate" called tai chi also made the body very fluid. Over the course of that year, I could visibly see people in the class losing their habitual tension bit by bit. Month by month, the students moved faster in the two-person fighting applications.

The strongest emphasis in the class was on a basic level of fighting applications and the choreographed two-person fighting set rather than on nonmartially oriented Push Hands. When Push Hands was practiced, the emphasis was on yielding, sticking, and connecting whole-body movements, but without fa jin (see p. 110). Some of the martially oriented Japanese students used to like to meet outside class. There, we would play and "mix it up" with an intensity significantly rougher than the general tenor of the class.

One: Ward Off (Peng)

Peng refers to energy rising or expanding from its source. It is the primary yang or projecting internal energy in tai chi, as well as all the other Taoist internal martial arts. It is equally defensive and attack-oriented in nature. It is the root of the yang energies in tai chi and can radiate energy from both the inside (yin) and outside (yang) surfaces of the body.*

In its expanding phase, peng is often compared to the energy that causes wood to float on water or a car tire to inflate, or the blood vessels to fill. The term *Ward Off* pertains to the expanding nature of peng, which, if directed to the arms or any body part, allows you to create a buffer zone that prevents the first shock of an incoming attack from penetrating your defenses; that is, warding it off with either your arms, legs, or body, and possibly even causing a blow to bounce off your body. Ward Off gives you the critical microsecond of neurological space to avoid being overwhelmed, before you begin your defense and deflect, absorb, or redirect an attacker's power. Equally in the limbs or torso, Ward Off also creates an expansion that prevents an opponent's force from getting past your skin and injuring you. This can happen because peng directly develops the body's protective chi, called **wei chi** in Chinese. According to Chinese medical theory, wei chi prevents illness from penetrating the pores of your skin.

This expansive energy can also enable you to move an attacking man's arms according to your will, by expanding past his strength and leaving him no choice but to move whatever body part or weapon you are touching out of the way. When your opponent hits your limbs, you can turn your peng on suddenly, and if your Ward Off is strong enough, your peng can cause pain or even severe damage to the attacking arm or leg.

Peng or Ward Off explains why the arm of an internal martial artist can be as soft as a baby's in one instant and, in the next, become exceedingly hard without registering any muscular tension. The development of this energy is the internal equivalent of the external martial artist's lifting of weights or striking the limbs against hard objects to toughen them up. As an attack technique, peng can enable your arm to hit like a lead pipe or painlessly cause opponents to be sent through the air without damage, unless, of course, they are hurt by the force with which they hit a wall or the ground. In its rising phase, Ward Off is responsible for the ability to attack and uproot an opponent. Uprooting causes your opponent's feet to leave the ground.

Peng or Ward Off is a yang energetic force. The original Chen tai chi manual states that peng is the source of all the other postures or internal energies in tai chi. It is not exactly unique to tai chi, being utilized as

WEI CHI
The layer of energy between a person's skin and muscle that protects against disease entering the body from the external environment.

---

*For body: from crown of head to tailbone, front surfaces are yin; back surfaces are yang. For limbs: inside of limbs is yin; outside is yang. Stand with your toes pointing forward and your arms held straight in front of your body, thumbs pointing up. The "inside" of your limbs faces your torso, the "outside" faces away from your torso.

much or more in ba gua or hsing-i, in which it is also called peng for the exact same reasons. It is peng that enables an internal martial artist to hit opponents and cause them, as the Chinese like to say, "to fly away." To achieve the power of Ward Off, a practitioner must have the ability to sink chi energy to the lower tantien (that is, drop energy from the upper body into the lower belly). This skill is absolutely required.

Two: Roll Back (Lu)

Lu refers to the ability to energetically absorb and/or yield to counter an incoming force, often with circular physical movements so tiny as to appear invisible. Its primary energetic direction is backwards; however, it can also be done going downwards, forwards, and upwards by fairly advanced practitioners. Roll Back is primarily defensive in nature, although it does have some use in attack. It is the primary yin energy in tai chi, and absorbs energy both on the inside and outside of the arms and the back of the hands.

The natural advantage of Roll Back is that it allows you to melt away, to release your own internal resistance to the power of your opponent's techniques. This kind of releasing causes opponents to lose their center of balance. It may be compared to the situation where a man rushes shoulder first to batter down a door, and the door is suddenly opened, causing him to fall on his face. Normal expectations have been reversed. The man you are fighting expects his force to be met by your force, and when it is not, his force projects forward, often taking his center with it; consequently, he loses his balance. In the second or less that exists between your opponent losing and recovering his balance, he is in effect existing in a state of defenseless suspension that creates the optimum conditions for a counterattack, which is tai chi's specialty.

If the Ward Off of a tai chi player is strong enough, it can be used to defend against someone of equal or slightly superior power. Roll back, however, is the primary technique that tai chi practitioners rely upon to defend themselves against a clearly superior force or during that fraction of a second when they may be using an unworkable fighting angle. Roll Back is the defining characteristic of tai chi chuan. As an internal martial art, tai chi specializes in this energy above all others.

Roll Back is what underlies the quality of "softness" in tai chi. The value of yielding to a superior brute force is self-evident to a matador as he yields his position and moves his body and cape out of the path of a charging bull's horns.

From the perspective of the internal martial arts, power can be either intelligent or stupid. "Intelligent" power is measured exactly, with sensitivity, and has the ability to change in a flash, according to the nature of the force with which it is dealing. "Stupid" power goes off in a direction with little or no ability to adjust to circumstances. Stupid power is like a bullet on a set trajectory it cannot control. Intelligent power can adjust its force and direction microsecond by microsecond between the beginning and end of a technique. Each of these types of power exists in both defensive and attack-oriented martial art techniques. Fighting angles, for instance, employ intelligent power.

The Roll Back technique, in its energetic and physical execution, allows a tai chi practitioner to successfully defend against the superior force of a *skilled* individual. If one person in a fight possesses superior brute force or speed and the other is skilled in fighting angles (like the bull and the matador), the knowledge of fighting angles can defeat the brute strength. However, if both individuals comprehend fighting angles equally, their knowledge will neutralize advantages on this level. The dominant position will then revert to whoever has the most power or speed, unless Roll Back enters the martial equation.

Roll Back's commingled qualities of yielding and absorption create a certain kind of amalgamated softness. As dedicated tai chi martial training progresses, one would expect this soft power to grow in the same way that weightlifters gradually increase the weight they can lift. It is the *practice* that increases the power, not merely the understanding of the mechanisms involved in Roll Back. Many tai chi practitioners mistakenly believe that, because Roll Back is an intellectually superior concept about how to handle overt force, it will automatically work physically against a person of superior strength. Nothing could be further from the truth. The mastery that comes with constant practice is the key.

From a martial art point of view, power is power. It matters not whether the power is "soft," or "hard," "external" or "internal," only that it is present or absent. The brilliant advantage of Roll Back's soft power is that it can be *relatively* less than the power projected toward it and still win the day. However, the soft power of Roll Back cannot be *dramatically* less or a stronger "hard" power will defeat it. This case is especially true the more your opponent is **rooted,** as are many top-of-the-line martial artists, both internal and external.

ROOTING
The technique of sinking body energy and rooting it into the earth.

It is always easier to develop any single skill if you focus on it to the exclusion of other agendas. Of course, if you do concentrate on learning multiple skills over time, you can end up with a superlative product when they eventually dovetail. This integration certainly holds true for martial arts. For example, during and before the eighteenth and nineteenth centuries, martial artists trained long hours with life-and-death seriousness. They worked with the intensity of top competitive athletes. In the hierarchy of internal martial arts of that era, tai chi, based on battlefield performance, ranked as a higher level or superior martial art to hsing-i. Yet, then and today, most hsing-i people will normally defeat most tai chi people in actual fighting. This situation may reverse itself when the tai chi practitioner has accrued ten years of experience. According to classical tai chi tradition, ten years was the minimum amount of training time tai chi players needed before they were fully prepared to successfully challenge martial artists of all kinds under lethal conditions. What accounts for this seeming contradiction?

Both hsing-i and tai chi share the same internal technology for developing hard internal power. Hsing-i, because it initially places less relative emphasis on yielding, focuses exclusively on developing hard, yang internal energy and efficient fighting angles. Hsing-i has a simpler agenda; thus, it turns out more winners sooner. Tai chi, on the other hand, has to fulfill not one or two, but three agendas. First, its specialty, the "soft" energy of Roll Back; second, its "hard" internal projecting powers, including Ward Off, Press Forward, and Split; and third, the complex multiple agenda of seamlessly melding the two, called in the tai chi classics *gang rou hsiang ji* or "hard and soft combine together."

This third empowers practitioners to smoothly and instantaneously shift back and forth from hard to soft. These shifts occur with an absolutely smooth changing of gears in the tai chi fighter's mind, physical technique, and emotions, during which changes many other martial artists often get "stuck." These critical microseconds occur in combat when a fighter becomes physically unable to move or is mentally disoriented, not knowing where, when, or how to move next. Because tai chi has a more complex agenda, fewer people learn it totally, but those who do really achieve something. However, for those who do hard or external martial arts, even mild exposure to tai chi and its Roll Back technique tends to increase the physical speed and smoothness of all evasive tactics.

It takes a lot of serious training to actualize the potential of Roll Back in tai chi. It is helpful to bear in mind two things about Roll Back. This "yin" internal technique requires a willingness to delve into the more subtle levels of the mind. The level of power of your yielding and absorbing has to be considerable if it is going to defeat an opponent with significant power and speed. Many undertrained tai chi proponents with insufficient Roll Back power fantasize that they can defeat a karate, gung fu, or boxing fighter because they hold their art to be superior—until, that is, they are soundly defeated.

Weak opponents can be handled with mediocre Roll Back skills; strong opponents require superior Roll Back, which is why, in Push Hands, Roll Back is the hardest and most essential skill to develop.

True, Roll Back is used mostly for defensive purposes in tai chi and is the reason why tai chi is often considered to have a noncompetitive flavor. Nonetheless, Roll Back is also, in its absorbing aspect, used for attack. Roll Back's attack phase strongly uses the closings of the body (see p. 63) to suck energy like a vacuum cleaner. If the closing action is connected to the edge of your hand, palm, or the back of your fist, it can cut through an opponent's flesh much like dragging the edge of a knife through a thick steak in order to cut it. This technique prevails using the fist, hand edge, and palm techniques throughout the Chen style with its strong circular slicing hand motions, and can easily be seen in the Yang style in the Chop with Fist, Pull Down, and Descending Roll Back Palm techniques.

Since Roll Back is a specialty of tai chi, it would be useful to look at the progression of its training, from the point of view of both the physical body mechanics and the energetics involved.

Mechanically, a physical turning or twisting action will deflect an incoming force, just as a whirling fan blade will throw off a pebble tossed at it. This principle works equally well if applied to the human torso, arms, or legs. The progression for learning the physical aspects of the Roll Back technique is:

Author (right) performs the fighting application of the tai chi posture Roll Back in its attack phase.

1. Focus on turning your waist and hips smoothly. As is often said in the Orient, "Hips as stiff as iron need to become hips soft and flexible as tofu (soy bean curd)."

2. Your arms and legs need to twist in coordination with the turning of your waist.

3. Your arms need to relax and soften until they offer minimal resistance to an aggressive force.

4. The opening and closing (as well as a deep relaxing) of all your joints needs to develop sufficiently in order for the joints to move unimpeded within their optimum range of motion in response to the slightest pressure from your opponent.

5. The twisting of your arms and legs needs to be established and sufficiently stabilized in order to amplify energy and bring it to the exact point where opposing bodies touch, which is most often at the forearm or hand.

6. Now the serious study of fighting angles using Roll Back begins. To be fully effective, this phase requires mastery of all the foundational skills learned in steps 1 through 5.

7. During the early stages of learning Roll Back, your movements will be large and obvious, both in your joints and in your waist. Over time, however, as your physical movements become more refined and circular, they can become extremely small, so tiny, in fact, that they are virtually invisible to the eye of someone untrained in observing subtlety of movement.

The progression for learning the energetic aspects of the Roll Back technique is:

1. You develop a sense of absorbing energy with your whole body.
2. You absorb energy on a line from the point of contact with your opponent, to beyond your body, either out from behind your back or out from your feet into the ground, preferably to the end of your aura, where it connects to the energy of the earth (that is, your energetic root).
3. You absorb and redirect your opponent's power at the exact point of contact, causing your opponent to seem to be suspended in space for a microsecond.
4. You extend the ability to absorb energy, pulling it from your opponent's body, which causes your opponent to lurch in the direction of the pull. Usually, this action happens without your opponent's perceiving a cause and effect relationship, which induces a disbelief along the lines of, "This can't be happening." This process is often likened to reeling in a fish, which causes the fish to land wherever you direct it.
5. If you can master all of the above, your hands become so soft that your opponent literally can neither feel them nor what they are doing.

Roll Back and Sticking   Intimately tied into Roll Back is the basic tai chi technique of Sticking, or adherence. Sticking is done both empty-handed and weapon-to-weapon. The focus here, however, will only be on bare hands. Sticking skin to skin is used after you have intercepted an aggressor's limbs or body with your own limbs or body. If a man attacks you and you keep bodily contact with him, you can stay with and control him, prevent him from harming you, or move him into position for a counterattack. Each progressive stage of training requires that you be able to interpret your attacker's force in ever-finer gradations.

There are four clear progressive stages* of Sticking, each one of which requires a higher level of skill, chi, and ability to intercept an opponent's force.

---

*Both the Chinese and English names are given for these stages. For some, however, I have never seen English translations that convey an authentic flavor of meaning. Accordingly, for these the English words used are not literal translations from the Chinese, but do reasonably fit the bill in terms of describing actual function.

1. Yielding (called **jan** in Chinese)   You yield by retreating from an attacker's force with great precision, staying just ahead of the attacker's power, thereby negating the ability of the oncoming force to reach or impact upon you. It is important that you let your attacker's force go wherever it wants to, without attempting to impede it; rather, you encourage it. This technique causes the attacker to feel that you are just within reach, if only a little more effort is made. The following three situations convey the essential "feel" of this procedure.

JAN/YIELDING
One of the four stages of sticking energy in tai chi chuan.

a. Attempt to punch a feather floating in the air. As your skin touches the feather, it recedes just slightly ahead of the force of your fist, avoiding any damaging impact.

b. As the bull's horn touches the matador's cape, the matador moves the cape just slightly ahead of the force of the horns. This action prevents any shock returning to the matador via the cape or stops the bull's horns becoming entangled in the cape, which could get the matador killed on the next turn of the bull's head.

c. Push your fingertips through water. You can feel some pressure from the water, but the water itself always recedes just ahead of your fingers, no matter how fast or slowly you go, and no matter how much power you use.

2. Merging (called **lan** in Chinese)   Next, you merge with the force of the man attacking you, so that at no point is your power and contacting body surface either ahead or behind his contacting body surface, regardless of what kind or how much speed or power is in play. When this merging occurs, the attacker does not consciously or subconsciously feel any resistance or difference between himself and you, which often subliminally causes him to lose the motivation to really go for it. At this moment, you can gently lead his arms or legs (or weapons) where you want them to go, just as a toy can easily and precisely be led around by a string that is neither too loose nor too taut. In the *Tai Chi Classics*, this activity is called **bu diu, bu ding** or, "neither leave the opponent, nor oppose him."

LAN/MERGING
One of the four stages of sticking energy in tai chi chuan.

BU DIU, BU DING
A tai chi chuan term for combat at touch, where the practitioner neither pushes against, nor lets go of, the point of contact between himself and his opponent.

NIEN/ADHERING
One of the four stages of sticking energy in tai chi chuan.

3. Sticking or adhering (called **nien** in Chinese)   You now do two things simultaneously: Apply very subtle pressure to your attacker's fascia just below his skin to stick to his muscles, and literally pull his energy from his body into yourself and through and past your body. If this is successful, when you move you will pull his body with you, by surface skin contact alone, without any use of grabbing. You can then move his arms or legs wherever you want, because they are stuck to your hands or legs like glue. This technique can be likened to three commonly experienced phenomena.

a. Wet your finger. Applying only gentle surface contact, you are able to move a piece of paper with your wet finger, just by the stickiness of the moisture, without the need to press down hard or exert pressure.

b. Put a piece of adhesive tape on a sheet of paper. Observe how, when the tape moves, it takes the paper along with it.

c. If your chi is really strong, the situation is similar to that where your hands are filled with static electricity. A piece of lint will move along with your hand, even though it barely seems to be physically connected.

SUEI/MAGNETIZING
One of the four stages of sticking energy in tai chi chuan.

4. Magnetizing (called **suei** in Chinese)   The first three sticking methods (yield, merge, and adhere) presuppose that your opponent is moving and that you have some momentum to work with according to the laws of physics. The fourth method—magnetizing—seems to go beyond these laws, as we currently understand them.

In method four, your hand magnetizes the attacker's body, allowing you to lift him off the ground just as a large industrial magnet lifts a heavy metal object off the floor. There is no momentum involved. You are purely controlling the chi of the attacker's body in a way that seems to negate laws of gravity.*

Three: Press Forward (Ji)

This internal energy projects forward from its source, on a straight line, along whichever angle you direct it: up, down, sideways, diagonally, or straight ahead. It is the primary attack technique in tai chi, and radiates energy on the outside of the arms and the back of the hands.

Press Forward is done in four different, progressively more powerful ways:

1. A simple straightforward punch with one hand. Here, you simply put the power and weight of your whole body behind the strike.

2. A simple straightforward hit with one hand, where you project a straight line of chi energy up from your feet through your legs, hips, torso, and spine to the part of your arm or head that is hitting the opponent. If you are kicking the opponent, the same thing applies. Again, you project a straight line of energy from your supporting leg and spine to the part of your kicking leg that is targeting the opponent. You

---

*This method may be lost to future generations. On the day before my mentor Liu Hung Chieh died, he demonstrated it on me. Liu did not explain it nor, at this point can I, although I'm trying to figure it out. The original masters of Chen style tai chi, as well as the original Yang, his son, and some of their students were said to possess the technique. T. T. Liang told a story about one of the disciples of the original Yang who, merely by putting his palms flat on the top of the armrest of a heavy chair, and not grabbing it, was able to lift it off the floor and move it.

should be able to generate tremendous internal power in this and the following two methods without any use of body weight to create momentum. (Obviously adding the use of body weight to this technique will enhance the power.) Methods 2, 3, and 4 allow tai chi, as well as hsing-i and ba gua, to generate full power from only a half inch away from an opponent and even closer, right to the point where skin has already touched skin.

3. One hand hits or touches the opponent, while the energy of the opposite arm and hand augments and amplifies the power of the blow, whether the nonhitting hand touches the opponent or not. Usually, when a person first becomes familiar with this technique, the nonhitting hand touches the actual hitting hand or forearm. Later, however, this progresses to just mentally projecting energy from the augmenting hand to the striking surface of the contacting hand or arm.

4. Energy from both arms is first focused at a point in space beyond the actual striking surface. The energy is then projected forward from that spot, which is usually deep inside the internal organs or brain or on the opposite surface of the body. For example, if you touched someone's chest, the focal point would be the spine, or even a point in space beyond the spine. Yang-style postures such as Step Forward, Parry and Punch, Press Forward, Shoulder Stroke, and Fan through the Back, typify this energetic technique.

Four: Push Downward (An)

An creates a downward movement of energy. It is a yin internal energy that can radiate energy from both the yin and yang meridians of the arms and hands. It is equally attack-oriented and defensive in nature. To get a sense of what Push Downward is and how it works, try one of two things. In a chair with arm rests, sit down with your palms firmly on the arm rests and raise your body off the chair by pushing downward with your palms. Or, sitting on the ground, lift your buttocks off the ground by pushing down on the ground with your palms. In both cases, you have applied the downward action of Push Downward.

Push Downward has three primary *defensive* functions:

1. It directly counters the upward expansive energy of Ward Off, preventing your opponent from controlling the upward movement of your arms or body against your will.

2. It enables you to prevent your opponents from raising their arms or legs.

3. It can cause an attacking man's center of gravity to be energetically forced to the ground, making him feel as if a huge sandbag had been dropped on him.

For *attack*, Push Downward has two primary functions:

1. It tends to make your hands incredibly heavy, so that they crash through your opponent's body, like steel through tin.

2. It can send a powerful wave of energy downward through an attacking man's body, down to the boundary of his energetic aura beneath his feet. This action can sever your attacker's energetic root. This downward wave can spark an ascending energy wave, which, when it moves upward, causes him to be uprooted — his feet leave the ground.

Push Downward can be compared to the downward energy exerted on a basketball during a dribble. This energy ultimately causes the basketball to bounce up in the air. Many shorter tai chi masters from Yang Lu Chan to Cheng Man-ching to Liu Hung Chieh favored this Push Downward technique, especially when they added a little rising Ward Off energy once the "basketball" (the opponent's body) was already bouncing upward, to make it go higher.

Ward Off, Roll Back, Press Forward, and Push Downward Are Both Obvious and Hidden

The four martial principles of tai chi just described (Ward Off, Roll Back, Press Forward, and Push Downward) comprise the core of all tai chi movements and fighting applications. The next four techniques (Pull Down, Split, Elbow Stroke, and Shoulder Stroke), represent various combinations of the original four.

The form movements of the main branches of the diverse schools the general public knows collectively as tai chi (that is, the Yang, Wu, Chen, Hao, and Combination Form styles) can look quite different from one another. They are all, however, composed of the same four fundamental moves. Most people have trouble grasping this point because they focus on external physical movements, and *not* on what the nonphysical energies behind the movements are manifesting. There are both overt and covert aspects concerning how the four basics are done in forms and applications. The obvious ones are virtually self-explanatory; the hidden elements involve the use of intent, and are usually part of the "secrets" that *require* you to find a tai chi adept willing to teach them. Such adepts are the only people who know the covert aspects thoroughly.

The Overt Level   In studying any tai chi form on its obvious level, you can experiment and often figure out which energy is at play by noticing how your hands move. In Ward Off, your energy will rise from your feet up your body and expand away from your body as your hands move upwards, away from your body at any angle, including vertically. In Roll

Back, you will be pulling energy from the air, from your fingertips through your arms to your spine, as your hands withdraw toward your body from an extended position in space. In Press Forward, the exact opposite of Roll Back, your hands move from being close to your body to extending straight ahead, as your energy moves from your spine, through your arms to your fingertips. In Push Downward, which is the opposite of Ward Off, you move energy from the top of your head to the bottom of your feet, as your hands move downwards at any angle, either toward or away from your body or vertically downward, as in the movement called Play the Lute/Guitar. What has just been described here, however, is only the visually obvious part of the story.

The Covert Level In the internal arts, chi energy is manifested not primarily by body movement, but through intention and the heart/mind (see p. 75). If a movement is to be effective in fighting, there must be a direct intent of what kind of power you want to manifest in specific types of situations. Like the thought behind the design of a modern stealth bomber, the ideal in combat is not to let your opponent know you are coming, or, at a minimum, to deceive your opponent about your plans and intentions.

Obvious physical movements alone carry minimal deception. Virtually all external martial artists have experience of hands moving up, down, forward, and back, and have developed tactics to counter and defeat such moves. However, they often have little or no experience countering the subtle energy movements of power at touch. Such techniques may not be present in their particular martial art system.

In many specific tai chi movements, the energy work is quite hidden. This is less the case in the original Chen style than in the Yang, Wu, Hao, and Combination Form styles. The cliche, "things are not always what they seem," applies to a significant number of internal martial art moves.

The Covert Energies: Embedded Ward Off, Roll Back, Press Forward, and Push Downward In some motions, as your arms are moving downward, either toward or away from your body, Ward Off energy can be projected from the outside of your arms toward the ground, causing an opponent to be bounced off your arm, as well as being simultaneously forced downward. For example, in the Yang style, this energetic projection occurs from the bottom hand in the Roll Back, Brush Knee, and Twist Step maneuvers.

Using the energy of Roll Back, but not its physical motion, you could be absorbing your opponent's energy as your hands are advancing forward or moving upward. This technique is sometimes referred to as "stealing your opponent's power." For example, this technique is executed in the first half of the upper hand of White Snake Sticks Out Its Tongue, before you stab your opponent's throat in the second half of the movement.

The energetic action of Press Forward, as well as going forward, is also present in many movements where the hands are returning to the body in a physical action that resembles Roll Back. Only here, as you are absorbing energy with the inside yin surfaces of your arm, you are either sequentially or simultaneously projecting energy from your elbows, along the outside of your arms, for a backward elbow strike.

The energy of Push Downward is often embedded and actively radiating along the underside of your arm, while your hands are moving straight ahead or upward. For example, in the Yang style, this radiating energy occurs in two (among many) clear places: (1) in the upper arm of the Brush Knee and Twist Step posture, as your hand moves forward, and (2) as your arms are rising and going forward when performing the basic Push Downward posture. In the basic Push Downward posture of the original Chen style, the meaning is not so hidden, as your hands move physically downward to face the ground at hip height.

Five: Pull Down (Tsai)

This move simultaneously combines the two primary yin energies of Roll Back and Push Downward, in the obvious, hidden, and embedded ways in many postures. Pull Down, for example, fuses these energies together moving in the same direction. You simultaneously yield to and/or absorb an attacking man's force while moving him downward, gradually or suddenly. The sudden variety is sometimes used to cause an attacker to fall to the ground, suffer whiplash, or dislocate a joint. The movement is most obviously seen in the posture Pull Down between Play the Lute and Shoulder Stroke, just before White Crane Spreads Its Wings, and in Needle to the Bottom of the Sea.

Six: Split (Lieh)

Split is the opposite of Pull Down. It combines the two primary yang energies of Ward Off and Press Forward. In this move, which requires turning the waist, the two yang energies do not join together but, rather, from a common point of origin, move apart in opposite directions. This creates a tremendous release of energy, just like a bomb exploding.

Split can be done two ways. Your hands and arms could be moving in opposite directions or one hand can remain fixed in space while the other pulls in the opposite direction. Split can be performed either forwards, backwards, sideways, or up and down. You could be combining two Ward Offs, two Press Forwards, or a combination of one Press Forward and one Ward Off. This method can be externally seen in the separating hands of the moves White Crane Spreads Its Wings, Fan through the Back, and Single Whip.

Seven/Eight: Elbow Stroke (Jou)/Shoulder Stroke (Kao)

Both Elbow Stroke and Shoulder Stroke are directly related to and commingled within the methodology of the Snake and the Crane in tai chi.

According to one of the main legends, tai chi was created by watching a long fight between a crane and a snake. Now whether this happened or not, it metaphorically describes the two main processes from which all tai chi applications are constructed. The first six basic energies (Ward Off, Roll Back, Press Forward, Push Downward, Pull, and Split) primarily focus on fighting applications that end in the forearms and hand, and are associated with the crane.

The last two, Elbow Stroke and Shoulder Stroke, are concerned with the snake. These movements use the elbow and the shoulder in some way. However, there is more to the story than the obvious implication that you are striking your opponent with your elbow, as you do in external martial arts like Thai boxing, or with your shoulder, as you would in a shoulder block in American football.

In the solo forms of the later styles of tai chi (Yang, Wu, Hao, and Combination Forms) the majority of the elbow and shoulder techniques are not physically shown. In their solo forms, the full covert range of the techniques does clearly exist; however, in order for them to be understood, they must be taught with full explanations at the level of mental intent. Only in two-person fighting application practice does the full range of elbow and shoulder methods have physical expression.

The situation becomes clear, however, if you examine how the movements of the original Chen style are structured, where that which is hidden in the Yang style is made overt. In the original Chen style, you will see clear elbow movements with visibly powerful discharges of energy and shaking of the elbow, as well as clearly defined large circular shoulder movements that rotate in every direction. During these overt elbow and shoulder moves, you will often see a hand that was distinctly moving cease its large movement and hover in space, making a tiny circle that follows the larger, emphasized shoulder or elbow movements. Like the undulating motions that happen in a snake, you may also see mini-sequences that powerfully flow through an overtly clear shoulder and then elbow movement before culminating in a hand technique. In other variations, the shoulder, elbow, and hands will move together in a smooth, fused flow that is totally seamless and connected, like that of a crane flapping its wings.

Elbow and Shoulder Strokes Relate Directly to the Crane and the Snake

The crane, which symbolizes unified movement, is an image that pertains to those techniques where there is a direct line of energy originating from the foot and lower tantien that completes itself in one clean movement culminating in the hand. This motion is said to mimic that of a crane flapping its wings to hit or block an attacking snake's head. The crane is an exceptionally graceful bird, a beautiful inspiration to watch as it languidly flaps its wings in slow, gently hypnotic, rhythmic waves. But it also can be fearsome. Indeed, when roused, it moves its wings at blinding speed.

In traveling over terrain, a snake undulates. It coils to store energy before it strikes, and it strikes rapidly, unfolding itself like a whip as it does so. Some snakes also coil defensively to wrap their attackers or to constrict prey to death. In the defensive stage of tai chi, if the hand is not enough to deflect an opponent's force, the elbow takes up the slack and, if that fails, the shoulder comes into play. Or you use various combinations of the multiple folding of the arms to pull the opponent's limbs, torso, or head closer and closer to your body.

In the attack phase of tai chi, a snakelike unfolding of the whip is expressed in a sequential series of rapid machine gun-like movements. A shoulder technique completing becomes an elbow technique, which becomes a forearm blow, which becomes an open or closed wrist and/or hand strike which, finally, becomes a finger thrust that finishes the opponent. If one technique is insufficient to do the job, you switch to the next. If one technique is partially impeded or completely countered, you move into the next with continuously connected rapid speed and fluidity. This method allows you to slither around and circumvent your opponents, who may at any given instant bring more power than you to a specific contested fighting angle. In the attack stage of tai chi, you do not resist superior power, but flow around it like water, using different joints, until the next good opportunity presents itself. Your undulating whip sequence could possibly consist of a hit, throw, or joint-lock.

As mentioned, snake techniques are more overt in the original Chen style, and more hidden in the Yang style.

The easiest place to witness this machine gun-like movement in the Yang or Wu style forms is in the transition sequence from right Shoulder Stroke to right White Crane Spreads Its Wings. In Shoulder Stroke, you could obviously be hitting someone with your shoulder, usually to break the sternum or ribs and/or knock the wind out of the opponent by hitting the solar plexus. Next, you would hit the opponent in the torso with your elbow, usually with cutting action, then a back of the wrist and hand strike (anywhere from the groin upward) and, finally, a finger strike or slap to the throat, face, or eyes.

In a second basic usage, you come up under an attacking man's body, grab his right leg with your left hand (or his left leg cross-body, if you can get the angle) and with your right shoulder press into his body attacking and sticking. Then slide your arm over until you have a good attachment on his right side, the soft part of his midriff, his ribs, or his armpit. You are now in position to throw him. Before turning to the left to complete White

Crane, you first turn to the right, beginning the raising of your elbow and hand. At this time, you pull whichever leg you are holding to your left hand (ideally, checking his left leg with your right leg, if your left hand is holding his right leg) and, with the turning of your waist and the rising of your right elbow, throw him sideways to your right in an up/down cartwheel-like manner. If this throw is done well, both his feet should leave the ground. On this way down, the side of his ribs initially faces the ground, however, people often twist in midair. He will land on his back or face depending on the kind of torque you have applied. During this whole procedure, your right hand does not touch his torso, only your right elbow and upper arm.

In the original Chen style, elbow movements are overtly shown at virtually every angle of a rotating circle: up, down, left, right, all diagonals, with the elbow both coming toward and moving away from the body. Beside serving as smashing and cutting strikes with the elbow tips, these elbow movements are also part of numerous joint and elbow locks. The outward and forward downward movements away from the body are used more, but not exclusively, to lock the opponent's elbows, knees, and **kwa**. The inward movements are used more, but not exclusively, to lock the wrist, ankles, hands, feet, and especially fingers.

The shoulder and elbow movements done together are also used to throw people on their backs, faces, and sides, when the front, side, or back of your own body is facing the opponent. These throws could occur in several ways. The shoulder could be the contact point for the throw, being accomplished by using fa jin (see p. 110) from the shoulder. Or if the contact point shifts from the shoulder to the upper arm to the elbow, the impetus for the throw would begin in the shoulder, but the throw itself would be completed by the elbow. Or the elbow contact point would break an attacking man's balance, getting him onto his toes. Once he is in the air, your hand would grab him or stick to him, and with circular arm motion he would be launched up and out, away from your body, and also possibly downwards.

The striking movements of the shoulder follow all the figure-eight rotations of the elbow, and originate in the shoulder blade. Especially for body blows, and specifically to the heart, shoulder strikes can implement more damaging blows than elbows. They perform another very important function, and that is defense against being grabbed and held by one person, while another hits you.

A primary goal of muggers, wrestlers, or joint-lockers is to compress your body sufficiently so that your body and/or limbs cannot move. In essence, they want to put you in a straightjacket, so you have no room to wiggle or break free. In the worst-case scenario, you are held fast by one attacker, so you cannot defend yourself as his cohorts hit you. Here, shoulder movements are used to counter in three basic ways.

KWA

The area of the body extending from the inguinal ligaments (on the left and right sides) through the inside of the pelvis to the top (crest) of the hip bones.

The first is to apply tai chi's shaking power (dou jin, see p. 96) to discharge the continuing force away from your body. If you are held in the upper body, having a strong sudden Ward Off energy in your shoulder blades as you move them is necessary for success.

A second way is to use less Ward Off, and expand your shoulder blades away from your spine, causing your shoulders, back, and ribs to either round forward or expand sideward, as your chest hollows. This action increases the surface circumference your opponent is grabbing, thereby giving the illusion that you are squeezed tight, when in fact you are not. Keeping the arm circumference steady, you then shrink your body and create a first physical gap of wiggle room with which to maneuver and create an advantageous angle. When you next shrink the circumference, a second little gap is created. This second gap then allows your arms to move again for a brief moment of time, which, if you are agile enough, is all you need to counterattack, first with an elbow and then a hand, often to the groin.

The third way is to shift whatever surface of your body an attacking man is holding by a rapid shoulder or hip turn or rotational movement, so as to create a gap of physical space. This created gap prevents your body and/or limbs from becoming immobile by compression, so you can break free during the gap that exists between his having touched you and his grip having settled in and accomplished its task. Rapid rotational shoulder movements here allow you to get the attacker to commit, and yet give you enough time to be gone when he arrives. In the internal martial arts in general, the tighter this gap, the more powerful and effective the counter.

It is worth noting that ba gua (more than hsing-i) also trains practitioners in the use of these shoulder and elbow techniques. Ba gua also has the overt technical shoulder and elbow aspects of Chen style tai chi, but with a larger throwing repertoire than tai chi. The shoulder and elbow training aspects of hsing-i are more similar to the hidden methodology of the Yang style. In terms of the eight basic tai chi techniques, they are all present in all three internal martial arts, with Roll Back being more emphasized in tai chi and Ward Off being definitely stronger in hsing-i, and usually stronger in ba gua.

FOUR PROGRESSIVE STAGES FOR LEARNING TAI CHI AS A MARTIAL ART

Long and Short Forms

Initially, tai chi forms were all long forms. The original Chen style had six forms, which condensed down to two forms over time. The Yang style began with 128 movements and then came the Yang styles with 108, 88, 66, 37, and 24 movements. In general, the shortest forms did not begin to appear until after World War II. Three basic procedures determined how all forms were originally shortened: (1) movements were cut out entirely; (2) original movements were left in the forms but the number of repetitions, each of which counted as a separate movement, was reduced; and (3) movements were simplified to save practice time. As leisure time to practice became progressively scarcer as the years rolled by, the pressure to reduce and condense created shorter and shorter forms.

The advantage of tai chi long forms is that they create energy flow rhythms inside the body not present in short forms. A long form will also generate much more chi for the same amount of practice time than an equivalent number of short forms done back to back. Long forms ultimately enable both the martial qualities and the health-giving aspects of the chi practice time to reach their maximum inherent potential. Looking at it from the other side of the coin, shortened forms take less time to practice. This attribute appeals to busy modern people who are more likely to practice a short form than a long form. The other martial opinion is that, if people only have limited time to practice, then it is better to practice a limited number of movements well than many that are mediocre.

Whatever forms you choose to become involved with, consider the following guidelines for learning the martial aspects of the art.

Left and Right in Form Practice

Tai chi forms are done on both the right and the left sides of the body, the direction being determined by which way you first move from the initial stance, which is usually assumed facing directly forward. For both long and short forms, from the martial and the health perspective, it is classically advised to practice your form for three continuous years first on one side (the right, say) before putting real effort in learning to do it on the opposite side. Then do the form two times on the left for each time on the right for three years, which is highly recommended to fully balance the body and enhance the ability to use the applications equally with both hands. This three-year period of practice provides the needed repetition to regularize and stabilize the body's chi and the stretching of its soft tissues. Next, spend three to four years doing the form equally on both sides until all your movements become comfortably ambidextrous.

Stage 1: Form Work (Long or Short Form)

To those whose devotion was strong enough to learn tai chi as a martial art, the form was classically taught in a series of progressive stages.

1. The student learns each movement separately. The conveyed posture is then held for 10 to 20 plus minutes, until the body settles and begins to learn to absorb the most basic internal components of the movement—physical relaxation, proper internal alignments, breathing, and lengthening of tissues. Then, you learn the transition to the next movement, holding each major juncture of the transition for at least 5 minutes. Then, hold the next posture for 10 to 20 minutes, then the pieces of the transition, etc., until the end of at least the first third of the form and, ideally, the whole form.

At this stage, your ability to visualize the fighting applications is general; detail here is neither required nor preferred, for it can distract you from focusing on connecting your body. Your mental focus should be completely on relaxing your mind, on letting your mind seep into, and be able to feel the inside of your body, and ascertaining if what you are feeling is indeed translating into your external posture. At this stage, the form movements begin with high stances and gradually work up to medium-height stances.

2. Next, you combine the separate movements together into a whole set of connected, flowing form movements. You may decide to begin combining movements at certain natural breaks in the form, for example, (a) at the end of the first section, (b) at the end of the first Cloud Hands in the second section, (c) at the end of the second section, and (d) just before the second and third Cloud Hands in the third section. While connecting up the separate movements, you also focus on learning the internal rhythms of the form, where you internally speed up or slow down and accentuate certain aspects of nei gung before emphasizing others. Your mind now learns to relax during fluid movements— a difficult task.

You now learn to see and feel imaginary opponents attacking you from all different angles, getting a full body experience of what it might be like to see and feel yourself defending and counterattacking according to the needs of the fighting applications of each individual posture. The form is usually done at this stage with medium-height stances.

3. Next, there is the question of speed. At what speed should you work? In general, the speed of a solo form is determined by the principle of not moving too fast nor too slow. Individuals at practice sessions must find their own comfortable speed, one which does not cause them to lose connection, power, and/or sensitivity in their movements. "Connection" means that your mind and your movement are together, with no "spacing out" and no sense of disconnection between the speed of your mind and body moving. If this disconnection occurs, you are essentially doing mindless movements. If mindless motion becomes a habit, or even occurs briefly, it will create subliminal gaps in real combat that will allow an opponent to defeat you.

4. Now go back and learn in more detail the separate postures of the form piece by piece, clearly. Focus on the yin and yang acupuncture meridian surfaces of your body, emphasizing the four main energies of Ward Off (*peng*), Roll Back (*lu*), Press Forward (*ji*) and Press Downward (*an*).

Begin with the standing postures and then move on to all the transitions of the form.

At this phase, you should begin to learn Push Hands (see p. 147). Through Push Hands, you discern what your body needs to feel and do, as you gradually make your skin able to listen to and interpret your opponent's energy.

You now imagine the sensation of the air being like a training partner and you listen to the feelings of the air on your skin and mind as you apply Ward Off, Roll Back, Press Forward, and Push Downward to the air as if it were a live human being. The form's speed usually has to slow dramatically for a while to give you the time to feel and be consciously aware of the nuances of your feelings. This phase is referred to by some as "swimming in air," because the felt sense of moving energy becomes as tangible to your body as the natural resistance of water feels to a swimmer. At this phase, stances are done slightly below medium height.

Courtesy of Caroline Frantzis

The author (right), defending against an attack, demonstrates a tai chi fighting application of the posture Single Whip. He captures the force of the attacking arm and redirects it through his body so that it exits from his palm, which strikes the attacker.

5. Next you relearn the form, classically called "form corrections" in tai chi, "hardwiring" one power aspect of the 16-part nei gung process at a time into your movements clearly and strongly, before attempting to learn and implement the next nei gung component. For example, correct breathing (in both its gross and subtle movements) is first stabilized in your movements until it becomes so hardwired as to be automatic, requiring minimal or no conscious attention on your part to do it properly. This process must be accomplished before moving onto the next nei gung component (body alignment, say) in order that you can devote your full attention to the next component without becoming overwhelmed at having to do two things at one time. This procedure

ultimately allows you to relax into learning and avoids wasted time and frustrations. The importance of this progressive learning with its *stabilized* plateaus becomes obvious as the number of simultaneously performed internal nei gung processes begins to mount up, eventually reaching 16.

6. This phase is usually done first by holding specifically selected standing postures, one by one, for a long period of time (classically, a minimum of one hour, which may not be a practical standard for us now). At this point, the stances gradually get lower and lower. The postures begin with Ward Off, Roll Back, Press Forward, and Push Downward, for obvious reasons. Then comes the form's most representative yin posture, Play the Lute, which completely incorporates Pull Down, where you are back-weighted (that is, your entire body weight rests on your back leg). Then comes the form's most representative yang posture, the forward-leg-weighted Single Whip, which completely incorporates Split. (Forward-leg-weighted means that 100 percent of your body weight is resting on your forward leg.) After this, the instructor will, if needed, teach and recommend other postures for practice at home, selected to correct energetic gaps in your form.

The nei gung component of each static posture is always physically tested both for its ability to absorb (yin) and project (yang) power. The early training concerning separately stabilized nei gung components usually progresses with a learning sequence like this:

1. dissolving relaxation process
2. breathing
3. internal alignments
4. bending and stretching the soft tissues
5. unifying the body and its chi
6. the twistings of the soft tissue
7. openings and closings of body cavities and joints (in the Chen style; reverse the previous two elements for the Yang style, that is, openings and closings first and twistings second)
8. lower tantien work
9. spinal pumping
10. energy channel movements

After these, the remainder of the 16 components (see p. 62) are taught.

Each separate nei gung component is first stabilized in the standing postures, and next practiced and cross-referenced throughout the whole form. In the final phase of stabilizing any given nei gung element, stances assumed during the form reach their lowest height. Lowest height means a crouch where one's buttocks and knees are on the same level. This height is considered the ideal for people of small to medium body types (provided you are not prone to knee problems). Each individual nei gung component that is separately emphasized in the static standing postures or the moving forms is also simultaneously worked on in Push Hands training. Form work and Push Hands reinforce each other until one's mind and body, which participate in both, become one.

If you see and/or feel something "energetic" in your form, it will directly translate into your neurological system and physically into your body and hands. At some point of practice, the form is usually done extremely slowly in order to, as mentioned, hardwire each nei gung component subliminally into the body. A 20 to 25 minute long form done slowly ordinarily takes a minimum of one hour and frequently much more. This also allows the practitioner's mind to fully and freely begin to imagine the nuances of applying the form movements to fighting applications.

7. After this phase, the form should follow a natural style of evolution throughout the decades of a practitioner's life. In general, stances are performed at a height greater than the low stances practiced when nei gung elements were being stabilized. When you begin the two-person sparring exercises, you enter into an interplay that uses the form to subliminally enable your body to release all resistance (psychological and neurological), to the fluidity needed to flow from technique to technique. If your primary interest is the martial rather than the health or meditation side of tai chi, you will now tend to do the form with three things in mind.

    1. You will focus on specific evolving combinations of nei gung work to enhance the power of your applications.

    2. You will use the form as a primary tool to repair any shortcomings made apparent from lessons learned in sparring or actual contests.

    3. You will practice without any thought of fighting applications, releasing any tension in your mind until it becomes empty and calm, losing all sense of the past and future and remaining in the present instant. In this state, you will be able to fully digest and integrate your fighting applications, eventually allowing them to become effortless and natural.

Stage 2 Push Hands

Push Hands, called **tui shou** in Chinese, is the middle ground between form work and fighting. Push Hands is not fighting itself, but is a two-person exercise that develops most of the skills and types of power practitioners will need in combat, both open-handed and with weapons. Push Hands practice is thus done empty-handed, as well as with poles, spears, and double-edged straight swords. Normally, you learn to do Push Hands empty-handed before doing it with weapons.

PUSH HANDS/TUI SHOU
A two-person practice where, in the Yang, Wu, and Combination styles, the partners try to unbalance, or "push" each other or defend against these actions while their arms or hands remain in continuous touch, and move in a variety of ways. In the Chen style and more advanced practices of the other styles, joint-locking or throwing may be added to the mix.

The goals of Push Hands are:

1. To maintain continuous contact with your opponent's arms, until one of you clearly discharges or completely unbalances the other.

2. To control your aggression and that of others by overcoming the instinctual animal stiffening of muscles associated with the competitive need to win.

3. To learn to relax under pressure.

4. To neutralize an opponent's power and speed and use it to your advantage.

5. To be able to remain calm, centered, and alert in the face of extreme physical or mental aggression, deception, or any other potentially destabilizing attitudes.

6. To be able to change instantaneously from defense to attack, without freezing, where half of a movement is a defense and the other half is an attack, with the same or opposite hands.

7. To be able to instantaneously shift seamlessly back and forth between hard and soft internal energy.

Means to Achieve the Goals of Push Hands

Push Hands has several emphases within its physical methods that allow practitioners to meet the goals of Push Hands. These are:

1. Techniques that provide the ability to stick to your opponent's arms, legs, and body (see p. 132).

2. Methods to develop your ability to have your limbs, waist, and spine move in an integrated, coordinated, and unified manner that satisfies the dictum of the *Tai Chi Classics:* "One part moves, all parts move. One part stops, all parts stop."

Courtesy of Caroline Frantzis

One type of basic stance used in both single and double Push Hands. Note that the opposite forward feet of the opponents face each other (that is, the left forward foot of one practitioner faces the right forward foot of the other). Here, the author practices with his teacher, Chen style adept Feng Zhi Qiang. Beijing, China, 1985.

3. Sensitivity training that develops an ability for you to feel, *directly on the surface of your skin*, how your opponent is moving. This physical sensitivity, once induced in your skin, can graduate to the greater sensitivity of being able to listen to your opponent's mental and emotional intent, psychic state, physical power, and energy. Then you can use this knowledge to instantly interpret what opponents are going to do at their slightest stirrings. Eventually, you can even predict their moves before they happen. In Chinese, this sensitivity is called **ting jin,** or "listening power."

4. Levels-of-force training. Initially, both partners do Push Hands gently, without using internal power. Once the basic physical coordination is established, both partners gradually increase the amount of internal power used.

5. The development of:
   a. Root, the ability to absorb power into your body, through it, and then discharge it into the ground. Rooting capability enables you to remain stationary and not be physically moved by an aggressor.
   b. Energy enhancement. Making the energies of Ward Off, Roll Back, Press Forward, and Push Downward more powerful, one at a time.
   c. Fa jin, or the ability to discharge energy and physical power from your body.

6. Cultivation of the many other kinds of internal power in tai chi besides the eight explored in this chapter. These include shaking, vibrating (see p. 96) drilling, scattering, shocking, penetrating, discharging, transforming, hiding and reappearing, being silent, and so forth. These internal powers are commonly taught through Push Hands, where the teacher does them to the student, letting the student feel them first gently, then roughly. Gradually, students are brought along until they can manifest these energies themselves, in both form work and Push Hands.

7. The development of advanced phases of tai chi power. This is done in three progressive steps:
   a. Power is trained to move in a general direction, without any accurate targeting.
   b. Power is trained to move specifically on a line from the tantien or from the foot to the point of skin contact.
   c. Power is trained to manifest directly at the point of contact with opponents, *with no warning whatsoever*. This is the most difficult to master. All these skills will be essential when you move to actual fighting. Without point power, it is nearly impossible to defeat skilled opponents (especially those who exhibit extremely violent intent) by discharging power at them without causing injury or pain.

(Text continues on p. 155.)

TING JIN

The ability to listen to and interpret the energy of another in tai chi.

Standing and Basic Power Training— Learning to Practice on My Own

Critical to attaining real excellence in internal martial arts is the ability to practice for long periods of time on your own. It is most often during these solitary practice sessions that you both find the true sources of your inner strength and discover and correct your most dangerously vulnerable weak points. Practicing standing chi gung can be a rigorous taskmaster that has the capacity to make an individual directly feel and work with the energy of the body. The ability to feel and adjust the inside of the body while moving externally at high speeds both in combat or during solo forms is an essential component for success in both the combat and chi development sides of all the internal martial arts.

Standing is of special value for those with no regular access to a teacher of the internal martial arts who can correct any wrong turns in the progression of chi development. The simple act of practice and "going inside" can gradually enable you to trust your feelings, not from wishful thinking but rather from a solid foundation of viscerally knowing your interior landscape. The ability to feel inside, which is most easily obtained through concentrated standing practice, is the best way to allow the Taoist 16-part nei gung system to reach its full potential in the martial arts.

Standing practice also develops a grounded ability to be self-motivated and to carry through on your intentions without needing the physical, mental, or emotional support of others to keep you going during the hard times. Within two years of beginning standing, there were occasions when I would practice standing without a break for up to six continuous hours. I considered myself fortunate to have had the free time to do so. Time for this kind of practice is difficult to obtain after one's relatively carefree college years.

In the late 1960s, it was no easy task finding a quiet place to practice in central Tokyo, where you would neither disturb people nor be disturbed by them. My tiny Tokyo apartment made it awkward to practice indoors much of the time. I usually began practicing after 10 P.M. When it was dry, my favorite place where privacy was guaranteed required me to climb over locked gates to gain access to a rooftop, or over a wall to practice on dirt in a small, walled graveyard. My least desired choice was on the tarmac in front of a large public building near the aikido headquarters across the street from where I lived.

After deciding to practice standing chi gung seriously, I spent about two months focusing purely on standing before working on any other basic

Standing and Basic Power Training—
Learning to Practice on My Own, continued

power exercises. In any given practice session, it was only after standing for a long time that I would begin to concentrate on doing a particular set of basic power training movements (called *ji ben gung* in Chinese—see p. 84). When done in a martial arts way, the first phase of standing addresses two things: maintaining proper body alignments, and letting all your strength and tension drop down your body. The next phase, which I learned years later, involves dissolving all your energy blockages.

Even in the most basic neutral standing posture where your hands are at your side,* every part of your body will probably ache sooner or later, as you personally experience your habitual tensions and blocked energies. Often, in the standing practice, the air can feel like an incredibly heavy weight on your arms. As your chi opens and clears out the blocked energy in your channels, the pain vanishes, and your energy level, sense of physical well being, and internal power all rise dramatically. If you assume a raised-arm standing posture, the higher and longer your hands are held up, the more the benefits will increase. However, standing for prolonged periods requires careful monitoring by a qualified teacher.

For most people, releasing energy blocked in the hips and legs is much harder than releasing blocked energy in the torso and arms. No matter how much your shoulders may ache, your legs will hurt more. The legs may shake and vibrate for varying lengths of time and not stop until your tensions release, your energy channels open, and your chi finally drops down your legs to connect with the ground. However, once your energetic root is fully connected, all shaking stops. It is replaced by a sense of being totally comfortable inside the whole of your body that lies underneath your skin.**

Only after I started doing the moving basic power training methods called "Cloud Hands" and the "Three Swings,"† did the process of being able to maintain my internal alignments really begin. In all sports and martial arts, maintaining good biomechanical alignments is much harder

---

*The I Chuan method encompasses eight arm postures for holding the arms in the air, whereas the original more complete Taoist method includes 200 standing postures.

**This same phenomenon also usually transpires during static tai chi postures as well as in hsing-i's San Ti (see p. 190).

†*Editor's note:* Instructions for doing the movements of Cloud Hands and the Three Swings may be found in *Opening the Energy Gates of Your Body* by B. K. Frantzis. (North Atlantic Books, Berkeley, California, 1993.)

Standing and Basic Power Training— Learning to Practice on My Own, continued

when you are in motion than when you are standing still. Maintenance of moving alignments requires the gradual connection and integration of the arms and legs with the hips and spine. As in standing, however, the hardest part is integrating the legs.

I can still remember my own process in learning to do Cloud Hands before my body became integrated. Years later, I would be able to move in a highly coordinated and relaxed manner, turning my hips significantly more than 90 degrees to the side, and being able to maintain fully aligned low stances with my buttocks near my knees. When I began, however, it was an entirely different story. I could not go lower than 3 or 4 inches from my standing height or turn my hips more than 15 degrees without breaking all my alignments. What I knew had to be done, and tried to do was, now *while moving*, to more or less maintain both the alignments and the level of internal sensations and chi that I had maintained during standing. I would move only an inch and then think "oh, there goes the alignment." Or, "I can feel the alignment ready to go." Or, "I can feel this or that body part less or not feel it at all any more." At this point, every ounce of impatience inside me screamed, "Wimp! Just move a bit more, you are not an old man yet!" Instead, I would stop moving in the direction I was going, reverse direction, and honestly try to perform the movement on the opposite side; be it Cloud Hands or any of the Three Swings. If I felt my internal tension level about to rise, rather than increase my range of motion and push on through the tension, stiffness, or pain, I would again decrease the range of my movement, until again my body felt realigned and integrated.

The hardest for me, and for most people I have met, were the leg alignments and dropping energy from my hips down through my legs into my feet, creating a root. From all my karate and judo training, and for all the physical conditioning work (push-ups, deep knee bends, muscle-tensing exercises, etc.), my muscles were tense. Getting to the point where I could move my hips and legs even one inch within their potential range of motion without tensing up required weeks. It took me nine months of practicing hours a day just to be able to maintain the stability of my internal alignments. As this process expanded and integrated into my tai chi form, I began to move dramatically more and more slowly. I had to be able to feel the nuances of how, while releasing my strength and tension,

Standing and Basic Power Training—
Learning to Practice on My Own, continued

my alignments either broke or were maintained during each and every movement. By following this unforgiving regimen month after month, my movements progressively became more and more free of tension; in fact, I became positively fluid. Eventually, it was taking me between one and two hours to complete a single round of tai chi. The result was that I had acquired a significantly stronger root and internal connections than I would have achieved from just doing years of the form alone.

The basic process was to release, soften, and seamlessly integrate the six combinations of the body (hip to shoulder, elbow to knee, and hand to foot). Then, only after determining that the previous steps were honestly completed (that is, "hardwired in") and not just half done, to increase the range of motion by only the tiniest of increments, usually less than a millimeter.

The Benefits of Basic Power Training and Standing

What I gained immediately from each day of standing was a concrete way to actually go inside myself and find out how my body and chi worked from the inside out. Although this initial intense focus on standing shifted and broadened, for more than fifteen years standing chi gung was a basic part of my personal practice.* The hard work it involved was more than justified by its multifaceted rewards.

Besides making me healthy and energetic, this chi development method directly strengthened both my karate and aikido. In aikido, my sensitivity regarding working with ki escalated radically. My softness was increasing more swiftly than it ever had with my aikido practice, both in the United States and while training with O-Sensei Ueshiba in Japan. Before I practiced standing, my hip turning actions and hand speed were never very fast in karate. I was primarily a kicker and a thrower, not a puncher. The chi work made a radical difference. As my nerves became released and relaxed, my hands started moving quickly for the first time in my life. My hand strikes also became much more powerful as a consequence of my legs beginning to root, my hips becoming much looser and

---

*For example, I also worked on the standing practice with Wang Shu Jin (a student of Wang Xiang Zai), with Han Hsing Yuan (a disciple of Wang Xiang Zai), and with Huang Hsi I, all in addition to the many long hours practicing on my own.

Standing and Basic Power Training— Learning to Practice on My Own, continued

more fluid, and the ever-increasing ability of my chi to sink. This increased speed and power in my arms, and changed my fighting style from one that primarily relied on kicks to one that was an even mix of punches and kicks. The rooting and newly acquired hip fluidity also dramatically improved my kicking speed, timing, and power, especially in front, side, and round kicks.

The injuries caused by both my active judo and sparring practices were a constant annoyance (as it is for almost all competitive and contact sport athletes). Standing was immensely helpful in healing these injuries. Previously, if hurt, I might have needed to grin and bear it, live in pain for weeks, and just carry on. The standing chi practices gave me a previously unavailable tool for removing the blocked energy within the injuries. This often enabled me to recover in a quarter of the time it ordinarily would have taken, so that I would be free of pain and completely mobile again.

Over time, as the seeds from the practice grew, and as both my internal and external coordinations improved, it was obvious that an internal infrastructure was taking root. From puberty, I had always felt exceedingly uncoordinated, no matter how well others thought I moved. This now changed as my whole nervous system was transformed month by month.

I could feel my arms and legs joining in an unbroken, connected way to my spine. Soon, bit by bit, I began to feel the sensations of chi in every place in my body. Some time later, I began to concretely feel chi motion emanating from my lower tantien, and feel it actually becoming the motivating force behind the movement of my limbs and hips.

The groundwork of standing chi gung laid during those first two years formed the firm foundation for all the subsequent chi and movement work I was to do for decades in the internal martial arts. This potential was fulfilled over the next fifteen years through learning the details of the 16-part nei gung system, which enriched and brought to fruition the promise of chi. All the accomplished internal martial artists I have met have that first something that made internal practices very real and immediate to them; for me, it was standing chi gung. My subsequent success and abilities, and capacity to persevere in the face of many odds, both in learning and practice, were based on this firm foundation. This ability to "go within" carried through in all my other internal martial arts trainings, and was vital to my future understanding of ba gua and Taoist meditation.

8. Speed training. This type of training employs both regular and broken rhythms. Speed mastery enables you to change techniques rapidly and fluidly with no hard edges or gaps that can be perceived by an opponent and used as an opportunity to attack.

9. The empowerment of different parts of your body to serve as the central axis of your internal power movements. These axes are often formed deep within the belly and require the ability to open and close every square inch of your abdominal cavity with speed and fluidity, while moving a literal untrappable ball of energy within your abdomen. When timed correctly, these actions enable you to project and absorb power from your belly and limbs in undetectable ways that seem impossible.

10. The wiring of whatever internal skills you learn in Push Hands directly into your form work. This process requires you to increase your ability to comprehend, feel, and imagine how you will be moving energy internally and externally with your intent while doing your form. This dimension continuously adds vitality and aliveness to form work as the years of practice pass.

Types of Push Hands   There are four basic styles of Push Hands: single hand, double hand, **da lu,** and free stepping. All perform different functions for martial development, and all are first done with fixed methods which, after competence is gained by the student, progress to freestyle methods. All Push Hands methods are initially done in fairly slow motion, with the spine straight, either vertically upright or leaning forward at a 45-degree angle. Gradually, this practice evolves into one in which the body oscillates between spine held straight and spine bending sideways or leaning backwards or forwards. The movements can become exceedingly fast at advanced levels.

DA LU
A moving form of Push Hands that focuses on moving to 45- and 135-degree angles.

Fixed and Freestyle Methods   Fixed methods of Push Hands dictate precisely how each partner will move or not move his or her hands and/or feet at each part of the exercise. All fixed methods begin with teaching a student how to move the hands, legs, and waist in specific patterns, with no attempt to discharge an opponent in any direction. The goal is simply to have the student learn the movements in their proper sequence, first with the physical motions and later incorporating internal energies. Single or double Push Hands works with Ward Off, Roll Back, Press Forward, Push Downward; da lu works with Pull Down, Split, Elbow Stroke, and Shoulder Stroke.

In the second stage of fixed Push Hands, within the mold of regulated hand and foot movements, each partner attempts to yield and discharge energy, thereby uprooting the other either up, down, sideways, or backwards.

In freestyle, both opponents are allowed to use whatever hand movements they like, in response to any technique. Freestyle Push Hands trainings are done with the feet fixed, the feet only allowed to move in certain specified ways, and the feet being allowed to move in all directions.

The Four Styles of Push Hands

Although done mostly in the Chen and Combination styles, there are also single and double Push Hand practices where the front legs of the partners face each other, and the legs either yield to each other, attempt to leg-lock each other, or do fa jin on each other. The four styles of Push Hands are:

1. Single Push Hands The partners' hands continuously touch at the wrists, and the palms continuously rotate from facing either toward or away from the body as the waist turns. Your weight shifts from your front leg on the attack, to being back-weighed on the defense. Your nontouching hand may either be fixed in space, at your side, or put on your hip or behind your back to maintain balance and ensure it does not get into the fray.

This method is initially done where your feet are fixed and do not move. Later, this way can be extended to moving your feet in order to simulate a worst-case situation. Suppose, during combat, one arm were broken. In order to prevent shock moving through your good arm to your broken arm or into something sensitive you may be holding, you have to move adroitly with the coordination between your hands, waist, and legs being extremely precise.

2. Double Push Hands (Three Kinds)

a. *The Middle Ground between Single and Double Push Hands* One partner's wrist touches the wrist of the other, while the opposite hands touch and attempt to control the elbow of the partner. This method provides practice in how to balance both arms against an opponent. It allows freestyle movement to loosen up the waist and begins the process of learning how to understand and maintain balance when attacks are coming from multiple horizontal vectors. This method then prepares you for full double Push Hands in a sequence where Ward Off, Roll Back, Push Downward, and Press Forward are being applied against you, both vertically and horizontally.

Courtesy of Caroline Frantzis

Large-style double Push Hands with same-side feet (in this case, the right side) facing each other. Done by Wu style adept Liu Hung Chieh and his student, B. K. Frantzis. Beijing, China, 1981.

b. *Large-Circle Push Hands* As you do large-circle Push Hands, your waist and arms are making large movements with very big turns, covering a lot of space. While doing a sequence of Ward Off, Roll Back, Push Downward, and Press Forward, your hands are moving vertically away from your body, to or above your head (Ward Off) towards your body and below your solar plexus (Push Downward), and horizontally from side to side (Roll Back), within a distance slightly wider than your shoulders and forward toward your opponent's body (Press Forward). This method ultimately prepares the practitioner for long- and middle-distance fighting, where strikes regularly come high and low, and roundhouse in from the side. Most styles begin with this method before progressing to the next level, which is a preparation for close-in fighting.

c. *Small-Circle Push Hands* This method uses the same sequence of Ward Off, Roll Back, Push Downward, and Press Forward, but primarily on a horizontal plane. Focus here is on smaller arm movements, rapid, tight movements of the waist, and foldings of the arm joints. This develops the critical skills needed for close-in fighting. (In the West, for example, this type of Push Hands is used almost exclusively within the Cheng Man-ching method of Yang style tai chi.)

In all three of these methods, your weight is constantly shifting between being forward-weighted and back-weighted. In single and double Push Hands, your feet and those of your partner are usually facing each other with your front leg adjacent to your partner's back leg, and vice versa. In terms of footwork, the progression is usually:

1. Begin with your feet fixed, not moving.
2. Take regular steps both forward and backward.
3. Step forward and backward with half steps. In a half-step, the lead foot remains forward and does not change position, as in a regular step.
4. Turn around 180 degrees.
5. Step in the pattern of a square (teaches how to sidestep fluidly).

3. Da Lu or Four Corners Push Hands This style teaches how to move to diagonals, spin, turn around at 135-degree angles, and attack and defend from off center and unusual angles. In general, da liu develops the footwork and the body's ability to move in most directions smoothly, although not to as great an extent as does ba gua chang.

Yang style Da Lu moving Push Hands. Done by Men Hui Feng (head tai chi instructor at the Beijing Institute of Physical Education) and his student, B. K. Frantzis. Beijing, China, 1981.

Photographer unknown

4. Freestyle Moving Push Hands   This style allows you to freely combine at will all the hand, waist, and stepping techniques of double Push Hands and da liu, in freestyle movement. Freestyle moving Push Hands sets the stage for you to begin to "cut your martial teeth."

In all these styles of Push Hands, there is also the issue of joint-locks and throws. In general, the Yang and Hao styles of tai chi allow throws, but do not encourage them, and actively discourage joint-locks, often forbidding them outright. The Chen and Combination Form styles, as well as allowing throws, permit and often encourage joint-locks to both the arms and legs. The Wu style encourages throws and is neutral on the subject of joint-locks. However, all the classical tai chi styles actively train students to make their joints exceedingly mobile and able to fold in order to deny an opponent the chance to put you in a joint-lock in the first place.

Stage 3   Baring Your Martial Teeth: Transition Methods Between Push Hands and Sparring

Push Hands is not unrehearsed sparring; nor by itself is it sufficient for genuine self-defense. As far as fighting is concerned, there are three tai chi methods that get you from Push Hands to sparring. These methods are:

1. Practicing Single Fighting Applications with a Partner   This methodology is not dramatically different from the fixed-step sparring of karate and tae kwon do, where the goal is to gradually become used to progressively more stringent levels of pressure, which demand that your level of skill rises. You begin with fixed feet. Only after your hand techniques, kicks, throws, and joint locks are up to standard, do you move your feet in accordance with the principles of Push Hands. Each partner switches roles at regular intervals determined by the participants or by the instructor. At each phase, always first develop your yin defensive capabilities before you begin to focus on the more yang preemptive attacks and counterattacks.

With feet fixed, use the following progressive steps:

   a. One person attacks with a prearranged technique at a prearranged fighting angle, and the other person responds with a prearranged defense and counter.

   b. The attack is prearranged, but you decide on your own defense.

   c. Your own feet remain fixed. Using a predetermined technique, your opponent can move his feet and attack from any angle, and you can use anything to counter, as long as you do not move your feet. In these fast exchanges, mobile waist turns, subtle weight shifts, and rapidly changing fighting angles must be developed.

   d. With feet fixed at predetermined distances of long, medium, and close range, both partners can attack and defend with any techniques at will, a fixed number of times. (You usually begin with one attack and stop at five.)

e. Now, moving your feet, use the same progressive steps of **a** through **e.** Work each and every type of footwork into all of tai chi's fighting techniques and appropriate fighting angles. Always begin with a preset response to a preset stimulus and progress to intuitively responding to an unpredictable attack, feint, or any kind of combination.

2. **Circling Hands** In this practice, the tai chi equivalent of ba gua's Rou Shou, you and your partner's hands attach at the wrists, stick together, and make large vertical circles, moving in the same or opposite direction. While circling like this, each partner attempts to create an opening through which the other can be hit with a tai chi hand technique. The circling is done both with feet fixed and moving. In its more advanced versions, kicks, throws, and joint-locks are added to the mix. Circling Hands, however is not as sophisticated as, nor as translatable to unrehearsed fighting as is ba gua's Rou Shou (see p. 235), due to ba gua's larger technical repertoire, especially in terms of fighting angles.

3. **Two-Person Sets** In these, two people attack and defend themselves over and over again in a long, prearranged sequence. A set is the equivalent of both sides individually doing a form, only here there is direct opposition from another human being. Initially, the forms are done slowly, with little or no power, to allow the student to memorize the moves. Some refer to the slow motion set as "the tai chi dance." Next, the form is still done slowly with little or no power, but the details of the form are examined down to the smallest degree, with respect not only to which move counters which, but exactly what internal power each side is using offensively and defensively. Gradually, the speed of the two-person set is increased, but not its power. In the end, the power is ratcheted up notch by notch until both sides are doing the form at full power. (This exact same methodology is used in the two-person sets of ba gua and hsing-i.) The two-person set done with and without power are two entirely different activities.

In all three of these transition methods, the focus is on gaining the skill to recognize what energies inherently defeat what other energies. The Chinese talk about this concept in terms of whether any technique (a) can rip a hole in the fabric of your opponent's attack-and-defense shirt, (b) is neutral in effect, or (c) will cause your own fabric to be torn.

Stage 4 Sparring and Actual Fighting

Sparring has a hundred times more variables to be handled than Push Hands. Yang Lu Chuan is said to have spent six years learning only the fighting and sparring strategies of tai chi. Even freestyle sparring is quite different from actual life-and-death combat. People respond very differently when they feel their survival is at stake as opposed to when only the ego gratification/humiliation of winning/losing is at risk.

From the traditional tai chi perspective, fighting (called *lan tsia hua*) is Push Hands with the following added:

1. Distance appreciation
2. Ability to flow between close, middle, and long fighting distances
3. Fighting angles
4. Hitting, kicking, throwing, joint-locking, and the ability to absorb blows
5. The ability to touch, disengage, and touch again, fluidly and without discontinuity
6. The ability to stay centered and calm regardless of danger, attempting to transcend the instinctual animal hormonal fight-or-flight reaction
7. Training aimed at being able to defend against high and low attacks from multiple opponents advancing at multiple angles
8. Bare hands versus weapons training

The classical fighting training exists on two levels. The lower level is concerned pragmatically with how to hurt or kill your opponent. The highest level, achieved by the famous Yang Lu Chuan who was called "The Invincible," is where, instead of hurting your opponents, you are, using nonviolent fa jin, able to throw them some distance through the air without hurting them at all. An opponent who is not physically harmed is often relieved of an inner need to seek revenge.

Classically, this training was done with open hands, which allowed a practitioner to use the sticking abilities of tai chi to great effect, as well as to throw, joint-lock, and use the fingers for nerve strikes. Today, there is also another emerging trend of practicing Push Hands open-handed, and then learning tai chi's fighting skills relying on sparring with boxing gloves, as is done in kickboxing. This has been done for basically the same reasons that karate also adapted the strategy and popularized kickboxing.

The use of boxing gloves gives an authentic sense of hitting and being hit, useful for getting past the first phases of the fight-or-flight syndrome. At this point in time, boxing with gloves is culturally accepted worldwide. It is easier for a teacher to control gloved rather than empty-handed encounters between students, where lines often blur between acceptable and unacceptable contact, as well as providing no-nonsense answers to the nagging question of how realistic were the attacks or defenses. With gloves, if you hit someone, there is no requirement to say you are sorry, or to justify whether you got hit or not. For highly motivated martial arts enthusiasts, there is usually a boxing gym to which they can go for genuine sparring with others. This activity may be lacking in a school where most of the students are there for health reasons and are not martially inclined to do intensive sparring. In the West, there is also a greater availability of gloved boxing skills to be had than there is tai chi martial training.

In classical tai chi, you learn to translate Push Hands to realistic fighting tactics. The practice of weapons sparring improves empty-hand skills, especially footwork and sensitivity to the issue of physical distance between fighters. Sword-play can be relatively easily translated into self-defense with canes and sticks. Whatever sparring skills you learn are always translated back to both form work and Push Hands.

In gung fu, boxing, street-fighting, or military combat you can get angry. Your mind can fill with all kinds of thoughts—malevolent, animalistic, pragmatic, tactical—and you can still fight very well. As a matter of fact, this way of being while fighting is often encouraged in many hard style martial arts, particularly those that are animal-oriented.

Tai chi is different. Training the mind to become still under fire is difficult, but is an essential component of tai chi fighting training, as the core of its physical fighting technique rests on this ability. When the animal fear/anger response rises high enough, the body begins to go into an extreme stress cycle that causes the human heart rate to increase dramatically. When the heart beat rate exceeds a certain number of beats per minute, our biological heritage causes our muscles to stiffen, vision to narrow, and fine motor control to be diminished. All tai chi touch techniques depend on fine muscle control. Loss of it dampens the effectiveness of most tai chi techniques. Developing a core of stillness, which keeps the heart rate down and naturally opens up the peripheral vision, has been a major element in tai chi and ba gua's whole ancient methodology of learning to fight well under real conditions.

Without a deep residual core of stabilized neurological relaxation and mental stillness, many of tai chi's techniques might not hold up under real violence, which can, unless mitigated, activate our biological animal heritage instantaneously. High-level tai chi is often likened to meditation because it contains pragmatic training that develops the ability to make the mind empty and calm. This characteristic is another reason why tai chi is sincerely respected by the captains of Asian industry as a method for managing stress and enhancing mental high performance. Tai chi is a tool that gives them a competitive edge.

We have seen that a major element in learning fighting strategies involves preparing for what can be foreseen. Even more important, though, is to have the capacity to become comfortable with unpredictability. This attribute requires a person to learn to fight with a mind holding no expectations of what is supposed to happen next, a mind able to respond to what it comes across with no hesitation whatsoever. The *Tai Chi Classics* express this concisely in the phrase, "Forget yourself and follow the other."

In fighting, once practitioners have been trained to move well, the critical component of success or failure under pressure is how well they can perceive the combat interaction. Can they neurologically process, interpret, and act on the information from their perceptions? Remember that in tai chi this is done by accurately reading the energy and mind intent of opponents, rather than their physical movements or muscular twitches. This approach is radically different from focusing on the opponent's physicality. There are many training techniques and strategies that, at the fighting stage, focus your capacity to interpret energy under real pressure.

Tai chi, hsing-i, and ba gua, unlike many other external/internal martial arts, do not use deceptive moves to set an opponent up for some kind of combination. These arts either execute a technique for real, or wait. This kind of training, combined with a calm mind, makes it difficult for someone to control a tai chi player with feints, a major tactic in fighting. Part of "listening energy" is to be able to discern if an opponent's threatening movement has any real energy behind it. Fake punches usually do not.

Integral to the whole method of tai chi fighting is learning how to wait, from the time an opponent has the intent to strike or actively begins the blow, before you act. Sometimes, the waiting is a second, sometimes a fraction of a second. Without this ability to wait, it is not possible to fulfill two primary strategic dictums from the *Classics*: "Seize the opportunity and then act" for a successful counterattack, and "The opponent begins the attack, but I arrive before he does."

At the unrehearsed fighting stage, tai chi people spend a lot of effort learning to expand their awareness in order to penetrate and become sensitized to the whole energetic field an opponent is generating. The training can get somewhat "psychic" in that, after your mind becomes sufficiently sensitive, quiet, and still, you can literally become one with an attacking man's energy. You literally slip into his mind space and his energy will tell you how to defeat him. It is energy that lets you know when and how to move, not your own ideas of what you should or should not do. Many of tai chi's advanced fighting strategies involve rigorous mental and psychic development, which is required to get over the last stages of hesitation, inertia, and noncircularity of technique.

Various Types of Sparring Practices Although tai chi has a full range of front, side, low roundhouse, and stomping kicks, it normally tends to focus on hand techniques. Its kicks tend to be done at or below the heart, rather than to the neck and head. Its armed and unarmed sparring techniques are first practiced one-on-one. Later, when expertise is achieved, the techniques are done to handle multiple opponents. In multiple-opponent sparring, there is a very strong emphasis on tai chi's freestyle Push Hands footwork methods and on being able to root at the end of each step. Tai chi always comes to a clear stop, roots, and discharges before moving on, unlike ba gua, which can discharge power on the run, so to speak. Five of tai chi's original thirteen postures—Step Forward, Step Backward, Gaze to the Left and Right, and Central Equilibrium—are concerned with footwork in fighting.

Both for single and multiple opponents, training is done standing upright, in extremely low stances, hugging the ground, sitting, and lying down. In specialized training, the student simulates various handicaps in order to be prepared to perform well under any adverse condition.

For example:

1. To simulate being wounded in the upper body—by putting one arm behind your back; in the leg—by letting one leg go dead or placing a heavy weight on a leg; to simulate a broken leg or ripped leg ligament—by being required to stand or move on one leg only, or with miscellaneous handicaps to mimic various adverse conditions

2. To be sitting down in a chair or on the floor

3. To be lying down, which extensively uses fa jin techniques, and nerve strikes

4. To be in the dark—done with blindfolds, but more importantly in totally blackened rooms

5. To be facing an opponent when the sun is directly in your eyes

6. To be with your back against the wall, with extremely limited options as to where you can move

7. To be with your back against a ledge, where the fall could be fatal—especially done against multiple opponents

8. To be faced with an overwhelming force where your only escape is to immediately jump to a higher place. Here, **ching gung** (see p. 310) or lightness skill (jumping ability) was employed. This skill seems to have disappeared from tai chi training after the Boxer Rebellion. Researchers have not yet been able to find a tai chi practitioner who could convincingly do ching gung.

CHING GUNG
Technique for making the body light by changing its chi, giving one incredible leaping ability.

DIFFERENT KINDS OF TAI CHI MASTERS OR TEACHERS THAT YOU ARE LIKELY TO ENCOUNTER

The vast majority of tai chi teachers in the West and in China today primarily teach tai chi (a) as a method for attaining health, (b) as a very effective method for learning to relax, and/or (c) as a kind of gentle nonimpact dance or as a refined method of physical education. This majority of instructors often only teach the form without Push Hands, or when they do teach Push Hands, it is usually devoid of martial content, conveyed solely as a kind of psychologically oriented centering exercise. In presenting it this way, such teachers genuinely benefit the people they work with, most often in terms of teaching a way to manage the horrendous stress placed on us by modern times. Martial tai chi teachers provide these same benefits in addition to self-defense skills.

The following discussion pertains strictly to those tai chi teachers who emphasize the martial side of the art, and are recognized as personally possessing tai chi's martial skills—a necessary prerequisite for being able to convey them to a potential student. Martial teachers in the West vary greatly in quality. Some are doing what they say, others are not. Some are highly qualified and know their subject, others do not. Some will have personalities you will find comfortable and pleasing, others will not. It is good to remember that, no matter what idea you have of what a tai chi teacher or master should or should not be, first and foremost they are all human beings, with the same kind of attributes and frailties that have comprised the human condition since our arrival on earth.

The following three issues concern the relationships of martial tai chi teachers to their students:

1. **Teaching and Form Work**   If you really want to learn the martial skills, and are willing to put in the work, it is achievable with the right teacher. In terms of learning form work, there are several critical attributes you should look for in teachers: They must know about rooting, relaxing the body, fighting applications, and how to transmit the nei gung internal power trainings. Some teachers can perform all of this material well, some none of it well, with all kinds of combinations in the middle. It is not wise to automatically assume that, because a teacher can do one part well, he or she even knows the other parts. Teachers may not deliberately withhold knowledge, they simply may not know other aspects of tai chi.

   Those that can teach simplified applications of the forms are not uncommon; those who know the full range are relatively rare. Those who know most of the internal nei gung power trainings are rarer still, as are those who even know three or four nei gung methods. Many gung fu teachers who teach tai chi can teach you fighting applications of a sort; however, these techniques may be those of their external martial art rather than of tai chi. Some teachers really can do Push Hands, but have not learned the sparring level of tai chi; others, for a variety of reasons, only do some of the Push Hands methods. Generally speaking, those who teach fixed-feet Push Hands are more numerous than those who can teach and perform moving Push Hands.

2. **Teaching and Sharing**   Assuming a given teacher is competent and has the ability to teach (which is a gift not equally given to all), the question arises, "How willing is this teacher to share what he or she knows?" Some instructors play the game of "teacher's pet"—if they like you and you are easy to teach, you get their full attention, and if they don't like you, even if you work ten times as hard, they will still withhold information. Some teachers are very fair and always reward honest effort with

more in-depth teachings. Some teachers will really try to help the untalented; others reserve their efforts for the middle of the pack and above.

The next question is, "Are teachers willing and able to put enough energy into the teaching task to make sure that students have a good chance of comprehending the material?" Younger people are often able to put in the energy to teach, but their knowledge still requires seasoning. In China, it is said that the best martial teachers are the middle-aged, those who have enough experience, have outgrown the impatience of youth, yet still have a zest for teaching. Elderly teachers usually have the most knowledge, but sometimes they lose their enthusiasm for teaching and prefer to reminisce rather than put in the necessary hard work. Teaching tai chi takes a lot out of instructors, presuming they do a good, rather than a superficial, job.

Different teachers can teach different things for all kinds of reasons that their students often conjecture about. Some are good at intellectually explaining what is supposed to be going on, but can't demonstrate the practical martial skills. Some are good at physically demonstrating the practical skills, but communicate poorly concerning how they were able to do it, which can leave the less intuitive student in a difficult learning position.

3. **Teaching Styles and Personality** Neither a pleasant nor a cold personality indicates the quality of a teacher's skills. The personality of the teacher does, however, create a social atmosphere, which can influence a student's attitudes about life. If you can, think deeply about whether you value the social interaction over obtaining the skills (gung fu) you really want, and about what is realistically available and being offered.

From the viewpoint of personality and teaching styles, internal martial arts teachers are of all stripes. They tend as a group to be highly individualistic people, and many of them could easily be called eccentric. They often hold very strong opinions, which they are not afraid to express. Some are strongly positive in outlook, others are not.

Tai chi books are often filled with inspirational stories of the martial exploits of previous masters. Some of the skills described seem to be lost in antiquity, unavailable to current and future generations. These abilities can return. One must pay attention not only to how high the old masters soared but also to the effort and depth of their practice. Many of these stories do point people down roads that eventually can result in exceptional accomplishments. Most of the stories are true. The question is: Are you willing to put in the time, effort, and creativity to help make them come alive in you?

A Wonderful Tai Chi Teaching Personality: T. T. Liang

An example of a wonderful tai chi teacher who was a true pleasure to be around was Liang Tung Ts'ai (T. T. Liang). Liang was a charming older man, balding, with a twinkle in his eye and a devilish "Who, me?" smile. He had what the French call joie de vivre, or joy of life. He was one of Cheng Man-ching's senior students in Taiwan. He came to America, taught tai chi in New York City at the United Nations, handed over the class to Cheng Man-ching, and moved to Boston, where he taught for years.

Liang taught a version of the Yang tai chi system.* No matter how cold the weather got in Boston, it was said, Liang always made your heart feel warm. He was an insightful teacher and excellent communicator. Students found that studying with him, hanging out in his apartment, or taking walks with him was always a genuine pleasure.

Liang was not the least bit sanctimonious about tai chi, as is the case with some elderly Chinese teachers. He was educated in both Chinese and English and had learned—and loved—many martial arts in his youth. In the 1930s and 1940s, Liang was a customs official in Shanghai. At that time, the Chinese underworld controlled the docks. Shanghai was then one of the most raucous cities existing, with perhaps the world's largest active red light district. Liang always liked regaling students with risque stories of those days in the "wild, wild East."

Liang would tell his students that he took up tai chi because he had ruined his liver by excessively partaking of the good life. He learned tai chi to recover his lost health, and although he had studied with 20 tai chi teachers, he considered Cheng Man-ching to be the best, even though he and Cheng disagreed on some issues.

Liang, always open-minded and willing to grow and learn, inspired his students. On the other side of seventy, in Taiwan he started learning Half-Step Praying Mantis from an eighty-year-old master from Shantung, Wei Shao Tang, who was as strong as a bull, and who did tai chi to keep his "gung fu" from deteriorating in old age. Not many men of Liang's age would have been open enough to start anything from scratch. Liang always said that, if you truly loved martial arts or had genuine passion for any other of the wonderful things life had to offer, you would never let your past achievements stop you from learning something valuable and new. With this attitude, Liang had in effect found one of the streams of the Fountain of Youth.

Yang style tai chi teacher T. T. Liang.

---

*Liang taught the Cheng Man-ching long form that Cheng first taught in Taiwan before he changed to teaching his 37-movement short form. Over eight or nine months in 1972, Liang taught me solo forms for sword, broadsword, double broadsword, two-person tai chi fencing sets, Push Hands, and his version of the two-person set he called the "two-person" dance.

Yang Shao Jung—Magnetic Hands

In 1977, I was given a letter of introduction to tai chi master Yang Shao Jung, who did not accept students without a recommendation. Yang was the eldest son of Yang Cheng Fu, great-grandson of the original Yang Lu Chan. His school, located in his walk-up flat in the Wan Chai district of Hong Kong, was announced by a sign in beautiful Chinese calligraphy above the second-floor balcony. As in many of the older buildings in Hong Kong, the stairway was particularly dark.

Two major tai chi masters, Yang Cheng Fu and Wu Jien Chuan, had fled to the then-British colony of Hong Kong for safe haven in the 1930s, a time of cascading troubles for China. Their oldest children remained in Hong Kong after World War II.

I knocked on Yang's door and gave over the letter of introduction. Once it was read, I was admitted. The flat was small, as were most of those in the older buildings in Hong Kong then. To the right was the family's private living quarters; to the left, the school. A few steps from the door was a small waiting area with a few places to sit. From this vantage, several things could be seen in the apartment. Straight ahead, a few feet away, you could observe Yang teaching in the next room, which seemed to be about 250 square feet. Toward the teaching room, above an opening in the wall, you could see pictures of Tung Ying Chieh and of Yang when he was younger. Tung was one of his father's main disciples who also taught in Hong Kong after the war and spread the teachings throughout Southeast Asia. To the left, next to the front door and against a solid wall, there were

usually one or two groups practicing Push Hands.

Yang was a northern Chinese, solidly built, relatively tall, and long-limbed for most in Hong Kong, being approximately 5 feet 10 inches tall. He was a warm, but very formal man, who stood extremely erect. Most of the time I saw him, he usually wore black pants, black gung fu shoes, and a loose-fitting shirt. The atmosphere of the front teaching room was businesslike, bare of furniture. Where the teaching room ended, the balcony began. On those many days that were hot and extremely humid in Hong Kong, any wind through the balcony window was a welcome relief. Yang taught most of his classes in Cantonese, but he clearly was more natural in his native language of Mandarin, which he spoke with a marked Beijing accent. Yang was pleased that I spoke Mandarin, and often gave me a little extra time, both because I had taken the effort to learn his language and because of his innate sense of graciousness toward visitors from afar. Yang taught his classes as private lessons, which usually lasted ten to fifteen minutes with one student before another came into the room.

In his early classes, Yang emphasized several things when he taught. First, clarity. There was never anything vague about the way he taught. He was extremely precise about how each of your body parts should be positioned, and he shaped them in each movement of the form. If you missed a critical detail after observing his demonstration of the movement, he would physically adjust your limbs to ensure that you understood

Yang Shao Jung—Magnetic Hands, continued

what was expected and what was necessary to maintain quality control. Second, he emphasized a clear 100/0 percent separation of weight in each stance. When I asked him why many others taught tai chi with other weight balances, he only said, "This is how my family back to my great-grandfather has always taught the form." Third, he stressed doing long stances, and especially encouraged younger students to go very low. Fourth, he advocated large extended movements where the hands were always stretched out and relatively far from the body, with the armpits extremely open. He encouraged the students to lengthen their arms from the spine, often gently pulling their elbows or hands forward, to set the feeling in their bodies.

I would often come early for his classes and stay after my form class so I could observe and learn more, which he graciously permitted. Sometimes, between students, when it was not my turn next, he would generously allow me to ask a question. It was very instructive seeing the source from which so many Yang style tai chi form versions derived. For example, once I asked about doing pushes in the form with the fingers facing straight ahead, as some did in Taiwan. He said this was not the way of the Yang family, maintaining that the fingertips should be facing vertically upward as the palm pushed forward, and advised me to look at his father's book.

On another occasion, several of the students in his school had recommended that I go to a Taoist to learn about meditation, and I asked Yang if he taught that also. He replied

that he did not, and the members of his family had not from the beginning. He taught the martial and chi gung aspects of tai chi, and that if my interest was meditation, I would need to look elsewhere.* Another time, he told me he taught his family's tai chi tradition because of the obligation to pass that tradition on. He admired the love and joy of martial arts that his great-grandfather had possessed.

Generally, Yang's students were well educated and some spoke English as well as Cantonese. Many with whom I talked were friendly and insightful individuals. The conversations were enjoyable.

Usually when I arrived for class, several people would be practicing Push Hands by the wall next to the door. They did a form of static Push Hands where both people would stand facing each other in a Press Forward position, without moving or yielding. The person who was facing the wall would attempt to discharge, uproot, and slam the other against the wall, with minimal or no obvious external movement. The person with his or her back against the wall would attempt either to absorb the other's power or to push the opponent only an inch or two (more, and the person pushed would land in the laps of those in the small

---

* Subsequently I learned Taoist meditation from Liu Hung Chieh, meditation that was directly related to tai chi. However, Liu was clear that he had learned this from Taoist meditation masters, not from his tai chi master, Wu Jien Chuan. Even though Wu prayed at a Taoist altar and practiced meditation, he did not teach it to Liu when Liu lived in his home.

Yang Shao Jung—Magnetic Hands, continued

waiting vestibule). Yang's small, thin wife loved to do Push Hands with the waiting students, bouncing them against the wall. The idea of doing Push Hands without turning the waist and yielding to a person's power was unusual, and different from everything I had previously learned. The Push Hands activity caused me to become skeptical and curious at the same time. Observing protocol, I mentioned to Yang, after I had been doing the form for a while, that I had some experience in Push Hands and would like to understand what they were doing at the wall. Yang agreed, and one Saturday I was invited to come to a Push Hands class.

When I came in, Yang was practicing with students in the main teaching room. He was putting his hands on their shoulders and bouncing them vertically in the air, always with a wide smile on his face. It was a small class of only six or eight people. In the waiting area, I asked one of them to do Push Hands. He showed me the two-person press method and explained that it was used to develop the ability to discharge. I was able to more or less

neutralize him. Then he said I should really go for it. I did what I was familiar with, yielded, moved my waist, and threw him against the wall again and again.

When Yang was done with vertically bouncing people in the other room, we all lined up against the wall in the main room and practiced the technique. Again, I turned, yielded, and turned and countered successfully with a student who had been at tai chi a few years longer than I.

Then came my turn to Push Hands with Yang. His power was significant, and he easily bounced me after I yielded. Then, as I next attempted to yield, he held me fast, with only his palms, locking me up tight so that it was not possible to yield or move my limbs or body in any direction, or exert any kind of power against him, in any way. It was like being held by a magnet. Due to circumstances beyond my control, I unfortunately had to leave Hong Kong shortly thereafter. The straitjacket experience with Yang remained forever embedded in my mind.

Liu Hung Chieh demonstrates the Five Element fighting application
of hsing-i's Drilling Fist, punching to the head of the author.

Hsing-I

Fighting Considerations and Applications

5

HSING-I CHUAN AS A MARTIAL ART

Like tai chi, hsing-i is a hybrid internal martial art. It exists in the middle ground between the psychological attitudes and emotional disposition of the Shaolin martial arts and internal power chi methods of the Taoists.

The name *hsing-i chuan* is composed of three terms:

1. *Chuan* (see p. 122), which translates as "fist." The word pertains to everything concerned with defeating a human being in physical combat.

2. *Hsing*, which means "the form of something." Everything that manifests, at the level of either energy or matter has in one way or another a form, a shape, a cohesion, a configuration—the form of a cup, the form of a thought, the forms of different species of animals. More specifically, hsing indicates the form or shape the body will take during a martial posture assumed for hitting, throwing, or controlling an opponent.

3. *I*, specifically in the phrase hsing-i, refers to the ability of the mind to create an idea and project it into the body, creating a functional physical form, that is, a way of moving, a fighting strategy, a fighting posture, or a kind of power.

The term *hsing-i*, then, can be looked at from two perspectives. First, it is whatever form that the mind—"I"—directs. If the mind imagines a concept, the body automatically molds and creates a bodily movement and form that pragmatically implements the idea. Second, by way of a computer analogy, the form (the hardware) can run varieties of ideas (software), and so there is a need to know and develop all the ideas that a form is capable of delivering.

Hsing-I Is an Excellent Bridge from the External Martial Arts to the Internal

Hsing-i's practitioners are military in approach—marching in straight lines, with a powerful emphasis at the end of every technique on mentally or physically taking an enemy down. In this sense, hsing-i is similar to most punch-and-kick martial arts. The obvious external attributes of punching and striking are inherent to the way hsing-i is practiced. For many external martial artists not satisfied with the slow-motion form practice of tai chi, hsing-i done at normal speed fits the bill.

Moreover, hidden within the apparently linear techniques of hsing-i is a significant amount of very small, almost unseen, complete circles that are normally lacking in external martial arts. In many ways, hsing-i is a kind of sophisticated internal karate. Rather than using muscular tension or anger for power, hsing-i focuses instead on utilizing relaxation, chi, and stillness of mind to accomplish the pragmatic martial goal of winning in a violent confrontation. Hsing-i possesses either the same or similar primary goals as other more external fighting arts, such as karate or boxing, but includes the chi work, health aspects, and ability to be martially effective into old age that most of the external martial arts lack.

The internal techniques of hsing-i can be as subtle and virtually invisible as those of ba gua or tai chi. However, hsing-i does not focus on the yin (soft), but rather on the yang (hard) internal energies of the tactics of repositioning, finding an effective fighting angle, and utilizing formidable internal power. Hsing-i's technique does not feel soft, but can appear so at touch due to its extreme flexibility and rapid ability to change from tactic to tactic. A majority of all the internal work in tai chi and hsing-i is exactly the same. The differences reside mainly in the fact that tai chi essentially seeks to fuse hard and soft energy, whereas hsing-i seeks only to maximize hard energy. The terms "hard" and "soft" do not refer to muscles at all but to the quality of the internal energy. Both arts require soft and relaxed muscles and never use muscular contractions.

The physical technique of hsing-i is based completely on efficient use of the nei gung internal power system; hence, it is internal. Because of this, it, too, is capable of making the weak strong and the sick healthy. However, its primary mental set is still the aggressive one of Shaolin, karate, or boxing.

The perspective of hsing-i is, as mentioned, militaristic: define the mission, do whatever it takes to win, preferably with minimal damage, but without qualms about inflicting whatever degree of pain or damage the situation calls for. Like many military personnel, hsing-i practitioners are often proud of their combat prowess. The stories about past hsing-i masters often tell of them simply brushing their opponents lightly yet leaving huge swellings and contusions on the body. Like tai chi and ba gua, hsing-i has the ability to deliver fa jin without inflicting pain, injury, or severe shocks to the central nervous system of the recipient. However, unlike tai chi and ba gua, hsing-i tends not to use its gentler side.

The vast majority of hsing-i schools emphasize the culturally defined "macho" attitude: Solve the problem in the shortest most direct way to gain the victory. Physically, this attitude translates into: get in position, attack, and take the opponent out with the least amount of wasted energy. This approach is rather different from that of the vast majority of tai chi schools, which encourage the yin attitude of yielding and cooperating to win, without hurting anybody, if humanly possible.

Historical Origin of Hsing-I

Legend has it that hsing-i was originally created by Yue Fei, whom many consider to have been China's best general. It is often conjectured in China that, if China's emperor had not become jealous of Yue Fei's military prowess and popularity, and ordered him to commit suicide, Yue Fei would have stopped the Mongol invasion dead in its tracks. The story is that Yue Fei invented two martial arts for his troops to use in battle. For his enlisted men, he created eagle-claw boxing, and for his officers he invented the more powerful hsing-i, based upon spear technique, which accounts for the linear appearance of hsing-i's movements.

There are many accounts concerning the history of hsing-i that are important to prospective students of the art in that they record the numerous hsing-i lineages. The closer the hsing-i teachings are to the original lineage material, the better they are for the student. Unlike practitioners of tai chi and, to a lesser extent ba gua, the stronger hsing-i people did not and still do not attempt to teach their methods purely for health. Unlike ba gua, hsing-i is not beautiful to watch. Given hsing-i's lack of aesthetics, its poor public relations concerning health benefits, and its strong no-frills martial orientation, it tends to attract a smaller number of adherents than other martial arts. No more than a skeletal history is provided here, one that focuses on the value of the art for practitioners going into the twenty-first century—that is, the value for health and healing, stress reduction, self-defense, and general balance in a breathless technological society.

After Yue Fei, the lineage moves through a variety of people. Usually one finds protracted stories about how the next heir is forced by the previous lineage holder to cultivate tremendous patience and resolve by undergoing severe hardships and tests of moral character. Only after the prospective lineage heir endured these tests would the current lineage holder agree to first give small parcels of knowledge and, eventually, the full teachings, allowing the heir to acquire the whole system of knowledge, and thereby the capacity to pass it on.

(Text continues on page 178.)

Northern Praying Mantis

The basic on-guard stance of Praying Mantis boxing resembles the manner in which the insect itself hold its forelegs when it is stationary. I learned Praying Mantis to find the answer to why so many martial artists in China frequently said, "Praying Mantis is most afraid of hsing-i." Then, too, I wanted to attempt to find out out what, if any, reality lay behind the story of the "death touch" (**dim mak** in Cantonese; **dian xue** in standard Chinese), which is often sensationalized in martial arts magazines. Praying Mantis, both in its Northern and Southern schools, was supposed to specialize in this technique. I subsequently found that much of the magazine writing about this subject was exaggerated.

Although the Northern and Southern schools of Praying Mantis are radically different in both appearance and technique, many in the West confuse the two. Southern Mantis focuses on close-in fighting; Northern Mantis on mid- and long-distance fighting. What the two schools share in common (besides an extremely aggressive nature) is the ability to execute fast, multiple strikes with deadly accuracy to an opponent's vital points.

Southern Mantis is a Canton province short-arm method, where the arms are kept close to the body. It focuses intently on arm-touching, hitting practices in the manner of Wing Chun and stresses breath work and being able to separately use and control the internal opening and closing movements of each and every joint in the body. There is a lot of chi gung work within Southern Mantis forms. Consequently, it is a true external/internal martial art. In this respect, it is related in technique to the Cantonese styles of White Eyebrow and Wu Mei. Most of its strikes are delivered close-in from a very short distance. It uses minimal kicks, mostly front kicks, usually only to below the waist.

Northern Mantis is another story. It is a Shandong province long-distance fighting style, with long, extended postures and a varied arsenal of long-range hand, forearm, and kicking techniques, generally done to, but not above, the neck. Northern Mantis is primarily an external martial art, without a well-developed chi gung method. It does, though, have highly developed touching practices, but does not place as great an emphasis on them as does Southern Mantis. Northern Praying Mantis has many styles. Many Northern Mantis practitioners would agree that Seven

DIM MAK
The art of hitting acupuncture points to cause harm or death.

DIAN XUE
Mandarin for dim mak.

Northern Praying Mantis, continued

Star is its most unsophisticated branch and Six Combination Praying Mantis its most sophisticated and effective branch. I learned three methods of Northern Praying Mantis: first Half-Step, then Seven Star, and finally Six Combinations.

My Half-Step teacher was over eighty, a solidly built man who emanated an immense sense of dignity. He preferred to use power hits rather than pinpoint strikes, and his forearm blows and hammer fists landed like lead pipes during applications.

True to the Northern Mantis style, he enjoyed using the staple technique of employing a pincerlike grabbing mantis hand to first pluck an attacking man's incoming fist out of the air, then break the attacker's balance using the opposite forearm, and finish the job with a counterstrike by the original grabbing hand. Part of breaking the attacker's balance involved first smashing the radial nerve in his forearm, which induced terrible pain that prevented him bracing against the next attack. This teacher loved using foot stamps in conjunction with grabbing an arm, taking a half-step forward, hitting, and shocking his attacker to within an inch of his life. Mantis, more than most forms of Shaolin, uses foot-stamping techniques that drive the stamper's chi into the ground, from where the natural energetic bounceback generates enormous power in the subsequent strike of the Mantis expert. Simultaneously to the chi going into the ground, a shock wave is created that penetrates an opponent's body. Another specialty of Northern Mantis is **shao twei,** a type of leg cut, ankle sweep, or kick directly aimed at several nerve-sensitive spots on the calf or the Achilles tendon, which it attempts to snap.

The teacher who introduced me to Seven Star Praying Mantis was a short, wiry man in his fifties. A former sergeant in the army, he spoke Mandarin with such a thick Shandong accent, I was never quite sure what he was saying. Students of his told me that this instructor was well known in the heavy drinking areas of Taipei for using his skill in several challenge matches that took place after he came with the army to Taiwan from the Mainland. The stories had it that his tried and true technique was successful against men much larger and stronger than he. From six feet away from his challenger, he would do a flying kick to chest or head. As his feet were coming down, he would attack with multiple hand strikes, and when his opponent would try to protect himself, he would find that his

SHAO TWEI
A Northern Praying Mantis leg cut, ankle sweep, or kick targeting the calf or Achilles tendon.

Northern Praying Mantis, continued

arms were trapped midair. Upon landing, the Seven Star teacher would throw his opponent down with shao twei and reverse feet, which left him poised to kick the thrown man either in the head, groin, or knees.

My Six Combination Mantis teacher specialized in strikes to sensitive spots in the body using fingers as well as cutting hands and palms. He was a muscular fifty-year-old with extremely long arms, whose tendons and muscles stood out when he flexed his forearms. He normally refused to teach anyone, and only taught me to repay a debt he felt he owed to a third party. As a man of means, all training took place privately within his large-walled courtyard. His teaching centered on fighting applications through sparring. He played rough as a matter of course, constantly accelerating speed, power, and ferocity during sparring to deliberately force his student to climb to the next level of martial competence. As his student, you absolutely had to progress in order to work out how to physically deal with him. If you didn't put up a defense with zest, he would really sting your sensitive points, such as the throat or the bones just behind the ear.

If you could not perform to standard (which was hard to do when fingers were continuously coming at your eyes and the most vulnerable parts of your throat, neck, and head), you would be thrown down hard with shao twei, left to contemplate whatever point had been driven home.

A phrase used to describe Northern Praying Mantis is, "Mantis hands and monkey feet." In the main, Mantis tactically focuses on skipping, jumping, and half-steps to close in on an opponent from mid- or long-range fighting distances. Mantis especially favors skipping steps where the back foot appears to be kicking the front foot into movement.

Northern Praying Mantis has, in fact, several distinguishing characteristics. It uses the elbow tip, which remains fixed in space like a multi-angle fulcrum around which the forearm rotates and the fingertips strike vital points on the body. From a starting position, where your forearm is vertical and its beak-hand fingers are directly in front of you, the Mantis fingers strike downward toward the inside of your body at any point on an arc of 180 degrees or more, and to the outside of your body up to 45 degrees. At each place, the Mantis fingers can deliver a full power strike to a vital point. Within a second, the beak hand can then change targets and hit with multiple finger strikes at radically different angles along a 225-degree-plus axis.

Fast and multi-angle snapping wrist movements that create all kinds

Northern Praying Mantis, continued

of knuckle strikes are also a speciality of Northern Mantis. Ba gua actually has a greater range of techniques, but rather than the strikes being linear and choppy like Mantis, they are done with very smooth circular and spiraling wrist movements that look like a moving gyroscope, where each several degrees of rotation creates a new hand weapon. Due to the emphasis in Praying Mantis on striking vital points, extreme speed and precision of strikes is usually valued over power. The power of Praying Mantis is derived from the forearm and its ability to suddenly grab and pull an opponent with significant shocking force. The style emphasizes extreme speed in changing from one hand strike to another. During one continuous attack, a Mantis person, using a different snapping hand technique each time, may strike five or six times, each from a completely different angle—high, low, or on opposite sides of the body.

The multiple strike aspect of Mantis was especially useful for honing my internal martial arts defensive techniques. There are ba gua methods that produce even faster and more varied continuous attacks than those of Mantis. Mantis, however, reinforced my perceived need to be able to defensively perform fluid multidirectional combinations when on the other side of a spectacularly aggressive and overwhelming attack. Knowing the internal logic of Mantis and its fighting perspective when dealing with multiple attacks made me appreciate the need to add layers to my internal martial arts defensive capabilities that I might otherwise have neglected.

It ultimately turned out that the reason Mantis most fears hsing-i is twofold. First of all, hsing-i's sunken and always dropped power elbows are able, at the critical change points between techniques, to simply nullify the less powerful elbows of Mantis. Secondly, especially during a multiple lightning attack, the constant forward motion of hsing-i takes away the gaps in awareness and physical motion which a Mantis player expects and needs to find in an opponent in order to locate a hole through which to get first and subsequent successful hits.

At the end of the day, given the fighting techniques involved, it is easy to see why, like the praying mantis insect itself that uses its legs to rip its prey apart, the martial arts style of Praying Mantis is legendary for its viciousness.

Modern hsing-i emerged from northwestern China in the nineteenth century. It began with an individual called Li Luo Neng (also known as Li Neng Ran), who successfully learned hsing-i not as a youth, but in middle age. Ultimately, Li persuaded his teacher Dai Long Bang to fully impart his knowledge by having Dai's mother plead his case. Many of the earlier hsing-i martial artists were illiterate people whose whole education was in how to acquire internal power normally beyond the reach of the most educated class. Hsing-i people often ran convoy agencies, which, in the era before firearms, provided protection from assassination as well as physical security against bandits out to steal shipments of valuable goods.

Li Luo Neng is a mythic source figure with many students. From this source, three clear schools of practicing hsing-i evolved over time. These schools are discussed in the sections that follow.

THREE MAIN SCHOOLS OF HSING-I

The Shansi School

After hsing-i moved from the legendary Yue Fei in the medieval Song Dynasty to Li Luo Neng in the nineteenth century, it underwent several changes, as Li's martial art descendants mixed the original hsing-i with other internal practices to create two new styles.

The original school is often called the Shansi school because that is where Li Luo Neng taught his students. In Beijing, although many schools identified themselves as teaching a Shansi style (because it was the original method), in reality they were closer to the Hebei style (see following section). Titles do not necessarily indicate a reality.

In the original Shansi* style there was an equal emphasis on the Five Elements and the Animal Forms. Besides doing the single movements in lines, Original Shansi had short forms or katas, such as **lien huan** (linking form), **ba shr** (eight forms) for the Five Elements, and **tsa jr chuei** (mixed or complicated fists) for the Animal Forms, which combined the individual line movements. Sometimes a single Animal Form would also have a short form that was designed to physically implement the single Animal Form's basic principles and mind intent. Originally, there were twelve Animal Forms. Today, some systems do not practice all twelve, some practicing fewer than ten.

In the West, the relevance of whether a hsing-i school is of Shansi origin usually does not help the student understand what the school actually does. In the original school, hsing-i was learned in three clear progressive stages: San Ti, then the Five Elements and their combined forms,

LIEN HUAN
One of the forms of hsing-i, based on the Five Elements.

BA SHR
One of the forms of hsing-i based on the Five Elements.

TSA JR CHUEI
One of the forms of hsing-i based on the Twelve Animal Forms.

---

*Editor's note: The author studied the Shansi methods of hsing-i from Liu Hung Chieh for three years in Beijing.

then the twelve animals and their forms. As the original hsing-i students spread out from Shansi province, other schools were founded and called by the names of the provinces where they had established themselves. The two most common provinces were Hebei and Honan. In Honan province, a Muslim style of hsing-i is said to have flourished. The practitioner who brought it there was a follower of the Muslim religion. The Hebei school often did not remain pure hsing-i, but commingled with ba gua.

The Heibei School

Many of the top students of Li Luo Neng ended up coming to Hebei province, especially to Beijing and its nearby port city of Tianjin. During this same period, the ba gua school was also in ascendancy, and the two schools trained with each other.

There are many accurate stories about the relationship between ba gua and hsing-i. One common myth that has been recounted in many books in English is definitely inaccurate. It concerns an alleged fight between the founder of ba gua, Tung Hai Chuan, and the famous hsing-i master, Guo Yun Shen, and how as a result of this epic battle the hsing-i and ba gua people came together for a mutual exchange of knowledge. This story is a good legend, but nothing more.*

In reality, the ba gua people and the hsing-i people were always friendly. As a matter of fact, at the turn of the century, there was a house in Tianjin where seven hsing-i and ba gua martial artists lived together as friends, including Li Tsung I, who was a top hsing-i man, Cheng Ting Hua, one of Tung's Big Four (see p. 309), and Chang Chao Tung, another top hsing-i/ba gua man. They were all dedicated to the martial arts and were all teachers. Rather than opposing each other, these two camps cooperated in their martial arts training. As a result of this interaction, the hsing-i people always wanted to learn ba gua, since they were consistently beaten when practicing with their ba gua friends. The ba gua people were open-minded and enjoyed learning hsing-i, but their interest in hsing-i did not match the interest the hsing-i people had in learning ba gua. However, the ba gua teachers saw that it might be useful for their beginning students to first get a solid grounding in internal power from a more linear, yet clearly internal method. Then they could start learning the more complex Circle-Walking methodology, which requires a more sophisticated mental process. It is as a result of this friendship, especially that between ba gua's Cheng Ting Hua and hsing-i's Li Tsung I, and not because of any mythical epic battle, that the trend for hsing-i and ba gua mixing originally began and continued on.

Editor's note: The author researched the accuracy of the stories concerning the relationship of hsing-i and ba gua. All his research done in Beijing indicated that Guo Yun Shen and Tung Hai Chuan had virtually no contact with each other.

There are ba gua schools where the techniques are done like hsing-i, and there are hsing-i schools in which the techniques are done in the manner of ba gua. One of many examples would be the hsing-i taught in the Tianjin school that mixed the teachings of Li Tsung I and Cheng Ting Hua, which through Chang Chun Feng came to Taiwan and to Hung I Hsiang. Its forms have the movements of classical hsing-i, but much of its methodology actually contains the basic internal body principles and techniques of ba gua, which are quite different from those of classical hsing-i. Conversely, many people practice ba gua's circular movements with the mind, energy, and internal mechanics of hsing-i. One example of this is the Sun Lu Tang method.

HEIBEI HSING-I
One of the main branches of hsing-i; a newer style that is heavily influenced by ba gua.

As the hsing-i and ba gua groups commingled, the new hsing-i method that was created often became called the **Hebei** school. In this strongly ba gua-influenced hsing-i school, the predominant influence and emphasis was on the Five Elements, with the Animal Forms being of secondary importance. In general, if teachers do ba gua as well as hsing-i, they will often focus their hsing-i teachings on the Five Elements. This tendency occurs because teaching students to obtain a solid foundation of internal power through the five elements is easier than to teach them through the basic ba gua Circle-Walking. However, once the student has some internal power, the Circle-Walking techniques of ba gua develop martial adaptability and the capacity to use sophisticated fighting angles in students much better than do the Animal Forms of hsing-i. Consequently, teachers put their energy into teaching ba gua rather than the hsing-i Animal Forms. When the Hebei school does teach Animal Forms, the internal content tends to be more similar to ba gua than hsing-i. They may use some of the external movements of the hsing-i system, or entirely different movements that use the hsing-i nomenclature, but are not the classical movements.

In the Western World, the greatest number of hsing-i schools belong to the Hebei method, although such schools may not be conscious of the origin of their material.

The I Chuan School

BENG CHUAN/ CRUSHING FIST
One of the five basic techniques of hsing-i chuan.

NEI JIA
A term used to describe all the internal martial arts or Taoist chi practices as being one family.

The I Chuan* is another mixed school. One of the finest students of Li Luo Neng, founder of the Shansi school, was a man named Guo Yun Shen, who had the "legendary" battle with ba gua's founder, Tung Hai Chuan. Famous for his half-step **Beng Chuan**, Guo produced two students who became important in the development of hsing-i. The first was Sun Lu Tang, who created a tai chi style that fused hsing-i, tai chi, and ba gua together. He widely spread the idea that all three were of one internal family, called the **nei jia.** As an adult, Sun learned the complete Shansi

*Editor's note: The author studied I Chuan during his undergraduate days in Tokyo with Kenichi Sawai, who called it Taiki-Ken, and later in Hong Kong with Han Hsing Yuan.

hsing-i system directly from Guo. Sun's martial descendants render the purest exposition of Guo's art.

The I Chuan branch of hsing-i was founded by Guo's student, Wang Hsiang Zai, who was Guo's last disciple when he was old. Wang only learned from Guo when he was a teenager. Later, Wang mixed Guo's hsing-i with Western boxing, Buddhist chi gung, and ba gua foot movement techniques he learned later in life to create I Chuan, or mind intention boxing. When he was older, his style was also called *da cheng chuan*, or Great Achievement Boxing.

I Chuan focuses strongly on San Ti (see p. 190). Practitioners often do the form for decades, frequently devoting half or more of every practice to San Ti. This is quite different from the Shansi and Hebei schools where, after the first few years, San Ti is only held for minutes at a time, between lines or at the end of forms. Moreover, the I Chuan school also does San Ti differently from the other schools. Here, Pi Chuan (see p. 187) is replaced by eight standing postures, at heights ranging from above the head to lower tantien level. The most well-known one is called Holding a Ball, or the Universal Post. The footwork of the standing postures is also different, and is of two types. The first is done in a modified horse stance with the feet parallel, and the second is done in a cat stance, which is completely back weighted, with the ball of the weightless foot on the ground, heel raised.

The Five Element practices of I Chuan emphasize an open centerline, where the hands are spread apart but the intention is always on the centerline. In contrast, the other schools emphasize closed centerlines, where the arms or hands are physically held in front of the centerline. I Chuan's Five-Element practices utilize hourglass-like walking with regular steps (such as are seen in karate and southern Chinese martial arts), which are not used in the Shansi or Hebei schools. I Chuan in general emphasizes regular steps rather than half-steps. Whereas the other hsing-i styles condense many large ideas into tiny components of the physical movements of the Five Elements and animal styles, the I Chuan school makes each minicomponent into a separate external movement.

In I Chuan, the emphasis on holding the standing postures is to develop fa jin. I Chuan's primary two-person training exercise is a form of touch training, where the arms of both partners move in circles, similar in concept but not with the same techniques as ba gua's Rou Shou (see p. 235) or tai chi's Circling Hands (see p.159). Each partner attempts to: (a) apply fa jin, discharge force, and uproot the other from arm contact alone; (b) completely trap the other's arms so there cannot be any resistance to being hit; (c) hit the other; (d) use arm contact alone to throw the other to the ground without using hip or shoulder throws. After this, the partners practice sparring, sometimes with boxing gloves.

(Text continues on page 185.)

The Hsing-I of Kenichi Sawai called Taiki-Ken

A member of the Shibuya tai chi school introduced me to Kenichi Sawai's hsing-i group, who were fanatics about developing chi through standing practices (see p. 86). Sawai had studied for ten years in China with Wang Hsiang Zai, founder of the I Chuan school of hsing-i.

At the time I was introduced to Kenichi Sawai's class, it was primarily oriented toward a love of fighting rather than health and fitness. Many of the students were the strong young men of the competitive martial arts scene in Tokyo at that time, and they were there to seriously learn how to fight. Many were third-, fourth-, and fifth-degree black belts in karate.* If a man came to Sawai's group and said he wanted to learn the fighting arts, he was usually tested to see if he was sincere and to see if he had a fighting spirit, a characteristic highly valued in the Japanese martial community.

After observing the class for a long time, I underwent the initial formalities that introduced me to the school, including revealing the nature of my previous martial background. I was then asked to spar in order to verify if I was a genuine fighting black belt or merely a dilettante. My first opponent looked grave. When it was mentioned from the sidelines that I was a black belt in karate, Sawai looked toward my sparring partner, who then took a bead on me and began to give me a much harder time. The next thing I knew, he kicked me in the heart (heart strikes were a speciality of that group). I crumpled to the floor, falling with intense pain and an imminent sense that this life was going to be over very soon. I had never experienced anything like this before in karate. Subsequently, I found out my sparring partner was a ringer —he had been a fifth-degree black belt in karate for years before studying with Sawai.

In a minute or two, someone helped me to my feet. It was extremely difficult to stand and begin breathing normally again. After giving me a little while to recover, they asked me to spar again, this time with a third-degree black belt, which was about my level at that time. In this

_____
*In Japan at that time, the strongest active fighting black belts were usually third, fourth, and fifth degrees. The third-to-fifth degree black belts in Sawai's group included a strong contingent from Mas Oyama's Kyokoshin Kai karate school. The late Mas Oyama was famous in Japan for killing bulls with his bare hands.

The Hsing-I of Kenichi Sawai called Taiki-Ken, continued

round, I did just fine, being able to get him fairly often with round kicks to the head. Later, it was explained to me that Sawai just wanted to see if I could go beyond my initial fear and maintain fighting spirit. After this interesting initiation, I was accepted into the class.

The class took place in Meiji Jingu Park, which was a major national shrine and the site of Japan's most important traditional New Year's event. The training took place in a clearing surrounded by trees. (Years later, as part of Japan's unrelenting industrial destruction of natural environments, the practice area, which was a rare natural spot in central Tokyo, had been cemented over to make a parking lot.) When I arrived at the class, students were standing in front of the trees. Their arms were held up in the air before their chests, as if each person were hugging a huge ball. Some stood with feet shoulder-width apart, body weight evenly placed on the ground. Others stood on one weighted leg, with the heel of the weightless leg slightly raised. This standing ritual was performed for an hour or two before anyone moved, usually with Sawai participating or sometimes walking up to individuals and correcting their postures.

After the standing was over, students started to practice the moving hand techniques—either individually or in groups. In the beginning, each complete step would take about thirty seconds. Progressively, however, as your chi got stronger, one full step with its attendant hand technique could take as much as ten full minutes. Next, students began Push Hands practice, the object being not only to break your partner's balance, but afterwards to either hit or apply a fa jin technique, which, unlike the fa jin of tai chi, often delivered quite a shock to the body. Then came free sparring, which was particularly interesting in terms of learning to defend against kicks and throws, as many sparring partners were high-ranking judo and karate black belts. Sawai himself was a former seventh-degree black belt in judo before his martial studies in China. At the conclusion of the session, the circle completed itself. The class finished with standing to stabilize chi, calm the mind, and fully absorb all that had been learned in class.

Sawai's love of fighting was downright infectious. A former combat veteran, he had a samurai's serious no-nonsense attitude toward the dance of life and death. He was not a sadist, but would not abide a dabbler's lack of martial intent and commitment. He assumed his students would settle for nothing less than maximum fulfillment of their

The Hsing-I of Kenichi Sawai called Taiki-Ken, continued

martial potential. Sawai could be gruffly playful, but when he got down to business, his manner was severe, and very down-to-earth. If you made a mistake in sparring, he would take you to task and, after a third failure, correct your mistake, often allowing you to painfully feel what your opponent would do to you—if given the opportunity. This approach strongly motivated all of us there to rapidly correct our faults!

A short, stocky man, Sawai particularly liked Pi Chuan (see p. 187) and the Monkey way of moving in hsing-i, especially its blocking methods and its rapid footwork that moved a fighter in and out of range. The offensive technique of which he was particularly fond was a heart strike, which he did both with the back of his wrist Monkey style or with the front of his knuckles, as in the animal form method of Horse. This bent-wrist fist technique mimics a fighting horse crushing its hooves down on its victim after it has stood on its hind legs. As Sawai's elbow descended vertically, his protruding front four knuckles would come cutting down on your heart.

If Sawai respected your sincere commitment to learning martial arts, he sooner or later applied this technique on you, allowing you to appreciate the nature of a martially induced heart attack. I can personally attest that it made a very real and lasting impression concerning the effectiveness of hsing-i that went deeper than mere words ever could.

A controversial subject often connected to I Chuan is the training technique of **kong jin,** or "empty force." In this technique, teachers move their students physically either backward, up in the air, or down to the ground by a wave of their hands from a distance, all without physically touching them. Unfortunately, although this works well with students, many incorrectly assume it can be done to strangers against their will, which, it can safely be said, rarely happens. Extensive research was done on this subject in Beijing to find out if empty force would work on unco-operative martial art experts—it did not. However, the technique of empty force chi training can, in fact, be useful for moving chi therapeutically to clear blocked energy channels.

Empty force is a training technique whose purpose is to sensitize practitioners to the movement of chi in themselves, in their opponents, in the space between themselves and their opponents, and in the psychic energy generated in combat. It aims to empower the recipient to be able to become sensitive and respond appropriately to the chi of others, whether during physical contact, or unimpeded in the gap before they touch your flesh or hit you. It requires cooperation at the psychic level between student and teacher, and often the histrionics seen during the encounter with empty force are incredibly exaggerated. The purpose of this exaggeration is simply to generate a sensitivity to energy and to be able to use that sensitivity to respond to a physical stimulus in real time, in a physical confrontation, rather than to gain the magical ability to knock King Kong down with an invisible force from a wave of your fingers.

KONG JIN
The energy technique of hsing-i where practitioners are purported to knock people down without touching them, solely by projecting energy.

THE TECHNIQUES AND TRAINING PRACTICES OF HSING-I

The hsing-i of Li Luo Neng had three components: San Ti, Five Elements, and various Animal Forms. It has large-, middle-, and small-**frame styles** (see p. 111). Hsing-i's basic qualities as a martial art include:

FRAME
The physical shape and energetic qualities that an internal martial arts posture assumes, ranging from small and condensed (small frame) to large and expansive (large frame).

1. The energetic and combat intent behind a movement is emphasized more than the physical movements of the form.

2. Functional power in each and every part of every movement, rather than only the ability to move well.

3. Movements that are designed purely from the viewpoint of combat effectiveness. In hsing-i, any movement that is not functional or is wasted in either solo forms, two-person practices, or in combat is considered to be the equivalent of a martial sin.

4. *Bu hao kan, hen hao yung* (the classic phrase in Chinese that describes hsing-i), freely translated means that hsing-i does not look pretty, it just works exceptionally well in combat.

5. A prime strategy that rests on the idea of never retreating. Hsing-i invades the space of opponents continuously, encroaching on their defenses until they are overwhelmed and defeated by the advancing motion. In hsing-i, even if you need to retreat for tactical considerations, your mind is just taking a short respite until it can reposition for its primary mission, which is to attack as soon as possible.

6. A mentality that is completely goal-oriented and based on a high level of aggression. Any defensive maneuvers are only interim tactics used until the hsing-i practitioner can get back to the main mission of attack. If the decision to commit to battle is made, there is little or no compassion for an adversary.

7. A primary focus on developing yang, not yin, methods of internal power; that is, hardness, not softness.

8. Developing the outside of a practitioner's body to feel extremely hard to someone touching it. Simultaneously, the practitioner's subjective experience is that the inside of the body feels soft and flexible. This chi balance of hard on the outside, soft on the inside is the exact opposite of tai chi.

9. A main philosophical orientation toward developing internal strength and unwavering focused intent.

The image frequently used to describe the technique of hsing-i is that of an iron ball rolling right over the opponent. Whether your body type is thin or heavyset, one of your major internal goals in hsing-i is to sink chi to make your body and arms become incredibly heavy, like lead. Yet you still need to retain the ability to move with sensitivity and be as agile as a leaf in a strong wind.

So heavy and dense do the arms become that practitioners, when they attack, can move their opponents arms out of the way as if they had no substance. The arms of opponents bounce off the heavier arms of the hsing-i adept like tin bounces off lead. During an attack, hsing-i practitioners use these heavy arms to completely control the arms of their opponents and move the opponents' hands away. The heavy arms of the hsing-i fighter can always open the defenses of their opponents for a clean and decisive attack.

The Five Elements

The Five Elements are in effect the five energies that, according to Taoist cosmology, comprise the energy matrix of the universe. In traditional Chinese medical theory, these five dynamic energies (Fire, Water, Wood, Earth, Metal) balance the internal organs of the human body. Each of the following hsing-i Five Elements utilizes a particular hand technique that moves power along a specific physical force vector. Each individual Five

Element hand technique has a slightly different way in which it is done: high (to the opponent's heart or above), middle (between the heart and the lower tantien), and low (to the opponent's hips, groin, or legs).

Chopping/Splitting Fist (Pi Chuan) In this Five-Element technique, physical motion goes from up to down, utilizing Push Downward internal energy (see p. 135). The final posture of the complete **Pi Chuan** movement is the one held in San Ti. Pi Chuan itself focuses on vertically downward-moving power. The internal pressures that this movement initiates in the body, in addition to its basic chi work, directly and positively affects the lungs. It is represented by the **metal element,** and focuses on making an extremely strong spine and hands as hard as steel.

The basic motion of Pi Chuan is a cutting action usually done downward with the palm or, in some schools, sometimes forward with the edge of the palm. In all schools, the fighting applications of Pi Chuan are also done with different parts of the closed fist. Pi Chuan is the primary on-guard defensive position in hsing-i. In this posture, one hand is held high, covering the middle and upper body sections, and one hand low, covering the body's middle and lower sections. Pi Chuan is used extensively against straight-line attacks. Many top hsing-i practitioners base their whole offensive strategy on only using Pi Chuan and Beng Chuan (Crushing Fist), defending with the upper hand of Pi Chuan and attacking with the bottom hand using Beng Chuan.

Drilling Fist (Tsuan Chuan) Here, physical motion goes from down to up and uses Ward Off, expansive internal energy (see p. 127). The internal pressures that **Tsuan Chuan** generates within the body during execution of the technique, in addition to its basic chi work, directly and positively affect the kidneys and the whole vitality of the body. It focuses on vertically upward-moving power. Tsuan Chuan is represented by the **water element,** and focuses on making the hands able to move around the opponent's arms like water moves around a rock. It is equally used for attack and defense. Its fundamental action brings one hand down your centerline as the other hand simultaneously moves upward along your centerline in a kind of drilling uppercut.

Drilling Fist twists the body and arms powerfully, and is done in three basic ways. In the first, after the upward motion, the hands come to a dead stop at the end of the of the technique. In the second, the hand first moves upward as if to go through its target (the head, for example) and then returns to a lower position in order to block a potential counterattack. With both these methods, the hitting hand proceeds forward on a straight trajectory along the centerline of your body from your lower tantien. In the third method, the hand moves in a zigzag, waterlike, formless manner that mimics the irregular motion of water going around a rock. The twist at the end of the punch is always emphasized.

PI CHUAN/ CHOPPING OR SPLITTING FIST
One of the five basic techniques of hsing-i chuan.

METAL ELEMENT
In Chinese cosmology, one of the basic energies or elements from which all manifested phenomena are created.

TSUAN CHUAN/ DRILLING FIST
One of the five basic techniques of hsing-i chuan.

WATER ELEMENT
In Chinese cosmology, one of the basic energies or elements from which all manifested phenomena are created.

WOOD ELEMENT
In Chinese cosmology, one of the basic energies or elements from which all manifested phenomena are created.

Crushing Fist (Beng Chuan) This technique uses straight-ahead physical motion along with the internal energy of Press Forward (see p.134). Beng Chuan is hsing-i's most well-known attack technique. It is often considered to be the most powerful straight punch in all the Chinese martial arts. The internal pressures initiated in the body by this movement, in addition to its basic chi work, directly and positively affect the liver. Beng Chuan is represented by the **wood element,** and focuses on making fists "grow" out of the body. It is often compared to the force of a powerful plant growing and expanding through concrete with a steady, inexorable force.

Beng Chuan is not like a normal straight punch, which depends on its momentum for much of its effectiveness. Rather, Beng Chuan's power is most likely to be applied from a very close distance, after, say, your arm has broken your opponent's balance in the act of moving forward for an attack. Beng Chuan is often used to stop the incoming attack of opponents and steal their power, after which either arm may attack. Beng Chuan is usually done with a quarter turn of the fist. It is applied both pressing down from above or pushing up from below an opponent's arm. Beng Chuan's retracting arm is used to push internal power downward to make the opponent's arm and body stand still (that is, not run away) while your other arm strikes. Beng Chuan also uses an elliptical rolling action to climb up an opponent's arms, and small defensive circular arm movements to set an opponent up for a counterattack. In back weighted stances, Beng Chuan is known for power punches with the arm of the forward leg. As the arm advances, Beng Chuan often neutralizes the opponent's attack with the front half of the extending punch and hits with the finishing second half of the arm's extension.

The first three techniques of the Five Elements—Pi Chuan, Tsuan Chuan, and Beng Chuan—are usually first practiced walking in straight lines only. They are considered sufficient for most to understand the basic internal substance of hsing-i. After these three are mastered, it then becomes profitable in terms of practice time to work with the next two techniques, which complete the full balance. The next two methods of Pao and Heng Chuan normally begin with using the seven-star stepping pattern of hsing-i. In these steps, the body moves in a zigzag pattern of connecting 45-degree angles. (The 45-degree angle way of stepping is also widely used in aikido and ninjitsu.) This diagonal stepping is used to move around the perceived superior power of a linear attack, as well as to get the body of one attacker between yourself and other assailants when you are attacked by several people at once.

PAO CHUAN/ POUNDING FIST
One of the five basic techniques of hsing-i chuan.

Pounding Fist (Pao Chuan) Pao Chuan focuses on diagonal physical motion, and uses the internal energies of Ward Off, Roll Back, Press Forward, Push Downward, and Pull Down (see p. 138). Pao Chuan concentrates on moving power diagonally in all directions and on explosive forward-moving power. In addition to its basic chi work, the internal pressures initiated in the body by this movement affect the heart and peri-cardium directly and positively. It is represented by the **fire element,** and focuses on explosive and rapid oscillating releases of power. In Pao Chuan, one hand initially defends and shifts the opponent's center of balance. Once your opponent's striking hand has been neutralized by your upper hand's Pao Chuan or Pounding Fist, your other hand attacks in a very smooth transition.

In Pao Chuan, the upper defensive hand is the more difficult to master and is the most important part of the technique. Often your upper hand, forearm, and elbow are used to twist an opponent's arm or leg out of the way. Then, in this newly created gap, you hit the opponent with your upper arm's hammer fist to conclude the movement. When your upper arm descends, a hammer or back fist is also used to either defend or smash the opponent's body in an inward-moving, Pi Chuan-like motion. The lead hand in Pao Chuan is especially used in defenses against high kicks.

Flames flick and move rapidly. The arms in Pao Chuan can either be light and seemingly weightless, representing the edge of the flame, or heavy and dense representing the core of the fire. Part of the intent of Pao Chuan is to be able to instantly explode with the hitting hand, in rapid strikes that, like fire, seek the tiny holes in your opponent's defenses. Done without physical tension, these punches often use the internal technique of "silk arms," where your arms can alter direction and move as smoothly as a silk banner in a changing wind. The bottom hand of Pao Chuan may either hit forward or upward. However, the blow is not like Beng Chuan. Rather, it is often done with a lighter feel, using vibrating rather than expanding power to penetrate opponents and take them down.

Crossing Fist (Heng Chuan) Here, the physical motion focuses on the inside of the fist moving horizontally. Heng Chuan is the most difficult of the Five Elements to do well. It focuses on horizontally moving power, and combines the energies and applications of the first four elements (pi, tsuan, beng, and pao) into one seamless technique. The internal pressures initiated in the body by Heng Chuan, in addition to its basic chi work, directly affect the spleen. It is represented by the **earth element,** and focuses on tightening the cross-linkages between the left and right sides of the inside of the abdominal cavity.

It is said it takes many hsing-i people ten years to fully understand Heng Chuan, because without completely grasping the internal mecha-nisms of the first four, the fifth and last punch always lacks important attributes in execution. The interchange between its hands is very circular as they move in opposite directions horizontally across the body, but this is difficult to perceive when observing an experienced practitioner. The basic punch combines the expanded action of a straight Beng Chuan-like punch with the twisting and sideways movements of Tsuan Chuan, as well as with inside and outside crossing blocks. Each of the two hands is making circles

FIRE ELEMENT
In Chinese cosmology, one of the basic energies or elements from which all manifested phenomena are created.

HENG CHUAN/ CROSSING FIST
One of the five basic techniques of hsing-i chuan.

EARTH ELEMENT
In Chinese cosmology, one of the basic energies or elements from which all manifested phenomena are created.

in opposite directions. When Heng Chuan is incomplete, its form movement often resembles a karate block with the thumb side of the forearm.

In application, Heng Chuan is used to go around the body of opponents and strike them from the opposite side. For example, without your feet moving, your hand begins in front of the attacking man's right hip, but it strikes him on his left kidney as your waist turns. From an advanced hsing-i practitioner's perspective, the blocking, pulling hand of Heng Chuan is even more challenging than the attack hand, and eventually opens many internal connections, which enable the Animal Forms to reach their full adaptability. Often hsing-i masters can see just how far a practitioner has penetrated the hsing-i system by having them just do Heng Chuan. Although Heng Chuan is the most difficult of the Five Elements with which to generate full power, once mastered it gives the ability to enhance the capacity of all your other hsing-i techniques.

San Ti

At the very heart of the martial practice of hsing-i and its Five Elements is San Ti, or the "trinity posture." San Ti is done holding a static standing posture, with your arms in the air. In the classic schools of hsing-i, the posture is held in Pi Chuan, which is the first of the Five Elements. Of all hsing-i schools, I Chuan places the greatest emphasis on San Ti.

There is a common story about the best people in hsing-i that says they were made to do San Ti for between one and three years before being allowed to learn anything else. Many interpret this type of demand as a useless hazing process. However, this process of standing is the most foundational power training in hsing-i, and without it the training of the Five Elements and the Animal Forms could easily become nothing more than Shaolin-type movements with minimal internal power.

Without internal power, hsing-i loses its quite legitimate claim to martial arts fame, as its fighting applications depend on that power. Good classic hsing-i usually employs the method of first developing a reasonable level of internal power, then skillfully learning fighting applications for how to use that power, while simultaneously continuing to upgrade it. Most external martial arts focus first on being able to move well and then develop power. Hsing-i, in contrast, focuses on developing power first, and afterward learning to move well, including refining and implementing fighting angles. Hsing-i has a lesser number of movements than does tai chi or ba gua (or, for that matter, most systems of Shaolin), but concentrates on making each of its relatively limited techniques count.

What San Ti Teaches

Aside from martial aspects, San Ti teaches how to make the mind calm and how to free it of accumulated stress. The process that San Ti sets in motion for balance, health, and healing is expanded and fulfilled in the Five Element practices. The primary energetic function of the metal element Pi Chuan, for example, is to move energy in the lungs. In Pi Chuan, the spreading of the open palm and the extending of the fingers has the effect of opening up the lungs, which then brings plenty of oxygen to the rest of the body.

Each of the energies of all your internal organs ends in acupuncture meridian lines at the end of your fingers and toes. Thus, moving your chi strongly to the ends of your fingertips and toes correspondingly stimulates all your visceral organs energetically, thereby increasing your strength. Because of this activity, Pi Chuan is called "the Mother of the Five Elements," and is the well to which hsing-i practitioners always return to increase their internal power (as ba gua players do with the Single Palm Change).

The first of the Five Elements, Pi Chuan or Chopping Fist, can be looked at from different perspectives. In its moving aspect, for instance, it can be considered a complete fighting technique. In its final position, though, often held unmoving for long periods, it is referred to as San Ti or "holding Pi Chuan." In the I Chuan schools, however, San Ti is not one posture that is held, but eight different standing postures that form the core of the I Chuan system. San Ti focuses on cultivating five critical processes: (1) breath; (2) legs and waist; (3) arms; and unifying the connections within your self, both (4) externally and (5) internally.

Breath   Like hsing-i in general, San Ti uses a wide variety of breathing techniques. Breathing begins with regular Taoist breath training, which emphasizes breathing from the lower belly, sides, kidneys, upper back and spine. In regular Taoist breathing, the belly is expanded on the inhale and deflated on the exhale. Later, regular breath work is extended by application of mind intent to breath energy, which is guided in and out of specific parts of the body in progressively more powerful sequences. Each level of breath practice must be stabilized before moving on to the next. If it is not, a couple of steps down the line you will find that your ability to advance to the next level of internal power will be greatly impeded by the limitations your previous incompleted practices have fixed in your energy channels. Moving on to each new type of breathing requires the guidance of an experienced teacher who has been through the process, experienced its results, and can recognize the nuances of how internal energy is developing in your body.

The next stage involves learning the various levels of reverse breathing and spinal breathing, including coordinating the breath with movements inside the joints and spine, and the moving of internal organs in various multidirectional ways. The final stage of breath practice includes the feeling of losing all sense of physical breath, even though your breathing processes are very strong. You shift your awareness from moving air in and out of your system to fully relying on moving chi energy first inside and then outside your body, as the sense of physical breath drops away.

Legs and Waist   San Ti develops your ability to root your energy and create and/or strengthen balance in your legs. As the methods for dropping your chi to your lower tantien are learned, your body (regardless of its shape or weight) will seem to feel heavier and heavier to someone's touch. When the sinking of the chi and all the other grounding techniques are accomplished, your body progressively becomes exceedingly stable whether hit from the front, side, or back. Being strong and stable against a frontal attack usually comes first, then strength comes to the sides of the body and, finally—the most difficult to achieve—to the back. Part of what you learn involves a separate ability to transfer the power of an incoming blow or touch into the ground. Upon contact, instead of the strike hurting you, some, much, or all of its power is diverted down your body to dissipate into the ground.

As your leg and hip flexibility grows, you become able to raise and lower your stance effortlessly. The internal methods for developing power in the legs come next. Then, techniques are learned for joining your leg, waist, and spine into one inseparable whole, with no energetic gaps or physical weakness in their unified power.

Finally, your legs and waist are trained to turn horizontally and rotate like a smoothly oiled wheel, where the power of each amplifies the other. When the "oiling" is complete, your waist is able to turn extremely rapidly, to both the left and right, whether you are front- or back-weighted.

Arms   Once your legs and waist are stable and you have a foundation to stand on, the next phase is infusing both attack-oriented and defensive power into your arms, from the shoulders to the fingertips, with the initial focus being on the elbows, forearms, and hands. To train for this power, you first learn to relax your arms and lengthen all the soft tissues in your body from your spine to your arms. During this process, the bending of the elbows with relaxed strength is critical to ultimate success. Next, the chi flow from your spine to your fingertips must become continuous and without gaps. This flow must become powerful until the chi in your palms and fingertips becomes full and extremely tangible, bringing with it a strong blood flow. The stronger the blood flow to your fingers, the softer and more full your hand should feel.

The next stage focuses on bringing downward vertical power into the elbows. As this training progresses, your arms begin to become heavy, extremely alive, and responsive to external stimuli. After elbow strength increases and your arms become heavy, the focus shifts to developing the ability of your hand to absorb energy back to your spine. As this process occurs, you concentrate on perfecting the clawlike grip of hsing-i.

After all the above are accomplished, the intent shifts to making the skin on your arms become extremely sensitive to the subtleties of air pressure. This sensitivity acts as a precursor to being able to feel your opponent's arms and body in fighting applications. Finally, through various forms of mind intent, you learn to absorb and to project power from your hands using various internal techniques, such as openings and closings and twistings.

Unifying Your External Physical Connections   Another major goal of San Ti is to connect your physical body into a unified whole. Such unification allows the movement of any small part of your arms or legs to be fully backed up by the whole of your body, thereby amplifying the power of the small body parts significantly. Several methods are used to accomplish this goal. The first involves connecting up all your alignments through the interior of your body. These include how to adjust the various soft tissues, joints, and bones of the body so they interconnect and reinforce each other, thereby maximizing the ability of the body to both absorb and project power. These alignments are also equally used in the internal arts of tai chi and ba gua.

Hsing-i particularly focuses on the six external coordinations or combinations of the body called **liu he** in Chinese. These six are the shoulder and the hip, the elbow and the knee, and the hand and the foot. Most who read about or practice hsing-i think that these six combinations are gross anatomical connections. In fact, each little sub-part of the arm and leg connects with each other tiny sub-part of its corresponding leg or arm or part of the torso, as well as the corresponding forearms/calves, upper arms/thighs of the trainee. These body parts must join so finely, that as one moves a micro-inch, its corresponding part moves the same proportional micro-inch. Any pressure exerted on one place in the body is immediately countered and amplified by its correspondent.

Along with the internal alignments and the six combinations, hsing-i shares several liftings, sinkings, and roundings of the body with tai chi and ba gua. However, given the relatively linear orientation to movement in hsing-i, linearity is much more expressed in this martial art than in tai chi and ba gua, whose natures emphasize motion that is circular or spiraling.

Liftings of the body refer to these locations: the top of the thighs, the back of the knee, the midriff, spine, top of the forearms, and neck and crown of the head. Hsing-i raises the neck in a much more pronounced manner and with more obvious strength than tai chi or ba gua. These liftings are integral to developing the Ward Off power (see p. 127) of hsing-i. Sinkings of the body include shoulders to the hips, elbows to the knees, wrists to the ankles, hands to the feet, chest to the lower tantien, ribs to the hips, tailbone to the bubbling well point on the ball of the foot into the ground, and from the feet to the end of the etheric body below the feet.

LIU HE
Six combinations of body parts that must be finely coordinated to maximize physical power in the internal martial arts.

These sinkings are integral to developing the Push Downward power (see p. 135) of hsing-i. Roundings of the body include: the shoulders forward and backward, soft tissue from the spine to the front centerline of the body in both directions, the elbows toward the centerline of the body, the ribs toward the sternum, thighs and calves slightly inward, palms slightly forward, simultaneously the inside of the thumb and little finger toward each other, and the outside nails away from each other.

Using the Gaze to Unify Your Internal Connections   The next stage of San Ti involves unifying your mind with the gaze of your eyes and your awareness. The object here is to fuse your physical power, chi, mind and perceptions into one unified entity. This training is done by fixing your gaze on the index or middle finger of your lead hand. You can either look into the far distance or at any intermediate length up to thirty or forty feet away. As you gaze, inhale. On the inhale, with your intent, breathe in energy from beyond your index finger to and through your index finger—to your nose, throat, and down the central channel (see p. 317) to your lower tantien. On the exhale, you reverse the pathway of the breath. This practice brings several effects.

By developing your gaze in coordination with your breath, you learn to clear out the gaps in awareness that often happen when you look at an opponent or the battlefield upon which you fight. These gaps create the mental states that allow you to become distracted, hesitant, or be fooled by feints or sudden movements. Through this process, your gaze is linked to your breath. Gradually, this enables you to simultaneously feel your body's chi and the energy residing in your lower tantien. With the four qualities of breath-chi-feeling-seeing acting as a unified whole, wherever you look, your awareness and power will automatically follow.

This gazing practice also opens up and strengthens your peripheral vision. Eventually, with this practice, you will be able to look straight ahead at an opponent, with a completely relaxed and expressionless face, while your field of vision extends from the ground to well above your head, and as far to the side as is physically possible. This extension of peripheral vision is critical for fighting multiple opponents, where visual tension impedes your ability to instantaneously adjust to new tactical conditions emerging either from the environment or the actions of your opponents.

This gazing technique sensitizes the mind, making it alive and calm with a relaxed concentration, the same state that comes from doing the "tradak" candle-staring exercises in yoga. When practiced sufficiently, this technique leads to an expansion of the mind so that it can link directly to the central nervous system, allowing you to feel the chi of your body with great clarity.

After San Ti has done the first phase of its work, the serious student is ready to begin to learn the fighting techniques of hsing-i chuan. No matter how long anyone learns hsing-i, they should never leave San Ti.

Gazing

I experienced the results of the gazing method for the first time in 1974, practicing at Hung I Hsiang's school in Taipei, Taiwan. In those days, the training used to occur on the concrete floor of an elementary school gymnasium. I often showed up to practice San Ti barefoot for an hour before the class started, before anyone arrived, by the light of a lone light bulb.

One day while breathing through my index finger for more than half an hour, all my attention seemed to be involuntarily drawn to the space in front of me at which I had been gazing. The space began to change. Soon my sense of the room began to visually disappear. Shortly, my index finger, hand, and then even my body itself seemed to vanish, as my mind began to expand dramatically, feeling as if it had no boundaries, only an ever-increasing crystal clear awareness. Soon the inside of my body began to feel as if it had no substance. Then, this changed. While feeling completely empty of any sense of physicality, at the same time I experienced the inside of my body to be just a living energy that was directly connected to my hand and the space inside me. Next, everything became empty of any sensations of any kind, with my mind being totally comfortable and content to be where it was, without needing or desiring to do anything or go anywhere.

Suddenly, my mind returned to its normal awareness. After this experience, my body began to become aware of how effortlessly chi energy was moving through my body whenever I did San Ti, or any other hsing-i movement for that matter. A few years later, I related this incident to my **kundalini** meditation teacher in India and asked him what had happened. Did that experience have any relationship to meditation? He regarded me awhile, and then explained that this was an experience of the first stage of **samadhi** or transcendental absorption into the absolute, as described in tantra and yoga.

KUNDALINI
A meditation method of India that uses energy work to unravel the mysteries of human consciousness and "enlightenment."

SAMADHI
A meditative experience that is indicative of a specific stage of "enlightenment."

Courtesy of Caroline Frantzis

The hsing-i Dragon Form depicted here utilizes the basic Five Element technique of Chopping Fist. which is done both jumping in the air and squatting on the ground. Dragon is used extensively in the ground-fighting techniques of hsing-i.

The Animal Forms

There are twelve basic Animal Forms, although some hsing-i schools may use a few more or less. Often, the same animal form can have different names in different schools.* The Animal Forms are all generated from the Five Elements and give full variance to all physical possibilities inherent in the Five Elements. For example:

1. Punching or chopping with one hand could become a double punch or double palm strike in the Tiger and mythical Tai Bird forms.

2. Punches or palm strikes where both hands are normally in front of the body could be done with one hand to the side or back of the body, as in Swallow or Dragon.

3. The Pao Chuan punch, which is normally done from the back leg, is done on the forward leg, as in some Horse and Sparrow forms.

4. The basic chopping action of Pi Chuan is done jumping in Dragon.

The principles of the Five Elements are done with different stances and footwork.

For example:

1. Squatting stances in Snake.
2. Jumping in the air and spinning in Monkey.
3. The back heel off the floor in Eagle.
4. Dropping to the ground in Swallow and Dragon.
5. Standing on one leg with the other high in the air, as in some forms of Swallow or Crane.

In beginning hsing-i practice, everyone learns all the Animal Forms to increase and balance their knowledge of the Five Elements, to broaden

*The Animal Forms in hsing-i include, but are not limited to, Tiger, Horse, Bear, Monkey, Snake, Water Strider, Chicken, Ostrich, Hawk, Sparrow, Crane, Eagle, Dragon, Tai Bird, and Unicorn.

their repertoire of fighting techniques, and to be able to create physical movement from mental intention alone. The mind training is especially critical in the Animal Forms, both in terms of developing intent, overall fighting strategies, and a whole-body style of movement.

Although everyone first learns all the Animal Forms, a majority find the most profitable next stage of practice is to concentrate on a few that fit the practitioner, these forms being determined by body type or the natural mental or emotional temperament of the learner. These forms are then practiced until they become embedded in the nervous system of the practitioner.

More about the Five Elements and Animal Forms In basic hsing-i practice, all the hand techniques of the Five Elements are initially performed at one height, usually at the level of the head or mid-torso. Later, however, both in form movements and applications, all these hand techniques are equally done around the upper, middle, and lower part of your own or your opponent's body. All the movements of hsing-i, both the Five Element and animal techniques, have certain qualities in common.

All the techniques are oriented to the centerline of the body, both in attack and defense, and all utilize both regular and broken rhythm. In the regular-rhythm methods, body and hand movements continue with ever-quickening drumlike cadences, overwhelming the opponent, who cannot keep up the pace and is defeated. Regular rhythms are used mostly when an opponent is retreating.

Broken-rhythm methods, in contrast, are by far more commonly applied in hsing-i. Broken rhythm does not repeat the same pattern twice. Thus, the opponent is denied the ability to predict moves and consequently work out a reasonable defense using the expectation of what is supposed to happen in the next likely rhythm. If your opponent does not know what is coming next, in either attack or defense, you gain a strategic advantage. In hsing-i and, for that matter, all internal martial arts, the basic timing mechanism involves a practitioner's concentrating on the "silent" space between the beats of an

Courtesy of Caroline Frantzis

The basic Five Element technique of Heng Chuan or Crossing Fist.

opponent's movements and intent. It does not involve focusing on an opponent's defending and attacking rhythms themselves.

This important timing consideration is another reason why stillness of the mind is so prized by internal martial artists—stillness is the underlying precondition necessary to stealthily and effectively slip in between the beats. The broken-rhythm method in hsing-i requires the mind and central nervous system to wait a microsecond before moving to break the rhythm of the fighting interaction. Often, the internal martial artist will allow the opponent to attack first, in order to ascertain the proper fighting angle for counterattack. This requires great composure in the midst of combat, a quality that is developed in the practice of San Ti.

In the hsing-i form and fighting applications, your hands are kept fully alive with mind intent and awareness held equally in each. One hand never moves perfunctorily, never only to simply complete the biomechanics of the other hand or in an automatic recoiling action. Hand techniques rarely use snapping actions, where the hands whip out or snap back to their original position. Rather, each hand technique inexorably keeps moving forward inch by inch, invading your opponent's space.

In hsing-i, Pull Back techniques are used specifically to neutralize an incoming attack, to pull an opponent or to tear skin. Each arm posture is designed to be stable at each point along its trajectory, so that it is difficult or impossible for an opponent to move your arms if you do not want them moved. This quality is well known and utilized in hsing-i's five element technique of Beng Chuan, or Crushing Fist. This point of stability also allows you to hold your ground. Remaining fixed in space, you have the ability to physically move the arms of opponents to a desired location, to redirect incoming aggressive force, and to stop opponents dead in their tracks before they move in for an attack.

In all hsing-i hand form techniques, the hand physically begins from the vicinity of the lower tantien, employing strong twistings of the arm during each micro-inch of movement, and especially accelerating the twisting of the whole body at the point of impact. The hand then returns to where it started, after moving the feet anywhere from either a half-step to several steps. All the hand techniques are designed to deliver full power, either from a dead stop or from half an inch or less away from your opponent's body. In all the specialized hand techniques, the elbows are always significant as their power is used to dig into and diminish the power-generating capacity of the opponent (called "cutting the opponent's power" in hsing-i terminology). The power of your entire body is concentrated in your hands, the principle of which is the origin of the common phrase in hsing-i, "You kick your opponent with your hand." As a practitioner becomes more advanced, this ability extends to being able to focus the unified power of your whole body in the specific body part of your choice.

(Text continues on page 201.)

Monkey Boxing

 I first became introduced to Monkey in high school by an older boy from Hong Kong. I helped him pass his exams, and, offering to teach me this martial art, he beat the stuffing out of me using Monkey and Cantonese White Crane on the grass in Central Park. My initial experiences with Monkey allowed me to take to another level all the rolling, falling, and groundwork techniques of judo, jujitsu, and aikido, as well as the ground-fighting techniques of karate. Later, I continued my studies of Monkey at various times in Taiwan.

I vividly remember the Monkey boxers who were training on the grass one grey afternoon in a Taiwan park. My then-future teacher, a small, middle-aged man, in a full squatting position was jumping around on the ground, making noises like a chimpanzee, open hands in front of his face and making all kind of grimaces and coy eye movements. His opponent was standing there, intently staring at him, getting ready to kick him in the head. Just as he began his kick, the small man on the ground made eye contact with him, used a weird face to distract him, and during the resulting fraction-of-a-second gap in the kicker's attention, jumped forward toward him, went airborne, and did a flip. Head down, the small man grabbed his opponent's thighs and simultaneously kicked him in the head, stunning him. Immediately thereafter, the Monkey boxer used his kicking legs to throttle his opponent's neck. Squeezing his opponent's neck strongly, the Monkey boxer, a sardonic look on his face, bent his own knees, crunched his own stomach, and threw his opponent down by twisting his head. Both men landed with a crash, the Monkey man on top, with his hand poised to either tear out the groin of his prey or rip out the tendons of his legs.

Like all Shaolin martial arts, Monkey has both Southern and Northern branches. I was most involved in the Northern style, which encompasses some chi gung methods. Above and beyond Monkey being extremely functional, it was, from the point of view of the joy of movement, a lot of fun to learn and practice. Monkey is a paradoxical martial art, which on the one hand is extremely playful and on the other raises viciousness to a malevolent art form.

Its primary techniques of cruelty involve striking the eyes, throat, and groin, tearing one's opponent's arteries or nerves out with one's teeth or fingernails, pinpoint knuckle and elbow tip strikes and rakes, wrist strikes, and striking the joints, especially during groundwork. On its more playful

Monkey Boxing, continued

side, Monkey practitioners, in a constant flow, deceptively and smoothly roll on the ground, jump and rapidly change height levels from deep squatting on the ground to being fully upright to being airborne. Monkey methods involve continuously moving toward and away from an opponent in a peek-a-boo manner, making it difficult to get a bead on a Monkey boxer, who all the while uses emotional trickery and distracting facial expressions.

The arm techniques of Monkey are both the long-range ones of the lumbering gorilla with hands that hang below its knees, and of the close-in fighting type of the smaller monkeys. This martial art uses jumps and rolling on the ground equally, offensively to get from out of range into attacking position and defensively for evasion. Hitting and kicking are used moving either toward or away from the opponent. Monkey boxers also like to literally climb up the body of an opponent. After attaching themselves to your body or standing on your shoulders or upper back, Monkey practitioners will control your head, take you down to the ground, and very rapidly finish the job.

My experience of learning Monkey was most valuable in its constant reminder never to assume anything, which is the essential ingredient a Monkey practitioner relies upon to deceive an opponent. Learning Monkey made me aware of the science of how to efficiently apply bites and nail-cutting pinches and scratches to especially vulnerable body points. When doing internal martial arts, I subsequently paid attention to how I could defensively assume dangers that most people would ignore and not let my guard down. Monkey forced me to develop countermeasures for attacks from bites and skin-tearing nail actions, kept me motivated to keep up work in tai chi Push Hands, and made me think about how to adjust my movements in order to reduce my vulnerability during potentially nasty close-in fighting conditions. Being aware of how fluidly Monkey people can move in and out of range in all directions greatly helped expand my ideas and focus during training on the absolute need to be able to follow someone rapidly while using various techniques of tai chi or hsing-i.

Recognizing how easily a monkey opponent could drop low, or rapidly move up and down, provided a good background for developing ba gua's vertical actions. It also made me appreciate a tai chi technique like step and punch downward. This particular tai chi move can crush a Monkey boxer to the ground and help defend against other excellent martial ground fighters and grapplers, who want to pull you to the ground and finish you off there.

Monkey Boxing, continued

Ba gua also has moves to counter Monkey mischief. Ba gua's footwork and ability to change directions, for example, can nullify the extreme movement and deceptive capacities of Monkey boxers. Ba gua can simply change more quickly and in more directions. Knowing I would really need these abilities after practicing Monkey drove me to achieving them in ba gua. Monkey practice made me realize not to take for granted ba gua's vertical movement techniques and enhanced ability to change. I believe this line of thought motivated me to increase my competence in ba gua.

Monkey boxing also has within it great ground fighting techniques, which are defensive weapons for countering judo and wrestling groundwork. Monkey also provided an excellent background for my later study of Eight Drunken Immortals (see p.228).

All the hsing-i hand techniques are done with various types of footwork, from very fast to very slow, including:

1. *Worm-walking*. Here, the same foot is always kept in the forward position. As you move the forward foot, the other one moves to fill the exact place the forward foot occupied. Worm-walking is used in conjunction with steps done going forward, backward, sideways, and diagonally.

2. *Regular steps*. Here, the left foot and the right foot change their forward and backward position with each step. These steps may be done with legs either front- or back-weighted.

3. *Half-steps*. These are a type of worm walk, often used to rapidly advance into an opponent's position. There are many kinds of half-steps. In short half-steps the distance moved is only a few inches to no more than two feet. In longer half-steps, up to five or six feet or more can be covered with a single step. In both of these, one foot is always in contact with the floor.

4. *Skipping half-steps*. Here, the body covers up to ten feet with a single half-step, as the feet, during the skip, seem to kick each other extremely lightly, propelling the body very far into space.

5. *Flying half-steps*. In this move, the practitioner leaps into the air and comes down again a great distance away to follow an opponent who is either jumping in the air or attempting to run away. This technique is

used extensively with Beng Chuan, one of the Five Elements. (Hsing-i in general uses half-step techniques much more than regular stepping, as well as mixing both steps within a single technique.)

6. *Seven-star steps.* Here, the feet step in diagonals 45 degrees in relation to the opponent, either forward or backward.

7. *Backward steps.* Backward steps are done in such a way as to initiate a full-power, forward attack as your retreating foot touches the ground.

8. *Side-steps 90 degrees to your side.* Moving directly sideways may be done to either the inside or outside of an attacking opponent's body. You may go directly sideways either from where you stand, or after first going slightly forwards or backwards.

Hung I Hsiang—Amazing Subtle Body Movements

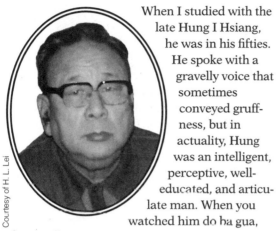

Courtesy of H. L. Lei

When I studied with the late Hung I Hsiang, he was in his fifties. He spoke with a gravelly voice that sometimes conveyed gruffness, but in actuality, Hung was an intelligent, perceptive, well-educated, and articulate man. When you watched him do ba gua, his small-movement precision was incredible.

The potential for misreading Hung based on interpretation of voicetone, raises an important point about ba gua people. I have met many over the years who practice ba gua for all sorts of animal, human, and spiritual reasons. Some have been saints, some sinners. The one thing in common about them was that they all tended to be people having exceptional innate intelligence, regardless of whether they had a formal education or not.

Hung had been in a lot of fights. In Taiwan, it was very easy to find a fight if you were so inclined. In the early and middle part of this century, all over the world men used to fight for the sheer joy of it. Such fights often took place in designated social places, such as bars. In Taipei, fights usually occurred near areas of prostitution. Very commonly, people were drinking in an underworld atmosphere and probably more often than not there were no hard feelings after a fight. Reputations were built, and rumors were spread: "So and so had such and such technique." It was also common for criminals,

military men, and law-abiding citizens to mix it up for fun, and for onlookers to make side bets on a fight, something that is also common today in saloons throughout the Western world. Hung was very well known, and his reputation led to many challenges. Those who challenged Hung suffered the consequences. He was a ferocious fighter who had the skill and the hard character that made many challengers regret their folly.

Hung was physically loose and flexible, and was very good at teaching minute martial arts movements and the technical skills of fighting. Hung's Rou Shou (see p. 235) was superb. He had an amazing ability to move. I had never before seen a person of his size who could undulate his body and move as if he had no bones. Hung had developed the Dragon Body* to the greatest extent possible. He could make his body twist, turn, and fold in ways that had to be seen to be believed. In addition, his hands were incredibly sensitive. He could feel minute shifts of a person's energy and counterattack instantaneously. It was as if his hands had eyes.

Hung's specialty was in the use of very tiny fighting angles based on the triangle, the square, and the octagon. Whereas most sophisticated martial artists use these angles, they usually need inches or feet to apply them. Hung, however, could apply these angles in less than a fraction of an inch of space. He loved analyzing the use of small circles and angles of attack. He was a truly creative martial artist who explored and extrapolated the knowledge he had gained. After three or four hours of class, Hung and his

---

*In the Dragon Body, the top, middle, and bottom part of the torso can move in different directions while simultaneously remaining completely connected internally.

Hung I Hsiang—Amazing Subtle Body Movements, continued

more committed students would drink tea, eat watermelon seeds, and talk about ba gua and fighting angles at open-air tables set up on the sidewalk near our practice hall. Hung's understanding and use of small circles and angles of attack made sparring with him fascinating, bewildering, terrifying, and a pure joy.

Hung was an excellent teacher of technical fighting applications. He always told me "I cannot teach you how to develop chi, but I can teach you how to use it." Hung always emphasized separating the different qualities of the martial arts. All too often people who study different martial arts do them all with the same quality of internal movement and chi.

Hung would constantly reinforce the thought that hsing-i, ba gua, and tai chi were very different. When I was initially with Hung during 1974 and 1975, this thought of difference in the internal arts was very difficult for me to grasp, as all this internal "stuff" was simply "different" from karate and Shaolin. Internal to me at the intermediate stage of learning hsing-i and ba gua meant soft, yet Hung's power was harder and stronger than any karate or Shaolin I had ever experienced. He was soft, and yet not as soft as tai chi masters I had met and studied with. Yet Hung was just as sensitive and able to react effectively in an instant, in just as mysterious a manner as the best tai chi people I had studied with, including Yang Shou Jung (Yang Cheng Fu's eldest son). Hung's hsing-i and ba gua were clearly better than his tai chi. The tai chi style practiced by both Wang Shu Jin and Hung I Hsiang was a tai chi/hsing-i/ba gua combination style developed by Chen Pan Ling, which also combined the essential elements of the Yang, Wu, and Chen styles of tai chi chuan.*

This was now further complicated by the fact that the hsing-i taught by Hung was a Hebei combination style, with hsing-i movements but ba gua dragon body motions and spiraling hand work. The internal quality of Hung's ba gua was only minutely different from his hsing-i, although it was much more undulating. All of this derived from the fact that his hsing-i and ba gua were fused together. Separating the nature of the internal movements from each other was most difficult. Even more so was clearly separating the different types of chi involved. This was very confusing, as Hung was constantly emphasizing to me and all his Chinese students that we had to clearly separate Shaolin and each of the three different internal martial arts. They were to be done clearly and separately, so that the unique qualities of each could be distinctly differentiated. It was only later, first through Bai Hua and later Liu Hung Chieh, that I was to clearly attain this ability to separate the different types of chi, which Hung expended much effort to drive home, but which was beyond my reach in those early days.

---

*Editor's note: The author also practiced and researched the Chen Pan Ling tai chi chuan form, which is composed of nine distinct levels of achievement. This research began in Tokyo in 1968 with Wang Shu Jin's student Chang I Chung and continued through 1987 with Wang, Hung I Hsiang, and Huang Hsi I, and with other students of Chen Pan Ling in Taichung, Taiwan, as well as with teachers in Mainland China. To complete this research and comprehend the roots of this style required an in-depth study of the Chen Village form of tai chi, which the author conducted with Feng Zhi Qiang in Beijing, the Wu style of tai chi with Liu Hung Chieh, and the Yang style with T. T. Liang, Yang Shou Jung, Bai Hua, and Lin Du Ying.

Hung I Hsiang—Amazing Subtle Body Movements, continued

In the 1970s, Hung I Hsiang had about a dozen exceptionally talented students. Many of his students dominated the full contact tournaments in Taiwan. One named Weng Hsien Ming, won the Taiwan full contact championships three times in a row when he was in his teens. He then went into the army and didn't practice at all for over three years. After returning to civilian life, he was able to train for only a few weeks and still capture second place. Another of Hung's students, Huang Hsi I, also usually won his all-Taiwan full contact tournaments with knockouts. Huang subsequently became one of the best chi gung tui na doctors in Taiwan. The youngest student was Lo Te Hsiu, known for his heel kick to the solar plexus. Over time, Lo researched and became highly skilled at Hung's complete post-birth ba gua system.

Hung I Hsiang's emphasis was not so much on maximizing internal power and chi development. Instead, he focused on the subtleties of how to effectively deliver the power one had and how to rapidly and smoothly change from one technique to another. He did this by showing how to make tiny circles deep within every crevice of the body and how to change internal body alignments with great speed. He spent a lot of time showing how tiny shifts in body weight could create unusual power vectors. He also made students feel this power not only in terms of strikes, but also by showing how changes in subtle body movements could achieve desired defense/attack application outcomes. He taught his students how to instantaneously release themselves from bad internal alignments that could normally paralyze the body, and resume their attack, much like you smoothly change gears in a stick shift car. Hung's emphasis was on how small changes of body movement or chi flow could produce superior practical fighting techniques and overall athletic capacity.

A ba gua fighting application. Liu Hung Chieh (right) defends against
both high and low attacks from his disciple, B. K. Frantzis. After controlling
both the hands of his opponent, Liu is in position to deliver a palm strike.

BA GUA

6

Fighting Considerations and Applications

BA GUA CHANG AS A MARTIAL ART

Many scholarly martial artists in the West have some familiarity with the three major internal martial arts of China—tai chi chuan, hsing-i, and ba gua chang. Of these three, tai chi chuan is by far the most widely known in the Western world, and ba gua chang probably the least. However, in Europe and particularly in the United States, there is a growing awareness of ba gua chang as a vigorous alternative to tai chi chuan.

Ba gua chang, often shortened to ba gua, or "eight trigram palm," is a unique Taoist art based on the ancient Chinese classic text, the *I Ching*, or Book of Changes. The fluid, circular art of ba gua places the same degree of emphasis on longevity, internal energy development, healing, and meditation as does tai chi chuan. Consequently, knowledge of ba gua is extremely valuable to all students of tai chi chuan and to those interested in practical ways of cultivating and using personal chi. Ba gua, though, is seen as being more effective in self-defense, specifically against multiple opponents.

Any comprehensive explanation of the fascinating and complex art of ba gua would require many lengthy volumes. This chapter serves only to give a brief introduction to this remarkable Taoist chi practice, conveying a flavor of its development and interconnected components. (For a brief history of ba gua, see Appendix B, p. 308.)

BA GUA'S CLOUDY ORIGINS

The Mysterious Tung Hai Chuan

The actual origin of ba gua is obscure, and Mainland China abounds with all sorts of popular histories of this complex martial art. There are claims that ba gua originated in this place or that place, but none of these accounts has been sufficiently substantiated to be considered fact. The author's ba gua teacher, Liu Hung Chieh (1905–1986) studied with a man named Ma Shr Ching (also known as Ma Gui), who lived and studied with Tung Hai Chuan (1798-1879), the man who brought ba gua chang out of complete obscurity. Tung would never say where his art came from. Near the end of his life, he lived in Ma's house, and in all of the many conversations that the two men had, Ma tried but could never persuade Tung to reveal the origins of ba gua. Other ba gua elders, who had known original members of the ba gua school, confirmed reports of Tung's staunch silence on this matter.

Given the circular nature of ba gua, it is most fitting that Tung gave circuitous responses to pointed questions about its origins, such as:

Question: Where did you learn it?
Answer: I learned it in the mountains.
Q: Who did you learn it from?
A: I learned it from a Taoist.
Q: What was his name?
A: He was a very old man.
Q: Where did he come from?
A: He lived in the mountains.

Tung Hai Chuan's own background is almost as cloudy as that of ba gua itself. It is known that he had studied many martial arts in his youth. However, there are many contradictory accounts about his activities during the period between his youth and his arrival in Beijing. Some stories have described him as having been either a bandit, a murderer, a thief, a eunuch, or a pimp, while other tales depict him as having been a much more benevolent individual. Whatever his character, prior to his arrival in Beijing, he was apparently injured badly. Tung is supposed to have met a Taoist who helped him recover and proceeded to teach him ba gua. However, all that anyone seems to know for certain is that he appeared on the scene in Beijing, gained fame for his fighting ability, and passed on his ba gua to a relatively small number of students, seventy-two of whom are officially listed on his tombstone.

THE UNIQUE MARTIAL ART QUALITIES OF BA GUA

Many legends tell of the effectiveness of ba gua chang as a fighting art. These legends include the numerous martial exploits of Tung Hai Chuan and his students. Despite Tung's vagueness regarding the origins of his ba gua chang, the art quickly gained a reputation throughout China for great martial effectiveness. One indication of this effectiveness is found in the fact that when the Dowager Empress Tzu Hsi fled Beijing after the collapse of China's Boxer Rebellion in 1908, she was protected by a single bodyguard—Tung's senior disciple, Yin Fu.

There is virtually no other martial art system or style, internal or external, that has combined and seamlessly integrated the whole pantheon of martial art fighting techniques in one package as effectively as ba gua. In ba gua, you can hit a person with an open hand, a fist, or a push. You can hit with your hand, your head, your shoulder, or any other part of your body. You can punch straight ahead, in a round fashion, or from every conceivable angle. You can also throw individuals without grabbing their bodies by tripping them through careful placement of your foot or by breaking their balance while controlling their arms or hands. You can use foot sweeps and leg cuts. In addition, you can lift an attacking man over your head and throw him on his back or on his face or his head. There are also chokes and joint-locks or chin na techniques as well as grabbing techniques in which you seize your attacker's skin and try to rip it off his body. Ba gua also has a range of kicks both high and low, knee butts, and stomping techniques, and a full arsenal of traditional weapons.

Fighting Eight Opponents Simultaneously

Ba gua was designed to fight up to eight opponents at once. This design is based on the inability of more than eight people to attack one person simultaneously without getting in each other's way (unless armed with long spears). When facing multiple opponents, the ba gua fighter flows through the group of attackers, constantly twisting, turning, and changing direction. From a defensive point of view, this minimizes the need to block attacks, since you are a continuously moving target that is no longer at the original location when the blow arrives. Never remaining in one spot for more than a fraction of a second, the ba gua chang fighter intends to disable, or at least bypass, one opponent and continue on to the next before the first attacker is replaced. This efficiency can only be achieved through deception and exploitation of angles of attack that most other martial arts do not utilize.

As a ba gua practitioner dealing with multiple attackers, your concentration on a single person should only be momentary as your focus immediately shifts to the next. This avoids being hit from behind, which easily happens if you spend more than an instant dealing with one member of the group. Thus, even when facing a single opponent, your perspective should always be toward multiple opponents.

The training for fighting multiple opponents simultaneously starts with the practitioner facing a single person. Then, as training progresses, opponents are added one at a time. To develop fighting prowess, ba gua people consider it necessary to practice fighting applications with real human beings, who are basically unpredictable during fighting. However, solo form work and Walking the Circle is the foundation of the training and the source of your energy, body coordination, and the freeing of your spirit to move spontaneously and to respond to attacks.

The movements practiced in the ba gua forms are the exact ones applied in combat. Many martial arts have hundreds of moves, but when it comes down to empty-hand fighting, they usually use only a couple, with the rest only serving to develop physical coordination. Every movement in ba gua has practical and usable fighting applications. In the traditional schools of ba gua, a wide range of applications is taught to people to make their body/minds more agile and adaptable to unexpected martial changes, rather than only to accumulate an inventory of specific techniques to respond to specific defenses or attacks.

PRE- AND POST-BIRTH CHI

In ba gua, the cultivation of energy and the fighting applications are based on two distinctively different practice methods. The first method taught by Tung Hai Chuan involves Circle-Walking techniques exclusively, and is referred to as the **pre-birth method** (or **hsien tien** in Chinese). The pre-birth circle methods can, depending on the teacher, be taught purely as an energetic movement art for health and meditation or in conjunction with ba gua fighting applications.

PRE-BIRTH/HSIEN TIEN
That which happens to a human between conception and the time they are born.

POST-BIRTH/HOU TIEN
That which happens to a person after they leave the womb. Talents and skills not inherent but acquired after birth.

The second method, called the **post-birth method** (or **hou tien** in Chinese), emphasizes ba gua's fighting applications, not its health and meditation aspects. The post-birth method is done in straight lines rather than by Walking a Circle. In these methods, created by Tung's students, each trigram of the *I Ching* is represented by eight sections of overt martial movements (with applications) categorized by fighting techniques, such as palms, fists, kicks, throws, joint-locks, etc. Each movement includes within it both specific fighting techniques and generalized tactical principles that must be creatively applied, often using different physical weapons (palms, kicks, and so on) from the form movement.

Ba gua is unique in that its most fundamental energy cultivation practices, derived from nei gung, are all incorporated into its pre-birth Circle-Walking, the use of which is not found in other martial arts. The Taoists believe that the way a human being is energized while in the womb (the pre-birth stage) differs from the way energy is received after one enters the world (post-birth stage). After birth, humans energize through exercising, breathing, eating food, and resting. In the womb, however, it is the cosmic forces, according to the Taoists, that charge the developing fetus much like a storage battery. A good deal of the charge received before birth will be used up in later life, and the amount of energy stored in the "battery" will determine a human being's general constitution and lifespan.

Pre-birth chi practices (including ba gua) attempt to reconnect with the original cosmic forces, charging the "battery" just like it was charged while in the womb, which may well upgrade a person's fundamental constitution. Post-birth chi practices are basically limited to optimizing what remains of a person's original pre-birth chi.

The simple act of Walking the Circle creates a vortex that allows the practitioner to amplify, mix, and control the natural energies that keep coming up from the earth and down from above. The twisting actions of ba gua create spirals of these energies according to the will of the practitioner. Also, these spiraling energies can involuntarily move the practitioner's chi and body. In later stages of practice, you are able to create energetic vortices that spiral up toward the sky and down toward the ground simultaneously. These energy flows are also used to create extremely powerful fighting applications.

Martial Training Philosophies of Ba Gua's Pre-Birth and Post-Birth Methods

In traditional tai chi and hsing-i schools, new students are first taught—without variation—the chi gung warm-up exercises and/or the movements of "the form." The tradition established by Tung Hai Chuan was not based on any one particular form. Ba gua students were taught the aspect of the art that suited their needs and individual interest. If they were studying ba gua for their health, they were taught the specifics of how to make their bodies extremely healthy and strong. If they were learning ba gua for fighting or meditation, the focus of instruction was in these areas. The position of the ba gua school and the Taoist martial arts in general is that a martial art must, first and foremost, be good for your body and for your mental and emotional well-being. Only when your body and character have become strong can you truly learn how to use the art for fighting, and fighting ability always remains a secondary, though very important consideration. Ba gua people believe that martial artists must be heroes, not cowards, and that this heroism must come from genuine internal centering, confidence, and skill rather than from bravado, raw physical talent, a violent mind, or a mere idea of the art.

Ba gua's initial goal is to open the body and thereby create health and strength. Continuing this, ba gua's intermediate and advanced levels progress to focusing either on its martial, therapeutic, or spiritual aspects. Tung taught different students different aspects of the art in different ways. Since Tung taught mostly in private one-on-one sessions or in small groups of three or four, he could tailor his instruction to the individual. He taught most of his students only the fighting applications of ba gua, leaving open the possibility of eventually teaching them the spiritual aspects as well. Others, he taught spiritual aspects as a way to access the power needed for martial purposes. Tung accepted experienced martial artists from a variety of backgrounds as his students. His instruction followed the path of least resistance for that particular student based upon the specifics of the student's previous background and experience.

Pre-Birth Training

Ba gua traditional Circle-Walking generally works on changing the inside of the body to create effects on the outside (that is, your external movements and applications). The pre-birth martial method, with its small number of external movements and large amount of internal content, could prove challenging for many in the West who want to learn ba gua. Our computerized culture creates an incessant drive for more information in less time. True knowledge or wisdom is not so much in demand. However, in terms of gaining benefits, information without wisdom is useless. Given our hectic pace, which usually leaves people with less than optimum time to practice, it is probably wiser and more satisfying to practice fewer movements in more depth to obtain maximum personal results.

Throughout history, most of the best ba gua fighters used only a small number of fighting techniques, done with such power and skill that no more was needed. In pre-birth ba gua, students are first taught the internal components through the Single Palm Change. Later, they are taught how to expand those components to direct and power other physical movements. At the initial training level, the hsing, meaning the forms or movements, come from Walking the Circle. Students typically would Walk the Circle over a period of one to several years. They would progressively add more and more internal nei gung elements while they opened up the energy channels of the body with specific static arm postures and the Single Palm Change. As each internal component stabilized, they then found that any applications they knew became imbued with power.

Through this process, the body becomes very strong. The student can start to realize how the energy that is inside connects to the energy that is outside: how the yin and yang energies inside the body equate to the sun and moon in the heavens, how the microcosm and the macrocosm interconnect. Once this foundation has been carefully laid, the student can next begin to learn the movements of the **Eight Mother Palms (ba mu chang)**, which, when done using the eight energies of the *I Ching*, are called the **Eight Inner Palms,** or **nei ba chang**.

Post-Birth Training

The alternative method was to learn post-birth ba gua. This method works from the outside to the inside and involves learning a tremendous number of outer movement forms, each with a few specific fighting applications. After years of this, when students are proficient at the outer forms, they

**EIGHT MOTHER PALMS/
BA MU CHANG**

The eight basic palm changes or movement patterns of ba gua chang.

**EIGHT INNER PALMS/
NEI BA CHANG**

Basic ba gua movement patterns that enable one to experience and ultimately embody the energies of the eight trigrams of the *I Ching*. (See p. 221 for Eight Outer Palms.)

would learn the internal power training. These post-birth linear ba gua methods do not use pre-birth circular walking as their primary solo practice. Instead, practitioners perform techniques and step in straight or zigzag walking patterns, in a manner similar to the Seven-Star walking pattern of hsing-i (see p. 202). After these post-birth methods are learned, the pre-birth Circle-Walking methods are incorporated into the system.

In general, the post-birth method was not related to the meditation practices of ba gua. A post-birth method of teaching large numbers of movements was first used to instruct army troops by Yin Fu and his students (see p.308). These simple and very effective straight-line techniques were easier to teach soldiers than the more complex Circle-Walking methods. A post-birth method later passed from Gao I Sheng's students in Tianjin to students in Hong Kong and Taiwan, including Hung I Hsiang. Cheng Ting Hua also had a 64-change method done while circling that is distinguished by specific fighting applications and throwing techniques.

Without the primary pre-birth power training, there is always the potential for ba gua to descend to a level where practitioners do external ba gua movements (hsing or form) well enough, but without sufficient power that is real, flexible, and fluid. The pre-birth method was used to train disciples in the most internal aspects of ba gua; however, ba gua's founder, Tung Hai Chuan, used both methods. If students had an external martial arts background with a tremendous number of movements, forms or hsing, he would teach them the outer forms first. Then, over time, Tung would add the internal power training to the skills already possessed to make the movements of his students come alive. If another student already had a good foundation of internal power, Tung would usually teach the power training first and fighting techniques next.* However, whatever way ba gua was taught, the internal power training remained primary and the applications secondary.

The core Circle-Walking pre-birth method develops a capacity for optimal chi generation and meditation. For the general population, this is where ba gua's most beneficial health and healing value is to be found. For martial artists, the chi generated by the pre-birth method provides significant internal energy that empowers techniques that may previously have been empty and functionless. Knowing the martial or healing applications of any ba gua movement is somewhat useless unless you have the power to make an application work on demand. Technique alone cannot

---

Editor's note: This training method was initially taught to the author by Wang Shu Jin and completed by Liu Hung Chieh. What the author's previous teachers (Hung I Hsiang, Huang Hsi I, and Bai Hua) had already taught him created a sufficient base of internal power, as well as post-birth fighting and healing techniques. Thus, Liu's primary objective was to teach the author the energetic pre-birth practices whose power created the applications and movements in the first place.

(Text continues on page 216.)

| PROFILE OF AN INTERNAL MASTER

Bai Hua—Clarity and Precision

Courtesy of Bai Hua

Bai Hua, a student of Liu Hung Chieh, was Beijing-educated. I met Bai Hua in Hong Kong and was lucky that he was an extremely articulate Mandarin speaker, because I spoke only Mandarin, the national language of China, and not Cantonese, the main language of Hong Kong. I shared an apartment with Bai Hua for a time, and he had as strong an influence on me as did Huang Hsi I (see p. 293), especially in terms of lengthening body tissue and opening and closing the joints and body cavities. Bai Hua's method of teaching was to focus on the most critical information. His emphasis was on creating chi and yang internal power. A former Red Guard general when he was a teenager, his martial approach was based on creating techniques that only required one or at the most two hits to completely incapacitate someone. Bai Hua also studied with other teachers besides Liu Hung Chieh.

Bai Hua began learning chi gung when he was six years old to cure himself of a case of severe hepatitis. He was sent to a village in the countryside that was so poor there were no herbs or acupuncture needles, so the local Chinese doctor taught him chi gung to survive. From that time, until he was thirteen and met Liu, he had learned chi gung, Northern Shaolin, and Eight Drunken Immortals boxing (an internal/external form of martial arts).

Bai Hua used to talk about the massive street fights in Beijing between the left- and right-wing Red Guard factions. There, he witnessed young Red Guard ba gua practitioners lifting and throwing their rivals on their heads, killing them. Over time, these battles escalated to the use of swords and spears. It was in these large-scale fights that Bai Hua gained his deep respect for ba gua as a martial art of the highest order, especially against multiple opponents in life-and-death battles.

Bai Hua's clarity about internal chi and his mastery of the movement of physical tissue below the skin was as astounding as it was precise. Everything Bai Hua did was purely Taoist with no Buddhist overtones. He emphasized the **fire method** of Taoism (which Liu taught him, as opposed to the **water method**, which Liu taught me), and was highly trained in inner **alchemy**. His knowledge of the Hua Shan chi gung tradition and the old Yang style of tai chi chuan he learned from Lin Du Ying was invaluable to me in my attempt to comprehend the fundamentals of chi gung.

Bai Hua stressed the chi chu dzuo practices (see p. 75). Like Huang Hsi I and Liu Hung Chieh, he emphasized personal practice above all else. Without both Huang Hsi I and Bai Hua, I would not have had the background or *gung fu* to have been qualified to study with Liu Hung Chieh, and would not have been able to comprehend Liu's work and transmissions.

How Bai Hua Taught

Bai Hua was a student of classical Taoism, in particular the *I Ching*. He saw all the chi processes of tai chi and ba gua as being nothing more than practical applications of the *I Ching*. Therefore he would be concerned with what one's goal was, what conditions were necessary

Bai Hua—Clarity and Precision, continued

to fulfill that goal, what specific techniques would be required to efficiently accomplish the goal, and what reinforced or negated that goal. He explained the framework of any problem in terms of the *I Ching* and the various Chinese classics, including the *Tai Chi Classics*. His way of teaching was to first have a student clearly understand the philosophical principles and theories. He would then focus on how to consciously turn the theories into practical applications for internal body movement (that is, the movement of chi inside the body and the specific mind states that would produce the required flow of chi). Bai Hua emphasized large power movements in the manner of Wang Shu Jin, rather than small movements and changes like Hung I Hsiang and Huang Hsi I.

In June of 1981, I visited Bai Hua in Hong Kong on the way to my first study trip to Beijing, where I had been invited to study tai chi at China's main Institute of Physical Educa-

tion.* I asked Bai Hua if I could train with his teacher while I was there. Bai Hua said he hoped that I could. He told me that Liu Hung Chieh was a recluse in the middle of the city and did not teach people very often. He then added that it was totally unpredictable whether or not Liu would teach me, even if he, Bai Hua, asked, as Liu kept his own counsel and often refused to teach people, even some very famous martial artists in China who had sought him out. Bai then proceeded to write me a formal letter of introduction. As I later learned, shortly before my arrival at his home, Liu had had a dream about teaching a foreigner, who fit my description, and consequently agreed to take me on as a student.

Editor's note: At the end of this training, the author became the first Westerner to be certified in the complete simplified tai chi system, including form, Push Hands, and weapons.

create spontaneous, powerful applications for strange situations that cannot be anticipated or preconceived. The more advanced training of the pre-birth method focuses on tapping into the matrix of the *I Ching* to manifest spontaneously arising chi. This enables the practitioner to better handle the totally unpredictable and to slowly grow the spirit of wu wei ("doing without doing"), which is the essence of all Taoist mind/body/spirit practices.

BA GUA TRAINING

The Stages of Circle-Walking

Ba gua's defining characteristic is its core training method of Walking the Circle. This holds equally true for its martial, energetic, and meditation aspects. During Circle-Walking practices, an individual walks around and around in a circle, regularly alternating direction between clockwise and counterclockwise and using various kinds of regular and specialized steps while simultaneously executing spiraling arm and waist movements.

Circle-Walking consists of several stages, each of which progressively builds upon the one before. The first is Walking the Circle while holding the arms in static postures, which, like the standing postures in I Chuan (see p. 181), is a method of basic power training. The second stage of

Courtesy of Caroline Frantzis

A lone practitioner Walking the Circle in a Beijing park wears a circular track in the winter snow.

Circle-Walking is based on a meditation method that existed within Taoist monasteries thousands of years ago: the Single Palm Change, which represents the first trigram of the *I Ching*, known as "heaven" (or *chien* in Chinese). It signifies the essence of yang energy, and is the prime chi power generation method of ba gua, focusing as it does on using power in one palm at a time.

The third stage consists of the **Double Palm Change,** which represents the second trigram of the *I Ching*, known as "earth" (or kun in Chinese). It signifies the essence of yin energy, and is the prime yin or soft power generation method of ba gua. It focuses on using the two palms together, coordinating them until they are as one and are able to move and change the quality of energy between them with fluidity and power. The fourth stage involves the basic Eight Mother Palms, where each palm represents the energy, characteristics, strategies and subtle qualities of each of the eight trigrams of the *I Ching*. In some ba gua systems, rather than the focus being on the energies of the *I Ching* itself, it is on the qualities of the animals associated with each of the trigrams. The fifth stage of Circle-Walking expands the repertoire to 64 techniques or hands, where each palm change attempts to represent the multitude of the qualities of the *I Ching*'s 64 hexagrams.

The Double Palm Change of ba gua.

Courtesy of Caroline Frantzis

Characteristics of Circle-Walking Although the essence of ba gua chang is moving meditation and energy cultivation, the initial training does not involve such esoteric considerations. Instead, ba gua's Circle-Walking methods first emphasize physical mechanics. The practitioner walks around a circle that is typically 6 to 12 feet in diameter, although many advocate that beginners use a circle that is 8 or 12 steps around in circumference. This walking is done with three primary steps: (1) a straight step that proceeds directly forward; (2) a toe-in step that propels and curves your leg and foot in toward your spine and moves your outside foot toward the center of the circle; (3) a toe-out step that propels you away from the center of the circle. (Other steps include backwards, sideways, spinning, jumping, zigzag, skipping, cross-steps, and half-steps.) If the walking is

DOUBLE PALM CHANGE
A movement that is the basis of all the yin, soft, or amorphous techniques of ba gua chang.

properly performed, the body will naturally open its internal energy channels, becoming healthy and strong.

As both a martial art and an exercise art, ba gua is known in China for its reliance on footwork. It is not uncommon for ba gua people to do 270-degree turns, while one foot is firmly planted on the ground and the other (the toe-out foot) opens around. These kind of steps can only be accomplished if the hips and the rest of the body have become open and relaxed after long practice, and the twisting motion of the body's deepest muscles is very strong.

Ba gua's palm changes are not normally practiced in slow motion. This is in direct contrast to the primary method of moving in slow motion in the solo forms of tai chi. Although the initial practices are done at a slow walk, the walking speed progresses over one to two years to the equivalent of the pace of modern speed walking, with lightning fast waist and arm movements, spins and constant changes of direction. The initial slow practice speed is done not because it is mandatory as in tai chi, but in order to stabilize ba gua's many indispensable technical requirements. The fundamental principles of ba gua must be integrated into the body. In ba gua's initial period of practice, it is virtually impossible to walk quickly without violating some or all of these principles. One of the most important involves the twisting of the body, particularly the legs and waist.

In ba gua, the body is constantly twisting and turning. No action in ba gua is done in a totally straight line, even in the relatively linear practice methods. Even a seemingly straight-line technique will be found, upon close visual analysis, to have a very slight curve. One of the unique things about this art is that many of its movements are completely spherical. The total flexibility of the body is critical in ba gua and, indeed, ba gua builds the most connected body flexibility of all the martial arts.

In addition to the twisting of the body and the smoothness with which it can flow in ba gua, there are many specific physical principles that must be followed when one is doing even the most basic practice of Walking the Circle, including the principle governing body alignments, which has these attributes: (a) the weight is sunk into the legs, (b) the spine and head are upright, lifted and very slightly bowed, (c) the entire body is relaxed but coiled toward the center of the circle, (d) the tailbone faces forward, and (e) both arms can either move in coordination with each other or simultaneously perform actions completely independent from each other.

The Physical Qualities of Circle-Walking

To repeat, the initial focus of ba gua training is on making the body healthy, flexible, and strong. This is the most immediate benefit that beginners derive from their ba gua practice. Many people in China practice ba gua for this reason only and are quite satisfied with the results. However, ba gua is not initially recommended for those with any kind of back or joint injuries. Ba gua walking, when practiced fast in a vigorous training program, puts a strain on the back and knees. Although this strain can easily be handled by an uninjured body, it may aggravate old injuries. It is best to heal any back or joint injuries first through practicing chi gung or tai chi. After such conditions have been alleviated, it may then be possible to begin ba gua practice.

Leaving aside for the moment the issue of chi (which is of absolute importance in ba gua), the continuous lengthening of soft tissue, opening and closing of joints and body cavities, and twisting of the muscles, fascia, and ligaments that this art requires is what makes the body physically strong. The movements of ba gua are extremely demanding on the body. To an untrained observer, it may appear as if a person is just walking senselessly in a circle, yet the body's twisting and turning while one is performing Walking the Circle invisibly puts massaging pressure on the internal organs and on the skeletal-muscular system.

Circle-Walking by itself will achieve the opening and strengthening of the lower body. To continue the process into the opening and strengthening of the torso and arms, dozens of specific extended arm postures have been developed for the upper body. These are performed while Walking the Circle. They are specifically designed to open the tissues and joints of the upper back, neck, chest, and arms to balance the body physically and energetically. The opening of the whole body happens gradually over weeks, months, and years of Walking the Circle. As the body stretches and strengthens, and more energy starts to circulate, the body progressively becomes more vigorous, as well as more relaxed.

The Energetic Qualities of Circle-Walking

Ba gua is first and foremost an art of internal energy movement. As mentioned, the basic internal power training of ba gua consists of eight palm changes. At ba gua's more advanced levels, each of the palm changes directly uses in fighting the inherent energy present in each of the trigrams or hexagrams of the *I Ching*. When initially entering this more refined level of practice, the movements might take on distinct internal power qualities. They might, for example, take on lightness or piercing for the trigram representing heaven, or heaviness, downward-smothering, or amorphousness for the trigram representing earth, or sudden abrupt shocks, vibrations, vortices, sucking in and spinning out, and so on, for other trigrams. Over the course of many years, the eight palm changes are integrated into Circle-Walking. These enable you to acquire self-defense techniques, to further strengthen and open the lower body, and to become aware of the eight primary energies of the *I Ching*. According to Taoist belief, the eight energies that correspond to the Eight Bodies of Man are:

the physical body, etheric/chi body, emotional body, mental body, psychic energy body, causal body, body of individuality, and body of the Tao. Each of these has a different energetic level of vibration.

In keeping with the *I Ching*, ba gua continuously combines and transforms the eight primary energies. In the beginning of training, metaphors that point toward the eight energies are translated into body and chi movement. The purpose of this early stage of training is to have the body become coordinated, the mind to become still, and the Taoist meditation state of "no mind" (wu wei) to appear.

THE ENERGIES OF THE *I CHING* — THE BEGINNING OF ADVANCED BA GUA

Once you are able to follow the fundamental principles while walking slowly, you are then able to start Walking the Circle at moderate and then fast speeds, incorporating spinning and arm movements with constant changes of direction. Over time, the rapid walking of the circle and the palm changes evolve into a swirling tornado with extremely rapid spiraling of the body and instantaneous changes of direction.

Once you have reached the "no-mind" state, your consciousness and then your body begin to glimpse, experience, and integrate into your being, one by one, the actual living reality of the eight energies. This understanding of the eight energies is experiential and impossible to portray accurately in words. Direct mind-to-mind transmissions are essential to teaching the process. Although the classic Taoist metaphors are pleasing to the intellect, the realities of these energies must be experienced in the cells of your body. You then begin to directly perceive how these eight energies combine with each other at ever-increasing levels of complexity both internally and in the continually manifesting world outside the body. This process is expressed in the art of ba gua as a smooth, unbroken flow through the eight palm changes. This flow is essential to the meditation and healing side of ba gua. It is also one foundation of ba gua chang's martial effectiveness, as the continuous changing of location and the direction and angles of attack confounds opponents.

The Eight Mother Palms

Each of the eight palm changes is designed to increase a person's ability to use its corresponding energy. However, each palm is also affected by the energies of the other seven to varying degrees. In the original ba gua school, many of the top people practiced the Single Palm Change for years before learning the other palms. For example, Shi Liu, who lived with Tung Hai Chuan and was one of his better students, practiced only the

Single Palm Change for his first six years. That is all he did, yet his applications were excellent because his efforts were concentrated rather than dispersed over many different forms. A modern example of such dispersion can be seen in some schools that use all the 64 hands for martial training. In such schools, often students cannot use the hand techniques effectively, which reflects a case of too much information and not enough true understanding and embodiment of the art.

There are many different versions of the Eight Mother Palms, depending on the lineage (see p. 308) and how it developed through the generations. However, there are two categories of the Eight Mother Palm sets that correspond to the pre-birth and post-birth methods. The post-birth sets involve learning all the movements and breaking down the hsing, or form, they contain in terms of how the movements are applied in fighting. This method approaches everything from the direction of the outside in, and uses the more external **Eight Outer Palms** training method. The **wai ba chang** movement is used more or less as the hsing in the form with little variation. In contrast, the pre-birth method approaches everything from the inside out, and uses the Eight Inner Palms training. With the pre-birth method, you internalize what you are doing so that a very small micromovement can contain all of the energetics, internal body mechanics, and fighting applications of a form. Although there may be a great deal happening internally, an untrained eye would be unable to see what is being done. Traditionally, seven of the eight palms are done with an open palm and only one of the eight includes using the closed fist.

In general, the Eight Inner Palms method is more powerful because its smaller internal movements allow you to change more quickly. Knowing a great deal of hsing, or form, does not necessarily increase your ability to change without inertia. The issue of change is the one that is most critical for martial or spiritual applications of this martial art. As a rule of thumb, the more you see on the outside, the less is happening on the inside. Conversely, the more that is happening on the inside, the less can be seen on the outside. This latter is the case for the top ba gua people. When they practice solo movements, what they are doing appears incredibly simple. However, when they apply it in combat, it becomes unimaginably complex. Just the opposite is often the case with practitioners who have complex outer forms. When they apply their art in combat, their application proves to be too simple and ineffective because they lack variety and do not respond well to change under the physical contact and pressure of combat.

Shi Liu and the Condensed Single Palm Change

For Shi Liu and others, Tung took the Eight Inner Palm set and further condensed it into the Single Palm Change. Within the Single Palm Change and the Double Palm Change there were included minute movements that

EIGHT OUTER PALMS/ WAI BA JANG
Basic pre-birth ba gua chang practice of secondary circle-walking techniques that function as fighting applications only.

contained all the principles, energies, and applications of the entire system of eight palms. This Single Palm Change was complete because it was fully developed inside the mind. There was no need for additional forms, because the "I," or intention, from which all of Shi Liu's thoughts sprang had a complete understanding of the nature of change and could instantly manifest whatever physical movement was required. This was quite similar to the intention-centered schools of hsing-i, in which, if the mind could conceive of a physical motion and move the chi through the necessary energy pathways, the body could instantaneously translate it into physical movement with full speed and power. This method of condensing all of the ba gua energy system into the Single Palm Change was the traditional Taoist monastic ba gua method, which was not concerned with martial arts, but purely with internal alchemy, Taoist meditation, and health practices.

For Tung's disciple, Shi Liu, tiny movements within the Single Palm Change became the means to cultivate his energy. It might have been just a movement of the finger into a new palm shape that linked deeply inside his mind, energy channels, and psyche to give him the ability to transform it into a fighting application. Another person doing ba gua might have needed to do two or three large, expansive movements to accomplish the same result. Shi Liu's movement might have been only one-hundredth the size physically, but it was equally or more effective, both in terms of moving chi inside the body and for purposes of fighting.

In such a detailed focus on the Single Palm Change, there are various levels of training with different objectives. Some training methods have the objective of strengthening an internal aspect of your body. For example, you might Walk the Circle concentrating on one specific internal process, such as the pulsing of the internal organs. At another time, you might focus on another process, such as varying the internal pressure of the cerebrospinal fluid, or perhaps you might concentrate on several processes simultaneously. This selective focus on an individual internal process is typically maintained for a period of time to "hardwire" that process into your mind and body. An observer would only see the same external motion repeated over and over and would be unaware of the varied internal processes that are being practiced.

Tung was the only one who has been credited with being able to fully use all eight palm changes. Starting with the third generation of Tung's original ba gua school and afterwards, it was rare for anyone to be able to use all Eight Mother Palm changes to maximum potential. Most, even the very best, used only three or four palm changes, since understanding just one palm change could take years. True understanding of a palm requires a detailed understanding of the internal mechanics of that palm, not just the external movements. Ba gua people consider the external movements to be more or less merely packaging. Currently in the West, a piece of food that weighs only a few ounces may have a great deal of packaging around it, but you can eat only the couple of ounces of food, not the packaging. Some of the top ba gua people learned to keep their movements condensed. Others, like Cheng Ting Hua and Yin Fu, expanded their movements. However, it is generally recognized that the essence of ba gua is contained in the Single and Double Palm Changes.

Spontaneous Movement

As your ba gua becomes more developed both internally and externally, there can be instances or periods of spontaneous movement. In ba gua language this is called, "When the dragon comes out of its cave." Spontaneous movement can happen while you are doing the form. You may spontaneously start releasing energy in very powerful ways, doing fa jin movements no one ever taught you. You may have psychic experiences of all kinds.

Liu Hung Chieh teaching the author the Single Palm Change.

Courtesy of Carolina Frantzis

BIEN HUA AND THE *I CHING*'S ART OF CHANGE

The *I Ching*, or Book of Changes, is about how one energy, event, situation, or thing changes into another. When used for purposes of divination, the *I Ching* is thrown to obtain a moving line, which in turn creates a new hexagram, and that new hexagram is a *bien hua*, or change. One of the core reasons for practicing ba gua is to viscerally (and not merely intellectually) understand the internal chi rules of change. When you begin to personally understand how chi changes inside your own body/mind, you also begin to grasp how the chi governing events and situations works. Ba gua, the personal practice of the *I Ching*, then shows you how to begin using the *I Ching* in the twenty-four hours of your daily life. You do this by learning how to feel and directly perceive within your own body the various kinds of chi and the energetic process that: (1) initiate a change; (2) carry through and support a change; (3) do not allow a change to progress through its natural unfolding by freezing it in place through inertia or unrecognized internal resistance; and (4) naturally or unnaturally terminate a change. The objective is not merely to intellectually comprehend the deeper meanings of the *I Ching*, but to make it personally relevant and spontaneously useful in daily life. For this, you need a regular personal practice. Ba gua was designed by the ancient Taoists for that purpose.

Whether it is practiced as a martial art, or a health, healing or spiritual art, one of the most important subjects of study in ba gua is the nature of change. In most martial art forms, as in many aspects of life, there is a perceived "right" way and a "wrong" way to do everything. For example, in external martial art forms, there is one correct way in which the strike can be done. If you wish to change the angle of attack, you must use a different external form that has the desired angle. Ba gua works differently. The ba gua person changes the internal resistances inside the body so the body can appropriately adapt and instantly strike or defend at the new angle, without assuming a new external form.

In the martial applications of ba gua, the use of bien hua is critical. It has been said that the Single Palm Change contains the ten thousand energy and fighting techniques/strategies of the *I Ching*. ("Ten thousand" is a common Chinese metaphor standing for "never-ending," "myriad," or "infinite.") The Single Palm Change alters as the ability of the practitioner improves in the same manner that you understand the inner meanings of the *I Ching* the more you work with it. The way practitioners move their insides, focus their attention, and change the energies inside their bodies all affect the possible angles of defense and attack of the Single Palm Change.

As taught by Tung Hai Chuan, however, there are only about ten or fifteen basic form movements that are all formally called the Single Palm Change. Tung adjusted the Single Palm Change to correspond to each student's unique body, mind, and energy. Tung passed down a physical form that allowed for many types of individual chi structures to undergo bien hua, or the possibility of change.

Sadly, down through the generations these variations on the palm changes have been codified into highly rigid forms. Some ba gua schools go so far as to say that there is only one correct way to do the Single Palm Change. However, the better students of Tung passed down how these changes could be created or modified, and they in turn created their own forms, which created their own innate bien hua, and so forth. This is what makes ba gua an evolving art, like a self-generating computer program with many permutations, that is capable of learning from its mistakes. This is in distinct contrast to the external martial arts, where the forms are often inflexible because the goal is to create a specific outer effect.

The Dragon Comes Out of Its Cave

 Until I met my teacher Liu Hung Chieh, I had never actually experienced spontaneous movement in the context of ba gua chang. When I talked to high-level ba gua people in Beijing, I was told that only those who are involved in ba gua meditation have this sort of experience. My first involvement with spontaneous movement was in 1981 with Liu at his home in Beijing. The experience lasted only a few weeks. One person who was watching described it as "shaking the dragon's tail" because my back and spine were vibrating so hard it looked as if a tail was coming out of my spine. The source of these incredibly rapid yet flowing movements is the release of a human being's internal consciousness. In this process, your energy starts mixing with the energy in the surrounding environment and you can tap into the primal energies that originated the ba gua lineage.

The metaphor of the dragon is appropriate for spontaneous ba gua movement. In Chinese thought, the dragon has a lot of meanings. It is the symbol of the Emperor as the Phoenix is the symbol of the Empress. It is the symbol of good fortune; and it is also the symbol of higher aspirations and spirituality. The spontaneous movements that I experienced are similar to what is called *kriya* or spontaneous actions in the Shaktipat meditation tradition of India's Kundalini yoga. The only difference is that this spontaneous movement took a form that is appropriate to ba gua and martial arts as opposed to an emotional or cathartic release.*

As manifested in these spontaneous movements, the energy of the universe is called "the dragon" by Taoists in China and "the snake" by Kundalini adepts in India. The spontaneous movement is not a matter of having permission to move freely as occurs in dance, psychotherapy, and some chi gung practices, or combining previously learned movements in free form like a jazz musician improvising, but something deeper and more powerful. A live energy simultaneously ascends from the earth and descends from the sky. When they mix, they become a living force inside your body that physically moves you. The experience has parallels to, but

---

*Years later in Taiwan, I again experienced a milder form of this with a group of Huang Hsi I's students doing spontaneous chi gung in central Taiwan. There I saw people who had never previously been involved in martial arts creating all kinds of martial art forms. Both with Liu and Huang, the method was done through purely energetic transmission without any verbal or psychological suggestions.

The Dragon Comes Out of Its Cave, continued

a very different feeling and flavor from, shamanic possession, the spontaneous movement of Kundalini energy, or the movement of the Holy Spirit in Christianity. It also spontaneously produces martial art abilities and chi flows that would be extremely difficult to gain through ordinary ba gua martial art training, regardless of effort and strength of will.

The dragon literally grabs your body/mind and starts moving and teaching you what to do. This is called "the celestial teachings of ba gua." These are teachings that come from heaven. It is not that you do a movement; instead you are moved, sometimes very forcibly. I clearly remember when it was occurring that I could spin on a dime in Liu's small room, whereas before I would normally have knocked something over. Spontaneous movement involved a level of physical coordination that even after twenty years of martial arts practice was beyond my capacities, yet I was doing it. My body was making impossible jumps in the air, jumps I could never have conceived of before. I was experiencing the beginnings of **ching gung**, or the lightness of body skill, which historically is a specialty of ba gua. There was not any particular technique; it was just happening to me suddenly. When this period of spontaneous movement ended, it never fully recurred. I wondered if all the kundalini work that I had done during the two years I had spent in India (and practiced for years) just happened to be coming out in ba gua.

I asked Liu. He said that spontaneous movement had first happened to him when he was in the mountains of Sichuan, and that it was a basic component of Taoist meditation. He was nevertheless surprised that it was happening to me so early in my training. When I explained my previous kundalini kriya training, Liu said that my background had exposed me to these energies and therefore I was perhaps open to this experience at an early stage.

Spontaneous movement is considered to be part of the spiritual side of ba gua. It releases bound emotions and gives one the ability to change energy to a degree that cannot be obtained from ordinary controlled ba gua practice. As these things start to happen, you can see into the root of what change in ba gua is really about. Spontaneous movement typically lasts for only a limited period of time, no more than a few years, and the levels of awareness it causes will not become permanent until the mind is sufficiently open, stable, and balanced.

CHING GUNG
Special technique, now virtually lost, for making the body incredibly light by changing its chi.

The subject of bien hua is also about how living things, including humans, change and transmute over time. Sometimes the changes occur over the span of weeks, months, or years with regard to form work, but there also can be ten changes in a half-second of fighting applications. The study of bien hua is lacking in most ba gua schools in the West. However, in the good ba gua schools in China everything is talked about in terms of bien hua, and all training is done with consideration of bien hua. Bien hua, or change, is the heart and soul of the *I Ching*. Hsing, or form, is the way in which your body moves and the specific outer shape it takes, and is the basic focus of external art forms. Bien hua is also concerned with how your internal chi/body shape changes when it encounters a situation either inside your body, as your chi jumps from a lower level to a higher level of capacity, or how it changes in a martial technique from a palm strike to a forearm strike to a shoulder strike, and so on. In the spiritual aspect of ba gua, bien hua is concerned with how you jump from one level of consciousness to another in internal alchemy.

In fighting, bien hua can be expressed in the way you change and how you perform a particular movement. The power can change minutely or dramatically to accommodate the way in which your opponent has changed the angle or power of an attack, and your body posture can change from attack to defense or defense to attack, possibly many times per second.

Changing Energy and Fighting Applications

There are three principal ways in which ba gua practitioners develop the ability to use energy changes for martial purposes. First and foremost is the practice of applying a technique as the body learns to mold to the energies of the environment, as well to one's own personal energy and that of the opponent. As a martial and spiritual art, ba gua actively uses the chi of the environment, drawing energy from the earth and sky. Ba gua is considered to be a celestial art rather than an earthly art because it is common for ba gua people to quite literally draw energy from the planets and stars. By forming psychic connections with these natural forces, ba gua people utilize them as they move through and interact with the energy of the practitioner's personal aura. Energies constantly coming up from the earth and down from the sky combine with the local energy of the environment around you. If, for example, you live near a mountain or the ocean, your body absorbs the energy of these environmental forces as well as that of the wind and the trees. It also absorbs the energy of the human being who is attacking you. The combination of all of these energies gives rise to an exactly appropriate energetic response, which becomes the martial application. In the external martial arts, fighting techniques are based on, "He does this and I do that." (He throws a punch and I do one of a potential multitude of reflexive applications.) However, in ba gua you do

(Text continues on page 231.)

A PERSONAL ODYSSEY THROUGH THE MARTIAL ARTS

Eight Drunken Immortals

 One afternoon in a Taipei park I saw a group of eight people doing an unusual martial art under a tree. The group was led by an old man who moved like a teenager. I watched for a while, and pretty soon the teacher and I got into a conversation. He was surprised that I could speak Chinese and had a love of Taoism. He said his method was called Eight Drunken Immortals, and that it was part of a Taoist lineage, not part of the Shaolin method. He asked if I would like to learn. When I inquired where to show up for training, he replied that if he was teaching, he would be doing it under this tree, on the grass, during the late afternoon Monday through Thursday. My attempts to have him or his students elaborate on any other training of this type got nowhere. The situation always remained the same. I came and learned fairly regularly under this tree for several years. Then, one day, without warning, the group vanished. No one knew where they had gone or even exactly who they were. I never saw them again.

Drunken boxers are constantly collapsing and then unexpectedly jumping up like a jack-in-the-box. They appear to completely lose their balance and/or roll on the floor, taking the most unbelievable breakfalls, and suddenly leaping up to attack. When upright, they often appear to have no body solidity at all. They look totally vulnerable and wide open, and yet when an opponent seeks to take advantage, he finds himself throttled without knowing why or how. All and all, it is probably the most playful martial art I have ever practiced.

There are two schools of Eight Drunken Immortals. The first comes from the Shaolin branch of Earth boxing called **ti tang**, which specializes in ground-fighting techniques. In Earth boxing, when practitioners fall to the ground, they may hit their opponents on the way down and/or drag them down, too. Once on the floor, an Eight Drunken Immortals boxer uses very sophisticated ground techniques, especially kicks, nerve strikes, chokes, and joint-locks, either on an opponent already taken down, and/or on a standing opponent who is trying to stomp him. The second school is purely Taoist. It is a martial art that Taoists taught to their children or teenagers to develop their physical body and chi while they were still too young to undergo the precise discipline required to be successful in the internal martial arts.

Eight Drunken Immortals provides training in the most basic principles used in the internal martial arts in excellent ways. However, it relies more on creatively manifesting the principle without being a stickler for the form. This martial art has a superb chi gung system. It develops

TI TANG

Various systems of Chinese martial arts concerned with fighting on the ground or earth.

Eight Drunken Immortals, continued

some elements of the 16-part nei gung system very well, but not the whole system, nor to the level of precision found in the internal martial arts. This style embraces a deep understanding of how human body weight and momentum work, and can manipulate these elements in the body as it is moving through space.

In some ways, I would say Eight Drunken Immortals took the flexibility, falling skills, and special ability to move in all directions of Monkey boxing to the next step. However, it substituted playfulness and a sense of good camaraderie for Monkey's viciousness, both in the way it defeats opponents and in its general philosophical mind-set. In softness, Eight Drunken Immortals is closest to tai chi. In attack mode, it is a mix of tai chi and ba gua principles with some of its own unique material. In its footwork, evasion principles, and emphasis on change and unpredictability, it is closest to ba gua.

Eight Drunken Immortals stresses several unusual martial qualities. It embodies more joint- and body-folding techniques than any other external or internal/external martial art. It imparts an ability to fold the human body like a rag doll, thus enabling the practitioner to both block and attack from quite unpredictable angles with every part of the body, including the buttocks and back. The extreme body-folding skill of the Drunken boxers makes it virtually impossible to apply joint-locks on them. Although some think Drunken boxers dislocate their joints to defend against locks, they do not. It is the extremely minute movements of the shoulder and area beneath the ribs that create this illusion. Eight Drunken Immortals is neither a "this or that" style, and equally uses punches, hand and finger strikes, and a large assortment of usual and unusual kicks from odd angles, joint-locks, all kinds of throws, both upright and crouching, and extensive use of the legs while on the ground.

Although Eight Drunken Immortals does incorporate developed chi work, its main emphasis for power and movement is mainly on weight displacement rather than pure chi work, which requires no physical body weight momentum for success. Consequently, this martial art studies the exact science of body momentum from every angle of body movement that can happen: upright, airborne, or on the ground. It is especially good for reversing the direction of body momentum within a tiny amount of space. This specific interest drives its practitioners until they are able to exert great control over how their body weight moves in space, both in projection, as in forward rolls, and while lurching both forward, backward, and sideways. These and any other movements, such as growing and shrinking, are analyzed in terms of the

Eight Drunken Immortals, continued

specifics of how shifts in the Drunken practitioner's momentum will correspondingly affect their opponent's momentum and body balance.

This precise control of their own and their opponent's space enables Drunken boxers to create optical illusions and use deception to great advantage. Another weight displacement focus is the ability to make any point on the body, say an elbow tip, head, tantien, or knee become the center of balance and movement, and then to rapidly change at will from any one of many multiple balance points to another. Such maneuvering allows Drunken boxers to appear totally unbalanced when in fact their balance is perfect. Thus, multiple traps are set for an unsuspecting opponent. In more advanced stages of practice, this ability allows Drunken boxers to smoothly segment their body into independent parts connected by a common thread of balance. This ultimately extends to being able to put the entire power or weight of one's whole body into a single part of the body, such as a shoulder or forearm, or at its best into only a tiny single point, such as a fingertip. This method is commonly done in the internal martial arts, only much more invisibly and with much greater internal power.

Eight Drunken Immortals includes a full range of chi techniques developed in both separate chi exercises and form movements. In the beginning, a Drunken boxer deliberately seeks to draw universal divine energy into the body from the heavens. In the Taoist method of Eight Drunken Immortals, it is this universal chi that makes practitioners "drunk," that flows through their movements. Neither real emotion nor acting is involved. Part of the training is to draw this universal energy into each of the three tantiens of the body, and move it between the three like a living force and next from each of the tantiens to anywhere in the body for specific effect.

The chi work of Drunken boxers makes their bodies become very light or heavy, gradually or instantaneously. Descending energy is used to sink their chi, which lets their hands sink to smash through their opponents. The heaviness allows defensive techniques that smother an opponent's attack and puts considerable power at the end of hits, using centrifugal force. In these, the lightness of the arms and body increases speed while, by the hand being heavy at the very end, the Drunken boxer amplifies the hit. The control of energy inside the body enables the practitioner to be able to move rapidly and impressively up and down, forwards and backwards, left and right, as well as to shrink and collapse into a ball, and then grow and shoot out like a lightning bolt.

not use reflexes to respond to an attack. Your mind is always present and still and, as indicated, you move spontaneously in response not only to the energies of yourself and your opponent, but also to the environmental energies around you. Most martial arts emphasize only having an awareness of the energy or body movement of your opponent.

Second, there are practices where one person attacks and one defends, spontaneously or with rules. Those ba gua schools that use pre-arranged two-person fighting sets are considered to be outside the gate of traditional ba gua. The true methods of change are learned when two people practice freely, attacking each other at will. This may be done while both are Walking the Circle together or engaging in some other two-person spontaneous interchange with a minimum of rules (for instance, the attacker may attack only particular parts of the body in any way, or only use a specific strike).

The third way to learn how to change energy and angles in martial applications is through Rou Shou (see p. 235), a training method much like Push Hands in tai chi except that, with Rou Shou, you are allowed to hit, throw, kick, and apply joint-locks. You hit or slap gently in the initial phase so that no one gets hurt, but hard enough that the strike is felt. It is not like karate or Shaolin where you pull a blow; rather, it is closer to light sparring in boxing. After you have learned the ability to absorb blows to the point where you can easily take strong blows, you start hitting and getting hit harder and more heavily.

The invisible changing of energy originating from your heart/mind is a critical component of ba gua as both a martial art and a spiritual art. It requires you to change within the hsing, or form, to match the change of your own energy or that of your opponent without being bound by your external form movement. One physical motion in ba gua can be done in several hundred different ways, each of which is considered a change (bien hua). Each change describes a different way in which the chi comes to a place in your body or your chi arrives at a specific energy level and changes into something else. Change is based on energy that is continuously coming together and separating. This fusion and fission releases tremendous energy and possibilities. It is the point at which this potential fusion or fission happens that determines the form that the energy will next take. Everything in ba gua is always geared toward allowing that sudden release or absorption of energy and using these intense mutating energies fruitfully.

Changing Angles of Attack:
Circles, Spirals, Triangles, and Squares

As pointed out, the changes expressed as bien hua can also refer to changes in physical angles of attack or changes in your energy or your opponent's energy. The most technically sophisticated external/internal

Courtesy of Caroline Frantzis

Liu Hung Chieh and the author begin ba gua's Circle-Walking sparring practice.

martial arts in China, as well as in Indonesia and Japan, use the techniques of the circle, spiral, triangle, and square. Usually, however, these techniques are performed only in large movements requiring inches or feet of space to be successful. Ba gua, in contrast, is able to successfully use these angles commonly in a fraction of an inch of space, due to the way the art can fold and mold the interior of the body. These ba gua techniques could be an extremely useful addition to aikido, for example.

Ba gua is concerned with the eight basic angles of approach to a person: front and back, left and right (both above and below the waist), and the four diagonal directions. In ba gua, the change of angles is a major concern. When skilled ba gua practitioners come into contact with their opponents, they may change an angle minutely, either through walking or turning the dragon body or folding the wrist, elbow, and shoulder joints so that it will seem as if they are moving in three directions at once. In the middle of all these directional changes, the opponent is hit without knowing how or from where. This rapid changing of angles makes a ba gua person disappear and reappear suddenly, leading many in China to liken ba gua to the actions of a ghost.

Ba gua chang as a martial art divides horizontal space into eight angles of direction that can be thought of in terms of personal (not geographic) compass points with north always being the direction in which one is facing. The eight points consist of the four main directions (north, south, east, and west) and their diagonals (northeast, southeast, southwest, and northwest). Walking in a circle allows for exploitation of these various angles for martial purposes. First, it develops an awareness of these angles. Second, by firmly rooting on one leg at all times you can, with sufficient training, move with full speed and power from any one compass point to any of the seven other directions.

Ba gua chang's rapid changes of direction are possible because each new step opens up another eight possible angles for movement. While this concept may seem simple, the practice is not. After an understanding of the horizontal angles is achieved through practice of Walking the Circle, a sense of the vertical is achieved through the eight palm changes. With these, the practitioner employs vertical up and down movements as the circle is walked, and thereby develops an insight into height and depth. By incorporating these dimensions, the angles of attack within ba gua chang's horizontal circular space are expanded immensely into the three dimensions of a sphere. Ba gua fighters, especially in the pre-birth practices, achieve an awareness of surrounding space in a 360-degree sphere, as well as being able to perceive the chi above themselves and below the ground.

Circles and Spirals

All martial arts are concerned to some extent with angles of attack. However, most involve angles that lie on one or two planes. Ba gua's consideration of these angles in three-dimensional space allows complete utilization of the spiraling energy developed through Walking the Circle. In ba gua chang, every angle has an arc no matter how slight. Using this spiraling energy allows you to attack with power from angles that other martial artists are normally unprepared to counter or to expect a counter from.

Both attacking and defending ba gua techniques may appear to move in a straight, curved, circular, spiraling, or snaking fashion. However, both ba gua and tai chi movements almost never follow a straight line. They are at least minimally curved, even if they appear to be straight. What appears to be a straight-line attack will actually be generated by invisible internal spirals caused by the person's chi and the twisting of soft tissue— the muscles, ligaments, tendons, and fascia. Also, spiraling and/or circular physical movement can create straight lines of projecting energy. A chopping or cutting action could be relatively straight, curved, or spiraling, depending upon your subtle movements. An upward palm strike could appear to be (a) straight, (b) curved, (c) straight coming out of a small circle, (d) curved coming out of a small circle, or (e) spiraling. Seemingly straight-line attacks can also include the transmission of force in the opposite direction to the trajectory of the attack. Circles, spirals, and straight lines can interact and combine with each other both internally and externally.

Triangles and Squares

The next important aspect of ba gua movement and strategy is the use of triangles and squares. In the same way that straight lines can interact and combine with circles and spirals, so can each straight-line component of a triangle or a square have these circular and spiraling qualities. The triangle is used primarily to triangulate force from two parts of the body to focus on a single point or to produce a power vector. For example, force originating from points A and B can combine to bring force to point C, or can combine to produce a line of force from point C to point D. This triangulation can take a number of forms; (a) your opponent's force hits your left arm and is rerouted in a triangular manner out of your right arm; (b) you triangulate force from your left rear leg and your right hand or (c) you triangulate force from your right front leg and your right or left leading arm. In this case, attacks and defenses with the arms and legs are performed at angles ranging between 30 and 75 degrees, with a 45-degree angle being the most common and 30 or 60 degrees being the next most common.

The square is employed when moving in a zigzag fashion, to the side and then forward, and then to the side again. Here, you might stay touching or completely disengage from your opponent and move to the side, where your opponent's force lines do not impact your freedom of movement or set you up for an immediate counter. Then, from the clear space, you can counterattack. The triangle methods commonly aim to intersect the opponent's line of force, immobilize it, and then counter. The square methods usually aim to disengage from the opponent's force lines or threat of attack and then counter at a 90-degree angle. Commonly, one can shift continuously back and forth between a triangle and a square, often in the space of less than one-quarter of a millimeter,* so that your shifts are utterly confusing to your opponent. This shifting is combined with rapid waist turns, joint folds, forwards and backwards body and footwork maneuvers, as well as sudden vertical body drops and rises. Considering this, it becomes easy to understand how ba gua confounds an opponent with its unpredictability as well as with its unique ability to project power from unexpected angles, which is its specialty.

---

*Sensitivity to touch, being centered, the ability to adhere to the opponent's arms, and fast, agile, tight waist-shifting become critical at this level of skill.

Sparring Practices

Like tai chi and hsing-i, ba gua develops fighting skills through a methodical sequence of solo exercises and practices with partners. As previously discussed, Walking the Circle while doing the 16 basic nei gung energy practices is the single most important exercise in ba gua for developing martial art power. When combined with holding postures, solo exercises, and palm changes, ba gua can be fully realized as a physical, energetic, and spiritual art. While these solo practices alone can even lead to some competence as a fighter, to fully develop ba gua as a fighting art requires that these solo exercises be complemented by very specific practices with a partner. There is simply no substitute for working with another person. The techniques for working two-person applications include: (1) Rou Sho; (2) Walking the Circle with palms joined and engaging in both pre-set and spontaneous attacks and defenses; (3) attacks and defenses executed from close, middle, and long distances (both pre-set and spontaneous); and (4) freestyle sparring.

Rou Shou or "Soft Hands"

One of the important martial practices in ba gua is Rou Shou, which means "soft hands." Rou Shou is used in different forms by different ba gua schools. The major objectives of the Rou Shou practice are to:

1. Develop sensitivity and aliveness of touch.

2. Overcome the tendency to experience paralysis or hysteria in combat.

3. Develop (as in tai chi Push Hands) the abilities to (a) root, (b) fold and twist the waist and arm joints, and (c) activate the springs in the legs for both vertical and horizontal movement.

4. Provide a safe, practical way to develop realistic combat techniques and fighting angles short of actual fighting.

Rou Shou could prove invaluable to tai chi people, as it forms a natural bridge between Push Hands (which is insufficient for practical self-defense) and sparring. This safe transition is unfortunately lacking in most modern tai chi schools.

Traditionally, Rou Shou was very popular with the ba gua schools in Tianjin, but less so with the Beijing schools. Like tai chi's Push Hands, Randori in judo and aikido, and Wing Chun's Sticking Hands* and all forms of grappling, Rou Shou is done with a partner. As is the case with

---

*Other well-known martial art two-person exercises include: (1) Joint hand exercises of Penchat/Silat; (2) Kaki Te of Goju Karate; and (3) joined-hand exercises of most Southern Chinese short- and medium-hand and Northern long-hand Kung Fu systems. Included would be any system in which through physical touching of the arms one is able to control and defeat an opponent.

tai chi Push Hands, Rou Shou develops your ability to root as you attempt to break the other person's balance. However, Rou Shou differs from Push Hands in that the object is to hit your partner, not just push him. You can push if you like, but this is not the primary goal. Instead, pushing is only one of many options, which include joint-locks, empty-handed hits, throws, leg sweeps, and eventually "pointing" on the body (that is, dian xue or dim mak). Rou Shou is similar to Wing Chun's Sticking Hands in that both seek to hit, but beyond that their differences are substantial. Wing Chun angles are very linear, while Rou Shou is circular and spherical. In addition, in Rou Shou, the hands are generally open, while in Sticking Hands punches predominate.

The reason that this practice is called "soft hands" is that you very deliberately keep your wrists relaxed and your hands soft. This allows you to hit your partners with power but without injury. Remember, the safety of your partner should be your highest priority.* An injured partner might not be able to continue to practice with you. Moreover, when harm is inflicted, unnecessary ill-will is developed. In modern society, it is important to avoid injuries during practice to be able to work and earn a living the next day.

Progression of Training   Rou Shou occupies the middle ground between ba gua as a solo exercise and ba gua as a martial art. It progresses from a very structured and soft interaction with your partner to free-flowing controlled violence (where no injury is inflicted). Rou Shou practices progress methodically, layering one skill on another. Do not be in a rush to advance to the next level. Like building a house, you must develop your foundation carefully or the whole structure will be weak. On the other hand, do not get stuck at one level of practice for years on end. Rou Shou, like Push Hands in tai chi chuan, is a means to an end (the ability to defend oneself), not the end in itself.

When beginning Rou Shou, do not move your feet. Using a bow stance, shift your weight back and forth from one leg to another. Keep your arms in a big horizontal circle in front of your body. Then move your arms in a circular fashion to get a sense of your body as a sphere. Soften your body as you shift your weight back and forth. Twist your waist and legs as you move. You and your partner can then join your wrists as you both continue to move them in large circles. Alternately have one of you lead the other, as the follower lightly adheres to the leader's wrists. Make all your movements light and circular. Avoid any breaks in your motion as your arms progressively begin to spiral and wrap around your partner's forearms more and more over time, like a corkscrew unwinding.

---

*Professional fighters, security personnel, bodyguards, policemen, gangsters, and combat military personnel commonly train more severely, as fighting is part of how they earn their living, and lack of skill can be fatal.

Rou Shou

(1) The author (right) turns his waist and defends, breaking the attacker's balance and making him come forward. Note that the author's lower hand is set to slap the attacker in the ribs. The slap would be generated by a waist turn.

(2) As the attacker attempts to escape backwards, the author separates and controls both of his arms, stretching one arm upward and the other outward.

(3) The author turns his waist to counterattack with a strike to the neck, which could continue into a throw.

Rou Shou has a very different character than Push Hands. It has a very defined yang quality. It appears solid and forthright. The skills learned in tai chi, (fa jin, rooting, yielding, circularity of movement, folding of the joints, and elasticity of the body) make an excellent foundation for Rou Shou. Conversely, Rou Shou will considerably improve one's tai chi and add interesting and valuable new dimensions to tai chi Push Hands. Rou Shou can also be of great value to aikido practitioners who wish to increase their chi and aikido skills in ways both subtle and gross. If done properly, Rou Shou's snakelike movements can be incredibly beautiful to watch.

Do not try to attack or defend in the initial phase of Rou Shou. After long practice in the initial phase, you can begin very gentle attacks and defenses. Continue moving your arms in a spiraling fashion, adhering to your partner at the wrist and shifting your weight back and forth. Feel the ebb and flow of your energy and your partner's energy. Where does your partner's incoming force originate? How is it moving? Where is it heading? How can you redirect it, change it, absorb it, or move around it? Conversely, how do you shape your force to contact your partner? How do you change it to respond to his or her defense? Which angles work and which do not? In which angles is your functional power strong, weak, or neutral? Does the attack/defense arrive weak or with strong energy? Which sequence of actions and reactions creates an opening? Ba gua people do not try to crash through an opponent's arms. The key to a successful attack is to create a clear opening, like a hole in a shirt that allows a mosquito to bite. In the case of ba gua, a mosquito-sized opening allows a tiger to bite.

For the intermediate student, the main point is to keep techniques rounded so that as you get hit, you can continue from one technique to another without pauses caused by inertia, emotional paralysis, or physical tension. This develops the ability to remain calm and not become paralyzed when the pressure is on. Since you must ultimately touch the opponent for a martial technique to work, Rou Shou begins the process of changes at the point where your body touches the opponent. This usually is somewhere on the arms. Rou Shou then forms the bridge between maintaining your distance and the shock of arms touching and hitting, throwing and joint-locking. Rou Shou is a practical training exercise in that it allows you to develop the ability to hit your partners (or opponents) with speed and power. It can also make your body accustomed to the shock of being hit or blocked. If this familiarity is not acquired, in a real fight you could freeze like a rabbit caught in car headlights at night.

The practice of Rou Shou develops your ability to move and eventually to fight. As you twist and turn your body, you should also open and close your spine and the joints and cavities of your body. This opening and closing, just as in tai chi and hsing-i, allows your body to act as a massive spring that can absorb energy and return it. It also enables you to move vertically up and down with great ease, which is crucial for attack and defense. The twisting and turning of arms, legs, and body is necessary to redirect incoming force. Often, one's hands and waist seem to be going in different directions, which creates deceptive angles of attack that most people would not consider possible.

Expand the limits of your Rou Shou practice over time. Do Rou Shou with as many different partners as possible. Each person will have individual physical, energetic, and emotional characteristics. At any given practice, you and your partner can agree on whatever variations of Rou Shou you desire. For example, you can alter the speed of your motions or the power of your strikes. Have fun with it! Just be sure that any escalation occurs slowly in accordance with your ability and that of your partner. People can be severely hurt in uncontrolled sparring. Permanently injuring your body to learn to defend yourself is not a very wise strategy. This is why two-person exercises were invented. Rou Shou does not have to be "wimpy" and devoid of physical power and surface bruises, but you want your practice to increase your chi, strength, and health as well as your fighting skills, without hurting yourself or your partner.

A major escalation of Rou Shou is to allow your feet to move. This in turn allows you to practice your footwork and coordinate your feet, hands, and body. Another escalation is to increase the power of your strikes to give your partner a more substantial hit. If your techniques include an ability to bend at the wrist, it not only gives you the flexibility for ba gua palm strikes but also allows you to strike your partner's body solidly, but without inflicting injury. The same strike could either be uncomfortable, very painful, potentially injurious, or even lethal, depending on whether your wrist and palm are soft or solid. "Uncomfortable" will be sufficient for you and your partner to register a score. Anything less than this may leave you unclear about what really happened, and you will not learn to act and react in a realistic way. As you escalate, negative emotions will tend to arise. This is where having a still, meditative mind will be realistically tested. Learning how to relax under intensifying force will also prove invaluable in learning to deal with stress induced by aggression and/or time pressures.

Do not add kicking to your Rou Shou until the advanced stages of practice. Your root must be very well established. If it is not well connected, you will unbalance yourself physically and energetically when you kick. Rather than gaining by executing a new kicking technique, you will be losing instead because you will be building a house with no foundation, which will make it easy for your partner to knock you down.

Rou Shou develops your ability to change extremely rapidly in response to your partner's actions. When you start Rou Shou, your awareness of your own chi and your sensitivity to your partner's energy may be very limited. Relax and don't worry. Be patient. Over time your awareness and ability to feel your partner's movements will improve. Practicing Rou Shou will develop your ability to move chi in your body and use it for martial purposes. In the initial phases of Rou Shou, you are in constant contact with your partner, which allows you to directly feel your partner's body and energy. However, after some time of practicing Rou Shou you can begin to step back from your partner so that you can gain an understanding of feeling your partner's energy from a distance, without touching. This begins the bridge between Rou Shou and practical fighting. You will find that as your sensitivity improves, the distance between you and your opponent makes little difference. You extend your mind to feel the other person's body, and you move accordingly. At this stage, it is important to begin practicing attack and defense training at close, medium, and long distance, where you do not begin by touching but bridge the gap in practical ways derived from the various form movements. At higher levels of ba gua training, there are quite sophisticated attacks and defenses that develop the ability to enter and exit the opponent's attacks and defenses by building on the skills and sensitivity acquired through Rou Shou.

Liu Hung Chieh—Possibilities of the Art Realized

Courtesy of Caroline Frantzis

My last teacher in China, Liu Hung Chieh, was a master of ba gua, hsing-i, and tai chi, as well as Taoist meditation. In addition, he was a master calligrapher and a classical Chinese scholar who also had a complete knowledge of traditional Chinese medical theory. Liu was able, by having his mind nonphysically contact my body, to use the energy in my body for literally moving me around the room when I practiced Walking the Circle. He could do this when he was either practicing with me, sitting meditating, or, most powerfully, when he was practicing calligraphy, which he did every day. When he wrote, it was like the stories of the classical Taoists, who by writing talismans could cause mystical events to happen.

Sometimes, when he would move me with his chi, I felt as if a mist were falling on me from the sky but, oddly, a mist that felt like a heavy weight. After I felt saturated with the weight of the mist, I would be moved around the room. At other times, it felt as if I was trying to walk through a solid wall of mud. It was incredible. Liu's chi focused through the calligraphy like a lens. Liu told of how his teacher Ma Shr Ching used to practice with swords or empty hands while Tung Hai Chuan was sitting meditating. With his eyes closed, Tung would correct Ma and tell him what to do. When Liu did it with me, I could feel his energy bubbling inside my system. He did not say anything. His energy would simply start coming through. His method of teaching involved some physical corrections and instructions, but he relied primarily on such chi transmissions. Since I had so much background in physical movement and martial art technique, Liu concentrated instead

Liu Hung Chieh—Possibilities of the Art Realized, continued

on showing how my internal energy was supposed to be moving by using and transmitting his own energy into my body/mind when I did solo work. He also trained me both in the freehand exchanges of fighting technique and the healing methods of ba gua chi gung therapy and **tui na,** a type of bodywork (see p. 282).

Wang Shu Jin, Hung I Hsiang, and Liu Hung Chieh all had incredible power. They all had the ability to discharge energy (fa jin), in which they could effortlessly and painlessly uproot and send the strongest of people flying for many feet in any direction they chose. They also had the ability to touch you with no apparent force and project their energy inside the body to cause injury or pain if necessary. Liu also had the added ability to heal with the same light fa jin touch.

Of the three men, Liu was the most powerful. This fact is hard to believe since Liu weighed less than 110 pounds, whereas Hung was in the 240-pound range and Wang was closer to 300 pounds.

On one of my first days with Liu, he asked about my martial arts background. Liu said that I looked big and strong, which I was, being over 200 pounds. As a small test, he got up and put his hand in the Single Palm Change posture and asked me to move it. I could not. I couldn't even move one of his fingers. This man never weighed more than 110 pounds and I could not move his finger with my entire bulk despite all the skill and power I had developed over twenty years of training. Like Wang, Liu said that having chi was more important than having size, youth, or strength.

Liu came from a wealthy family. He was originally a very studious nonphysical young man who focused on classical Confucian studies. In fact, he graduated from university in Beijing, which was highly unusual in that era for a future major martial art master.* Frail as a youth, he reasoned that if he did not strengthen his body when young he could easily have health problems in later life. Unlike many famous future martial artists, he did not come from an urban or rural working class background where physical strength was acquired through intense manual labor. Wanting to be strong like most male youths, and being a fan of the martial art novels of the day, he asked his parents if he could learn martial arts.

Liu came from a family that had produced many generations of Chinese doctors. As such, his parents were motivated for Liu to strengthen both his chi and his blood and to learn and experience in his own body the tenets of Chinese medicine. They thought also that being able to protect oneself against physical violence was useful and especially necessary in politically unstable times. Thus, when Liu was eleven years old, his family granted his wishes. They took him to learn the Six Combination Northern Shaolin external martial art system from a reputable master. Liu's situation then was similar to most contemporary middle- or upper-class urban-dwelling Americans or Europeans who want to learn martial arts. Taking to martial arts with great enthusiasm and diligent practice, Liu progressed rapidly, to the point where his teacher felt that he had learned his

---

*In the later days of the Ching Dynasty and the early days of the Republic, many of the most publicly known internal martial art masters were people of minimal formal education, who were even, in some cases, illiterate.

Liu Hung Chieh—Possibilities of the Art Realized, continued

basics well. His teacher also felt that it was his responsibility to pass the talented Liu on to a higher-level master who could better help Liu fulfill his potential.

Liu's Shaolin teacher took him to the last intact school of the original Beijing ba gua tradition. This was the school of Cheng Ting Hua at Chang Wen Men Wai Hua Shi, which hosted the largest gathering of ba gua practitioners in Beijing. Liu was formally initiated into the lineage by Cheng Ting Hua's son, You Lung.

At fourteen, Liu was the last person admitted to the original ba gua school. The next youngest person was thirty years old. Here, not only the students who practiced the Cheng style but also all styles of ba gua people came and practiced together. The younger students were taught by the senior students, who may have been thirty to forty years older and had been practicing ba gua for decades. As well as learning the Cheng Ting Hua Dragon style, Liu also learned the Yin Fu Willow Leaf Palm style.

Every evening for two or three hours in a large training hall, the individual senior students would take a younger student and work with him intensely in the techniques of walking. Each student was expected to practice what they had learned the night before by themselves in the morning, which Liu did. After the solo work, Liu would practice two-person fighting exercises, empty-handed and with weapons (sword and spear), and sparring. Every night after his homework was finished, Liu would go to the school. This routine lasted for over two-and-a-half years until the school was disbanded. Liu formally kowtowed to Cheng You Lung and Cheng taught him. Being much younger than

everyone else in the school, Liu became the school mascot. He gained insights and practice methods from many of the seniors. Here, he was introduced to, and began to practice, hsing-i chuan. This school was a true meeting ground for all the top ba gua people of Beijing.

After the school disbanded, Liu continued to learn from the people he had met there for another decade. Ju Wen Bao initially taught Liu the ba gua meditation techniques. However, the person whom Liu credited with teaching him the most about ba gua both in terms of its meditation work and in the mastery of chi was Ma Gui (Ma Shr Ching). One of the top four students of Tung Hai Chun, Ma took no formal disciples. However, Ma liked Liu and introduced him to the higher-level energy work that Ma had learned from Tung. Very old at the time and fond of drinking, Ma said it was a pity he had not met Liu when he was younger. Liu always said that although his ba gua movements were basically those of the Cheng school, the most critical aspects of his internal chi work came from Ma Gui.

Liu told me that prior to 1928 there was a very strong martial art community in Beijing consisting of people who really understood gung fu and were truly able to use martial arts. He said there were many who played at it and did not "have" gung fu, but that there were about 200 who really had it. These were the people of legends, each of whom could manifest the potential of their gung fu system. Today, that level of skill can no longer be found concentrated in one geographical location. Much in the manner of the literary and artistic boom in Paris of the 1920s, the era was a Golden Age for martial arts in Beijing.

Liu Hung Chieh—Possibilities of the Art Realized, continued

In 1928, China held its first modern national martial arts tournament. Liu Hung Chieh was the representative of the Beijing school at this tournament. Except for strikes to the groin, eyes, and throat, everything was legal. The tournament was especially brutal and had to be called off after a day or two. It was deemed that there would be too much death and maiming. There was so much violence that, midway in the tournament, the winners were decided by vote. The decision went to the Hsing-i school. Although the ba gua practitioners were at least as capable of inflicting damage as the hsing-i people, they were not as willing to casually exercise the option of maximum violence simply to win.

Liu won all of his matches, but with one interesting twist. The parents of the young man

China's first full-contact National Martial Arts Tournament held in Nanjing in 1928.

Photographer unknown

Liu Hung Chieh—Possibilities of the Art Realized, continued

who was his last opponent pleaded with Liu not to harm or maim their son. This was standard behavior in most matches so as to leave no doubt as to who really won. The parents told Liu that they would suffer greatly if their son was not able to take care of them in their old age. At that time, Liu was a devoted follower of the Confucian tradition and realized how genuine their request must have been, as the parents lost great face

just by begging. As a compassionate act Liu honored the parent's request, and after clearly showing sufficient superiority to win the match, he stayed away from the young man rather than fully engage him to produce a definitive ending, as had been his original strategy. Also at the tournament was Liu's friend Wang Lai Sheng, as well as Wu Jien Chuan's student Wu Tu Nan, who was three or four years older than Liu.

The arrow identifies Liu Hung Chieh.

Liu Hung Chieh—Possibilities of the Art Realized, continued

It was primarily because of Liu's performance in this tournament that he became the head instructor of the Hunan province Central Government Martial Arts Academy in Changsha from 1932 to 1934. During this period, Wu Jien Chuan's two sons, Wu Gong I and Wu Gong Zao, were junior instructors under Liu. Wu Jien Chuan and his father, Chuan You, co-founded the Wu style of tai chi chuan, the second most popular tai chi style in China after its parent Yang style. Although both were not strong enough to physically convince Liu of tai chi's merit, their long discussions about the tai chi philosophy of softness and yielding kindled Liu's interest. This connection ultimately led to Liu living and studying in Wu Jien Chuan's house in Hong Kong, and becoming his disciple.

Liu then became interested in Buddhism and its spiritual way of life after meeting the enlightened Tien Tai sect Buddhist master Tan Hsiu Fa Shr, who invited him to come to his monastery and learn from him. Liu rejected the monastic life. His master did not require Liu to become a monk, but simply to learn at his monastery. Again, Liu proved to be particularly talented and Tan Hsiu began to teach him privately. After a relatively short time, Tan Hsiu recognized that Liu had realized the Nature of Emptiness, the major objective of Buddhist Mahayana spiritual practice, which in the West is often called enlightenment. After having realized the spiritual tenets of Tian Tai Buddhism from Tan Hsu Fa Shr, Liu spent ten years alone in the mountains of Western China, training with several Taoist masters from whom he learned the methods of Taoist internal alchemy.

His initial exposure to Taoism occurred when he was around ten years old. At New Year's time the White Cloud Temple in Beijing was open to the public. It was a magical place to the boy, and the thing that stuck most in his mind was a group of adepts who sat unmoving twenty-four hours a day for over a week.

In Western China, Liu studied with individual Taoist adepts, bypassing the monastic route that he had experienced in Buddhism. Not being a talkative man by nature, Liu focused in his communications with me on the practices more than on his own learning situations from his past. It was with the Taoist adepts that Liu said he completed his studies about chi and realized the root of the *I Ching* and its manifestations. After this, Liu shifted his primary work away from the efforts and responsibilities of martial arts to Taoism, which included the totality of ba gua. Over the next thirty-seven years in Beijing, Liu worked primarily for the spiritual benefit of humankind, as he had become the head of a Northern Taoist lineage.

While instructing me, there was a constant ebb and flow of subjects through which Liu passed on his Taoist teachings. He said it was fortunate we both shared similar loves—chi gung, internal martial arts, meditation and internal alchemy. He would have liked to have used the methods of literature and calligraphy, but since my classical Chinese was not up to standard, Liu trained me with direct experiential chi transmissions rather than through a literary intellectual tradition.

The day before he died, and many times before that, Liu told me that he had transferred all his knowledge into my consciousness and that practice would cause the seeds to grow into full trees. Being just an ordinary mortal,

Liu Hung Chieh—Possibilities of the Art Realized, continued

the seeds are growing slowly in me, and yet Liu still remains a source of never-ending inspiration about the possibilities of spirit.

On the last day that he was alive, Liu taught me the internal aspects of the final ba gua palm, as well as the last piece of Wu tai chi's transformational energy work. It was the most intense energetic work I had ever been through. When I told this to Liu, he said it was even harder on him. He spent much time that day sharing his knowledge and clearing up loose ends with me. The next day Liu died only an hour before our usual lesson. Three days later, his body was still soft and flexible, a sign that an adept had died. He was cremated. A great sadness filled me for a long time.

Teaching Style of Liu

Liu used all the teaching methods of Wang, Hung, Huang, and Bai Hua, tying the strands of their teachings together into a coherent whole. He then went into entirely new realms. In martial arts, he favored the large movements of Wang and Bai Hua because they were better for the body's health and for developing the greatest degree of raw power. He then took all the internal components of small movements and internally combined them into large movements. Thus, when Liu did a strike, he would change the internal pressures of his blow (with the same degree of precision that Hung and Huang did with small movements and shifts of body mechanics) without his outer form changing at all.

Liu was also able to understand and communicate the whole interconnected overview of chi gung. This experience for me was different from that obtained from my other teachers, who were adepts at specific areas of chi gung, but were unable to connect all the various divergent threads of the complete chi gung tapestry. Liu was also extremely skilled at explaining how different martial techniques, when done separately or in various combinations, affected the chi of the body medically. He also knew which chi combinations mixed well, neutrally or to ill effect. Liu also went into great detail about how the martial techniques of ba gua, tai chi, and to a lesser extent, hsing-i could be applied directly in Taoist meditation to turn them into genuine spiritual practices.

Liu's Teachings on Morality

Liu was very clear about the spiritual nature of Taoist morality, which shares much in common with, yet is often quite different from, normal Chinese martial arts or Judeo-Christian morality. These basic moral values included a directive not to interfere with or manipulate the natural chi or the freedom of another individual or spontaneously arising event unless specifically requested. Pragmatism and integrity were based on internal awareness and clarity rather than specific outer forms, rules, or self-interest imposed by society. You were supposed to do what you said you would, and say only what you genuinely intended and were willing to do. The Golden Rule was to "do to others what you would want or be willing for them to do to you" and "do not do to others what you would not want or be willing for them to do to you." You were to try your best, within your capacity of clarity and awareness, to balance and bring to harmony whatever life spontaneously threw your way.

Speed can be crucial in every martial art. During karate sparring, a roundhouse back kick is used to defend against a straight punch. Here, the speed and timing of the kick are of paramount importance.

SPEED

7

The Nature of Speed in All Styles of Martial Arts

ACHIEVING THE FOUR BASIC TYPES OF SPEED

In the flesh-meets-flesh combat of all martial arts, speed is a critical component. There are four major types of speed in martial arts, each with distinct shadings. If two opponents are evenly matched in all other aspects, the winner is usually the one who possesses a type of speed the other lacks. Different martial arts schools tend to focus on different kinds of speed, with many ignoring important types of speed that are not part of their system's basic philosophy or storehouse of techniques.

Often, speed of one type may look similar to that of another, but in fact the two differ radically. Because many practitioners think that their speed should transfer across all lines, they remain puzzled that they never seem to acquire speed in all arenas. Sometimes merely by paying attention to the simple fact that there are different types of speed, martial artists can beneficially develop their speed skills and thereby come to value what they had previously derided as being "different."

The four types of speed in martial arts exist for all styles, be they external, external/internal, or purely internal.

Type I: Speed from Point A to Point B

This type concerns how fast your body or its various parts can move from point A to B through unobstructed space or water, measurable in feet per second.

Hand and Arm Speed   Hand and arm speed is critical to most martial arts. If the object is to hit your opponent, the need for speed is obvious. Wrestlers also require hand speed in reaching out to grab their opponents, especially in sensitive areas such as the private parts, the ears, the hair, or the throat. With weapons, the faster your hand and arm moves, the faster the weapon moves. Often the weight, point, or edge of the weapon is sufficient to do the required damage, making speed, not power, the only critical issue.

Movement of an Arm Using exactly the same arm movement, you may strike faster or more slowly depending on what kind of hand position you assume. Bear in mind that it is a challenging tenet of martial arts to keep your hands neither too flaccid nor excessively tense under combat conditions. There are a number of ways you can shape your hand as your arm moves to deliver a blow. These include:

1. Various types of fists—flat, vertical, uppercut, hammer-hand, thumb side of the closed fist, and with various knuckles protruding
2. Whips with the fingers, palms, and back of the open hand or fist
3. Cuts with the knuckles, heel of the palm, and edge of the open hand
4. Finger strikes and rakes
5. Open-hand strikes—ridge of hand, heel of hand, wrist, and center of the palm

Moving the Arms Quickly in All Directions Different muscles may be used in one arm movement that are not used in another. The same muscles may be used in different sequences, each being stressed differently, with the neuromuscular changes being completed when changing from one arm movement to another arm movement in a different direction. The basic arm motions that need separate training to attain speed are forwards, backwards, sideways, on the same side of body (right arm moving on right side of body) and across the body. Backwards, sideways, and across the body are the most challenging. For martial purposes, it is generally easier to move the arms forwards than to move them backwards with speed.

The Speed of Different Hand Positions There are several factors that are equally true when hands touch, which account for the speed differential between different hand positions. These are:

1. *Hand position and soft tissue* In different sequences, various hand positions engage some of the same soft tissue or different soft tissue; that is, the muscles, ligaments, and tendons in your hand. Your hand may shape itself faster or more slowly, according to the specific sequence of soft tissues activated. This variance happens because some of the soft tissues may be underdeveloped, lack tone, be too tense, or have fibers that are either overly loose or shortened. The more strain there is in the hand, the more slowly the arm and hand are going to move together when you want to do a fast technique.

2. *Interrelationship of soft tissue* As you deliver a hand strike, the soft tissue formed by your hand position engages other soft tissues all the way up your arm to your shoulders and, depending on how loose or tight you are, to your chest, back, and waist, and even down to your feet. Some of these muscles in your arm and elsewhere may be more stretched (looser) or less stretched (tighter). Consequently, some move faster or more slowly than others. Some of these soft tissues may even have restrictions. If you use a specific hand position that engages poorly functioning soft tissues further up your arm or body, your hand will move more slowly than otherwise.

For example, let's say that you do three different hand strikes (fist, open palm, and edge of palm) at maximum speed, using the same extended straight arm motion. The result: vertical fist goes very fast, vertical palm goes moderately fast, and a sideways palm goes less fast. Why? The vertical fist punch uses common muscle pathways that in most people are usually fairly open and unobstructed. The vertical palm strike naturally pulls on muscles at the top and inside of the shoulders, which are naturally tighter in most of us, unless we have specifically stretched or trained them. The sideways palm strike not only uses the normally tight muscles of the top and inside of the shoulder, but also requires the latissimus dorsi muscles to be very stretched (normally, they are not), or they will inhibit the speed of the hand movement. To overcome these speed problems, which is essential for those interested in high performance, martial arts use a range of sophisticated training techniques.

In most of us, these soft tissues become developed either through involvement in natural movements (probably less intensely in city dwellers) or in specific physical activities (sports, climbing trees, etc). If you are not active in ways that would normally develop the soft tissues involved in hand strikes, then you would require some remedial exercises or some activity that would change the internal sequencing of the soft tissues used. Otherwise, years of practice later, your hand strikes will still be relatively slow. Repeatedly practicing the slower technique alone may not be the answer to closing the speed gap between the different hand techniques.

3. *Condition of connective tissue* Bound connective tissue (fascia) will bind up muscles and ligaments that could normally move freely, inhibiting their ability to move smoothly and quickly. To correct this situation, the fascia will need to be stretched and separated; if this is not done, the tight fascia will not release the unseparated muscles and ligaments bound to it. Methods for loosening fascia while moving are specialties of the internal martial arts of China. For those involved in external martial arts, deep myofascial massage, yoga-like stretching, and tai chi can be especially helpful.

4. *Nerve signals* Neurologically, there may be significantly stronger signals to certain select muscle groups than to others. The body has many energy lines. If these energy lines are fully or partially blocked, they impede the speed with which signals move through the nerves.

5. *Circulation* Poor circulation can also impede all kinds of body speed, especially hand speed.

Leg and Foot Speed

Kicks Kicks are a necessary component of martial arts because you never know if your hands will be bound or otherwise occupied. Some martial arts specialize in kicks, especially high kicks. You could attain speed in certain kinds of kicks, but not in others. For example, you may have speedy high, middle, or low kicks, kicks done while the kicker is sitting or lying on the ground, sitting in a chair, or jumping in the air. The speed of a kick can vary depending upon the position you start from. You may be faster or slower with the same kick if you begin flat-footed in a strong stance or on the balls of your feet. Kicking speed is normally faster when your body weight is well balanced; however, can you maintain speed if you are in an unbalanced position? The factor of balance may determine your survival during real combat.

Footwork Test yourself to see if you have some level of speed in all kinds of footwork. Is there some footwork that you can execute swiftly? Some you are very slow at? Some you cannot do at all? Can your feet move rapidly over short distances, but not over long distances or vice versa? Are you very good at holding your ground and shifting your weight, but slow when you move your feet in almost any direction? Can you shift your weight quickly? What about your linear foot speed forwards and backwards and from side to side? Most people usually can move faster stepping forwards than backwards or to the side. Then there are half-steps, skipping steps, jumping steps, and back-pedaling—are you fast or slow with these? There is also the issue of speed when you are moving forwards and backwards at various odd angles, such as 30, 45, 60, or 135 degrees. Then there is circular stepping, including hourglass stepping and the toe-in and toe-out steps used in sword techniques, the internal martial arts, aikido, ninjitsu, judo, and many other throwing arts.

Check yourself. Do you have equal speed in all kinds of footwork or are you faster in some than in others?

Waist and Body Turnings The turning of the body and waist is one of the basic power generators in all styles of martial arts. Many people who can move their hands or feet quickly cannot do so when turning their waist or body. In all martial arts—external, external/internal, and purely internal—

the ideal is to move your arms, feet, and waist with equal speed in a coordinated fashion. The different types of speed variables at work when turning the waist and body are as follows (each of these requires mastering different kinds of leg speed, some being easier than others):

1. Using one or both hands to strike, grab, pull, or guide the opponent
2. Kicking with either your front or rear leg
3. Kicking and striking simultaneously or in tandem
4. Raising or lowering the body
5. Feet fixed and flat-footed
6. Feet fixed with one or both heels raised
7. Front foot fixed with rear foot pivoting, either flat-footed or heel raised
8. Both feet pivoting and moving simultaneously or sequentially with and without hand movements

Each of these requires mastering different kinds of leg speed, some being easier than others.

Type II: Speed-at-Touch

The speed of an object moving from point A to point B is relatively easy to gauge. You can see it and measure it—it is obvious in a moving foot, hand, or waist. In contrast, the speed involved at touch is much more subtle. It cannot be easily measured in any visibly objective way, but can be subjectively felt. It involves sensitivity as well as pure athletic ability. These factors are present because, at touch, besides pressure and power moving between two opponents, there is the added factor of one individual attempting to counter every move another is making, all within fractions of a second.

Many top wrestling, judo, and aikido practitioners can move incredibly rapidly at touch, both upright and on the ground, but are relatively slow at throwing punches and kicks. Conversely, many fast punchers and kickers are fairly slow at touch so that when they get in close and are grabbed, they are in trouble because they cannot move quickly enough. Most martial arts that extensively use speed while touching tend to focus almost exclusively on either hitting or throwing. For example, among those well known in the West, Wing Chun and hsing-i concentrate primarily on hitting with minimal throwing techniques. Judo, jujitsu, and aikido focus primarily on throwing and joint-locks. Some cross over into both areas, such as ninjitsu, tai chi, and ba gua.

When we watch two fighters maneuvering, we usually see the contact of arms, legs, hips, and even backs. We may be able to observe limbs touching quickly, although not with the same drama as arms, legs, or hips moving fast through unobstructed air. What is not obvious at all to the uninitiated is that the speed of moving limbs depends on the speed of small internal muscular shifts inside the torso, shifts that seem invisible, and yet are essential for providing speed to arms, legs, and hips at touch.

There are varying basic types of speed at touch, all of which must be practiced separately and extensively for each to bear fruit. Being quick in one mode does not guarantee that the speed will transfer to another. The basic types of speed at touch are:

1. *Hand and arm to hand and arm* At touch, the speed of palms, fingers, back and sides of the hands, and wrists is quite different from speed in the forearms, elbows, upper arms, shoulders, and shoulder blades. Many practitioners have speed in the hands but not in the arms, or else the opposite—they have fast arms and slower hands. A person could even have speed in several parts, but not all of them simultaneously in a coordinated fashion. The combined speed of all parts working together seamlessly, quickly, and sensitively is one of the telltale signs of a high-level martial arts master.

2. *Leg to leg* This contact can be seen in throws, foot sweeps, joint-locks of the knee, ankle, and lower back, and in the striking of acupuncture points with your knee while your opponent's leg is trapped at the ankle by your ankle. When two legs touch, there are two kinds of speed. One is necessary to counter an attacking man's moves or countermoves. The other is the speed necessary to overcome his balance, roots, and various strengths in order to set him up for a throw or leg-lock, or to hit his leg with your leg, or unbalance his whole body while your hands hit or do something else to him.

3. *Hip to hip* Hip-turning speed and sensitivity of touch are very important both for executing throws, as well as for countering someone trying to throw you, and for destabilizing your opponent's balance before you hit or kick. This at-touch speed is essential in any form of ground-fighting, or where your back is pressed against a wall.

With all the above, speed is very different when your feet are moving rather than still. In general, it is easier to maintain touch speed when your feet arc still. Many individuals perform well flat-footed, but become ineffectual when they step. It takes an entirely different type of calmness and control to maintain speed at touch when you are moving around.

The speed factor in your hands and feet is contingent upon whether or not your waist is moving. Lack of balance affects speed. It is more difficult to maintain internal balance when the waist is moving than when it is still. Mostly, it is initially easier to generate hand and foot speed when the waist is not moving. However, coordinated use of the waist allows your hand and foot speed to reach its maximum. This is also true when your hands are moving through the air and not yet in contact with an opponent.

Northern Shaolin

The continuous tensing at the end of every punch and kick of the karate I practiced in youth made a serious impression on my body, emotions, and central nervous system. I practiced karate intensely during all my teenage years, so tensing myself physically and emotionally to accomplish a goal was drilled into my very way of being throughout an important developmental period.

Looking back, it seems that this habit of tension spilled over into all aspects of my life well into my thirties, causing a lot of general stress, and making it difficult to fully relax in the practice of internal arts. The catalyst that changed this habit turned out to be a style of Northern Shaolin. I learned Northern Shaolin Six Combination boxing from Bai Hua in Hong Kong just before returning to study with Liu Hung Chieh in Beijing.

Shotokan karate (the most popular in Japan and the style I had studied for so long) and Northern Shaolin parallel each other in many respects. Both are primarily mid- and long-range styles that emphasize power and aggression. Both use low stances, long extended hand techniques, strong, fast waist turnings, and both regular and jumping kicks, especially high front, roundhouse, back, and side kicks. Both practice forms at fast fighting speed. There is, however, one notable difference between these two types of fighting: In Northern Shaolin, the muscles are never tensed, they always remained relaxed, whereas in Shotokan karate the muscles always tense for power at the end of a technique. Yet Northern Shaolin is able to provide as much striking power as karate without muscular tension. It accomplishes this feat by using two components of the 16-part nei gung system (see p. 62). One component involves breathing techniques and the other involves the rapid stretching of the soft tissues outward along the muscles associated with the yang acupuncture meridians and inward toward the body along the muscles associated with the yin acupuncture meridians. The outward stretching creates projecting power for striking through an opponent, and the inward soft tissue movement creates pulls, power blocks, parries, and cutting actions. The power of a blow in Northern Shaolin comes from the speed at which the soft tissues move, not by tensing the muscles at the end.

The general mind-set of doing a Northern Shaolin form and doing a karate form are almost identical: After the initial defense, you punch, kick,

Northern Shaolin, continued

strike, and take out an opponent with one clean blow. However, the underlying fundamental principles of these two fighting systems are the opposite of each other. In Northern Shaolin, at the end of your technique, when you take the opponent out, you project infinitely into space, without mentally locking onto a specific place in space before you. At the point of focusing your blow, you do not contract your large muscles, abdomen, face and jaw, as you do in karate, but rather open and relax these muscles in a short, concentrated explosive burst, like a laser firing. In karate, on the other hand, at the point where you take someone out, you focus your attention on the opponent's body or your visualization of it, tense your body, yell,* and become fierce.

Because the movements of these two martial arts are so similar, I would, when initially practicing the Northern Shaolin forms, always overtly or subliminally tense up at the end of a strike. After a while, though, with consistent inner mental reminders to relax and let go, I was able to avoid tensing and became able to only use the nei gung tissue-lengthening technique. Initially, I could only do this for one or two movements at a time, but after a few weeks it was possible to do it over the entire length of a form.

Through releasing tension while doing form after form, my speed began to gradually increase. The general intent to accomplish the goal of taking an opponent out was still present, but it was not accompanied by inner mental contractions of destroying a specifically focused-upon enemy, nor was there the ego charge that often follows that mentality like a dark shadow. Then, one time for three sets, my speed started to dramatically accelerate as though on its own. Each time I did a strike with total intent, I could feel some level of deep subliminal tension from my karate days disappear. Finally, at the end of the third form, that subliminal tension vanished completely, never to return. This change allowed me to move unimpeded into the depths of the internal martial arts. It became viscerally evident to me that there was as much strength, power, and martial effectiveness to be had from relaxation as my mind in youth thought could only be derived from tension.

---

*The yell, known in Japanese as a *kiai* (spirit shout), can be overt and loud or subtle and virtually inaudible. Its function is to focus the practitioner's inner power.

Speed in the Gaps between Touching and Disengaging   In any fighting situation, there is usually a time lag in the gaps between the engaging and disengaging process. During such gaps, the practitioner is especially vulnerable and may be unable to follow up on any advantage that may have been gained. Beginners especially tend to freeze or slow down dramatically in the gaps between hit and grab, touch and hit, and so on. During these intervals, time is usually measured in fractions of a second. It is not easy to naturally recover and shift gears smoothly without a loss of speed. To develop speed in these gaps, you must, when you train, pay conscious attention to the various internal mechanisms governing freezing or stiffening up, and work out ways to relax both your body and mind during these difficult transitions. Tension, fear, or anxiety is usually the source of the temporary paralysis.

A Note about Touch and Nontouch Speed   For all kinds of speed at touch, fine motor control is required. As the heartbeat raises dramatically (due usually to fear or lack of internal calmness in the practitioner), two things happen. First, conscious control of fine motor skills begins to diminish, making it more difficult for a fighter to feel and react. Second, the vision progressively narrows. Thus, it is necessary to ensure that your speed responses at touch are sufficiently practiced until they are imprinted so strongly on your subconscious that they can come out reflexively without the need for conscious thought. It is as important to achieve stillness and calmness of mind through training as it is to master actual fighting techniques themselves—so that under severe pressure, your mind remains calm and your pulse does not rise alarmingly.

By the same token, if you primarily practice touch martial arts, it is tremendously useful to learn some very simple hand strikes and kicks that require minimal fine motor coordination, as a backup (that is, if pragmatic self-defense is one of your goals).

Type III: Speed under Differing Conditions

Tracking and Timing—Changing Direction in the Middle of a Motion   For all types of touching and nontouching techniques, physical speed is bound up with timing. Timing involves telling the body when to move, and how quickly or slowly. Besides moving faster than your opponent, you can win a fight moving at the same speed as or even more slowly than your opponent if you move at the right moment and/or at the correct angle. Timing is essentially a link between your body's ability to move quickly and the mental ability to perceive when and how it is best to move. The essential central ingredient—the coordinating link—is the capacity of the nervous system to connect these two mechanisms. The fluidity of your motion, as well as your skill at changing techniques rapidly, is determined by the speed at which the signals move across all the body's nerves and energy channels, including those in the upper tantien, skin, spinal cord, and brain.

Increasing the reaction time of the nervous system requires you to develop your timing abilities and engrave them in your subconscious mind. The thinner the barrier between your conscious and subconscious mind, the easier it is to coordinate speed with timing. What does this mean? The sense of slow motion or time distortion (where things seem to be happening in surreal slow motion) experienced by many when they have a peak speed experience, comes about partially because the subconscious does not possess a sense of linear time. When things appear to you to have slowed down, it is not necessarily the external happenings that have slowed; instead, it could be the case that your central nervous system has speeded up dramatically and is linking to your subconscious mind at a rate much faster than you are used to. ("It was over before I realized what I was doing.") Let's say you are moving at an accelerated speed and this time the veil between your conscious and subconscious mind thins. This experience is one of being very relaxed, with a sense of having all the time in the world at your disposal, without any attendant feelings of surreal slow motion. This timing effect can have these implications:

1. Speed that has a fixed or constantly accelerating trajectory (like a bullet fired from a gun) is different from speed that can change at any point in mid-motion (like a heat-seeking missile that zigzags to track an evading aircraft). Fixed-trajectory motion requires only one clear signal from the central nervous system; motion that constantly changes direction requires multiple outputs from the nervous system within a condensed period of time. Speed that continuously alters direction is a specialty of internal martial artists as well as sword and knife fighters using double-edge blades.

2. Speed is different depending on whether you begin any martial technique from an unmoving start or execute it when your body is already in motion. Fighters often use feints to work themselves up to speed before launching into a real attack. Conversely, if in combat you can recognize how your opponents are accelerating their nervous systems, you can figure out ways to interrupt and confuse their patterns, thus turning the situation to your tactical advantage.

3. Speed during the gap (whatever its size) from the conclusion of one technique to the beginning of another new technique, within the same medium of touching or moving through open air, directly depends on a sense of timing.

4. Speed in reversing the left-right direction of the waist is also a critical ingredient of martial arts mastery.

Linear and Circular Techniques   Circular techniques are inherently more complex, and therefore much more difficult to learn, than linear techniques. Generally speaking, it is initially easier to achieve exceptional speed in the linear techniques, where your hand, foot, or body moves in a simple straight line from one point to another. Ultimately, however, circular techniques have the built-in speed advantage of reducing inertia. Inertia places a drag on speed and can cause the nervous system to slow down or freeze. Circular techniques reduce inertia more than the linear ones can because using circularity, it is easier to both relax your muscles and utilize the speed-generating capacity of centrifugal force.

Type IV: Speed in Relation to Power

Speed with Minimal, Middling, and Maximum Power   One of the distinguishing characteristics of high-class martial artists of every body type from razor-thin to heavyset, is that speed, grace, and power are equally displayed in their movements. Although this combination is the ideal, it is not so easy to achieve, taking years, perhaps decades, of arduous discipline before it is perfected.

However, it is not unusual in martial arts to see practitioners who can move beautifully or with amazing speed, but who have no power. What accounts for this? A certain amount of your speed is employed deep inside the body below the skin to connect up your body so you can project power toward someone else or absorb the power of someone else without being knocked down. When parts of the body are floppy and unconnected, they cannot reinforce each other or amplify each other's power. The faster the connections are made, the stronger the end ability to both project and absorb power. The internal speed needed to cause internal body cohesion is different than that speed which makes body parts move in space. True speed means having your internal connections solid and being able to move your body rapidly through space at the same time.

One of the joys of having a physical body is to make it move fluidly and fast, which are qualities of a number of martial arts and dance styles. However, if you have any aspirations toward being skilled in the art of combat, it is necessary that you recognize the levels of speeds you can realistically attain with differing levels of power. To hit someone in the testicles or the eyes, or to get out of someone's way as long as there is no physical contact, does not require power, only speed. It is good to learn how to generate maximum speed with minimum power.

Of course, it is also useful to learn how to be effective at the level in which both your speed and power are put to work somewhere in the middle of their range. Maybe you only want to control someone in an encounter that is not life-threatening, and you do not want to harm them or get hurt yourself. Here, dodging has importance, however there may also be a need to deliver a stinging or warning blow to keep the situation from developing into one where the offending person has to be hurt to be stopped.

It is also useful to be aware of the fastest speed you can generate while delivering your maximum power, and progressively working to increase that speed. Training for this level is the most sophisticated and requires the hardest effort.

Again, the speed-to-power ratio must be practiced with your hand and foot techniques. Practice with your feet fixed and your waist turning or not, as well as with your feet moving with your waist turning or not.

THE FAST/SLOW PARADOX OF THE INTERNAL MARTIAL ARTS

The internal martial arts, especially tai chi, are often practiced at very slow speeds. Extrapolating from watching these slow form movements, many reckon that internal martial arts are too slow for fighting. This has even become a subject for jokes, such as one told in a San Francisco comedy club. "It was noon and on my way to lunch I saw this tai chi guy getting mugged. He punched so beautifully, I stuck around to watch. But I had to get back to work at one, so I didn't get a chance to see the punch land."

Like external martial arts, the internal martial arts can and do indeed fight and move at lightning speed during fighting, both at touch and from point A to B. Operationally, however, they work differently from most external martial arts. The performance of these internally driven speed techniques also requires good muscle tone but most importantly, an efficient and unblocked central nervous system.

Each of the three internal martial arts also has specialized training methods and martial techniques for creating the externally visible speed of moving in space from point A to B. In tai chi, the clearest examples are silk arms, multidirectional punching, and straight-line punches using rapid openings and closings. In silk arms, the fist moves very fast, covering both sides of the opponent's body from top to bottom, fluidly changing from straight hits, to sideways cuts to hooks, like the tip of a piece of silk blowing in a high wind. This allows punches to rapidly change direction (as much as ten short-, medium-, and long-range punches in three seconds), using the front of the fist and the hammer part of the closed hand to strike. As this occurs, the arms and elbows appear to be boneless as they seamlessly fold and bend like undulating cloth. Ba gua has a similar technique, only here the punch is not silky, but moves in spiraling motions, criss-crossing the opponent's body, hitting equally with all parts of the fist from every conceivable angle, raking, drilling, and cutting as well as making direct impacts. In hsing-i, the chi that the lower-exploding hand of the fire element manifests (pao chuan) clearly can be done as a speed punch, or adapted to external speed in any hand strike. In certain types of ba gua form work, as well as in the Chen style of tai chi, the speed of both body movement and hand strikes is visibly obvious and not hidden at all. In the internal arts, any punch from point A to point B can function like a heat-seeking missile that tracks and hits a moving and evading target, or it can go like a bullet on a fixed trajectory. Although, in general, nontouch speed from point A to B is vibrantly present in internal martial arts, it is emphasized less than speed-at-touch.

More emphasized is timing and at-touch speed, either physical or mental, especially the speed to recognize and move to advantageous fighting angles. There are two important structural aspects of the internal arts that account for this focus: (1) the methodologies behind power generation and 2) an emphasis on the nonphysical aspects of combat rather than just the physical.

In drumming, there is a beat, then a space, and then another beat. In method 1, in terms of speed, the internal martial arts work more on the space between beats, rather than the beats themselves, as is more common in the external arts. This is due to the internal martial arts principle succinctly stated in the tai chi classics as, "From posture to posture the internal power is unbroken." This means continuous internal power is maintained at all times. Looked at from another perspective, at no time during any part of a movement are your limbs or body slack and without power. Let's assume that your output of power is considered to be the equivalent of hitting the drum (a beat). In the internal arts, continuous power is maintained equally both between the beats and during the beats, without discrimination. Power at the point of contact is amplified by increasing the speed of internal movement below your skin (a process invisible to the naked eye), and not by tensing your muscles. In external martial arts, power is usually exerted during the beats, not necessarily by increasing the momentum of the action, but by instituting muscular contractions that conceivably could actually slow down the velocity of the action. After these muscular contractions, there is a momentary gap in which there is no power, allowing the body time to recharge before power is again exerted.

This principle of shifting your internal speed up or down to increase or decrease your output of power at any point of contact is utilized in the same way both at touch or in the air going from point A to B. In a punch, for example, the internal arts practitioner's hand may not move any faster in an external A-to-B way but, depending on whether or not the internal speed increases or decreases as it approaches the target, the power brought to bear on a point of contact will be greater or less. This increased internal speed could be related to and/or generated by any one of the chi movements of the 16-part nei gung system (see p. 62), including: the speed of opening or closing joints or spinal vertebrae, the release of energy from the lower tantien to the hand, or the lengthening of soft tissues on the inner (yin) or outer (yang) surfaces of your body (see p. 127).

For hitting, the general use of speed in the external arts is quite different, especially in karate (which provides a strong image of the external martial arts to the public). The general external principle of speed and power follows an ever-repeating three-part cycle: explode, relax and rest, and rev up for the next explosion. In other words:

1. Fire and explode your power, usually tensing your muscles,* which is never done at any point in any internal arts technique.

2. Have a brief rest space where the muscles and nerves relax and regenerate. This gap allows a necessary space to recharge, much as a weight lifter rests between sets of lifting weights. It is helpful to remember that there are physical limits to how long muscles can continuously tense before fatigue occurs or the nerves that signal the muscles to tense can no longer operate at maximum efficiency.

3. Rev up the muscles and nerves to bring them back on line as you move into your next attack or defense technique.

Physical speed of moving from point A to B, or even at touch can be quantified to some extent. Touch- and timing-speeds focus on the nonphysical qualities of speed that are not so easy to externally quantify, although these qualities are definitely critical to the effectiveness of internal martial arts fighting applications. This method is used equally for attack or defense. Its focus is the internal speed of perception, which can translate into action that allows you under pressure to rapidly cycle through synchronizing with your opponent's energy, interpreting it, finding a weakness, mentally slipping into your opponent's gaps of unawareness or unchangeable physical momentum and applying an appropriate technique or using a fighting angle that wins the day (or, at a minimum, leaves you unhurt and able to continue seeking another chance). This process can be successfully accomplished with you physically moving either faster, at the same speed as or more slowly than your opponent. As such, physical speed is a by-product, not a primary goal. In fact, the equivalent process to seeking the "Holy Grail" in internal martial arts is the ability to move more slowly than your opponent and consistently win.

Slower speed that wins out requires three types of speed coming together simultaneously: (1) timing, (2) the signals required to maintain some level of continuous power (or your opponent's power can shock your body and break your attention), and (3) the ability to release the internal gears of the body, which, if they freeze up, can also create a momentary mental gap that breaks the connection between you and your opponent.

---

*See Chap. 1, p. 5, "Animal, Human, and Spiritual: Three Approaches to Martial Arts."

This method is referred to in the tai chi classics in the form of a question: "How is it possible that an old man can defeat a group of younger men?" Obviously, elderly men, even the most talented, are not physically capable of having the speed of young men. Virtually by definition, the elderly move with slowness, and yet those "old men" internal arts masters, by slipping in between the gaps, are justifiably well known for defeating younger and faster men.

Qualities in Common

There are also common elements used in all the previously mentioned types of speed in the internal martial arts, with or without touch. Your mind needs to tangibly move both within and through your body, and must have a concrete sensation of the air surrounding you. As your mind is able to develop these subjective but very real sensations, your chi will begin to follow.

As your mind travels through your own body, or into an attacking man's body to connect with his energy and intent, it must do so smoothly, and without gaps. The objective is to become completely connected, gradually diminishing those places where your awareness lapses, until there are no gaps. Over time, this skill requires extreme relaxation and development of a very smooth sense of internal nerve flow. Creating a "smooth-running" nervous system is necessary for developing speed in the internal martial arts. This achievement also results in a generally more comfortable body, and is a strong component of the stress relief and stamina development aspects of the internal martial arts.

After your nervous system starts functioning smoothly without experiencing gaps, simply by having your mind move through your body faster or more slowly you can increase and decrease the speed continuum of your movements or fighting applications instantaneously. A primary principle is that the mind moves the chi, and the chi moves the body. The faster your mind and chi move within your body/mind in a relaxed manner, the faster your body can move. Where the chi is blocked or its movement is consciously slowed, the body itself slows down. The more your mind and chi are comfortable within your body and can internally move effortlessly and unimpeded within, the faster your body can move externally in space or change from one technique to another, both without freezing up or having to rest and recharge.

Your mind, through the medium of your chi and nerves, becomes like the control knob of an electric dimmer switch, where you can change the neurological signals to your muscles effortlessly. Turn the mind one way and you can instantaneously accelerate or overcome body inertia. Turn the mind another way and you can instantaneously stop or control the speed of your deceleration.

A primary goal either in form or in fighting applications is to have the body move as a completely connected and integrated unit from one of two centers: the lower tantien or the central energy channel. (See Appendix C, p. 317.) This goal, even for the most talented, takes some time to achieve. Especially in applications, the speed and power of movements progressively originates in different parts of your body, until finally after a rigorous development period, the body's connection, speed and power can unify. When observed carefully, it is perceivable where in the body the originating point of power is. Is it developing from shoulders, back, chest and arms, waist or upper body, legs or any other possible permutations? Likewise, it can be seen where the speed inside someone's body is originating; for example the arms, hips, or legs. Also, the flow of speed within someone's body movement can be detected to be disproportionately faster or slower in some parts of the body than others.

During fighting applications, beginners of internal martial arts usually originate their speed in some part of their arms and chest. For example, they feel an upper arm, shoulder, or chest muscle, and however fast that muscle moves sets the tenor and motivates the rest of the body to move, following its lead. Even though beginners may ideally want their speed to originate in their waist and legs, the reality is that their actual originating point of speed in the body is usually somewhere else. A good strategy for overcoming this lack of body unification is to:

1. Carefully and realistically observe where your speed is originating in your body.

2. Allow yourself some time to become comfortable there, both mentally and neurologically, until you can move without self-consciousness from this speed origination point, whether it is in your hand, foot, hip, torso, or anywhere else.

3. Focus first on single techniques. Consciously work on progressively moving your point of origination to more useful areas of the body—your shoulder rather than your elbow, your hip rather than your chest, etc. At each new more useful point and training plateau, you must always stabilize and become comfortable before moving to the next better point. Otherwise you may later have difficulties in your upward climb to achieving your maximum speed potential. If you want greater arm or hand speed, move your attention from your shoulder, say, in progressive stages downward to your shoulder blade and upper back (but not your chest or solar plexus), then move to your lower back, abdomen, lower tantien, hips, and buttocks, and from there down each lower part of the legs to the foot, until eventually your sense is that your hand speed is originating from the earth itself. This should increase both speed and power. It gives the sensation, when you do a hand strike, of kicking someone with your hand. Before foot move-

ments, progressively shift the originating point of the movement from the foot up the body to the lower tantien and spine for stepping and other nonkicking actions. For kicking actions or sweeps, continue the progression from the kicking foot to the tantien and spine, all the way down the supporting leg to the foot and into the earth. For torso movements—in throwing for example—the nexus of your movement should run from both your upper and lower extremities progressively to your hips, lower tantien and, eventually, your central energy channel.

4. Reusing all the exact same procedures just covered, next focus only on the transitions from technique to technique. The speed needed for a single technique is easier to acquire than the the speed needed to transit between continuous multiple techniques. The originating point of transition speed is most effectively located in the lower tantien and/or central energy channel. Emphasized methods and trainings differ from school to school.

Specialized Strategies

All the internal martial arts share speed-training methods to some extent, although each art has its favorite. Hsing-i's training strategy to increase speed proceeds along two paths. The first is focusing your mind on strongly occupying the space in front of you, either holding a posture or moving relatively slowly. You literally take possession of the space and all the energy in it. The slower your physical movement, the faster and more totally your mind occupies that space. The second path involves increasing your neurological speed through the practice of walking long distance lines doing the Five Elements (see p. 186). In this, the faster and more completely the mind occupies the space around you, the faster, with sufficient training, the body follows and moves through that space.

Tai chi uses three primary strategies to create speed in fighting applications. The first, which most are familiar with, is training in the fast forms of tai chi. In these fast forms, there is a continuous back and forth repeating rhythm of moving in slow motion and then doing bursts of fast, explosive movements that issue fa jin, and then returning to slow motion again.

The second is to move in extremely slow motion, where you train to put your mind in your body, until you can control your speed with an internal dimmer switch. Whereas normally a tai chi long form usually takes approximately twenty to twenty-five minutes, with this method a form would take a minimum of an hour. In order to do this, specific instructions are given regarding the exact mental and physical processes of how to most efficiently wire and build your internal dimmer switch. To get a sense of this, try this experiment using some kind of reliable timing device: Beginning with your hands at your sides, time how long it takes you to go at your top speed from a dead stop to hitting a head-high spot on a wall. Rest a little and try again, then rest and try again. With three tries you should be able to get an accurate sense of your maximum hand speed. When you feel completely rested, repeat the same action, only this time move in extremely slow motion, taking five minutes to accomplish the same action. Rest, and being timed, repeat at top speed. You may find that your speed has increased. Moving in extreme slow motion is a very powerful, if paradoxical, tool for increasing speed.

The third method is related to the technical nature of Roll Back (see p. 128). At touch, Roll Back does not depend upon physical speed but instead upon the ability to time the pulling of opponents to where they do not want to go. At the critical moment, when they lose their center, there is often a tiny period of time when opponents are unaware of where they are going. By capitalizing on this blank spot in an opponent's mind and using a small change of angle, the tai chi player slips in before the opponent realizes what is occurring. Although this seems as if the tai chi person has moved very fast, this is not the case. Rather, the practitioner has simply used subtlety and precision to great effect.

Ba gua chang uses most, if not all, of the strategies of both tai chi and hsing-i. Its unique material, not present in the other two arts, comes from Circle-Walking and from continuously projecting energy from the feet. This action not only creates foot speed, but enables hand speed to build by changing the tuning of a person's central nervous system and chi. After the knots in the nerves and energy channels are released, the arms begin to become energetically fused into the torso, and the hands can fly. The second strategy relies on the speed that is generated from the centrifugal force of the spinning and waist-turning. The full payoff in terms of speed ultimately depends on the nei gung techniques for mobilizing the energy of the central energy channel.

A Comparison of Five Masters—Their Differing Types of Speed

Wang Shu Jin

When I knew him, Wang was a very large man and past the age of 65. He was able to move reasonably quickly over short distances of four or five feet. What was so unusual about his speed was that, given his age and how large he was, it was amazing that he was moving quickly at all. Wang was not lightning fast, but he was fast by any standard in the martial arts game, and he could be called exceedingly fast for an aging heavyweight.

His power was formidable. Wang had an extra advantage in that he did not really care if you hit him, as he could absorb virtually any blow effortlessly. Being able to take full kicks to the knees and shins and being able to withdraw his testicles into his body, he could not really be hurt. About the only thing that you could hit that might make a difference was his head. I never attempted that, because given how Chinese are about "face," hitting Wang on his head might be interpreted as issuing a challenge that I wanted no part of. Consequently, I never tried.

Besides, Wang was able to guard his head with near perfection. He would perhaps leave an opening for his body, but would never leave a gap that would allow a head hit. Wang was fast enough to block most straight-on strikes thrown at him, but most of the time he did not bother, much like you might not bother stopping a tiny mosquito from biting you.

Although his speed during Push Hands and Rou Shou was not exceptional, Wang had the uncanny ability to get behind opponents very quickly. The speed he used was not that of stepping immensely rapidly, but was rather that of being able to slip into the gaps of an opponent's awareness. Consequently, when fighting those who were extremely fast, he would be swift enough (and sufficiently sensitive to the space in which the opposing fighter's mind resided) to slip through the gaps. And he had enough power that he only had to slip in once.

Hung I Hsiang

Hung I Hsiang had remarkable hand-touch speed, as well as sensitivity. He could move his hands up and down the inside and outside of your arms while each one of his five fingers operated independently, moving your arms and/or body in different directions. His fingers changed direction with the speed of a concert pianist. The various parts of his hand, moving like a rapidly coiling snake, could adjust pressures on your arm or hand, changing the force vectors ten times within a second.

In terms of speed through space from point A to point B, Hung was not particularly fast. However, the speed with which Hung could fold his joints and the inside of his abdomen and legs in coordination at touch was astounding. Hung was also very fast at slipping into the movement of an opponent, especially in terms of fighting angles and moving his body to the side. This skill more than compensated for any inability to move exceptionally fast through physical space.

Hung always emphasized the speed required to make the angles of the hand and the waist coordinate swiftly with the angles of the circle, the spiral, the triangle, and the square.

Bai Hua

Bai Hua's speciality was unbelievably rapid openings and closings and linear speed from

A Comparison of Five Masters, continued

point A to point B. In fact, he was a heavy-weight who could move *exceedingly* fast between points. In any sort of Push Hands or touch-fighting application practices, Bai Hua's speed came out of his ability to fluidly change from technique to technique.

Although he was faster than Wang in touch practices (being much younger), he clearly was not as fast as some of the other masters. In touch practices, Bai Hua emphasized power over speed. He strongly favored speed during openings and closings of the body. However, rather than focusing on speed in getting to the target, he emphasized the speed of blasting through it once he got there.

Bai Hua had exceptional elbow control, and in all his touch and nontouch practices, he emphasized the springiness of the elbows and on increasing their striking speed. Bai Hua was especially fast when using weapons, particularly the spear and the straight sword, which he clearly used physically faster than any of the other masters.

Huang Hsi I

Huang was extremely long-limbed, with huge hands the shapes of which could change with lightning speed. During touch practices, he always stressed the ability to rapidly change between the permutations of any single technique. Although he had a vast technical repertoire, rather than using a different technique each time an opponent changed on him, he would himself rapidly change into another permutation of the technique he was using, so as not to break his flow.

Huang stressed power over speed in Rou Shou. He invariably defeated his opponent at the instant a contested fighting angle arose. He would be able to stop an opponent's power and then go right around his joints and strike him.

Huang had an interesting type of speed in sparring. Although his main technique was slipping into the gaps of an opponent, he was also excellent the moment he gained an advantageous fighting angle, stepping in extremely fast and knocking his opponent out with a hsing-i technique. He also frequently executed the dimmer-switch quality of radically slowing down his action in mid-motion, waiting, and, when his opponent committed to the trap he had laid, instantaneously turning his internal switch up full-bore to attack. He performed this feat in the middle of either a defense or attack. To his opponent, this action seemed to be amazingly fast, when in fact Huang was not physically moving quickly at all.

Liu Hung Chieh

Liu had transcended physical speed in the martial arts. He was not particularly fast physically in the last years of his life when I knew him, yet he had found the "Holy Grail" of speed within the internal martial arts. He was able to move at any speed, no matter how slow, and yet always beat his opponent. He accomplished this feat through complete mastery of energy, both his own and that of his opponent, in terms of speed, subtlety, direction, and power.

There were no gaps in Liu's defense, and it was as though he knew what you would do before you did. In nontouch practices, he was a

A Comparison of Five Masters, continued

member of the minimalist school of movement, sometimes not moving his hands more than two or three inches no matter what type of attack I brought against him. In general, his power was such that once he touched my hand there was no way to budge him if he did not want to move. The more I tried, the greater the holes in my defenses became and, at will, he could move through and hit me or apply some other internal martial arts technique.

At touch, whenever I would try to apply power against him, there would simply be nothing to apply the power against, and I would find myself slightly off-angle no matter how fast I readjusted the angle. Of course, he was able to either apply fa jin instantaneously, no matter what the position, or move my arms out of the way, easily touching me gently after opening up an unimpeded highway to some target on my body. Liu did not emphasize speed but rather ability to slip inside a person's movement or, at any contested fighting angle, to exert a light, irresistible force that always put an opponent at a disadvantage. Liu is the only person I ever met who could move significantly more slowly than I, and yet always easily prevail.

Chinese people of varying ages practicing tai chi for health in a Beijing park.

USING ENERGY TO HEAL

8

The Health Aspects of Martial Arts

THE INTERNAL MARTIAL ARTS AS ENERGY-HEALING SYSTEMS

The healing, meditation, and martial aspects of internal martial arts, especially ba gua and tai chi, are completely intertwined. This chapter completes a circle as we move from the martial to the healing side of the internal arts, whose power can be used to fight disease. In fact, for most people, the fame of the internal martial arts comes not so much from their excellent martial capacities, but rather from their superlative ability to treat disease that other methods cannot, as well as from their ability to enhance other healing methods. The practice of internal martial arts supports lifelong vitality and suppleness, especially into old age, and consequently can serve as a useful adjunct to any longevity program. Of the three internal martial arts that are the focus of this book, tai chi is the most popular. Its popularity is due in large part to its initial relative ease of practice and to its accessibility because of the larger number of active tai chi teachers. This being said, ba gua and hsing-i also have the same abilities, although they use different methods. Many throughout China turn to tai chi and chi gung to heal themselves of all manners of illnesses and injuries.*

All the internal martial arts are used therapeutically in China to reduce blood pressure, improve nerve function, regulate the digestive system, and treat what is becoming known in the West as chronic fatigue syndrome (or burnout). The internal martial arts are also well known for helping to rehabilitate traumatic injury to the joints, muscles, and spine. The therapeutic aspects of the internal martial arts have as much depth, breadth, and complexity of skill as their martial side. Essentially, the healing techniques are based on sophisticated chi gung therapy.

*Editor's note: The author himself used the Wu style of tai chi taught to him by Liu Hung Chieh to recover from serious injury to his spine caused by an automobile accident.

The Difference Between Health and Fitness from an Internal Viewpoint

The approach to health taken by many external hard-style martial artists, as well as those in competitive sports, is to create an extreme state of physical fitness. If you look at any heavy-duty sport (contact or noncontact), you will find that the primary goal is maximum performance that demonstrates speed, power, strength, and agility. In Taoism, however, health is defined not so much in terms of superior performance, but more as a state of overall wellness in which your mind is clear, your emotions balanced (that is, you are mentally healthy), your body is free from organic illness or injury, and you have strong vitality coupled with a sense of well-being.

A person who is considered to be fit in the West may be able to do over 100 push-ups, run a marathon, possess a beautiful, muscular physique—and yet not be internally healthy. He or she may have a bad back, damaged joints, liver problems, unbalanced emotions, an inability to handle stress, and sexual weakness or dysfunction. On the other hand, an internally healthy person may be frail-looking, unmuscular, or fat, be able to run only a few hundred meters, or lack physical strength. Yet this person may have a strong, healthy back, good joints and blood circulation, be emotionally balanced, have no internal organ or central nervous system problems, be able to do all of life's normal activities with stamina, have a full sexual life, and be able to handle heavy stress in a relaxed way.

From this framework, it is easy to see that someone could be considered fit and yet not healthy, or healthy and not fit. In the Taoist chi development arts, the first goal is to make a person healthy, a goal that is useful and accessible to everyone. That level of chi development actually takes less work than becoming "fit." To become a superior martial artist or athlete, you must first become healthy and *afterwards* work harder to achieve fitness, maximum competence, and peak performance.

If your primary goal is health, the most important area to concentrate on is bringing the chi to the state the Chinese call *tong*, which is the ability of the chi to completely circulate throughout the body without being obstructed. To accomplish flowing chi circulation, it is critical to thoroughly learn the basic Taoist 16-part nei gung program (see p. 62). To go beyond simply being free from illness to developing superior mental and physical functioning takes more effort. Usually, one progresses from the easier health practices to a general overall fitness to more involved training to encompass maximum physical speed, power, vitality, and mental clarity.

Personal Health: Jack Pao and the Nature of Limitations

Ba gua was clearly one of Jack Pao's passions. His original introduction to it came from a private instructor his family had employed to teach him as a boy. Jack had a cryptic, quiet sense of humor and a way about him that

Westerners would call "mild-mannered."* He was a very private man in his late forties, about five-and-a-half feet tall and very thin, who did not like to talk about himself or his previous life in China. A kind man with a liking for Russian food, Jack worked for a furrier. Unlike most in the emerging economic powerhouse of Hong Kong, he did not seem to have much interest in money. By demeanor, language, and obvious education in both English and Chinese, he appeared to have come from a middle- or upper-class background in Beijing.

When sparring, Jack would spontaneously attack and defend. In conversation, he would share his knowledge of solo palm changes and the do's and don'ts of how to practice to restore health.

Jack had an acute case of some form of hereditary rheumatism. If he practiced well and sensibly, his pain would go away, but if he did not practice, his health would reverse and his power in applications would weaken significantly. One could see clear differences in him over a month, a week, a day, or as little as an hour. Being totally fluent in English, he was often willing and linguistically able to share his experiences. He provided tremendous insights into how the middle-aged body works with chi for maximum health, and specifically how either overdoing or underdoing causes diseases to accelerate, stay the same, or get better.

Jack Pao specialized in hit-and-run fighting. Being small, he had less reach and power than bigger people, so he concentrated on avoidance and rapid in-and-out counterattacks. Jack Pao was a living example that even those with handicaps, congenital or otherwise, can realistically defend themselves if they put in the time and effort.

Do You Have To Learn Self-Defense To Get the Health Benefits?

Many people who study the internal martial arts in the West are interested in only some of the five aspects of the practice. These aspects are personal health, high performance, healing others, self-defense, and meditation. In China, you learn what your teacher teaches. If you don't like one aspect of what is being taught, you simply ignore it and go through the motions for the sake of politeness. A Chinese student will recognize and accept that individual teachers will impart similar and different slices of the whole internal arts pie.

In the West, students often have unrealistic expectations of what a teacher can, should, or is willing to offer. A frequently asked question is, "If I do tai chi or ba gua, do I have to learn fighting, healing, meditation, etc? I only really want...." The truth is, you do not have to if you do not want to. It is best, however, to discuss these questions with your teacher

---

Editor's note: The author met Jack Pao while practicing in Kowloon park in Hong Kong in 1974. Throughout that year and the next, the two practiced ba gua walking fighting applications together.

because he/she may only know how to teach by also including the parts you don't like. Even if a teacher can leave out parts that you personally dislike, it would be wise to get some information about those parts and listen to the teacher concerning their potential value in regard to your own long-term progress.

Because so many confusing questions arise in the minds of students, it is worthwhile to discuss how you should go about successfully pursuing your perceived goals in a balanced and intelligent way. One individual might feel this way: "I care about getting healthy and really like the way these chi practices make my body feel, but I do not like this fighting stuff, and am neutral toward healing others and meditation." Another person might be an athlete who wants to use the Taoist internal arts to better excel in a given sport, and couldn't care less about meditation or other elements. A healer might not be interested in the fighting aspect, and a fighter might be totally uninterested in healing others, while either might or might not take to meditation. A meditator might or might not want to be involved in high performance, self-defense, or healing others.

To attain the fruits of any one of these five aspects of Taoist personal practices, you will have to emphasize those methods and strategies that will bring a particular result. There are both major overlaps and clear distinctions between methods of training, in terms of how your mind operates and where you put your effort. To obtain peace of mind or realize the Tao does not require you become a great fighter, or vice versa. It is possible that you could transcend your personality and yet have little skill at healing somebody else's physical disease. In the same way, you could also become either a great physical healer or martial artist who nevertheless lives in emotional or psychic torment and imbalance.

So the issue is how much weight you should give to each aspect of your personal chi practice at any given point in time. What benefits do you wish to obtain at this time? Where do your interests now lie? Your emphasis may shift over a period of years, months, weeks, days, or even within the span of a single practice session. The nature of internal martial arts practice is that the basic needs of health are always met with the development of chi, which naturally brings good health. There is a great difference between being minimally healthy (that is, not obviously sick) and being in a superb state of health and vitality. You may not care about healing others professionally, but if a close friend, relative, or loved one becomes ill, you may suddenly develop an interest in healing another. You may not care about fighting skills for a long time until some violent event touches you or a person close to you. Meditators years later may find themselves becoming interested in action and directly overcoming physical fears and limitations. Accomplished fighters may one day become interested in conquering nonphysical fears and transforming the power of their blows to the power of peace and kindness. In terms of the context of the whole system, the five beneficial components of ba gua, tai chi, and all internal arts are assigned values of "weight." At any given point in time, depending upon your specific interest or level of progress in your own personal practice sessions, you should weigh your present attention against your goals and aspirations.

The following tabulation gives suggested amounts of time to spend on each aspect of practice according to various specific interests.

SUGGESTED PROPORTION OF PRACTICE TIME

	Average Person (% of time)	Meditator (% of time)	Elderly Person (% of time)	Fighter (% of time)	Healer (% of time)
General Health	60	20	20	20	15
Rejuvenation	20	20	50	10	15
Fighting	10	–	–	60	–
Healing	–	–	10	–	50
Meditation	10	60	20	10	20

These numbers could change over time as your interest and expertise in an area grows or as it becomes necessary to bolster a weakness to maximize and/or balance your capacity in your primary areas of interest. For example, a meditator may need to address physical fears about fighting to progress with meditation, or a healer may need to address his or her personal imbalanced psychic or emotional chi using meditation in order to be able to better serve patients.

Bear in mind that if you go to an internal arts supermarket, you normally buy the staples (health) no matter what else you get, and then the specialty items (fighting, meditation, longevity, healing). The larger the number of your specialty items, the higher the price (effort, practice time, study, etc.), but the greater the enjoyment and satisfaction. As time goes on, it is not uncommon to get more of a particular category of special goods, as well as specific items (specific techniques). It is the responsibility of individuals to decide what they want, and how much they are willing to do for the benefits. You get what you pay for—there are no free lunches in any genuine internal practice.

Real ba gua and tai chi teaching masters are a bit like food store owners. Some have small stores (one or two categories) with a few items of high quality. Some have big supermarkets with all five categories, but with a mix of high and low quality items. The stores where everything is of the highest quality are exceedingly rare. The challenging job of a ba gua or tai chi master is, from the categories available, to teach students in a progressive manner tailored to what they want, what they are capable of achieving, and the balanced development and integration required for their bodies and minds.

Health and Fitness in Internal Martial Arts

When practiced for health and fitness, ba gua, tai chi, and hsing-i have three basic aspects: physical motions, the development of chi, and the releasing of stress from the nerves and mind. For achieving both health and fitness in ba gua, the physical motions of Circle-Walking and the changing techniques will keep your body active. These alone will help keep sedentary workers healthy. The chi work will balance the energies of your body. The meditation techniques of calming the mind will be of immense help in balancing your emotions. Ba gua practitioners who train for fitness attempt to create superior balance, speed, and strength while upgrading their internal organs, glands, and joints in order to gain superior vitality and mental alertness. All this must be combined with a mind and central nervous system that is relaxed, calm, and flexible.

The central technique for internal development in ba gua, the Single Palm Change (see p. 217), was practiced in Taoist monasteries for at least 1500 years with *no martial applications*.* It was done purely to enhance health, fitness, mental clarity, and meditation practices. Therefore, it is not necessary for you to actively pursue the self-defense aspects of ba gua in order to attain these benefits. At the initial level of training for health, a more easy-going practice approach will help to promote chi circulation to take care of everyday physical discomforts with the least effort. If you are after greater benefits, you will have to pay the higher price of greater effort and longer practice time. As the intensity of the practice increases, the benefits increase proportionately.

If one wishes to add martial applications to the mix, forms done at slow and medium speed are sufficient for health, while full-speed, rapidly changing defense/attacks are necessary for full fitness. For personal health and fitness, the solo work is sufficient, and neither the fighting applications nor the practice for applying therapeutic healing work to others are required. The beginning level meditation work of spirituality is helpful to calm the spirit and promote better chi circulation, but intermediate or advanced level Taoist mediation and internal alchemy work is not a prerequisite for a healthy mind and body. Merely having the chi sink to the lower tantien and having the mind become focused, calm, and relaxed is sufficient for health or fitness.

---

*Bai Hua interviewed monks at the Lung Men Gate Monastery in great detail in 1985 to verify this history.

TABLE 1 Parameters for Practicing the Single Palm Change for Health and Fitness

Aspect of Palm Change	To Achieve Health	To Achieve Fitness
Walking speed	Slow or medium speed is sufficient	You must be able to speed-walk and execute lightning fast steps, waist turns, and arm movements
Stamina	Initially yields only low-to-medium stamina	You must develop significant stamina to achieve genuine high-performance abilities
Stances	High or medium stances only	Low or squatting stances are necessary
Twisting of tendons, muscles, and fascia	50 to 60 percent of capacity is sufficient	70 to 90 percent of capacity is necessary
Leg strength	Medium is sufficient	Superior leg strength is necessary
Breath	Must be deep and slow	Must be deep, slow, and exceptionally long
Weighted objects	Weights or weapons not necessary	Training with iron balls or heavy weapons is recommended
Movement	Airborne techniques are not needed	Airborne techniques (leaps, kicks, spins) are needed
Size of circle	Big or medium circles; middle-sized organ-twisting	Small circles for maximum organ- and muscle-twisting
Minimum time	20 to 30 minutes	30 to 60 minutes

TABLE 2 Parameters for Practicing the Tai Chi Solo Form for Health and Fitness

Tai Chi Solo Form	To Achieve Health	To Achieve Fitness
Practice speed	Slow to medium	Extremely slow to extremely fast
Stamina	Initially yields only low-to-medium stamina	You must be capable of significant stamina
Stances	High or medium	Low or medium
Twistings	40 to 50 percent of capacity is sufficient	70 to 80 percent of capacity is sufficient
Leg Strength	Medium is sufficient	Superior leg strength is necessary
Breath	Must be deep and slow	Must be deep, slow, and exceptionally long
Weapons training	Not needed	Regular and heavy weapons training preferred (straight sword, broad-sword, spear)
Movement	Kicks only to knee or groin height	Kicks to solar plexus or higher
Postures	Done using the 16-part nei gung system in an internally gentle way	Done using the 16-part nei gung system to create steel-like internal compressions
Duration of posture	5 minutes maximum	15 minutes plus
Daily practice time	20 to 30 minutes	30 to 60 minutes minimum

TABLE 3 Parameters for Practicing the Hsing-I Five Elements for Health and Fitness

Five Element Form	To Achieve Health	To Achieve Fitness
Practice speed	Normal walking speed	Extremely slow or extremely rapid
Stamina	Initially yields low-to-medium stamina	You must be capable of significant stamina
Stances	Medium to high	Medium to low
Twistings	50 to 60 percent of capacity is sufficient	70 to 80 percent of capacity is sufficient
Leg strength	Medium is sufficient	Superior leg strength is necessary
Breath	Must be deep and slow	Must be deep, slow, and exceptionally long
Heavy weapons training	Not needed	Preferred with broadsword and spear; the heavier, the better
Movement	Kicks above groin or leaps in air not needed	Kicks to solar plexus and airborne techniques
Postures	Done using 16-part nei gung system to create moderately strong, steel-like compressions	Done using 16-part nei gung system to create maximum steel-like internal compressions and internal strength
Duration of posture	5 minutes for San Ti; 1 minute each, maximum, for other postures	Capacity to do San Ti for 30 to 60 minutes
Daily practice time	100 yards of hsing-i stepping, 20 to 30 minutes	30 to 60 minutes or minimum 1000 yards of hsing-i stepping

HOW THE INTERNAL MARTIAL ARTS
AND CHI GUNG PRODUCE HEALTH

In China, the most popular view of internal martial arts is that they are primarily sophisticated chi gung systems for manipulating the chi of the body for purposes of healing. The perspectives of Traditional Chinese Medicine and orthodox Western medicine differ on how to promote healing and relieve human suffering. Chinese medicine seeks to heal the body by balancing the energy flows within it, strengthening that which is deficient and reducing what is excessive. Among the therapies used to alter chi imbalances are herbs, acupuncture, therapeutic movements (including those of chi gung and internal martial arts), and therapeutic massage. These Chinese therapies usually do not have the invasive quality and detrimental side effects at times associated with strong pharmaceuticals and surgery.

Chinese and Western medicine also differ in methods of diagnosis. Western medicine checks for material changes in the body through a range of clinical biochemical and biophysical testing, some of which utilize highly technical equipment. Chinese medicine checks for how the chi flows of the body are imbalanced, utilizing sophisticated observation techniques that can include pulse and tongue diagnosis, palpation, aura analysis, and taking the patient's emotional and spiritual chi patterns into account. Consistent practice of Chinese diagnostic methods can ultimately bring extreme sensitivities to internal chi into the conscious awareness of the practitioner. In like manner, one can gain these sensitivities and then apply them through specific chi gung healing techniques appropriate for healing various conditions in oneself and others.

The methods for correcting one's own health conditions or helping another with a problem are both contained within the 16-part nei gung system (see p. 62). These methods may be taught by competent internal martial arts teachers with varying degrees of expertise and communication abilities. Yet all three internal martial arts are so sophisticated that their healing techniques still work wonderfully in watered-down versions. Some of the first places to look for the healing powers of solo form work lie in balancing the left and right sides of the body both physically and energetically, releasing the nerves and sinking the chi. Leg, hip, and lower back injuries, as well as other chronic problems, can be greatly helped by aligning the body properly. Learning to open and close the joints can prevent or help arthritis. Stimulating the external aura of the body, as well as systematically stretching the muscles and fascia, can stimulate the practitioner's acupuncture meridians.

All this occurs merely through movement exercises whose primary aim is the systematic moving and balancing of the chi of the human body. For the majority of the practicing population, the most powerful self-defense techniques of the internal martial arts are those for defending yourself against both illness and the ravages of old age. This is why huge numbers of Chinese practice internal martial arts and/or chi gung every day.

There are two major aspects to the energy movements of internal martial arts that are done for health. The first concerns how any specific movement or series of movements is done as a therapeutic whole. The second concerns how they are done as a whole emphasizing each individual nei gung component. This requires detailed knowledge of how the whole form may or may not need to be adjusted to accomodate any additional single or multiple series of nei gung components. Someone who only knows a form as a whole will not normally be aware of the exact energy qualities and permutations specific to each individual movement.

Repairing Agitated Chi

One of the things a good energy teacher imparts to students is how to smoothly develop chi without side effects. Unfortunately, there are incorrect chi gung practices that can negatively impact a student's chi and/or central nervous system.* Chi gung exploded in popularity in Taiwan and Mainland China during the latter half of the 1980s. At the International Chi Gung Conference in 1994, held in San Francisco, California, professionals in the field reported that the improper practice of chi gung was a problem escalating throughout Asia, and even more in Mainland China.

The *I Ching*-based ba gua healing techniques are particularly effective for repairing the aftermath of improperly performed chi gung. Unfortunately, these skills are extremely rare even in China. The nei gung downward energy and dissolving practices** usually form the beginning of these procedures. In many cases, this alone is sufficient for straightening out problems stemming from improper chi gung practice. If you need help in this area, seek it from a willing and experienced energy-work adept familiar with the Chinese methods. Usually chi gung tui na practitioners have the requisite expertise. The ba gua healing system, for example, specifically uses the eight primary energies of the I Ching, along with diagnosing the energies of the three tantiens, to treat what has gone physically, emotionally, psychologically, or spiritually wrong with the body from improperly performed energetic practices. This three tantien pulse-taking is a highly sophisticated technology that is a specialty of the Taoists. The Buddhists and medical chi gung practitioners have alternative ways of approaching the problem.

Editor's note: For more information on this subject see B. K. Frantzis, *Opening the Energy Gates of Your Body*, North Atlantic Books, Berkeley, California, 1993, Appendix C, "The Importance of Correct Chi Gung Practice."

**Editor's note:* For more information on these subjects see B. K. Frantzis, *Opening the Energy Gates of Your Body*, North Atlantic Books, Berkeley, California, 1993, Chapter 3.

INTERNAL MARTIAL ARTS AS A NATURAL ROUTE TO BECOMING A HANDS-ON HEALER

The internal martial arts, along with their associated methods of chi gung, have, in China, traditionally been a consistent training ground for empowering energetic healers. All the internal martial arts and chi gung techniques and movements (as well as the techniques of Taoist meditation) can give you the knowledge and ability to move your energy for healing. The hands-on healing technologies of tai chi, hsing-i, and ba gua are all derived from chi gung. They are collectively called tui na, or more specifically, chi gung tui na (*tui* means to push, *na* means to grab or pull.) Chi gung tui na can be thought of as energetic therapeutic bodywork or massage.

Each of the internal martial arts has energetic therapeutic massage methods directly associated with it. While the three systems of hsing-i, tai chi, and ba gua share many techniques, each has its own particular specialty of energetic medical bodywork. The arts themselves contain the specialities; practitioners may or may not have learned them. Generally, hsing-i adepts are well-known for their bone-setting skills and deep tissue work and are also skilled at repairing heavy traumatic damage to the body, called **die da** in Chinese. Tai chi includes very sophisticated techniques for working with the yin aspects of chi that are particularly effective for treating diseases of the internal organs and cancers. Ba Gua adepts are also proficient in all these areas and have specialized skills* in working with the spine, central nervous system, and nerve damage.

In China, only a small minority of internal martial arts practitioners are interested in, or learn parts or the whole of, any system's energetic healing technologies. Hung I Hsiang (see p. 203), was one. He was very adept at "hit medicine," therapy applied to people who have had heavy injuries to their bodies from accidents, sports, or fights. The late Han Hsing Yuan (of I Chuan) also worked as a chi gung tui na practitioner in Hong Kong, as does Huang Hsi I (see p. 293). On one side of the traditional Chinese medical approach, healers learn to indirectly observe the shadow of chi by reading wrist pulses, doing tongue diagnosis, urine analysis, and asking questions of the patient. In contrast, those training in the internal martial arts methods of chi gung tui na learn how to directly feel and see both balanced and imbalanced chi in the body. By directly perceiving the 16 components of the nei gung system at work in the body, these practitioners can detect how a particular chi changes and mixes

DIE DA
The traditional Chinese medical practice that deals with immediate bruises, swellings, and broken bones from accidents.

Editor's note: The author, for instance, has used his specialized training in the ba gua and tai chi healing methods (studied over a period of ten years in China) to help formulate a comprehensive chi gung program that promotes wellness (see p. 344).

with other energies in the body. They may read the energy of the external aura or the three primary energy lines of the body (left, right, and central channels) as well as the several thousand secondary energy lines in the body, including the acupuncture meridian lines.

In order to practice the methods of the energy therapies of internal martial arts, significant training in cultivating one's own chi is required. Generally speaking, a practitioner should be able to feel the chi inside his or her own body before undertaking the more difficult task of feeling chi in someone else's body. Ordinary tui na massage, on the other hand, does not require its practitioners to have the ability to feel the chi that is directly used in chi gung tui na. Instead, it relies on the indirect methods of diagnosis and on treatments based on physical, not energetic, technique, such as Chinese acupuncture and acupressure or methods that have points in common with Western chiropractic, structural deep tissue work, or ordinary massage. It is for these reasons that a would-be practitioner of chi gung therapy or bodywork must first have a solid background in personal chi practice before being able to competently learn chi gung therapeutics. Ordinary tui na, however, can be learned by anyone.

The Connection between Internal Martial Arts and Healing Work

According to legend, Tung Hai Chuan was found injured in the mountains by Taoists who healed him and went on to teach him ba gua to complete his healing process. Whatever the truth of the many legends about Tung, this story illustrates the traditional linkage in Taoism between the healing arts and the martial arts. In fact, it is common for high-level Taoists to be trained in tai chi, hsing-i, and ba gua, all of which cultivate the ability to project chi, a skill that can be used to heal people or to hurt them. The ability to project chi to kill or harm a violent assailant becomes a valuable tool in the hands of an accomplished chi gung doctor when that chi is used to kill cancerous cells or shrink tumors, a speciality of some of the best and most experienced chi gung healers in China. To hurt and heal are two sides of the same chi coin.

The healing systems of the three internal martial arts are very sophisticated and extremely effective. They probably first arose from the need to treat martial arts injuries and, over time, evolved to treating disease. The more advanced techniques from the ba gua school, for example, include raising the vibratory levels within a person's body, done by using specific mantra-like sounds to activate dormant or underused capacities and/or to influence the energetic functions of each of the eight energy bodies. Various oscillating Chinese mantras and tones are coordinated with vibrating one's body and energy channels. This complex system ranges beyond the basic Six Healing Sounds that some are familiar with in the West.

Using the same chi diagnostic and treatment principles, a chi gung therapist who does not do hands-on bodywork will attempt to get the same results by specifically designing (prescribing) chi gung exercises to be done standing, moving, sitting, or lying down. These exercises will function to affect both the body's tissues and its chi. The patient will be shown where, why, when, and how to move his or her chi inside the body, and for what specific effects. The patient is also shown what to work with and what to avoid, as well as how to recognize positive and negative results. Patients will also be shown how to physically re-educate the internal muscles, joints, spinal vertebrae and internal organs of the body in order to maximize motor function and alleviate pain. Just as the newly emerging cutting-edge somatic (body) therapies in the West have discovered, the ancient Chinese knew full well that the best therapeutic results occur when the body tissues, the mind, and the central nervous system are all worked with simultaneously.

The Value of a Personal Chi Gung and Internal Martial Arts Practice to Western Healers

Energizing the Hands   The practice of chi gung and the internal martial arts, both in their solo forms and their Push Hands and Rou Shou practices, can dramatically energize and increase the tactile sensivity of all manner of bodyworkers. In various bodywork schools in the West, people frequently spend some months or years learning a range of somatic bodywork and manipulation techniques, along the way accruing great technical knowledge of anatomy, acupressure or trigger points, physiology, and so on. Without "the hands that can intuitively and accurately feel," it will be less than totally effective to apply a good part of hard-earned and learned book knowledge appropriately on a live human being. A bodyworker has a critical need to know how to vary pressure to discover when the body is being forced against its will (which can cause resistance or damage) and when the body is giving its permission for a procedure to continue. Sensitized hands allow the therapist to gather critical information that a pair of "dead" hands cannot. Excellent hand sensitivity makes it possible for the bodyworker to know how to track the chi in someone's body. With this knowledge, it is possible to change techniques appropriately and instantaneously for the most effective possible therapeutic intervention.

This precise systematic development of the capacity to feel chi in the body is a very useful tool generally lacking in current Western bodywork. It could, in fact, prove to be a next great leap forward in the West's rapidly evolving field of somatics.

Burnout Prevention and Recovery   Chronic fatigue, burnout, Epstein-Barr, and nervous exhaustion are all Western terms for what is traditionally referred to in Chinese medicine as *shenti swai rou* (exhaustion of the body's constitution) or *shenjing swai rou* (exhaustion of the body and its nervous system and energy channels). This condition is endemic in our society, especially among high achievers in whatever field. Burnout often affects the best and the brightest.

The internal martial arts and chi gung are very helpful for reversing this problem of energetic exhaustion. They rebuild the energy channels of the body that have been depleted or imbalanced in some way. Increased and rebalanced chi causes the nerves to cease being continuously agitated, to truly rest, and, over time, to regenerate. When the nerves regenerate, the internal organs again begin to re-energize, and the body slowly comes out of its stupor.

Burnout is especially prevalent in all the healing professions, affecting psychologists, counselors, nurses, doctors, bodyworkers, acupuncturists, chiropractors, or anyone involved in healthcare. Patients in China as well as the West can drain the healer. If the patient is grasping for life or has a neurotic obsession, he or she will literally pull chi from the therapist's body/mind. Over prolonged periods of time, this process brings exhaustion to the care-giver and is one of the main reasons why many talented practitioners quit their professions.

It is consequently imperative that healers learn how to systematically prevent energetic burnout. In China, the skills that chi experts found to be most necessary for actively working therapists concern: (1) how to protect yourself, as a healer, from having your patients pull energy from you; (2) how to use chi gung exercises to regenerate the depleted chi of your system; (3) how to avoid patterning your own body's chi after the chi of the sick patient. This latter is a particularly necessary skill for naturally intuitive healers. Such healers often psychically meld with the energy of their patients. A healer does so in order to feel inside his or her own body what is ailing the client, to understand at an experientially visceral level how to fix the problem. Without being clearly able to separate yourself from the condition of a patient, the danger exists that you will pattern yourself into the problems that your patient is exhibiting or that you will simply exhaust your own energetic reserves.

Some of the energy techniques used to achieve these three goals include gaining skills in:

1. Sealing your chi so that it cannot be pulled from your body.
2. Moving energy from the outside environment into the patient's body so that you are not using your own energy and depleting your reserves.
3. Becoming consciously aware of how deep and strong your energetic reserves are at any given point in time. If you have depleted your reserves to a dangerous level, you must learn how to use specific techniques from the 16 basic components of the Taoist nei gung system to replenish your reserves.

4. Reclaiming the chi you projected from your own body into your patient to re-pattern his or her dysfunctional chi.

5. Clearing from your body/mind any emotional or psychic influences that you have picked up from your patients during therapy.

6. Checking yourself at regular intervals during the day for the presence of any subliminal residues. This is done so you can take remedial measures using your chi gung techniques to clear the negative influences the same day they occur, thus preventing cumulative buildup—being your own human Geiger counter, so to speak. It is the cumulative buildup of emotional/psychic residue over time that physically wears people down and results in emotional burnout.

THE VALUE OF LEARNING THE INTERNAL ARTS FOR OLDER MARTIAL ARTISTS

Typically, the ranks of sports (with the exception of golf) are mostly populated by the young. In karate and tae kwon do, half to two-thirds of all participants are in classes for children and teens. As people age, fewer of their peers actively practice martial arts, and are relegated to being spectators. As opposed to being a spectator sport, the internal martial arts can become a lifelong pursuit that equally allows an average person or a dedicated martial artist to age with vitality and grace as the decades go by. Internal martial art practitioners, like great wine vintages, get better with age. There are solid reasons why this phenomenon occurs.

Most external sports, with the effort and strain they require, take a toll on the body. When you are young, injuries heal more quickly, your body stretches faster and more easily, your nerves recuperate more rapidly from exhaustion, and your blood circulates more efficiently. For most people, unless they have specialized chi gung or yoga training, these qualities fade with age. There is normally more body pain associated with aging in all rigorous external practices, from martial arts to sports. Back problems are legion in the Western world, and this one problem alone dramatically thins the ranks of martial artists over the age of forty, especially in those arts that emphasize jumps, throws, and falls.

In China, tai chi especially is used as a supplement to train competitive athletes of all kinds. This training is provided to improve the athlete's reaction times, reflexes, and rate of recovery from injuries, as well as to oil their joints, increase their range of motion, and, most importantly, extend the length of their competitive careers. Now the West is just beginning to pick up on this approach, which will most likely sooner or later be adopted by our professional sports teams and individuals as a competitive adjunct.

Active fifty-year-old gymnasts, boxers, and karate, tae kwon do, external kung fu, and aikido practitioners, both in the Orient and the West, while existing, are few and far between. Above the age of sixty-five, they are virtually nonexistent. In actual fights, where no quarter is given or taken, it is doubtful how many of the martial arts seniors could defeat much younger, stronger martial artists. The elderly silver-haired grandfather or grandmother who begins karate and becomes good at it, is sufficiently rare to merit appearance on a television show or at least a news spot.

Contrast this situation with that of the internal martial arts, where half of all practitioners in China are over fifty, and where it is not an uncommon event when an internal martial artist who is a senior citizen soundly defeats a much younger, stronger martial artist. In fact, at the master level, this is a normal state of affairs. In this sense, the internal martial arts is the Western equivalent of golf. Indeed, these two activities have many parallels. Both have a steady, even flow to them, and have a tradition of being done outdoors in parklike settings. Both are low-impact sports that rely on skill much more than on brute strength and genetically determined athletic ability. As such, both are widely taken up by middle-aged and older people as well as youth, skill being equally available to all ages. Players of both golf and internal arts will practice for hours on end to experience the clarity of the "perfect shot," where the mind and body become one, without demanding it happen instantly or every time. Both can claim a high percentage of educated and successful people who appreciate the level of competence and perserverance involved in achieving effortlessness and subtlety under challenging conditions.

Who Should Practice Internal Martial Arts after the Age of Thirty

There are essentially three groups, ranging from martial arts experts to complete novices, that should actively practice internal martial arts after thirty years of age. The first category consists of people over thirty who are currently practicing external systems and who wish to maintain their physical skill level and, ideally, to see it rise rather than fall. The methods of all the internal martial arts can help external martial artists move better and more smoothly in their choosen art. The emphasis of the internal arts on relaxation going deep into the nerves and muscles of the practitioner upgrades the speed and reflexes of practicing external martial artists. For example, the well-respected Shotokan karate adept H. Kanazawa has his black-belt students learn tai chi to enable them to do their karate better. The more that individuals can learn to relax the body, the more powerfully they can tense the body, if they so choose. The opposite, however, is not true. Bodies habituated to tension often cannot

Martial Arts and Aging

 I am no longer a young man. In my youth, I lived through and enjoyed the fire that the young get from practicing martial arts. Most of my friends who were dedicated no longer practice martial arts due to the normal consequences of aging, and I have felt sadness over witnessing them doing without what had once been a great joy to them. Echoing the words of millions in China, I can honestly say that by using internal martial arts and chi gung, this state of affairs does not have to be. I say this being a martial arts insider approaching fifty at the time of writing this book, a person who has loved and practiced external, external/internal, and internal martial arts until they became part of my blood and bones.

The therapeutic health aspect of the internal martial arts is as deep a science as its combat aspects. Although I had also, along with its fighting techniques, personally specialized in the health side of the internal martial arts throughout the 1970s, it was not until I worked with Liu Hung Chieh in Beijing that I learned just how deep and beneficial this other life-serving aspect of the internal arts could be. Slowly and meticulously over the years, Liu went through all the movements patiently with me again and again from an energetic and therapeutic perspective, just as we also looked at them from the point of view of combat, Taoist meditation, and internal alchemy. We continuously analyzed the effects of internal martial arts movements on all kinds of chi flows and health, equally for those who were healthy and wanted to stay that way and for those with problems that needed help.

In Japan, America, and Europe, the general populations are graying, which makes the health and longevity to be derived from the internal arts of prime importance. All aging people, whether martial artists or not, can deeply benefit from learning some of the internal methods that can bring vitality to anyone of any age. Quality of life has become a major issue for aging populations. I would argue that practicing the techniques of chi gung and nei gung can be a remarkable way to increase the quality of life for the aging.

relax well. In youth, such tension brings on stiffness and slowness, which continues to increase as the body ages. Being able to move powerfully without stiffness is one major difference between mediocre and superior martial artists. The techniques of internal martial arts soften the joints and muscles appreciably, loosening up tight elbows, knees, shoulders, and hips. Practicing these techniques invariably increases the hip-turning speed and power needed in all martial arts and many sports. When older martial artists learn the internal arts and chi gung, they can normally perform their already acquired current techniques with more speed.

The second category includes those older martial artists who wish to increase their already-mastered arsenal of martial techniques. Expanding your knowledge base can be fascinating and exhilarating as the infusion of new material makes your current art ever more alive. Learning internal martial arts never fails to give insights into external martial arts practice. There is real value in cross-martial research, which has been amply demonstrated by highly accomplished martial artists such as aikido's founder Morihei Ueshiba and the film star Bruce Lee.

Internal martial arts skills can help to significantly mitigate many of the difficulties arising from an aging body that lets you down. This applies to pre-black belt practitioners who are trying to sort out what makes a martial technique practical or not. It also applies to junior and senior black belts or their equivalents in other martial arts who want to achieve the highest level of skill possible in their lifetime. If your primary interest is to learn those aspects of the internal arts that relax and smooth the inside of the body, then you do not have to find a powerful internal martial arts fighting master (not too commonly available in in the West). However, if your desire is to go as far martially in this life as possible, then you need to go to a teacher who can also perform internal fighting methods rather than just talk about them.

The third category consists of people over thirty who did martial arts, benefitted from it, wanted to continue, but had to stop due to the pressures of work and family life. Most did tae kwon do or karate and quit. Now middle-aged or older, they want to return to martial arts and find something that can maintain or upgrade their health, heal their old injuries, and also enable them to gain the stamina that will give them the edge to persevere and succeed, whatever their line of work. Because there is no falling, excessive arm-smashing, and considerably less contact sparring in fighting internal martial arts schools, older people are less likely to receive injuries that can interfere with work time. You can grow old with the internal martial arts; you do not have to quit or practice half-heartedly after the flush of youth. Today, many external karate and gung fu schools are adding tai chi or ba gua to their repertoire for just these reasons.

THE INTERNAL MARTIAL ARTS AND MENTAL HEALTH

Internal Martial Arts for Teenagers

Some internal martial arts may well be able to help with problems of mental health, especially with youth. Currently, and most likely for a long time in the future, we are in an era of overpopulation, one result of which is widespread violence, particularly among urban teenagers in the Western world. The Taoist art/meditation aspect of ba gua for learning to resolve internal conflicts without the violent behaviors inherent in other more aggressive martial arts makes the internal martial arts potentially valuable for helping our youth "tame the savage beast within." Beneath the violence of teenagers and young men in their early twenties lies tremendous apathy, denial, hopelessness, and fear of the dark, unconscious spaces inside society as well as inside their own personal body/mind. To relieve a major source of violent crime and human dysfunction, including drug addiction, it could be very useful to develop new methods of liberating these dark spaces before the dysfunctional teenager becomes the self-destructive adult.

Random youth violence eats away at the fabric of society. Youths with a strong, clear, and positive self-image are much less likely to uselessly damage themselves and others. Violent teenagers often need a coherent structure they can believe in. Such a structure can be found in martial arts. Its elements include ranking systems based on merit that encourages individuality and leadership, development of physical strength and coordination, and a highly interactive group that a teenager can belong to and identify with in a positive way.

The Mental Health Benefits of the Internal Martial Arts

This book now comes full circle and returns to the subject of Chapter One: animal, human and spiritual martial arts. Animals respond to uncontrollable instinctual urges, which determine their external behavior. Humans have the ability to recognize when they are possessed by their animal instincts. Often however, they do not have the patience or psychological centering to step back, realize that their animal instincts are overpowering them, choose to decide if they want to go the animal or human way, and act accordingly.

The consistent practice of internal martial arts trains people in the ability to witness their emotions, and to wait for that critical moment when they can decide to override their instinctual animal-like modus operandi. This ability to watch and make a conscious choice before acting is honed every time practitioners do a solo form or a fighting application. In solo movements it occurs during the wait for that critical fraction of a second needed to mobilize the mind before the chi follows and tells the body to act. In fighting applications, it occurs as practitioners wait, initially observe an opponent's intention, and interpret the ramifications of an action (a potential attack, defense, or counterattack) before they slip in the gap and turn the martial situation to their advantage. Humans have the ability to wait and observe themselves before taking action; animals often do not, as they instinctively react from their hormones.

Psychologically, "yang" emotions of anxiety, rage, unending wanting and its attendant frustration are all gradually reduced with internal martial arts practice. Several internal practices contribute to lessening these very human emotions that reduce the joy of living. The first is the breathing techniques, which tend to calm the mind and smooth the tendency of the mind to erupt and explode. The second is the stilling of the mind, which is a basic goal of all internal martial arts solo practices and a fundamental ingredient of their fighting applications. As this mental and emotional stillness begins to settle into the nervous system, becoming "embodied," it balances, calms, and changes the physiology, thereby removing many of the unconscious biological triggers that hormonally maintain a predisposition to frustration and anger.

The internal martial arts develop patience. Developing patience gradually creates a sense of psychological equanimity and acceptance about life and its often uncontrollable changing circumstances, which in turn, creates a healthier sense of internal balance and the ability to comfortably live with oneself. Psychological health at some level requires humans to come to realistic terms both with external events that are commonly beyond our ability to control, (much as the human need for control wishes they were not) and our own human limitations, (such as wanting to do a movement well before one has put in sufficient practice), which invariably will take time and patience to smooth out.

Psychological "yin" emotions of lack of self-esteem (which can lead to all kinds of compensatory negative "yang" emotions), self-destructiveness, apathy, lack of follow-through, and depression are also helped by internal martial art practice. Anything that gets a person's energy moving can have the ability to shift the physiology that predisposes a person to many types of depression. The high-energy practices of moving quickly (such as rapidly Walking the Circle in ba gua or doing speed punching or fast forms in tai chi or hsing-i) can be especially useful for moving someone's energy out of a depressed state.

The act of achieving competence in the internal arts can gradually raise a person's self-esteem in several ways. First, by realistically becoming competent in something that by its nature is not easy, a person develops follow-through and realizes what can be accomplished in life, which gives a realistic counterforce for overcoming previous tendencies toward failure and a sense of worthlessness. Second, the internal arts can make people aware that they can "get in touch" with their insides for long periods of time, without discomfort. The more a person delves into the spiritual practices of martial arts, the clearer and more magnanimous their self-perceived internal environment becomes. Once this happens, the need for unconsciously driven self-destructive behaviors may well begin to diminish of its own accord.

Finding out that positive action yields real internal benefits and competence also gradually cuts out the ground from which apathy takes root and grows. Moving beyond apathy towards a more positive direction in life lies at the core of all spiritual martial arts practices.

When a practitioner enters the active spiritual stage of martial arts, he or she deliberately seeks to resolve all that which prevents the full flowering of love, compassion, equanimity, forgiveness, justice, generosity, and wisdom. These qualities all contribute to a healthy psychological environment and have the possibility of transcending all psychological limitations.* In this way, people can "defeat" their own "lower nature" and possibly emerge "victorious" to fulfill the potential with which all humans are born.

---

*It is important to note that, whatever mental health benefits they may bring to a practitioner, the internal martial arts are not a substitute for psychotherapy. Those with mental or emotional problems should seek help from a qualified mental health professional.

Healing Others — Huang Hsi I and Therapeutic Chi

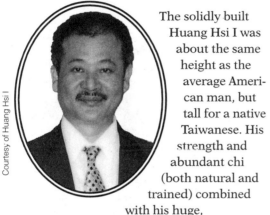

Courtesy of Huang Hsi I

The solidly built Huang Hsi I was about the same height as the average American man, but tall for a native Taiwanese. His strength and abundant chi (both natural and trained) combined with his huge, immensely sensitive hands, made him a superb healer in Chinese chi gung therapeutic bodywork and osteopathy. Like many in Taiwan, he came from a farming background, and consequently had a strong affinity for living things, including plants and herbs. He loved to cook for people, and was one of the few men I ever met who could prepare food with medicinal herbs and make the dishes taste good. Very flexible physically, Huang had an endearing habit of squatting flatfoot on a tiny stool while talking on the telephone.

Although he dressed in modern clothes, he was a very old-fashioned, conservative Chinese, with a heart of gold. Even by Chinese standards, he was an eccentric. For several years while we were roommates, Huang lived from a rural sense of time based on the seasons. He did not pay much attention to clocks, which caused me, as well as many others who knew him, extreme frustration. Eventually, we all gave in to Huang's sense of the natural flow of events unfolding, ignoring our own schedules and expectations. When Huang and I were together, he was just learning to use Mandarin naturally, rather than his native Taiwanese, which I did not know. Although his Mandarin eventually became just fine, at that time it made for a linguistic and cultural comedy of errors. These communication problems could have made the situation intolerable if we had not had such natural affection for each other, and I had not had such immense respect for his accomplishments. I also enjoyed his sense of humor. Besides being an exceptional internal martial art adept, Huang was without doubt one of the most gifted chi gung therapists and bodyworkers I had met during all my time in the Orient.

I lived and studied with Huang Hsi I in 1978 and 1979. At that time, he was one of Hung I Hsiang's most powerful hsing-i students. Huang, before, during and after his time with Hung, had quietly studied with some of Taiwan's most adept old internal masters from the Mainland. During those years when we were roommates, Huang— of all of Hung's students—clearly had the finest and most subtle command of Rou Shou that I had ever seen.

Huang introduced me to spinal chi gung, and was a major influence in my chi gung tui na training. In my second long trip to Taiwan, I studied much less regularly with Hung I Hsiang (see p. 203), filling in many critical gaps with Huang. Huang took me on as his younger brother, avoiding much of the strange Confucian structure of disciplehood that culturally would have made life immensely complicated for me as a foreigner. Huang's hsing-i and ba gua skills were very high, and

Healing Others — Huang Hsi I and Therapeutic Chi, continued

his grasp of Taoist internal chi gung was of a rare level for such a young man.

Huang's method of teaching was that of the traditional school: have students struggle to find the essential meaning of an internal technique within themselves from information imparted but not precisely spelled out. Huang was extremely talented at instructing without being directly explicit, which is one of the classic Taoist methods of teaching.

It was primarily through Huang's teaching that I was able to completely understand much of what Hung I Hsiang was imparting. Huang also was the first to make me understand the importance of the Taoist method of working with the spinal vertebrae and cerebrospinal system. It was the personal applications of many of his techniques that allowed me to begin recovery from the severe back injuries that I sustained in a car accident (cracked vertebrae and rippped soft tissue) in 1982. Without the life-giving spinal chi

gung knowledge that Huang Hsi I, Liu Hung Chieh, and some other Taoist chi masters had taught me, I would never have walked again after that crash, and most likely would have died in the crash itself. Huang's methods helped me greatly with the continuous pain I suffered in the immediate aftermath of the accident. Later on, the Old Yang style tai chi of Lin Du Ying helped heal my upper back and neck, and finally the Wu style tai chi taught by Liu cured my lower back.

Huang was a specialist in the standing chi gung postures of Taoism, the chi work of hsing-i, and the methods of manifesting light in the body through standing and spontaneous movement chi gung. Huang took his knowledge of chi, the hand movement work of ba gua, and the internal martial arts, and directly moved it into the beneficial arena of therapeutics and healing. He started and developed a highly successful practice as a chi gung doctor.

APPENDICES

THE DIFFERENT STYLES OF TAI CHI · A

A Brief History

ORIGIN OF THE DIFFERENT STYLES OF TAI CHI

Many have claimed to know the exact origin of tai chi. Some of these claims seem fairly reasonable, some clearly need scrutiny, and others seem to be created out of self-interest. There are so many books written on the origins of tai chi, both in Chinese and in other languages, that only a skeletal history is presented here. This brief history concerns points that are of value for tai chi students who will benefit from this art in the highly technological environment of the twenty-first century. As well as imparting combat skills, all the internal martial arts, including tai chi, are extremely valuable for health and healing, reducing and managing stress, and providing a sense of much-needed balance in one's general life.

The origins of tai chi before it reached the Chen village are open to controversy, and would be exceedingly difficult to verify historically beyond a shadow of a doubt. One thing, however, can be said with certainty: In modern times, the clear source of what is commonly recognized as high-level tai chi originates from the Chen village in central China.*

To truly understand the origins of any specific style or school, it is much more revealing to look at what it actually does now, rather than study its early history. In this way, one can discover what kinds of gung fu skills its teachers now possess and its diligent students are beginning to manifest. In order to differentiate hyperbole and wishful

thinking from substance, look into the nature of the external fighting movements a school is teaching, the internal work being imparted, and the group's most emphasized verbal directives. ("Relax!" "Drop your tailbone!" "Sink your chi!" "Open and close your joints and spine!" and so on.) In short, focus on the real structure of what they do, because ultimately that is all any student will become exposed to. The historical story of a good meal might entice, but is usually less satisfying than savoring the flavors of today's dinner.

Original Chen Family Village Tai Chi

There are four main theories concerning how tai chi first found its way into the Chen village (that is, the origin of tai chi chuan). Theory One says that the famous Taoist Immortal Chang San Feng watched a snake and a crane fighting. From this observation, he created a new soft internal martial art that was different from the external Shaolin Temple gung fu, and which he infused with all the wisdom, military strategies, and longevity methods of Taoism. This knowledge passed down to Wang Tsung Yueh, who arrived at the Chen family village in central China, which was clearly off the beaten track and located roughly about a week's horse ride away from the Shaolin Temple. Theory Two says Wang Tsung Yueh learned tai chi chuan from one of several possible lineages whose sources are not completely clear, possibly that of Chang San Feng, or lineages hundreds of years older. At this point, Theory One and Theory Two dovetail.

One night, Wang arrived at the local inn of the Chen's family village, where almost everybody was

Editor's note: The author studied the Chen style of tai chi in Beijing during the mid-1980s with Feng Zhi Qiang, student of Chen Fa Ke of the Chen village.

a relative by blood or marriage. Conversation ensued. Gradually, Wang proceeded to first disparage and then insult the village's martial art, of which the Chens were very proud, and upon which the village depended for defense against warlords and bandits. In time, the villagers became greatly outraged. They exploded and attacked Wang. He accepted the challenge, and then proceeded to beat the stuffing out of them in a most convincing and spectacular fashion. The next day, the villagers asked Wang if he would teach them this amazing martial art. He agreed. However, he did not have the time to teach them the physical movements of his martial art. Instead, he adapted the principles of his Taoist martial art to their Shaolin-like external martial art style of Cannon Fist.

In Theory Three, tai chi chuan was created by Chen Wan Ting of the Chen village, who had been a fighting general in the army of Chi Chi Guang, China's most famous general of the period. As such, Chen was expected to perform the actual art of combat equal to or better than his troops,* and could be required to accept physical challenges to prove his worth at a moment's notice. Chen Wan Ting is said to have combined the principles of Chinese medical theory and the acupuncture meridian system with Chi's martial art methods. Twenty-nine of the thirty-two basic techniques in Chen tai chi are more or less identical to those in Chi Chi Guang's military training manual for his troops. Chi's method was clearly Shaolin-based.

In Theory Four, tai chi was brought to the Chen village by a man named Jiang Fa, who was

on the run for unspecified reasons. Jiang was given political sanctuary and protection by General Chen Wang Ting in exchange for teaching him and his clan tai chi chuan. In this theory, Jiang Fa knew both Wang Tsuang Yueh's internal power system and Chi Chi Guang's martial methods. Chi called these Chang Chuan, which was in effect a compendium of the best Shaolin fighting techniques of sixteenth-century China.

However, details of how Jiang Fa came to possess all this knowledge is left vague. In this fourth theory, Chen Wan Ting was still a fighting general but under a different Ming Dynasty general than Chi Chi Guang. After Jiang Fa taught Chen Wan Ting the material that eventually* became the first tai chi form of the Chen village, Chen Wan Ting on his own created what eventually became the second set of Chen tai chi called Cannon Fist.

In the author's view, only two sensible things can be considered. First, that the Chen family style of tai chi chuan directly derives from, or has a common antecedent with, the military manual of Chi Chi Guang. Second, although the Chen style clearly uses acupuncture points and meridian-line theory, it is consistent, especially in its middle- and upper-training levels, with the more complete traditional Taoist nei gung method, of which the acupuncture meridian system is only one part.

TAI CHI CHUAN LEAVES THE CHEN VILLAGE AND BECOMES THE YANG AND THEN THE HAO STYLE

Chen Style Begets the Yang Style of Tai Chi

Over the next century, the Chen village developed this internal martial art to a very high level. The village prospered by growing and selling herbs and was successful partially because of the ability

---

*The Chinese military structure was often different from the Western one, where the general sits back far from the fray, directing the battle. In ancient China, when two armies were squared off on a battlefield, at times two top generals would ride right out to the middle of the field for single one-on-one combat, as both sides watched. These generals trained their troops, and the troops were using their fighting methods. If one general lost, his troops would interpret this as the other army having superior military technology (that is, martial arts). The losing side might then surrender or scatter.

---

*Originally, the Chen tai chi style had six forms which, over time, were condensed to two forms — the First Set and Cannon Fist.

to guard the transit of its valuable products. In the nineteenth century, Yang Lu Chan (1799-1872), a talented and motivated young man with a great love of martial arts, was told by his teacher, a decent man of integrity, that he could take him no further. The teacher said the martial art of the Chen village was up to the standard of the young man's talent, and the ideal place for him to go. However, the teachings of this amazing martial art were secret and forbidden to nonfamily members.

Possessed by a desire to learn this art, Yang devised a scheme to enter the Chen family village, which was barred to outsiders. Convincingly pretending to be deaf, he managed to become a servant to the family of the clan's martial art leader. Yang worked hard, reliably accomplished his tasks, gradually became completely trusted, and was given keys to all the rooms. The keys allowed him to watch the internal training unobserved as it was done behind locked doors. After the training was done, Yang assiduously practiced what he had seen late into the night, arising earlier than the others to fulfill his role as trusted servant. This clandestine process went on for several years.

One day, Yang got caught. Some trainees demanded that he be thrown out of the village on the spot; others wanted to rip him apart. The head teacher allowed Yang to demonstrate the movements he had learned through spying. Next, Yang was allowed to take the challenges from the trainees, whom he soundly defeated. The head of the clan pondered the question, "If this young man has come so far without instruction, what could he do with it?" Chen was impressed with Yang's good nature and character, and appreciated the great patience the young man exercised to gain the opportunity to learn. Deciding that Yang's obvious talent, perseverance, and competence were not to be denied, Chen gave him a final initiation, testing his sincerity and traditional Confucian respect for a teacher. Yang passed with flying colors. He shortly became Chen's favorite student.

The first six years of Yang's training were focused on teaching him the internal power work of the form, accurately and precisely down to the minutest detail. In the next six years, concentration was on refining his listening, interpreting, and discharging energy abilities to a high degree with Push Hands training, and training both with and without weapons. The last six years of Yang's training were devoted to learning the fighting techniques and strategies to be used against lethal, motivated opponents, both empty-handed and armed.

Yang completed his martial education and left with his teacher's best wishes and willingness for him to spread tai chi outside the village and teach whomever he wanted. Yang traveled throughout China, challenging every highly respected fighter and master to test the truth of his art, both empty-handed and with his favorite weapon, the spear, known as the "king of traditional Chinese weapons."

No matter where he went, Yang unequivocally defeated everyone, without hurting them, even those who tried to maim or kill him—a superlative level of skill that made him universally recognized as a martial master of the highest level.* From these challenges, he earned the name "Yang the Invincible." His skill level eventually landed him the job of martial art teacher to the Emperor's personal guard, a position reserved for the man proven to be the best martial artist in China. In time, the system that Yang taught became known as the Yang family's tai chi or, simply, Yang style tai chi.

---

*The stories of Yang Lu Chan are legion. He was a deservedly mythic figure in Chinese martial arts. Legend has it that once he left the Chen village, he never lost one of his many matches. Numerous Yang style tai chi books in English and Chinese tell wonderful inspirational stories about his martial exploits as well as those of his sons. These stories illustrate the skills of which tai chi is capable, but often lack sufficient details as to how these skills are acquired. Many of these skills still exist today, while others seem to have been lost to later generations.

Yang Style Plus the Chen Small Style Begets the Hao/Wu Style

While continuing to teach the Emperor's elite, Yang also taught regular citizens in Beijing. One of Yang's first students was a man named Wu Yu Hsiang. After initial study with Yang, Wu decided to go to the Chen village to widen his exposure to this wonderful art. On the way to see Yang's master, he instead was introduced to a top Chen style master of the small-movement method. Wu studied with him and learned the small style well. In a corner of a salt store near the Chen village, Wu, perhaps along with his brothers, discovered the Tai Chi Classics, which described the philosophical and operational underpinnings of the Chen family's internal martial art. Around this time in Beijing, the name tai chi chuan was first coined, based on Taoist philosophical principles. The name continues to this day. Wu's art focused on the small-frame aspect of tai chi (see p. 111), which today is rarely found in its pure form. In the twentieth century, the Wu Yu Hsiang style changed its name and ultimately became known as the Hao style, after Hao Wei Zhen. It eventually fused with the hsing-i and ba gua practices of Sun Lu Tang to become Sun style tai chi.

Old Yang Changes to the New Yang Style

Before the twentieth century, the economic success and status of tai chi martial arts professionals was primarily based on their ability to convince people that they were superior physically in real, potentially lethal confrontations with or without traditional weapons. Moreover, they had to be able to pass on their martial knowledge in ways that would also allow their students to gain their extraordinary abilities. From their inception in China, martial arts were often considered to be supernatural or divine. Automatic firearms were not yet widely available and the use of the relatively superior power of the gun, the old "equalizer," had not yet penetrated conservative Confucian

thinking. This situation changed abruptly in 1900 with the Boxer Rebellion, where martial artists—called Boxers by the Western press—were recruited by the dying Ching dynasty to fight and eject the Western powers from Beijing. The Boxers lost, with terrible consequences.

The Boxer Rebellion shocked China into the modern world with machine gun fire, and Beijing was effectively conquered by the Western nations and the newly industrialized Japan. The foreigners burned the impact of their victory into the Chinese consciousness by carving China up into "concessions," or colonies. Before this defeat, the Chinese often believed martial arts could border on the "supernatural," and many were not convinced that guns were superior to the martial arts. Now they were. Although the internal martial arts had a clear edge over external martial arts, they hardly had one over repeating or automatic weapons. The martial tai chi of Yang Lu Chan changed emphasis after the Boxer Rebellion, when the Chinese clearly realized what guns could do, and that guns were here to stay.

Old Yang Style   The emphasis in Yang's method before the Boxer Rebellion was on fighting techniques. The training focused on both producing power and how to effectively use that power under lethal conditions.* During the lifetimes of Yang Lu Chan, his son Pan Hou, his grandson Shao Hou, and Wu Jien Chuan, Push Hands was not equated with combat training. The motions of peng, lu, ji and an (see pp. 127-135) were much more emphasized before the Boxer Rebellion. The students of this generation were taught tai chi as a fighting

---

*Japanese martial arts underwent this same conversion for different reasons. After the Meiji restoration, samurai were no longer allowed to wear swords and legally fight duels or challenges to the death. Martial arts that seriously focused on the actual techniques of lethal combat were termed *jitsu* as in jujitsu. Those that primarily focused on the physical education, spiritual, and character-building aspect of martial arts were called *do* (Tao in Chinese), as in judo.

martial art, and the forms they did were called the Old Yang style.* Forms and Push Hands were viewed primarily as useful preparatory skills, the stepping stones toward the actual ability to successfully perform fighting applications in unrehearsed combat. Many of the students of that generation were taught the tai chi fighting skills fairly directly. These martial teachings, while being in the minority now still exist and continue to be taught today.

New Yang Style Most of the Yang style done today comes from Yang's other grandson, Yang Cheng Fu, who did not come into his own until after the Boxer Rebellion. When he was young, Yang Cheng Fu took up a dissolute life of drinking and living in red light districts, and did not complete the classical combat training. However, he was very good at Push Hands.** In his era, the 1920s and 1930s, students were very interested in becoming healthy and strong, which is what the practice of Push Hands accomplishes.† They were not, however, too excited about the next level of martial expertise, which often required more work than they were ready to put in to gain high-level "gung fu."

It is equally difficult today to find those who can teach the martial side and those willing to put

---

Editor's note: The author studied the Old Yang style with Lin Du Ying at the end of Ying's life in Xiamen, Fujian (Fukien) province, Mainland China, in 1983. Lin had originally learned this art in Beijing and Shanghai. His teachers were Tien Chau Ling and Wu Hui Chuan, two of the top tai chi fighters in North China, and students of Yang Pan Hou.

**The story goes that his uncle locked Yang Cheng Fu in a room for several years, and would not let him out until the young man could beat him at Push Hands. In China, there is another common oral story, which is more likely to be true. It conjectures that after the death of his father and uncle and the realization of his family responsibilities, Cheng Fu was primarily taught by his older brother Shao Hou and other senior members directly connected to the Yangs, such as Wu Jien Chuan.

†Two commingled aspects simultaneously exist in human beings: the psychological need to be right and feel victorious and the biological need to survive. Push Hands provides the first, but not the second.

in the time and effort required to attain mastery. As we move more toward the next millennium, most tai chi schools do not even seriously practice Push Hands, and even fewer reach the level of fighting applications. There is much value in terms of personal cultivation to be had learning both Push Hands and the fighting applications side of tai chi, based on calmness and clarity rather than an animal hormonal rush.

The Yang Style Begets the Wu Style

During the time Yang Lu Chan taught the Emperor's guards, he had three top students: Wang Chun, who was the most proficient with hard energy, Ling Shan, the best at using soft energy; and Chuan You, the most adept at transforming energy, the highest level of tai chi. After the fall of the Manchu Ching dynasty, Chuan You's family changed their Manchurian name to the Chinese name of Wu, to be more politically in tune with the times. Chuan You's method of tai chi is still taught in Beijing,* although not very widely, as he was primarily a working rather than a teaching martial artist.

Chuan You passed all his knowledge to his son Wu Jien Chuan, who also learned from Yang Lu Chan's son, Pan Hou, teacher of many of the better tai chi fighters to emerge in the early part of the twentieth century. Wu Jien Chuan taught along with the Yang family members at their association in Beijing before both he and Yang Cheng Fu left Beijing to spread tai chi to Shanghai and southern China. Wu, however, was almost twenty years older than Yang Cheng Fu and more immersed in the martial way of the Old Yang style. On many occasions, both Wu and Yang Cheng Fu did their tai chi forms together in demonstrations, and it has often been said that Wu sharpened Yang Cheng Fu's skills at Push Hands when they were together in Shanghai. Wu Jien Chuan, however, became more involved with the small-movement side of tai

---

*See *Wu Style Taijiquan* by Wang Peisheng and Zeng Weiqi, Zhaohua Publishing House, Beijing, China, 1982.

chi rather than the large and medium movement method of Yang Cheng Fu. The form movements Wu himself taught are basically the same as the modern Yang Cheng Fu form, as both of them collaborated. However, because the form is a small-movement style, its movements are more compact, and because it derived from the Old Yang style, it holds much of the old knowledge of fighting applications, with a strong stress on throwing techniques.* Wu Jien Chuan was a prolific teacher who spread his tai chi throughout southern China as much or more than Yang Cheng Fu. For those who do traditional tai chi, the Wu style is the second most popular in China, the Yang family and their students having had a generation's head start. In the next generation, Wu's sons changed the form, emphasizing higher stances and less circularity than their father's form, shifting in the manner of Yang Cheng Fu toward a less martial orientation. The Wu style has three main branches: those of Wu's father, Chuan You, mostly centered in Beijing, which has the least number of adherents, the students of Wu himself, which is the most prevalent; and those deriving from his sons, the number of practitioners falling somewhere between the other two branches.

Traditional Martial Arts Thinking

Before the Boxer Rebellion, people studying one kind of martial art did not learn with people devoted to another martial art. In order to become genuinely trained in a Chinese martial art, a beginning practitioner had to undergo a formal disciple initiation ceremony. During this ceremony, disciples had to take many oaths and "kowtow"— knocking their heads to the floor, often with significant force, to demonstrate sincerity. The teacher became your surrogate father; you as disciple became his surrogate son. The strong Confucian

---

Editor's note: The author learned this method from his teacher Liu Hung Chieh, who lived and studied with Wu Jien Chuan.

nature of the ceremony powerfully bound you to your teacher and fellow students, your new martial art family. Students were not allowed to study outside their systems, unless given express permission. Those who disobeyed this dictum were given the silent treatment by colleagues, and a martial family member might even challenge the offender, with mutually understood lethal intent.

Good-hearted teachers felt the same responsibility toward the learning of the student as a father would feel toward the education of his son. A good teacher would only release a disciple to study with another, second teacher, if it was felt that: (a) the disciple had learned the first teacher's system completely, could honorably demonstrate it, and would profit from new useful, knowledge and the upgrading of skills; (b) there was something lacking in the student's education that another specific teacher, whose integrity the original teacher respected, could teach better. These cross-teaching situations were quite rare because the content of the more powerful martial art systems were considered life-and-death military secrets. Teachers did not want their material getting into the hands of their rivals.

Wu Yu Hsiang, for example, was only able to study small-style Cheng tai chi because he was already a "family member" having been formerly taught by Yang Lu Chan, who opened the door for other outsiders in future generations. Vestiges of this thought still prevail in "closed-door systems." This mentality also accounts, even today, for the intense competitive spirit of, "My style is better than your style" and, "You are a traitor if you study outside your own style." These feelings are not uncommon in the modern martial arts community. For instance, this old feudal mind-set is a popular theme in the Chinese martial arts movies coming from Taiwan and Hong Kong in the last half of the twentieth century. Unfortunately, old habits die hard.

The Confucian social structure venerates the past and demands strict conformity to the exact forms of its tradition, to an extent that is hard for most Americans or Europeans to comprehend. As a rationale for their behavior pertaining to whatever is happening currently, Chinese will cite, both verbally and in writing, incidents from thousands of years ago as though these long-gone events had happened last week. It is expected that the listener understands and will react correctly to the merest nuance of an implicated historical event that enters into the conversation. All these expectations, inculcated by Confucianism, carry sanctions if transgressed. In China, the martial arts tradition was especially orthodox. Today, because Westerners do not have an understanding of "implied Confucian expectations," Western students often become confused by and have difficulty learning from Chinese martial art masters. There is a large cultural gap to overcome, particularly when both sides have grown up with very different kinds of social, behavioral, and psychological boundaries. Often, a few bows or handshakes are not sufficient to smooth over misinterpreted expectations, implied in the mind of one, but never overtly or coherently expressed to the other. Often, each side feels exploited by the other.

Before the Boxer Rebellion, people of one internal martial arts style normally did not share knowledge with those learning another style, just as during the Cold War, the American and Russians did not openly share their military technology with each other. The reality of guns took away a good part of the pragmatic need for the separation. Afterwards, teachers began to become more willing to teach those who had studied other styles. The trend began just before the Boxer Rebellion with the hsing-i and ba gua schools, and extended to the tai chi schools by the next decade. By the 1920s, the central government had set up national martial arts schools where many styles were taught under one roof, sometimes by the top people in their respective styles, including tai chi's Yang Cheng Fu and Wu Jien Chuan. During this time, the internal martial arts began to be practiced increasingly by the more educated members of society, a trend that continues to this day.

Combination Styles

Life was fairly stable in China before the Boxer Rebellion. People did not move around much. Afterwards, the Chinese population became extremely mobile: railroads were built, a warlord period began, the country was invaded by Japan, the Communist Revolution brought on a civil war, all displacing massive numbers of people. All this movement caused a mixing of martial art styles to an extent unprecedented in China's history.

Tai chi began to mix with other styles in three main ways. First, in 1914, the small-movement Hao style (of Wu Yu Hsiang) was taught by Hao Wei Zhen to a famous hsing-i master called Sun Lu Tang, after Sun did him a good turn in Beijing. Sun, like many hsing-i and ba gua people after him, was intrigued by tai chi's idea of softness. Sun combined the soft-body method of tai chi with the rooting and tantien techniques of hsing-i and the stepping methods of ba gua. He subsequently wrote a series of internal martial arts books stating that the three internal arts are of one family. This unification becomes the first of the tai chi combination styles and the only one widely known to be based on the small-movement style.

Second, there are a number of tai chi/ba gua combination styles patterned directly from the large-or middle-frame Yang style. In some of these styles, the hsing-i and ba gua predominate; in others, the Yang tai chi prevails. Tai chi, hsing-i, and ba gua share an incredible number of crossover techniques; in these cases, each of these arts are essentially executing the same fighting application, but with their own particular flavor. These styles usually use the basic form sequence of the Yang style, but in numerous specific movements covertly or overtly incorporate elements of hsing-i and ba gua, such as:

1. Substituting a hsing-i or ba gua arm/hand movement for its specified tai chi movement. For example, a rounded horizontal Ward Off tai chi movement could change to something more like a vertically oriented rise and drill hsing-i/ba

gua move, done with the softness of tai chi. Tai chi's Fair Lady Weaves the Shuttles becomes more like hsing-i's Pounding Fist. These substitutions occur throughout combination forms. In effect, a hsing-i/ba gua technique is done in a tai chi way.

2. Ba gua footwork is often substituted for tai chi footwork. A ba gua "toe out" step being used to change directions or turn the body around is the most obvious giveaway, as this movement does not exist in traditional tai chi.

3. The presence of the hsing-i animal form movements within the tai chi form.

4. The palm is formed in a hsing-i/ba gua way, not that of tai chi.

5. The obvious rising neck of hsing-i can be seen, which is not normally done in tai chi.

6. Stances utilizing 60/40 balance of weight on each foot begin to come into play, rather than the 100/0 balance of the Yang style.

One of the most martially complete of these combination forms is the one created by Chen Pan Ling,* in committee, for the Martial Arts Institute of the central government. This form was created to preserve the martial arts during the Japanese invasion. At this time, China's future was uncertain, and it was not clear which of the great masters might be killed, along with their great legacies. The chairman of the committee, Chen Pan Ling, an engineer by profession besides being a formal disciple in hsing-i and ba gua, trained in the Chen village and also studied extensively with Yang Shao Hou (Old Yang style) and Wu Jien Chuan (Wu style). Other styles in this combination paradigm that have found their way to the West are the Fu style of Fu Jien Sung, and the Kuan Ping style of Guo Lien Ying.

Editor's note: The author studied this style during the late 1960s, 1970s, and 1980s in Japan and Taiwan. Both Wang Shu Jin and Hung I Hsiang practiced this tai chi style, which is composed of nine levels of teachings.

The third main way that tai chi mixes with other styles is where a person proficient in a particular Shaolin martial art loads up the external movements of a tai chi form with the flavor of those Shaolin techniques. (A similar situation also happened to ba gua chang (see p. 313). Through this sort of combining, Shaolin martial artists gain the body and health benefits of tai chi and, simultaneously, augment their primary "Shaolin gung fu" with new useful tai chi techniques. At the same time, they continue to stay focused on their original martial art. A good example of this would be the tai chi form of Chang Tung Shen, Taiwan's highly regarded Chinese wrestling adept.* Chang had studied with Yang Shao Hou. It was extremely obvious when he did his tai chi exactly how his throwing movements completely permeated his form. Chang once stated that the older he became, the more he enjoyed practicing tai chi, and the more he gained from it, especially its ability to extend his martial career into his later years. This evaluation is heard from many top martial art masters of all kinds in China.

Other Tai Chi Styles: Family, Secret, and Lost Lineages

There are a lot of claims around purporting that this or that form of tai chi came from a lost ancient or secret lineage. Many of these types of claims for special history are dubious. They are generally advanced under the heading of lost lineages prior to the Chen village (such as from Chang San Feng or Wang Tsung Yueh), of family styles, and of secret styles coming from clandestine studies with the inheritors of regular lineages. Some of these styles are clearly variations of the major ones; some have high-quality content, whereas others are extremely watered down. Some of these "lineages" are obviously mostly Shaolin done in the slow motion

---

Editor's note: The author studied with Chang Tung Shen briefly in the 1970s.

way of tai chi, incorporating a few tai chi moves. These usually originate from the Yangtze Valley.

What Caused New Styles to Be Created?

New and Improved vs Watered Down As tai chi mutated into new styles—Chen to Yang to Hao to Wu to Combination styles, each new style changed its form movements slightly or significantly. These core changes were not originally made for their health benefits to the general public, but for their ability to pass on the original teacher's martial skills to the next generation. Two competing partisan points of view are held about the effective result of these changes. The first is that it is the earlier style that contains all the original material and that the new was a watered-down version of the old. The opposite view states that the new model improved the old, taking it to new heights with new material, eliminating the deadwood of the parent forms.

Either point of view may more accurately state the case, depending upon which specific surviving lineages are being discussed. For example, the movements of the original Chen and Yang forms are strikingly different. If neither one is more advanced nor complete than the other, what might have accounted for the changes? In their methods, certain basic differences are visibly obvious.

1. **Stances** Unlike the Yang style, the Chen style utilizes stances where both feet are not pointing in the same general direction. Chen style also often utilizes forward stances with 55/45 percent leg weight distribution. Yang style classically uses 100/0 weight balance of the legs (that is, 100 percent of your weight is on your front leg, zero percent is on your back leg), and only the forward bow stance.

The Chen form derived from battlefield military movements, where people wore medieval body armor that had to be compensated for. The Chen-style stances in question were specif-

ically designed to achieve these compensations and obtain a workable position from which to realistically throw an armored opponent. By the time Yang reached Beijing, times had changed. With the advent of firearms, battlefield armor became obsolete; hence, the need for techniques to deal with armored foes had passed. Yang and his students had to deal more with situations encountered by bodyguards, not armies opposing each other.

Yang was also teaching people who had clear training in Northern Shaolin, which uses bow stances. By capitalizing on what they already knew to train them, Yang, in the opinion of some, simply adapted to the needs of his environment. The 100/0 weighted bow stance is also an excellent way of working with the basic tai chi technical requirement of "empty and full" (one leg is full of weight but empty of internal power and vice versa), which has exceedingly practical reasoning behind it.

2. **Arm Movements** Chen style emphasizes overt "silk-coiling" movements. In these motions, during the inward and outward twistings of the body's soft tissues, the elbow tip is constantly moving between two poles (that is, forearm parallel to the ground— the elbow at 90 degrees and the forearm perpendicular to the ground with the elbow facing the floor. Yang style emphasizes the "pulling of silk" technique. In this, energy is pulled directly from the spine to the joints and the twisting of the body's soft tissue is clearly present but hidden in subtle body movements. The elbow tip is fixed somewhere between facing the ground and a 45-degree sideways angle. The elbow tip never faces 90 degrees to the side, or alternates between moving up and down between facing the ground and 90 degrees to the side, as in the Chen style.

Exactly why Yang changed his form only he truly knew. However, the standard story is that he probably changed the Chen style for several basic reasons. Many of the chan sz jin motions utilizing the moving of the elbow tips were designed to move around the bulges that body armor created. These techniques were especially good for the throwing or joint-locking of armored opponents, unarmed or with weapons.* (Throwing and joint-locking soldiers wearing body armor is much more practical than hitting them.) The Chen's method also equally worked with those not wearing armor. Without the need to maneuver around the bulkiness and protection created by armor, the need to move the elbow was no longer necessary. Yang adapted his techniques accordingly, to maximize the efficiency of practice time.

Cause of Variations Within the Same Style

Within the same tai chi style, movements changed for many reasons. The Yang style is a good one to illustrate the situation because it is the most popular and has produced the greatest number of practitioners, not because it is the "best style."** (The other styles of tai chi usually experienced changes within themselves for the same reasons as the Yang.) In the Western World alone there are now at least 20 clearly definable "Yang style" sets of movements. These emphasize some, but not all of the same principles. These forms have anywhere from 24 to 128 movements, all of which collectively are called the "Yang" style. So the name "Yang style"

---

*This same need was recognized by the samurai of Japan, who developed jujitsu along the same lines to work under all conditions, against opponents with or without body armor, in both armed and empty-handed encounters.

**Editor's note:* The author researched the relative popularity of tai chi styles in Mainland China in the 1980s. Then, the Yang and the Wu (a basic variant of the Yang) drew almost 90 percent of tai chi practitioners, the combination styles were the bulk of the rest; the Chen style was a very small part of the remainder, but was undergoing a revival, and the Hao style was exceedingly rare.

alone does not indicate with precision what any Yang style tai chi school is actually doing. The reasons for changes within the Yang style are:

1. The desire of a teacher or group to trademark what they are doing, to distinguish their specific philosophy or their training methods within the Yang-style universe. Often, you see the desire of a group to differentiate its material from variations that are, in its view, of a lesser quality or from a more "impure" lineage. In America, for example, there is the Tung Family style and the Cheng Man-ching style, each of which has either a completely distinct form or several distinctive trademarking movements within its form. The Tungs have several unique movements within their slow long form, as well as a modified fast form,* which is not exactly how their teacher Yang Cheng Fu performed tai chi. Then there is the modified 37-movement short form of Cheng Man-ching, which again is not exactly what the Yang family did.

2. Individual variations personally favored by the teacher are institutionalized into the form. One good example is the Fair Lady's hand position of Cheng Man-ching's Yang style form. This position was clearly not present in the classical Yang family forms.

3. Tai chi teachers themselves learned only fragments, not complete forms, and they pass their incomplete knowledge down the line. Thus, students through the generations continue or escalate the watered-down version.

4. A student learned well from his or her teacher, but changed the moves to conform to a personal viewpoint on what was valuable in tai chi. Such changes can become institutionalized.

5. A branch exclusively focuses on one or only a

---

*The Yang family always did both slow and fast forms, which derived from the two original forms of Chen tai chi. The first focused primarily on slow movements with a few fast movements sporadically thrown in to practice fa jin. In the second form, the emphasis was more on the fast movements than the slow.

few parts of the complete internal 16-part nei gung system and fashions the form to fulfill its chosen aspects of tai chi's energy work, leaving aside other important considerations. Gradually, the physical movements are molded to fit and express the partial energy work.

6. Movements can look quite different, based on what principles teachers most valued for creating fighting applications.

7. Original Yang transmissions concerning tai chi's internal techniques are incompletely received, so the principles of other martial arts are thrown in to make up the difference. This process makes the hybrid tai chi form a kind of mixed drink, one part Yang tai chi, two or three parts something else. This situation happened commonly using Northern Shaolin in Mainland China and adding in Fukien White Crane in Taiwan. Often, the "secrets" of these styles are based on Shaolin, rather than tai chi, methods. Bear in mind that teachers can only teach what they know. Three generations down the line, a student having learned an incomplete system only knows that this is "my style." Such students are neither aware of their form's possibilities nor shortcomings.

8. Measures are taken to make tai chi easier to learn. Consequently, forms are shortened, movements deleted, precision in specific movements becomes vague, all under the banner of reducing a learner's frustration level when faced with challenging material. Usually, this "dumbing down" of tai chi is done to either help spread its genuine health benefits to a wider audience (as something is better than nothing), or to acquire more paying students. When simplification occurs, sometimes the martial and energetic content of the form suffers—it is either greatly diminished or is completely dropped.

9. Many teachers in their older years lose the motivation to put forth the necessary energy and care required to maintain the form and/or present it in its full details.

Considering all of the above, it is easy to see how changes can and do occur. The process is likely to continue long into the future.

BACKGROUND OF BA GUA

A Brief History

THE FOUNDATION OF THE BA GUA SCHOOL IN MODERN TIMES

Some things about the mysterious founder of modern ba gua, Tung Hai Chuan (1798-1879), can be said with certainty. One is that his method of teaching was unique in that he did not teach anyone who was not already a martial arts expert. A prospective student would have had to have practiced martial arts for many years before Tung would even talk to him. Ba gua was a graduate school for martial artists, not grammar school, high school, or even college. It was considered to be an extremely sophisticated martial art, and anyone Tung taught had to have a demonstrated commitment to study. A student had to be someone who embraced martial arts fully, who had already gone through an initial five or ten years of training, and who considered martial arts to be a life's work. A number of Tung's senior students became the backbone of the modern ba gua school and went on to teach many people themselves. However, there were four in particular whose skill or gung fu rose above the others. These are known as the Big Four.

Tung's Four Main Students

Yin Fu (1842-1911) Tung's most senior student was Yin Fu, who was so slim he was nicknamed "Thin Yin." Liu Hung Chieh, the author's teacher, kept photographs of Yin Fu practicing with a broadsword in an old dust-covered album he kept in his room. The sword was significantly larger than Yin. Despite his diminutive size, Yin Fu was known to be incredibly powerful. His fighting techniques, using his Willow-Leaf Palm, were based upon being able to cut right through an opponent's arms to hit his body. Yin Fu made his living as a professional bodyguard, but he also taught many people while he was in Beijing, and in Shandong province when he was older. He had a number of famous students. Unfortunately, many who claimed to have come from Yin Fu's school probably did not. When Walking the Circle (a basic ba gua training technique—see p. 216), Yin Fu's students walked with their fingers pointing horizontally toward the center of the circle instead of pointing up toward the sky, which is the usual manner the movement is done. They were known for training in this walking style, as well as for their ability to pierce their opponents' bodies with their fingers.

Yin Fu had already mastered *lohan chuan*, a Northern Shaolin system of boxing, before studying ba gua with Tung. By incorporating his lohan into Tung's ba gua, Yin Fu developed an entirely new methodology for teaching ba gua, one that used linear rather than circular techniques. Ba gua is basically a circling movement art that develops what is called hsien tien, or "pre-birth" chi, but these linear methods develop what is called hou tien, or "post-birth" chi. Yin Fu's purpose in developing these linear methods was to teach the basic self-defense techniques and body mechanics of ba gua before introducing Circle-Walking. Walking the Circle can be somewhat abstract for beginning students. Word in Beijing and Tianjin had it that Yin Fu's students taught the straight-line methods to the Chinese army troops. The straight-line approach may not have come entirely from Yin. It is clear that linear methods of ba gua were also influenced (although to what degree is speculative) by the large number of hsing-i people who also learned ba gua. Yin Fu's linear method was carried by some of his students to the city of Tianjin, sister city of Beijing, and located only 35 miles away. Tianjin is a port city, and it was quite common for martial artists from Beijing to go there to teach. The linear method was learned by Gao I Sheng, who came to Beijing to study with Yin Fu, Cheng Ting Hua, and perhaps other masters.* These straight-line methods are primarily concerned with the projection of power for fighting and have no discernible application to Taoist meditation. Early in his ba gua training, Liu Hung Chieh also studied Yin Fu's walking method. He trained with some of Yin's students, who worked out at Cheng You Long's ba gua school. At that time, ba gua was one school without branches. It was only later that styles became separated.

Cheng Ting Hua (1848-1900)   Another of Tung's famous students was Cheng Ting Hua. More people who practice ba gua today come from the Cheng Ting Hua school than from any other. Cheng Ting Hua had studied suai chao, Chinese wrestling, when he was young. As a result of following the path of least resistance, Tung taught more of ba gua's throwing methods to Cheng than to any of his other students. Cheng was known for his throwing abilities. He was a short, stocky man built somewhat like Tung himself, and was very strong. Cheng Ting Hua developed a method

---

*Yin Fu's method of linear ba gua became well known in Tianjin, as did the linear methods of a few others, such as Wu Meng Sha. Gao I Sheng's linear ba gua methods (which may well have come from Cheng Ting Hua) eventually came to Taiwan through Chang Chun Feng and passed from him to Hung I Min and Hung I Hsiang (with whom the author studied).

of 64 changes that are only done while circling. While Yin Fu's method is known for its straight piercing movements done with a tremendous amount of power, Cheng Ting Hua's ba gua is known for extremely fast and complicated snake-like shifts of direction, which leave opponents completely disoriented and thus easily defeated.

Ma Shr Ching aka Ma Gui (1853-1940)   Ma Shr Ching (also known as Ma Gui) studied with Yin Fu for the first several years of his ba gua training and afterwards studied directly with Tung in his house. Much of the first-hand history of ba gua given to the author came directly from Liu Hung Chieh, who heard it directly from Ma Shr Ching when he was Ma's private student. Ma took no formal disciples, and he taught Liu only when he was older. Ma did not like to teach. He owned a successful lumber business in which he made enough money to make it unnecessary for him to earn his living as a professional ba gua teacher. Another of the Big Four, Ma Wei Chi, owned a successful coal business. Together, these two were called collectively "Mei (coal) and Mu (lumber) Ma".

Ma Shr Ching told Liu how Tung had taught. Tung frequently would sit with his eyes closed, describe every motion Ma was making, and tell him to adjust it one way or another. Tung used to sit and meditate for hours every day. The basis of his martial power, at least according to Ma, was at least as much due to his sitting practices, which were pure Taoist meditation, as to his martial arts techniques.

One well-known story about Ma Shr Ching goes as follows: Yang Lu Chan of Yang family tai chi fame had three students who were considered to be his best. There was Chuan You (who, along with his son, Wu Jien Chuan, founded Wu style tai chi), known for his transformational energy, the highest level of energy in tai chi chuan; Ling Shan, who was known for his soft energy; and Wang Chun, who was known for his hard energy and straight, solid power. On one occasion, Wang Chun and Ma Shr Ching came to blows. Wang Chun went flying out of the door twice, the second time taking the door with him. This incident is probably the only reported case of fighting between the top tai chi and ba gua people. As a rule, in the ba gua school, there has never been bad blood with any members of the tai chi school, as has sometimes been the case between different Shaolin gung fu systems. Tai chi chuan and ba gua chang share most of the same basic principles. They differ only in the specific ways in which they apply these principles.

Ma Wei Chi (1851-1880) The fourth member of the Big Four was Ma Wei Chi. Liu had many stories about Ma Wei Chi, who was known for being extremely powerful and violent. His nickname was "Ten-Day Ma" because when he hit someone that person usually died after ten days. It was not that ten days were needed before an opponent's injuries would finally kill him; Ma Wei Chi could easily kill an opponent outright, rarely needing to strike more than once. Rather, Ma Wei Chi's strikes were designed to cause latent internal damage that would only later cause death. The ten-day delay would prevent Ma Wei Chi from being considered the legal cause of the death, keeping him out of trouble with the authorities.

There are two stories about Ma Wei Chi's early death. The first, told by Liu Hung Chieh, is that the relatives of a challenger who became a victim of Ma's ten-day procedure took a cowardly form of revenge and had him poisoned. The second, told by Jang Jie of Beijing, was that Ma was killed in a challenge match by a Buddhist monk who was a martial arts master. The killing was done to prevent his excessively immoral violent behavior from continuing.

Ma Wei Chi was famous for his fist techniques, which are not as common in ba gua as palm strikes. He was also well known for his ability to circle around an opponent and use his forearms and fists with devastating effect, as well as for his straight palm work. As a general rule, most of

Ma's students were not considered to be that good, which was probably a result of Ma's incredibly violent temper. He liked to prove that what he did worked. Unfortunately, this inclination resulted in frequent bodily harm to his students. Consequently, they often did not complete their training.

No Students with Ching Gung in Modern Times

True or untrue, the stories about Tung Hai Chuan are legion. Hundreds of them exist and, if these tales were collected together, they would make a hefty tome. Among these stories are those that speak of Tung's ability to jump up in the air to great heights (ostensibly, as high as twenty feet). This ability is what the Chinese call ching gung, or making the body extremely light. Tung was renowned for being able to leap up and hang by his fingertips from very high objects, such as ceiling beams. However, it appears that he did not pass on his knowledge of ching gung to anyone. None of his students could duplicate this ability.

It is told that Tung taught ching gung to one person while traveling before coming to Beijing. He taught this person ching gung for two or three years while he himself was still perfecting the skills he had learned in the mountains. Tung had taken pity on this individual, who was poor, and had helped him. A couple of years later, this same person turned up in Beijing as a cat burglar. He was using his ching gung ability to leap over fences and walls. Tung is supposed to have found out about this and ordered the burglar to get out of town or else he would kill him for immoral use of his teachings. Unfortunately, this sour experience is supposed to have deterred Tung from teaching that particular skill. Many ba gua people can jump very high, but the actual method of ching gung was not passed down. Many contemporary ba gua researchers have failed to uncover one single person in any tradition who had this ability.

THE SPREAD OF BA GUA OUTWARD FROM BEIJING

Ba gua was originally centered around Beijing and Tianjin, since this is where Tung and his disciples taught. When Tung died in 1879 at the age of 81, a number of his students left Beijing and settled in North China, carrying the art with them. Yin Fu left Beijing and went north to Shandong Province, where he died in 1909 at the age of 69. Yin Fu's lineage was passed down through many people, including Kung Pao Tien, who also went north to Shandong Province. Cheng Ting Hua died young, and some of his better students also settled in North China, while his two sons continued to teach in Beijing. However, until the 1920s and 1930s, the strongest ba gua was without any doubt still to be found in Beijing and Tianjin. Then two events produced great turmoil in China: the Chinese Civil War and the war with Japan. During this period, massive migration from North to South China and from China to Hong Kong and Taiwan occurred, including many ba gua masters and practitioners.

During the 1920s, 1930s, and 1940s, the Civil War between the Kuomintang (Nationalists) and the Communists in South and West China, along with the war with Japan in North and East China, caused massive relocation of the civilian populace as well as government and military personnel. Transportation was improving, and a journey that used to take weeks or months now took days. Many northern Chinese martial artists, including ba gua people, moved south. A large number of ba gua people ended up in Shanghai, a city that was becoming a great commercial center. Professional teachers were attracted to it for its financial opportunities. In addition, a number of the ba gua people were members of secret societies, which also followed the commercial activity to Shanghai. Others, involved with the Nationalists as high officials or as members of the upper strata of society, stayed with the seat of government, which was forced by the fighting to move to Nanjing in

the south, then Chongqing in the west, and ultimately to Taiwan. Many ba gua people joined the military and died in the wars.

Tai chi chuan came to the West largely as a result of this migration. Yang Chen Fu (of Yang style tai chi), his son Yang Shou Jung, his disciple Tung Ying Chieh, and Wu Jien Chuan (co-founder of Wu style tai chi) all ended up in Hong Kong and became very well known, while masters such as Cheng Man-ching went to Taiwan. From Hong Kong and Taiwan, tai chi came to the West.

Many of the ba gua people who relocated were not of the highest rank in Beijing; as such, they did not have great face in Beijing. Of course, the Beijing and Tianjin people were fairly conservative. When they taught, they liked to go into great depth. They rejected anything less than serious training. Only extremely dedicated people were involved in ba gua in Beijing and Tianjin. One migrant wave occurred at the end of the 1920s, when a particular group of five famous martial artists, including representatives of the ba gua/hsing-i school (Fu Chen Sung and Gui I Jai) went south. They were called the Five Tigers, and were sent by the northern military people to Canton in the south.

Liu Hung Chieh was a friend of Wan Lai Sheng, one of the famous five tigers, and studied for a short time with Wan's Natural Gate Boxing teacher, Tu Hsing Wu. Liu and Wang both had the same Six Combination Shaolin Boxing teacher. After Liu defeated Wan in a friendly match, Wan introduced Liu to Tu, who accepted him as a student. Liu studied briefly with Tu Hsing Wu, but stopped when Tu wanted him to start the practice of kicking big wooden logs barefoot. Liu continued with his ba gua practice instead.

In general, ba gua did not become well established in South China. Most of the people who migrated to the south from Beijing after the civil war ended up either in Hong Kong or in Taiwan. From these two locations, ba gua spread to the rest of the world. Despite this diffusion, first to Southeast Asia and later to North America and Europe, the center of the ba gua chang universe within China has always been and continues to be Beijing and Tianjin.

Ba Gua in Hong Kong

With the re-emergence of the Chinese Civil War after the defeat of the Japanese in 1945, and then the Communist takeover of China in 1949, ba gua was further dispersed. During the 1940s and 1950s, many people fled Mainland China to Hong Kong and Taiwan. A few high-level ba gua people went to Hong Kong, such as Shun Hsi Kun (who went to Taiwan at the end of his life). However, as a general rule, most of those who went to Hong Kong did not take on students. Jack Pao (see p. 272), a colleague of the author, is a case in point. Jack had severe rheumatism and practiced ba gua primarily to keep his body from disintegrating. He had studied ba gua in Beijing when he was a child. His family was wealthy, and they had a very good ba gua person teach him. Because he had previously been well connected with the ba gua crowd, when he moved to Hong Kong he persuaded several of the ba gua people there to teach him more before they got too old. He would probably not have been accepted as a student without his background and former ba gua connections. At that time, it was incredibly difficult to be initiated into the ba gua school. However, if you had already entered the gate through another teacher, it was much easier to persuade someone to help you to continue your studies.

This way of proceeding is similar to the Western tradition in which it is hard to become a member of the club, but once you become a member, the other members are more willing to help you get along. Taking one into the ba gua club in China presumed, of course, that the seniors could see that the ba gua the student had learned was the real stuff and not a diluted version for which they would take no responsibility. Ba gua people traditionally were absolutely strict about whom they would teach. In Hong Kong and Taiwan, this tendency was reinforced by the deep-seated pre-judices of northern people against people from South China, whom they generally considered to be frivolous.

Generally speaking, from 1974 to the present, the ba gua scene in Hong Kong has been relatively quiet. Students of Fu Chen Sung of Canton and Gao I Sheng of Tianjin taught on a small scale publicly, but in the main most ba gua taught was not widespread throughout the former Crown Colony. However, hsing-i was another matter. The most well-known public hsing-i person in the early 1970s was the late Han Hsing Yuan, who was one of Wang Xiang Zhai's four main disciples from the I Chuan school. This school of hsing-i (see p. 180) focused on standing rather than moving practices. Han did some ba gua, but it was not his principal interest. There are a few other top hsing-i people in Hong Kong, such as Chen I Ren and Liang Jr Pang, and quite a number of competent middle-level people.

Ba Gua in Taiwan

More top ba gua people went to Taiwan rather than to Hong Kong. In Taiwan, too, however, not many of the top people took on more than a few students. There were also many good hsing-i people in Taiwan, but only a few taught in each major area. In Taipei, there was Chang Chen Feng and, later, the Hung brothers (Hung I Hsiang and Hung I Mien), and Chao Lien Fang, who was personally very good at hsing-i, but did not really impart his knowledge. In Taichung, there was Chen Pan Ling and Wang Shu Jin, as well as many other more good small and secretive hsing-i/ba gua schools.

Many of the people teaching ba gua publicly in the parks of Taiwan were not very good. They would write Chinese characters in the dirt and say, "This is what we mean," but then be able to put little of it into practice. There were many people doing ba gua in Taiwan, but most were not ba gua *men*, people in the lineage. There were, however, individuals scattered about the island who did have the skill, but most generally maintained a low profile.

Another problem with ba gua in Taiwan was that the Mainlanders, the ones the locals called the *wai sheng ren*, or out-of-province people, looked down on the native Taiwanese as socially and racially inferior—country bumpkins, in effect. Generally, the Mainland ba gua people preferred not to teach Taiwanese. They considered it below their dignity to do so. Chang Chen Feng outraged many Mainlanders by teaching Taiwanese. In addition, if you were Taiwanese (as was Hung I Hsiang) or if you had a Taiwanese teacher, you were automatically dismissed by the Mainland people as not being any good, regardless of whether you had a high level of skill or not. Over time, these attitudes have changed somewhat, in part because many of the Taiwanese became better at ba gua than the children of the Mainlanders and in part because Mainlanders and Taiwanese have become more socially integrated.

As a general rule, most of the really good ba gua teachers had only a few students who were closely connected by family or friendship. Convincing a teacher to accept you as a student could take years of trying to meet him, talking to him, bringing him gifts, and using all of your powers of persuasion. Many seekers of the art considered themselves fortunate just to meet and talk with the top instructors, and the acceptance of a person as a student or disciple was rare indeed. The traditional training that ba gua teachers demanded was difficult and strict. It was very different from the easier training that goes into the physical culture ba gua you now see on the Mainland or the more watered-down ba gua one commonly saw in public parks.

In Taiwan, you had to search to locate the qualified ba gua people and you had to persevere to persuade them to teach you. Wang Shu Jin was in Taichung, as was Chen Pan Ling. Unfortunately, Chen Pan Ling was weakened from a car accident in his later years, but he remained an excellent instructor. There were also people teaching in the southern cities of Taiwan, Chiayi, Tainan, and

Kaohsiung. There were poor instructors who would teach anyone and good instructors who would teach virtually no one. This situation has led to great confusion about ba gua in Taiwan.

BA GUA IN MAINLAND CHINA TODAY: TRADITIONAL AND WUSHU

When Mainland China opened to the West in the 1970s and 1980s, and the traditional ba gua people in Mainland China, Hong Kong, and Taiwan improved their communication, it became obvious to them that their beloved art was being severely diluted. The Mainlanders who did their training in the 1920s and 1930s had a skill level that was appreciably higher than that of those who had trained in the 1950s and 1960s. This discrepancy was not only a function of the number of years of practice, but of the purity of the ba gua learned. The difference was not trivial—it was like night and day. The art appeared to be dying, as each succeeding generation exhibited a lower-quality ba gua. The same situation existed for hsing-i and tai chi chuan.

Some of the people in Taiwan went to extraordinary prolonged efforts to learn ba gua, and spent fortunes trying to track down the authentic teachers of the art. Nevertheless, the ba gua masters were getting old and passing away, and their knowledge was often not being fully transmitted to the next generation. To make matters worse, the lower-quality ba gua was commanding much more credence, especially where it was being mixed with external gung fu arts.

As ba gua came to South China from Beijing and dispersed from there to Taiwan, Hong Kong, and the rest of the world, it became mixed with various Southern as well as Northern Chinese martial arts. When lower-level ba gua people left Beijing, they may have carried only 10 to 20 percent of the entire art, and the blending of this partial ba gua with other arts resulted in a great deal of dilution and contamination of pure ba gua. It was common for a person to learn some ba gua from here, some hsing-i from there, a bit of

Chinese wrestling from over there, and maybe some other martial arts or chi gung from who knows where, and then to start teaching their own hybrid version. Even the better mixes would be only 30 percent ba gua, with 20 percent hsing-i, 30 percent tai chi, and 20 percent miscellaneous arts. This hybridization did not happen in every case, and many high-level people remained selective in their choice of students and traditional in their teaching. However, it is accurate to say that as ba gua spread outward, its quality diminished and that clear transmissions from the original ba gua school were few and far between. A similar situation existed with tai chi, where the majority of tai chi teachers who left China for Taiwan were not exceptionally schooled in tai chi.

Many factors disrupted the transmission of ba gua in the post-1949 era. First of all, in 1949, China was politically torn in two. Many people who as Nationalists were subject to execution or long-term imprisonment tried to flee to Hong Kong, Taiwan, or Southeast Asia. For those who remained on the Mainland, admitting that they knew ba gua was risky. They could be placed on the "to be observed" list, which was potentially extremely dangerous. Many ba gua people fled to remote areas of China and "hid their light," not showing what they knew. If they were over 60, they may have "hid their light" until death. If they taught at all, it was probably only to one or two individuals in secret, hardly what could be called optimal learning conditions.

Secondly, before the Cultural Revolution in China, there was the "Great Leap Forward" in the late 1950s and early 1960s, when 30 million people died of starvation. During this time, there was almost no food in China. For any serious athlete doing heavy training, sufficient food is necessary to train well. Since food was not available, the ba gua training of the generation of the 1950s and early 1960s suffered accordingly.

During this period, some things actually helped the ba gua school slightly: One of Mao's most trusted bodyguards was a ba gua man; then Mao promoted tai chi strictly for health and the ba gua people could sometimes hide behind that authorized sanction.

The third weakening factor was the fact that "the old" became a primary target of the Cultural Revolution and was to be fought against, just as Confucianism and Buddhism were to be opposed. The ingenious solution to this problem was the creation of Wushu, or "martial techniques arts." Instead of Wushu being military or meditative in nature, it was instead a state-sponsored performing art system. Wushu is based on a mixture of martial arts movements, dance, and gymnastics. From a battlefield perspective, martial arts were downgraded to "martial movements," commonly performed more like dance than boxing. The emphasis was placed on physical education, with a bias toward visual beauty in performance. Wushu was also designed to catalog and preserve the martial movement forms, essentially creating a living encyclopedia of Chinese martial techniques. Backed by the central government, the Chinese martial arts were thus promoted both to the mass of the Chinese people, as well as to other nations through official government-sponsored international goodwill Wushu tours. The emphasis was on athletics, stretching, beauty of movement, and the Chinese spirit. This agenda was an entirely different one from that of traditional martial arts, which incorporated the battlefield virtues of courage, spirit, power, fighting competence, meditation, as well as Confucian, Buddhist, and Taoist moral values. Whereas traditional martial artists will spend anywhere from five to thirty years perfecting one integrated martial art, the Wushu performer is similar to a dancer using the modern dance method.

In the beginning, a modern dancer starts with a general core movement foundation that emphasizes stretching, balance, good body control, and the ability to manifest stage presence by expressing emotion or charisma through movement.

The Wushu method, which, like dance, does not include any practical power training applicable to self-defense, uses as its foundation the art of chang chuan (long-fist Northern Shaolin) to teach the basic skills of stretching, gymnastics (aerial flips and tumbles), balance, good body movement, stage presence, and representations of martial movements with minimal physical power.

Just as the modern dancer then goes on to continuously learn new pieces of choreography, the Wushu person will next learn hundreds of sets from dozens of martial arts performed as permutations on the basic chang chuan training. Wushu practitioners usually study the outer movements (sets) of a martial art for a few months and then add the new "martial art" to their teaching or performing repertoires, normally without having gained any significant fighting competence in the "new" martial art. Traditional teachers, aware of the Wushu approach, have often voiced reservations about it. In the 1990s, traditional approaches have begun to re-emerge within Wushu, especially with the reinstitution of full contact competitions in China.

Wushu people work very hard at the "Modern Martial Art." Their effort and thousands of hours of diligent practice merit genuine respect. However, performing arts and martial arts are entirely different creatures with respect to what they give to the individual practitioner and to society. Wushu is primarily concerned with the surface external movements of ba gua, while traditional ba gua is concerned with the internal development and practical skills that can be gained from this ancient art. The values and skills of someone concerned with chi cultivation and fighting abilities are quite different from those of someone interested in stage performance. Wushu has made valuable contributions in terms of physical culture and organizational skills. Overall, however, Wushu has been one of the streams that has diluted the art of traditional ba gua chang.

DIFFERENT LINEAGES

The schools of Cheng Ting Hua and Yin Fu have become the two dominant ba gua schools inside and outside China. Of all the ba gua practitioners the author saw in Taiwan, Hong Kong, and Mainland China, the majority of the people that were able consistently to use ba gua as a martial art came from one or the other of these two lineages. Other disciples of Tung Hai Chuan, namely Sung Shr Rong, and Shr Liu (with whom Tung also lived), passed down their arts, but it was their students who also studied with Cheng Ting Hua or Yin Fu who were, in the author's opinion, the ones who could in general truly use their arts to the fullest extent.*

There are many other schools, often called ba gua this or ba gua that, claiming to have originated somewhere other than with Tung Hai Chuan, though all the ba gua schools respected for their fighting technique came from Tung. There were many stories about secret ba gua schools in remote areas of China. Invariably, whenever these claims were investigated in depth, it always turned out that these schools came from either the Cheng Ting Hua or Yin Fu lineage. If not, what they were doing did not compare to Tung's ba gua in content or effectiveness.

Currently in China, the majority of the strongest fighters and the most skillful physical technicians of ba gua without doubt come from the Cheng Ting Hua school. The Yin Fu school is still strong, but the number of people who can practice this line of ba gua with a high degree of skill seems

---

Editor's note: Although the author "exchanged hands" (that is, sparred or did Rou Shou) with over 200 practitioners, he did not personally track down each and every branch of the other schools, and therefore his observations may not be completely accurate. He has studied both styles, and has no particular preference for either. They each have their own characteristics, positive and negative. The Yin Fu school is more linear, and the Cheng Ting Hua school is more circular and spiraling.

to be shrinking, while the number of high-level Cheng Ting Hua practitioners seems to be relatively growing. This state of affairs may be due to the fact that Cheng attracted better students or may be because his system is more learnable. In the United States and Europe at this time, the vast majority of practitioners descend from the Cheng school.

Not every lineage will have intact the physical/chi aspect, the martial aspect, and the spiritual aspects of ba gua. Teachers can only teach what they know, which may not necessarily be what a student wishes the teacher had. True high-quality ba gua and other internal arts teachers are rare. Consequently their methods should be honored. Usually, something of quality that enhances your life is remembered—long after the price and effort paid have faded from memory.

ENERGY ANATOMY OF THE HUMAN BODY   C

The Main Energy Channels and the Three Tantiens

WHAT IS COMMON TO THE LEFT, RIGHT, AND CENTRAL ENERGY CHANNELS

Three main energy channels, or paths of flow—the left, right, and central channels (see Figures 1 and 2)—begin at conception and remain within a person throughout life. Other important energies move in the human body according to meridian patterns that have been well mapped by Chinese medicine. Any text on acupuncture should include charts that identify them. The left, right, and central channels, however, according to Taoist chi gung theory, come into existence before the acupuncture meridians and create these meridians during fetal evelopment. The three main energy channels have certain characteristics in common.

All three, for example, are located in the center of the body; that is, in each, the energy flows occur midway between the skin in the front of the body and the skin in the back of the body.

Also, the central channel joins the right channel on the right side of the body and the left channel on the left side at the tips of the fingers, the tips of the toes, the center of the armpits, kwa, and at the *ba hui* point, which is located on the center of the crown of the head.

THE PATHWAY OF THE CENTRAL CHANNEL

In the torso and head: The central channel runs from the center of the perineum (the area between the anus and the posterior part of the external genitalia) through the center of the torso to the bai hui point on the center of the crown of the head. The channel runs through internal organs, soft tissues, blood vessels, and the brain.

In the arms: The central channel runs from the heart center (middle tantien) to a meeting point in the center of the armpits, where the energies of the central and left or right channels temporarily join. From the armpits, the energy of the central channel moves through the bone marrow of the arm bones, through the center of the elbows and then the wrist joints to the center of the palms and from there, via the bone marrow, to the fingertips. In the fingertips, the energies of the right and left channels on their respective sides merge with the energy of the central channel and, once joined, continue to the edge of the etheric body.

In the legs: The central channel runs through the bone marrow from the perineum between the legs along a line continuing across the pelvis to the kwa and hip sockets. From there it travels through the bone marrow of the leg bones, through the knee and ankle joints, then through the center of each foot along a midline from the heel to the ball of the foot and then through the bone marrow of the toes.

Where the central channel exits the body: The energy of the central channel mingles with the energies of the right and left channels and the commingled energies exit from the physical body to the etheric body at these points:

1. From the end of the fingertips and the tips of the toes, extending to the boundary of the etheric body.

2. From the bai hui point at the crown of the head to the boundary of the etheric body above the head, where one's own personal energy connects with the energy of heaven (cosmic energy).

3. From the center of the ball of each foot extending out to below the feet, to the boundary of the etheric body beneath, where one's personal energy connects with the energy of the earth.

Figure 1
THE CENTRAL CHANNEL

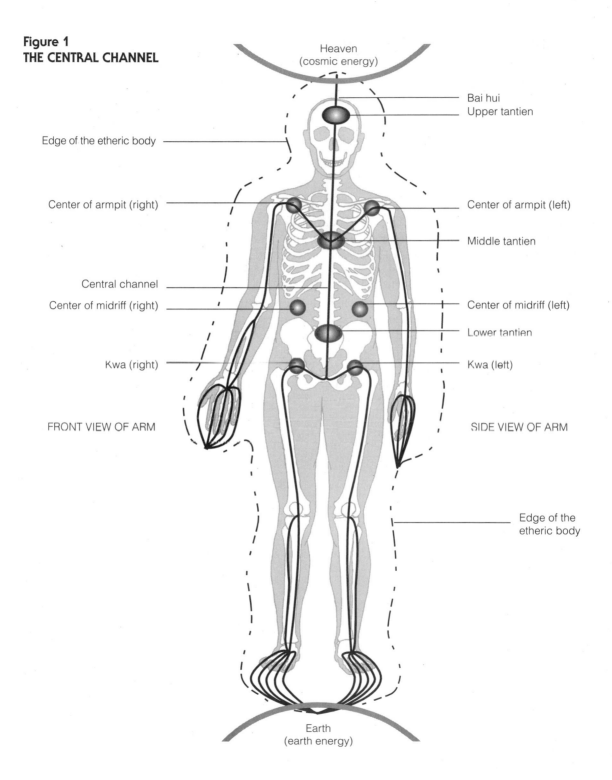

Heaven
(cosmic energy)

Bai hui
Upper tantien

Edge of the etheric body

Center of armpit (right)

Center of armpit (left)

Middle tantien

Central channel

Center of midriff (right)

Center of midriff (left)

Lower tantien

Kwa (right)

Kwa (left)

FRONT VIEW OF ARM

SIDE VIEW OF ARM

Edge of the
etheric body

Earth
(earth energy)

THE PATHWAY OF THE LEFT AND RIGHT CHANNELS

In the head and shoulders: From the crown of the head down to the collarbone, at no time do the left and right channels intersect the central channel. The left and right channels begin at the bai hui point at the crown of the head (where their energies are merged with that of the central channel). They continue down the center of the brain going parallel on either side of the central channel at an imperceptible distance away from it. At the upper tantien (third eye), the distance between the left and right channels widens, and they continue down to the center of the eyes, to the nostrils, down each side of the mouth, down the throat, to the level of the clavicals, close to but without intersecting the central channel. At this point the left and right channels branch off on a line to the left and to the right along the centerline between the clavicals and back, where they join temporarily with the central channel in the center of the armpits, before splitting off again.

In the arms: From the center of the armpits on their respective sides of the body, the left and right channels run down each arm to the fingertips within the bone matrix (calicum) of both the bones of the arm and the joints to the ends of the five fingertips. Here, the left and right channels merge with the central channel.

In the legs: Beginning from the kwa (inguinal fold), both the left and right channels run within the bone matrix of their respective hip sockets, thigh and shin bones, knee and ankle joints, within the small bones of the feet along two thin parallel lines on either side of the central channel, to the center of the ball of the foot where the left right and central channels merge. They then split again and go to the tips of the toes, where again the left and right channels merge with the central channel and the commingled energy continues to the boundary of the etheric body.

The control gates of the left and right channels: There are three energetic "sluice gates" that either allow energy to pass unimpeded through the left and right channels or diminish it or completely cut off its flow. These are located in the center of the armpits, the center of the midriff, and the kwa.

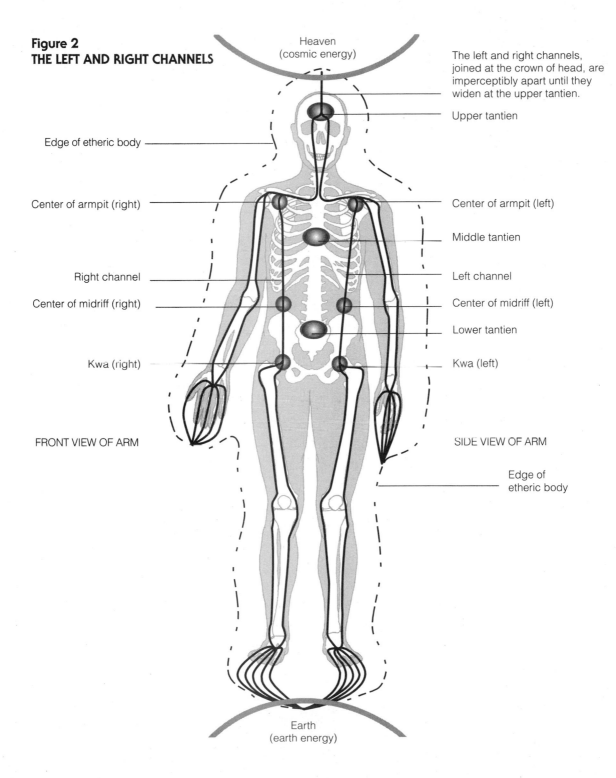

Figure 2
THE LEFT AND RIGHT CHANNELS

Heaven
(cosmic energy)

The left and right channels,
joined at the crown of head, are
imperceptibly apart until they
widen at the upper tantien.

Upper tantien

Edge of etheric body

Center of armpit (right)

Center of armpit (left)

Middle tantien

Right channel

Left channel

Center of midriff (right)

Center of midriff (left)

Lower tantien

Kwa (right)

Kwa (left)

FRONT VIEW OF ARM

SIDE VIEW OF ARM

Edge of
etheric body

Earth
(earth energy)

D LINEAGES AND TRAINING CHRONOLOGY
Summary of Martial Arts Experience of B. K. Frantzis

A CHRONOLOGY OF THE AUTHOR'S MARTIAL ARTS TRAINING

Martial Art	Location of Training	Dates of Training
Judo	New York; Tokyo	1961-67; 1967-70
Karate	New York; Tokyo; Okinawa	1961-67; 1967-69; 1970
Jujitsu	New York	1962-66
Aikido	New York; Tokyo	1963-1967; 1967-69
Iaido	New York	1965-66
Cantonese White Crane	New York	1966-67
Monkey Boxing	New York	1966-67
Ba Gua	Tokyo/Taiwan	1968-71
	Taiwan/Hong Kong	1974-75, 77-79, 83, 87, 89
	Beijing	1981, 83-86
Tai Chi	Tokyo/Taiwan	1968-71
	Hong Kong/Taiwan	1974-75, 77-79, 83, 87, 89, 97
	Xiamen	1983-84
	Beijing	1981, 83-86
Hsing-I	Tokyo/Taiwan	1968-71
	Hong Kong/Taiwan	1974-75, 77-79,83, 87, 89
	Beijing	1981, 83-86
Fukien White Crane	Tokyo; Taiwan	1971; 1974-75
Wing Chun	New York; Hong Kong	1972, 76; 1974, 75, 77
Chinese Wrestling	Taiwan	1974
Northern Monkey Boxing	Taiwan	1974-75, 78
Eight Drunken Immortals	Taiwan	1974-75, 78
Praying Mantis	Taiwan	1974-75
Northern Shaolin	Hong Kong	1983

Note: At the time of these trainings, traditional Chinese teachers of the internal martial arts usually did not issue certificates to students. However, certain documentation was presented to the author, some of which appears in the following sections. The above chart does not include the author's training in the related arts of meditation, chi gung, tui na, and other bodywork disciplines, nor does it cover his two years in India studying Yoga, Kundalini, and Tantra.

THE CERTIFICATES

Ba Gua Certificate

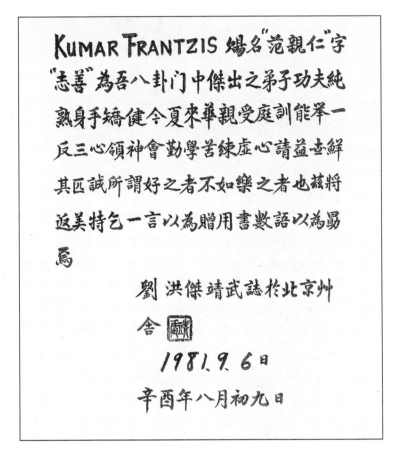

Kumar Frantzis, whose bestowed names are Fan Qingren and Fan Zhishan, is an outstanding disciple of our ba gua *men* (tradition). His art is highly skilled and his body and hands are strong and vigorous.

This summer, Kumar Frantzis came to China and was personally trained in our courtyard. He is able to draw inferences about other cases from one instance, to understand tacitly and to study diligently and train hard. He is open-minded and is good at learning from others. Few people in the world can match him. It is said that people who are professional are not as good as people who really enjoy what they are doing.

Upon his returning to the United States, it is my honor to write a few words to praise and encourage him.

Liu Hongjie (Liu Hung Chieh)

In teaching courtyard, Beijing, September 6, 1981

Tai Chi Certificate

C E R T I F I C A T E   No. 80853
September 11, 1981

Kumar Frantzis completed his further studies of tai chi chuan in 24 patterns, tai chi sword in 32 patterns, tai chi knife and Tui Shou (Push Hands) at Beijing Institute of Physical Education, Beijing, People's Republic of China, from August 4, 1981 to September 10, 1981. He is qualified to be a coach.

Beijing Institute of Physical Education
Beijing,
People's Republic of China

Hsing-I Certificate

KUMAR FRANTZIS 賜名范親仁字志善為吾
形意門中傑出之弟子功夫純熟身手矯健今夏來
華親受庭訓能舉一反三心領神會勤學苦練虛心
請益大有一日千里之勢余深喜之誠屬不世出之奇
才也茲將返美特乞一言以為贈用書數語以為嘉勉
焉

劉洪傑靖武 [印]
[印] 誌於北京艸堂

1981. 9. 11.
辛酉年八月十四日

Kumar Frantzis, whose bestowed names are Fan Qingren and Fan Zhishan, is an outstanding disciple of our hsing-i *men* (tradition). His *gung fu* (skill) is very good, and his movements are quick and perfect.

This summer he came to China and I personally trained him. When I tell him "A" he already knows "Z." He understands everything from his heart and soul. He is diligent and practices hard. He is very humble when he asks questions. In one day of practice he can go a thousand miles. I am very happy that he is a very special and outstanding student.

Upon his returning to the United States, it is my honor to write a few words to praise and encourage him.

Liu Hongjie (Liu Hung Chieh)
In teaching courtyard, Beijing, September 11, 1981

THE LINEAGES

This lineage information was provided to B. K. Frantzis by Liu Hung Chieh. Liu said that it was not possible to list all the lineage masters. In Liu's words, "The masters listed here are the important ones, and their art is handed down directly by the Old Generation."

八卦掌師傳系統表
一代 董海川
二代 尹福 馬維祺 程廷華
三代 馬貴 李永慶 劉棟臣
　　 饅頭郭 程有龍
四代 朱文豹
五代 劉振麟
六代 劉洪傑
七代 白樺 范覦仁
KUMAR FRANTZIS

其餘本門師友尚多不及
備載, 僅擇其尤要而又有
直接系統者錄焉
1981. 9. 9.

The Name List of Ba Gua Masters

The First Generation:
Tung Hai Chuan

The Second Generation:
Yin Fu,
Ma Weiqi,
Cheng Ting Hua

The Third Generation:
Ma Gui,
Li Yongqing,
Liu Jianchen,
Mantou Guo

The Fourth Generation:
Zhu Wenbao

The Fifth Generation:
Liu Zhenlin

The Sixth Generatiion:
Liu Hung Chieh

The Seventh Generation:
Bai Hua,
Fan Qingren (Kumar Frantzis)

The Name List of Tai Chi Masters

Chang San Feng (A legendary Taoist figure)

Wang Tsung Yueh

Chen Wang Ting

Chen Hsing

Yang Lu Chan

Yang Pan Hou   Chuan You

Wu Jien Chuan

Liu Hung Chieh

Fan Qingren (Kumar Frantzis)

The Name List of Hsing-I Masters (Since Li Luo Neng, Shen County, Hebei Province)

1. Li Luo Neng

2. Liu Qilan,   Guo Yun Shen

3. Li Tsung I,   Chang Chao-Tung,   Li Kuiyuan

4. Li Yunshan,   Shang Yunxiang,   Sun Lu Tang

5. Li Jianqiu,   Jin Yunding

6. Liu Hung Chieh

7. Bai Hua   Fan Qingren (Kumar Frantzis)

E CHINESE TERMINOLOGY

The Romanization of Chinese Words in This Book

HOW CHINESE WORDS, PHRASES, AND NAMES ARE TRANSLITERATED IN THIS TEXT

English translations of Chinese words and phrases have been used in this text extensively. Due to the nature of the contents, however, it was not always possible to avoid using a transliteration of the actual Chinese. Thus, a back-of-the-book glossary has been provided that incorporates definitions of all transliterated Chinese terms. Any attempt to transliterate the sounds of Chinese words into English with any accuracy is bound to fall short. One reason is that Chinese contains sounds that English simply does not have; another is that Chinese uses a system of "vocal tones" that do not exist in English. Moreover, English has sounds that are not present in Chinese. English speakers attempting to pronounce Chinese words will invariably add sounds from their own language, which distorts the pronunciation of Chinese.

Each of the major systems for romanizing Chinese words has its flaws. Written Chinese is composed of ideogram pictures, each of which may convey one idea or several combined ideas. These ideograms, when spoken, are pronounced differently in the different Chinese languages. To the foreign ear, these languages can sometimes seem as far apart as French and German. For example, the word for family is *jia* in the National Language, Mandarin, but it is *gar* in Cantonese, a regional Chinese sublanguage, or dialect, spoken by over sixty million people in the province of Canton and by the people of Hong Kong. There are yet more regional languages, again with different sounds for the same character, such as Szechuanese (which is a language of a greater

number of people than Cantonese) and Minnanhua of Fujian province (which is an older language than Cantonese). To make matters worse, there are subdialects within each major dialect. In some instances in Old China, people from the same province only one or two hundred miles away from each other could hardly communicate with one another.

There is no single correct system for writing standard Mandarin Chinese words in English or Roman script. Currently, there are three major systems of transliterating the Chinese language, which spell the same Chinese word sometimes in the same way and sometimes in different ways. Each of these three systems is a valid method of transliteration to render the pronounced sounds of standard Mandarin Chinese using the English alphabet. These three are the Pinyin system of Mainland China, the Wade-Giles system, and the Yale system.

The Pinyin system of Mainland China, which is being used with increasing frequency in academic circles and in popular literature, has been officially employed by the United Nations since 1972 when China displaced Taiwan there. Since then, Pinyin has become the "official" way of romanizing Chinese words. This system uses the English letter *x* as a "hs" or "sh" sound, the letter *q* as a "ch" sound, and the letter *z* as a "dz" sound. The Wade-Giles system was the standard used most commonly before the 1980s. In this system, the most confusing notation is the use of the apostrophe, which is all-important in pronunciation. Thus t' is pronounced "t" as in Tom; (while "t" is pronounced "d" as in "David"), ch is pronounced "j"; and ch' is pronounced "ch."

Accordingly, in the Wade-Giles system you will see *t'ai chi ch'uan*. This is pronounced "tie jee chewan."

Using the Pinyin system, it is written as *tai ji quan*.

Using the Yale system, it appears as *tai ji chuan*.

The Yale system is the least commonly used. It was specifically created by Yale University to render to the greatest extent possible a reasonable representation of how the Chinese language is accurately pronounced using the letters of the English alphabet. For example, *chi gung* in the Yale system is *chi gung;* in Wade-Giles, it is *chi kung,* and in Pinyin, it is *qi gong.* Actually, the way it is said in China is closest to *chee gung.* The *qi* of Pinyin and the *kung* of Wade-Giles are the most confusing here.

Another way of demonstrating the considerable differences in the three transliteration systems is to look at the manner that each transcribes the internal martial art that is a major subject of this book, the art based on the *I Ching*.

In the Wade-Giles system, the art is *pa kua chang*.

In the Pinyin system, the art is *ba gua zhang*.

In the Yale system, the art is *ba gua jang* (closest to the actual spoken Chinese).

This book freely mixes and matches transliterations from the existing systems on two levels. First of all, the cognitive. For those who have read related literature on martial arts, chi gung, meditation, and so on, we have taken license to make it easier to recognize what word or phrase is being referenced by spelling it in the manner most likely to be unambiguous. Secondly, we shuffle transliterations on the level of the phrase. For instance, we have standardized on the spelling of "ba gua chang" for this internal martial art. "Ba gua" from Pinyin and Yale, and "chang" from Wade-Giles. Why? (1) Because "ba gua" is reasonably close to the pronounced Chinese, where "pa kua" is nowhere near close. If you are schooled in Chinese, the word "jang" is clearly the closest to Chinese sound, but if you are not, then "jang," "chang," and "zhang" are equally useless and "chang" is at least widely known from " pa kua chang." (2) To the average Westerner untrained in Chinese, the spelling of "ba gua chang" will evoke vocalized sounds that are the most likely to be closest to what a native Chinese speaker would say.

This discussion on language may seem burdensome to some. However, there are over a billion Chinese in the world and miscommunication can waste a lot of time and energy. The choice was made to have this book use transliterations that allow English speakers to best mimic what the original Chinese actually sounds like. Consequently, the concern has not been to adhere to any one formal system of transliteration.

GLOSSARY

Chinese words and phrases in this glossary are sometimes followed in parentheses with alternative transliterations, either in the Pinyin, Wade-Giles, or Yale systems, or combinations of these systems. Japanese words have no alternative transliterations.

A

Aikido   A Japanese internal energy-based martial art. Aikido was created by Morihei Ueshiba in the 1930s from a unique blend of Daito Ryu aikijitsu (a form of jujitsu), sword techniques, and the teachings of a mystical Shinto-like religion that included mantra and sound work called the Kototama. In addition, aikido incorporates certain realizations encountered by Ueshiba during his journey towards his own spiritual enlightenment, and (as hypothesized by the author) ba gua chang and other chi gung methods learned by Ueshiba during his time in China.

Aikido styles   Originally aikido was only one school, where its founder Morihei Ueshiba taught and where members of his family continued to teach. This is called the *Hombu* style, which means headquarters. As time passed, Ueshiba's senior students created their own different styles. For example, the *Tomeki* style, a fusion of aikido and judo, emphasizes competitive practices. Other formal styles include the *Yoshinkai, Ki Society,* and *Iwama.*

Alchemy   The process of changing one substance into another. In the esoteric field, alchemy has two main branches—external and internal. *External alchemy* occurs in a laboratory in order to focus human spiritual energies to transform ordinary herbs and minerals into super medicines, to change base metals into gold, to create the Philosopher's Stone (which alchemists believed conferred physical immortality), and to gain direct knowledge of God. *Internal alchemy* (known in Chinese as *nei dan*) seeks through meditation and certain mind/body/spirit exercises to: (1) work with the consciousness of an individual in order to become aware of the cellular vibratory energetic level of the body to heal disease; (2) raise, bring out, and transform normally hidden capacities of the body/mind; and (3) elevate ordinary consciousness to higher and more refined levels of superconsciousness until the mind expands to encompass the whole of the universe. All this is done inside an individual's mind/body/spirit without the use of any external laboratory equipment.

An   In internal martial arts, any downward-moving energy or power.

Application   The practical use or range of uses of a particular technique in the martial arts, Chinese medicine, or meditation.

Aura   The energetic or bioelectric field that surrounds the living human body. *See also* Etheric body.

B

Ba gua or **ba gua chang** (ba gua zhang, pakua chang, ba gua jang)   Eight trigram palm ba gua is one of China's three main internal martial arts. It is a Taoist practice based on the *I Ching,* which is simultaneously a longevity practice, a martial art, a healing modality, and a spiritual/meditation practice.

Ba gua men   A ba gua chang school that has the complete martial tradition of ba gua chang intact, usually from a lineage source.

Ba ji chuan (pa chi ch'uan)   An external/internal martial art of North China.

Ba Mu Chang   *See* Eight Mother Palms.

Ba shr   One of the forms of hsing-i, based on the Five Elements.

Bai bu (pai pu) Toe out. The toe-out step of ba gua chang Circle-Walking, which allows a practitioner to step outside the circle.

Bai shr (bai shi) The formal initiation ceremony that confers discipleship upon an individual in Chinese culture. Also known as a kowtow.

Bando A martial art from Burma.

Basic Power Training *See* Ji Ben Gung.

Beng chuan (beng quan) Crushing Fist. One of the five basic techniques of hsing-i chuan.

Bien hua (pien hua, bian hua) To change; changes. The nature of change itself. Basic to Taoism and the *I Ching* is that everything in the phenomenal universe is in the process of changing, except the Tao, which remains changeless. What occurs during the shift, how that change transpires, and the final result of the change are all aspects of bien hua. The term also applies to the shift experienced during Taoist alchemy between one level of energy or consciousness and another level, either higher or lower. Refers also to the way you change from one fighting technique to another technique in internal martial arts or from one healing intervention to another in chi gung tui na.

Broadsword or knife (dao or tao) Both English terms are used interchangeably for the primary curved blade weapon used in Chinese martial arts for fighting multiple opponents. This sword is relatively narrow at the bottom, widens in the top third of the blade, and again narrows down to a sharp point at the top. Either one or both sides of the blade may be sharpened.

Bu diu bu ding A technical term in tai chi chuan for combat at touch, where the practitioner neither wants to push against, nor let go of, the point of contact between himself and his opponent.

Buddhism One of the world's major religions. Buddhism is based on the meditation teachings of Gautama the Buddha who lived and taught in India in the sixth century B. C. Buddhism has mostly vanished from India since the Muslim invasions occurring from the thirteenth to the sixteenth century, and is most prevalent in the cultures of Oriental Asia—China, Japan, Korea, Southeast Asia, and Tibet. The four main branches of Buddhism mentioned in this book are , Tibetan, Tien Tai (Tian Tai), Vipassana, and Zen/Chan.

Budo Japanese martial arts whose goal is to simultaneously cultivate martial technique, character, and spirituality.

Bujitsu Japanese martial arts whose sole goal is the development of efficient fighting and killing techniques.

Bunkai The fighting applications of a Japanese martial art move.

C

Central channel (zhong mai, chung mai, jung mai) The main energy channel located in the exact center of the human body between the perineum and the crown of the head and extending through the bone marrow of the arms and legs.

Chan sz jin (chan si jin) The silk-coiling technique of Chen style tai chi chuan, wherein the soft tissues of the body twist and turn dramatically.

Chang chuan (chang quan) Long fist. The basic method of Northern Shaolin external martial arts that forms the core of the official, state-sponsored Wushu martial arts program in Mainland China.

Chen Pan Ling style tai chi A specific combination form of tai chi chuan.

Chen village tai chi The original form of tai chi chuan.

Cheng Ting Hua ba gua The most popular style of ba gua; uses the Dragon Palm.

Chi (qi, ch'i; ki in Japanese) Energy, subtle life force, internal energy, internal power. Manifested energy that empowers something to work and function. This concept underlies Chinese, Japanese, and Korean culture, in which the world is perceived not purely in terms of physical matter but also in terms of invisible energy.

Chi chu dzuo (qi chu zuo, ch'i ch'u tso) The method of moving a felt bodily sensation of chi as a live force from the lower tantien into whichever energy channels the practitioner consciously directs it.

Chi gung (qi gong, chi kung) Energy work/power. The ancient Chinese art and science of developing and cultivating chi by one's own effort. Chi gung techniques may be done standing, moving, sitting, lying down, and during sex. These exercises balance, regulate, and strengthen energy channels, centers, and points of the body.

Chi gung tui na (qi gong tui na, ch'i kung twei na) Therapeutic bodywork with chi. A specialty of Chinese medicine, where the healer directly emits and rebalances the chi in the patient's body to bring about a therapeutic result. Its diagnostic techniques are based on reading the energy of the external aura, as well as the subtle energy of the internal tantiens of the body.

Chi sau The two-person touch sparring practice of Wing Chun, where both partners attempt to strike, block, and counter each other.

Chin na (ch'in na, qin na) Seizing the joints. The branch of Chinese martial arts concerned with using joint-locks to immobilize and capture someone, as well as to dislocate or break arms, leg joints, and spinal vertebrae. Also used to pull, rip, or tear skin by grabbing.

Chinese calligraphy A method of writing Chinese characters or symbolic concepts with pictures using a brush and ink. Calligraphy is considered by the Chinese to be a high form of fine art and a form of intellectual chi gung, one of its distinguishing characteristics being that chi, or energy, is projected onto the written surface.

Chinese medicine (Traditional Chinese medicine, TCM) The 3000-year-old traditional medical system of China. Its basic branches are acupuncture, bone-setting, chi gung, chi gung tui na, herbalism, and moxibustion. Its therapeutic interventions are not based so much on regulating the physical matter of the body but rather on regulating the subtle energy (chi), which tells the matter how to behave.

Chinese wrestling (shuai/shwei jiao, shuai chiao) China's traditional martial art of throws. It includes grappling (standing only, no matwork), joint-locks, and low kicks. Also *shuai fa* is a generic term in Chinese used for the throwing component of any martial art.

Ching gung (qing gong, ch'ing kung) Lightness skill. The special technique in Chinese martial arts (which seems to have died out in the present generation) of making the body incredibly light by changing its chi, giving one the ability to jump up 10 to 20 feet or leap down from three or more stories

unharmed. Ching gung is a favorite technique of cat burglars and bodyguards in Chinese novels and martial arts films.

Choi li fut (choy lay fut, choy lee fut) A Southern Shaolin fighting style from Canton province.

Circle-Walking The primary training method of the internal martial art of ba gua.

Combination Form tai chi A form wherein one or several styles of tai chi and/or hsing-i, ba gua, or Shaolin are mixed together within a single form.

Cotton boxing An external/internal martial art of North China.

D

Da Cheng Chuan Another name for I Chuan.

Da lu A style of moving Push Hands.

Dai An energetic technique in ba gua chang for leading a person's energy. One's energy and that of the opponent blend into one nonseparate stream. Then one can gain control of the opponent's power and direct it to one's advantage.

Daito Ryu The style of Japanese jujitsu from which aikido originated.

Di pan gung fu (di pan gong fu) The skill of the lower body. The chi cultivation skill wherein the chi from the lower tantien to the feet fully and completely opens. In martial arts and chi gung, this is considered the highest level of skill, for if the lower-body chi opens fully, the chi automatically reaches the upper body. This is summed up in the classical chi cultivation phrase, "The deeper the root, the higher the tree and the more abundant its branches."

Dian xue (dien hsueh) Mandarin for dim mak.

Die da The traditional Chinese medical practice for dealing with the immediate bruises, swellings, and broken bones of physical accidents and trauma.

Dim mak (Cantonese) The art of hitting acupuncture points to cause harm or death.

Dissolving process A nei gung technique for releasing bound energy both from within the human body and the etheric body.

Dojo Japanese term for a martial arts training hall.

Dou jin (dou jing)   The internal martial art technique of vibrating or shaking the body suddenly and with great force. Dou jin is used to issue power at a short distance, deliver powerful strikes when one is smothered with little or no distance to hit or do fa jin, or to change direction mid-motion and hit opponents who bob and weave like Western boxers.

Double Palm Change   A movement that is the basis of all the yin, soft, or amorphous techniques of ba gua chang.

E

Earth element   In Chinese cosmology, one of the basic energies or elements from which all manifested phenomena are created.

Eight Drunken Immortals   An external/internal martial art in which practitioners mimic the lurching, falling, rolling movements of a drunk.

Eight energetic bodies   In Taoist philosophy, eight clear vibratory frequencies of energy that comprise a human being. Each is called a "body." These are identified as the physical body, etheric/chi body, emotional body, mental body, psychic energy body, causal body, body of individuality and body of the Tao.

Eight extraordinary or special meridians   The eight meridians that have special uses in acupuncture above and beyond the normal vertical and horizontal meridians.

Eight Mother Palms (ba mu chang, ba mu zhang, pa mu chang, ba mu jang)   The eight basic palm changes or movement patterns of ba gua chang. Each of the energies of the eight trigrams of the *I Ching* is embodied in one of the eight mother palms.

Emptiness   A profound state of spiritual, mental, and psychic equilibrium that is a major goal of all Asian meditation practices and that lies at the heart of the higher levels of achievement in the internal martial arts.

Empty/full (xu/shi, hsu/shi, syu/shr)   A fundamental concept that exists throughout chi gung, Chinese medicine, and internal martial arts. Empty refers to a lack of, a deficiency of, or less of something. Its opposite, full, refers to an abundance of, an excess of, or simply more of something. Commonly used in reference to the chi of a body part or internal organ being full or empty.

Energy channels of the body   All the subtle energetic channels of the body through which chi travels.

Etheric body (chi body)   The bioelectric field that extends anywhere from a few inches to a few hundred feet from a person's body. Commonly called the aura in the West.

External/internal martial arts (nei wai quan/chuan)   Those martial arts that use both a clearly developed internal chi gung program and external muscular practices based on contracting the muscles through physical tension.

External martial arts (wai jia quan, wai chia ch'uan)   Martial arts that focus on physicality, muscular strength, reflexes, tension, mental discipline, and body conditioning (push-ups, sit-ups, weight-lifting, and running), and not on developing and cultivating the chi.

F

Fa chi (fa qi)   To discharge, emit, or issue chi. The action wherein chi is projected from one individual's body or mind to another person or object, for any reason. Called *wai chi* or external chi when used medically for chi gung therapy. Called *fa gung* when used for transmissions in meditation.

Fa jin (fa jing, fa chin)   To issue or discharge power. The internal martial arts technique of issuing power so it passes through an opponent (without physical harm), moving him in space just as a gust of wind blows dust away. Fa jin can also be used to focus power inside an opponent to break bones or rupture organs.

Feng shui   The mathematical occult science of Chinese geomancy where one locates the energy lines, relationships, and points of a physical site on the earth. The site could be a piece of land, a building, or arrangements of the objects within a room. The chi of the site is then analyzed to determine its positive or negative effects on manifesting wealth, love relationships, family harmony, spirituality or on whether certain types of events will be successful or not. Techniques can then be employed to mitigate bad fortune or enhance good fortune.

Fighting application   The practical use or range of uses for combat of a specific technique of a martial art.

Fire element   In Chinese cosmology, one of the

GLOSSARY **335**

basic energies or elements from which all manifested phenomena are created.

Fire method   A meditation or energetic technique that emphasizes pushing your limits and using full effort to 100 percent of your capacities.

Five Ancestors   A Fukien (Fujian) province, Southern Shaolin style that contains within it the core material of most Southern short-hand styles.

Frame   The physical shape and energetic qualities that an internal martial arts posture assumes, ranging from small and condensed (small frame) to large and expansive (large frame).

Fut gar   An external style of Southern Shaolin from Canton province.

G

Gang rou hsiang chi (gang rou xiang ji)   The ability of a tai chi practitioner to fuse hard and soft power together and to switch instantaneously between them.

Goju karate   A karate style that has strong Fukien province Southern Shaolin roots. It has both Okinawan and Japanese branches.

Gung fu (gong fu, kung fu)   (1) A level of skill usually gained through long continuous effort in anything. (2) A generic term for all the Chinese martial arts. (3) Refers also to the Chinese external and external/internal arts as opposed to only the internal martial arts ("Do you do internal martial arts—tai chi, ba gua, hsing-i—or gung fu?").

H

Hao style tai chi   The least widespread style of tai chi; based on small external and internal movements.

Hard martial arts   Those martial methods whose techniques rely on superior force and strength to defeat inferior strength. Practices of the hard martial arts are aimed at making the body as hard as steel, especially the arms and legs. Hard approaches may be used in both internal (hsing-i, for example) and exter-nal schools, but prevail mostly in the external martial arts.

Hebei hsing-i   A branch of hsing-i where hsing-i and ba gua are commingled and not distinct.

Heng chuan (heng quan)   Crossing Fist. One of the five basic techniques of hsing-i chuan.

Hexagram   One of the sixty-four energetic changes of the *I Ching*.

Hinduism   A major religion of India that reaches as far back as recorded time. Its most important texts are the Vedas, Upanishads, and the Bhagavad Gita. Hinduism gave birth to Yoga, Tantra, and Buddhism.

Hit medicine (die da, tie da, di da)   A branch of Chinese medicine that deals with the aftermath of traumatic injuries, such as broken bones, swelling, soft tissue damage, spinal misalignments, joint dislocations, and internal organ damage.

Hombu style   *See* Aikido.

Hou tien   *See* Post-birth.

Hsien tien   *See* Pre-birth.

Hsin (xin, shin)   Heart/mind. The ultimate source of a person's being according to classical Taoist and Buddhist thought. The hsin is both subtle and non-physical, and is located near the physical heart.

Hsin-i   Heart/mind boxing. Another term for hsing-i chuan.

Hsing (xing, shing)   The form or shape that any manifestation takes, be it a concrete object, a martial art movement, a subtle energy or feeling, or a mental construction of the mind.

Hsing-i or **Hsing-i Chuan** (xing yi quan, shing yi chuan)   Mind-form boxing. A hard internal martial art created by the Chinese general Yue Fei in the thirteenth century. Hsing-i emphasizes all aspects of the mind to create its forms and fighting movements.

Hsing-i men   A hsing-i chuan school that has the complete martial tradition of hsing-i intact, usually from a lineage source.

Hung gar   An external style of Southern Shaolin from Canton province.

Hyung (*Hyung* is Korean; in Chinese: *tao lu*; in Japanese: *kata*)   A form. A set of prearranged choreographed martial movements done either alone or with a partner or partners.

I

I (yi)   Will, intent, intention, mind, and projecting mind. In the chi world of China, "I" (pronounced yee) denotes the specific aspect of mind that projects. If a person sees something and wants to acquire or move toward the object of their intentions (be it concrete or mental), that person mobilizes the "I," and after an infinitesimal gap moves into action.

I Ching (yi jing)   Book of Changes. This 5000-year-old book is considered to be the classic Taoist text about the nature of change and how change occurs. The *I Ching* encompasses eight trigrams that embody the eight primal chi energies of which the universe is composed, according to Taoist thought. The eight expand to sixty-four by detailing how each of the individual trigrams impacts, mitigates, and expands the others when they are mixed. Ba gua chang is a mind/body/spirit practice that seeks to have an individual experience within his or her own being what the *I Ching* communicates intellectually.

I Chuan   Also known as Da Cheng Chuan. A style of hsing-i that is based upon eight standing postures rather than on the classical movements of hsing-i. I Chuan was developed by combining classical hsing-i with ba gua footwork, Western boxing, and Buddhist chi gung.

I chu dzuo (yi chu zuo, i ch'u tso)   A basic chi cultivation method where one uses the "I" to create a mental picture (visualization), which then indirectly moves chi through the human body according to the classic Chinese principle: The "I" leads or moves the chi.

Iaido   Japanese martial art of the sword; practiced with actual samurai swords.

Inner-dissolving process   A basic Taoist chi (nei gung) practice for releasing energy blocked anywhere within a person; used primarily to heal and strengthen an individual's emotional, mental, and psychic aspects.

Internal arts (nei jia, nei chia)   Those energy arts in China that are concerned with cultivating meditation, the internal chi, and the inner aspects of a person's being rather than only his or her quantifiable external manifestations in the physical world.

Internal martial arts (nei jia quan, nei chia ch'uan)   Those fighting systems that base their power on cultivating chi, the mind, total relaxation, longevity, and meditation rather than the purely physical means of the external martial arts. Although there are internal aspects to some of the external Shaolin martial arts, in China the term "internal martial arts" usually refers to the three Taoist martial arts of tai chi chuan, hsing-i chuan, and ba gua chang.

Iron shirt chi gung   Classically one of the many terms used for the ability to take heavy physical blows without pain or injury, as though you were wearing a protective shirt of iron.

J

Jan (rang)   Yielding. A technical term for one of the four stages of sticking energy in tai chi chuan.

Jeng chi (zheng qi, cheng ch'i)   Unifying chi. The one chi that unifies all the chi of the body, which the practice of all the Taoist internal arts, including ba gua chang, seeks to cultivate.

Ji   In the internal martial arts, any energy that presses or projects in a forward direction.

Ji ben gung (ji ben gong, chi ben kung)   The basic power training through which all the Chinese martial arts develop the type of power they specialize in.

Jin (jing)   Power.

Jing luo   Collateral meridians. The acupuncture meridians that horizontally wrap around the body and connect its vertical acupuncture lines.

Jou (zhou, chou)   Elbow stroke.

Judo   A Japanese external martial art based on wrestling, joint-locks, submission holds, and chokes. A descendant of the Chinese martial art of shuai jiao and the Japanese martial art of jujitsu. Judo has been an Olympic sport since the 1960s.

Jujitsu   The unarmed combat external martial art of the samurai during Japan's feudal period. Based primarily on throws, joint-locks, submission holds, and chokes, with punches, kicks, and strikes being secondary.

K

Kai-he   Opening and closing.

Kao   Shoulder stroke.

Karate   The Japanese external martial art based primarily on kicks, punches, hand strikes, foot sweeps, and a few throws. Karate is primarily an empty-handed martial art, with limited weapons training. The major styles of karate mentioned in this book are: (1) *Japanese karate,* primarily a hard style that concentrates equally on kicking and punching, its four major branches being Shotokan, Goju, Wado, and Shito; (2) *Okinawan karate,* an original form of karate based on training for raw physical power; (3) *Shorin Ryu karate,* a major Okinawan hard style based on short stances, low kicks, and power punches. It is one of the major antecedents of Shotokan karate; (4) *Uechi Ryu karate,* a major Okinawan hard style known for using muscular dynamic tension techniques in training; (5) *Korean karate* or *tae kwon do,* which emphasizes kicking (especially high kicks); historically originating from Northern Shaolin.

Kata (*kata* is Japanese; in Korean: *hyung*; in Chinese: *tao lu*) A form; a set of prearranged choreographed martial movements done either alone or with a partner or partners.

Katana A Japanese curved samurai sword.

Kendo The Japanese art of swordsmanship, where participants practice with lacquered armor and swords made of bamboo.

Kenkyusei A special research student in Japanese martial arts—especially in judo and karate—usually the student must be a third-degree black belt or above.

Ki *See* Chi.

Kickboxing An external martial-based full-contact competition sport done with boxing gloves, which combines boxing skills with karate kicks.

Kong jin (kong jing, kung jin) Empty force. The energy technique of hsing-i where practitioners are purported to knock people down without touching them, solely by projecting energy.

Kou bu (k'ou pu) The toe-in step of ba gua walking.

Kundalini A meditation method of India that uses energy work to unravel the mysteries of human consciousness and "enlightenment."

Kung fu (gung fu) family A Chinese surrogate family structure based on martial arts or meditation. The teacher symbolizes the father, the students become the children, the people who studied earlier become older brothers/sisters, new arrivals are younger brothers/sisters, and so forth.

Kuntao An Indonesian martial art that has extremely strong Chinese influences.

Kwa (kua) The area on each side of the body extending from the inguinal ligaments through the inside of the pelvis to the top (crest) of the hip bones.

L

Lan Merging. A technical term for one of the four stages of sticking energy in tai chi chuan.

Lan tsai hua The sparring techniques of tai chi chuan.

Lao gung (lao gong/kung) The energetic point in the center of the palm; the easiest point in the body from which to project chi externally.

Left channel One of the three primary energy lines in the body (on its left side), the other two being the right channel (its paired opposite), and the central channel. The paired opposites of the left and right channels of subtle energy are responsible for all the yin/yang dualistic functions of a human being, including the functioning of the body, emotions, psychic activity, and the manifestation of events in the outer world.

Lieh (lie) The splitting energy of tai chi chuan.

Lien huan One of the forms of hsing-i, based on the Five Elements.

Lineage In the martial arts, an unbroken line of teaching that runs from one master through successive generations of worthy students, who become masters in their own right and pass on the knowledge.

Lineage disciple A formal disciple who is chosen to learn and carry forth to future generations all the intact knowledge of any specific internal martial arts lineage.

Listening power (ting jin, t'ing chin) The ability to accurately feel and interpret the energy of another with one's hands and mind.

Liu he Six combinations of body parts (shoulders and hips, elbows and knees, hands and feet) that must be finely coordinated with each other and the nei san he to maximize physical power in the internal martial arts.

Liu he ba fa (liu ho pa fa) A completely internal martial art of China that combines movement elements of tai chi, hsing-i, ba gua, and Shaolin. Noted for its exceedingly long form, which can reach 700 movements in some of its branches. Relatively rare in the West.

Lohan Arhat Boxing; a Northern Shaolin style.

Lost Track Boxing (mizong quan, mi tsung ch'uan) An external Northern Shaolin fighting system.

Lotus kick   A sideways kick in tai chi chuan that begins from the front of the body and moves to the outside of the body at least as far as the shoulder or even farther. Uses the shin, instep, the outside edge of the foot or the heel as the kicking weapon.

Lu   Roll Back or the absorbing, yielding energy of the internal martial arts. This term is especially used in tai chi chuan

Lower tantien (dantian)   Located below the navel in the center of the body, this energetic center is primarily responsible for the health of the human body. It is the only energy center where all the energy channels that affect the physical body intersect. Also known in Japanese as the hara and in English as the elixir or cinnabar field.

M

Martial arts   Various fighting methodologies, both empty-handed and with weapons, that are concerned with formalized techniques of injuring or killing an attacker in the most efficient manner with the least harm to oneself.

Meditative stillness   A level of accomplishment in meditation where the practitioner's mind becomes exceptionally quiet and rests relaxed and centered within itself.

Metal element   In Chinese cosmology, one of the basic energies or elements from which all manifested phenomena are created.

Middle burner   Located in the torso between the solar plexus and the lower tantien. The energy that exists in this middle area of the body coordinates and harmonizes the chi of the upper and lower burners, which lie above and below the middle burner.

Middle tantien (dantian)   One of the three major energy centers in the body. Two separate places are considered to be the middle tantien. They are located near each other, each governing different energetic functions. The point located at the solar plexus just below the sternum is responsible for the physical functions of the middle internal organs of the body (liver, spleen, and kidneys), as well as the will to persevere. The point located near the heart on the central channel governs physical, emotional, mental, psychic, or causal relationships.

Mok gar (*mo jia* in Mandarin)   A Southern Shaolin fighting style from Canton province.

Monkey boxing (hou chuan)   A martial art system that mimics the movements of a monkey, which is known for viciousness in fighting, as well as for jumping, rolling, and extremely deceptive movements.

Moving meditation   Any method of meditation wherein a practitioner is able to actualize the goals of meditation (including stilling the mind) while the body is in continuous motion.

Mudra (seal)   A hand/finger/body position that automatically activates a person's energy channels in a specific fashion or creates a particular mind or psychic state in the practitioner.

Muslim hsing-i   A specific style of hsing-i.

N

Nan chuan   Southern Fist. All the southern schools of Chinese martial arts.

Natural Gate Boxing   A Northern Shaolin external/internal style known for its kicking techniques.

Nei ba chang   The eight palms of ba gua that are designed to put an individual in direct contact with the living energies upon which the eight trigrams of the *I Ching* are based.

Nei dan   Literally, "inner cosmic egg/pill." A term for the internal alchemy methods of Taoism. *See* Alchemy.

Nei gung (nei gong/kung)   Internal power. The original chi cultivation (chi gung) system in China invented by the Taoists. The Taoist nei gung system forms the basis for the internal martial arts of ba gua chang, tai chi chuan, and hsing-i chuan.

Nei jia   A term used to describe all the internal martial arts or Taoist chi practices as one family.

Nei jin (nei jing, nei chin)   Internal power. A specific form of chi that integrates all the various energies of the body into one unified chi that can manifest physical power.

Nei san he   The three internal components of the mind in Taoist theory: the "I" (intention), chi (energy), and shen (spirit or consciousness), all of which must be united in Chinese internal martial arts practices.

New Yang style   Tai chi methods taught by the third and later generations of the Yang family, which reduced the emphasis on fighting applications in favor of Push Hands.

Nien (nian)   Adhering. A technical term for one of the four stages of sticking energy in tai chi chuan.

Ninjitsu   A specialized Japanese martial art style historically used exclusively by professional assassins in Japan.

Northern Praying Mantis (tang lang quan, t'ang lang ch'uan)   An animal-form Shaolin method that specializes in mimicking the actions of the praying mantis insect. Mantis has both Northern and Southern branches. Northern Praying Mantis is known for its stamping footwork, finger strikes, complex arm motions, and extremely aggressive attack-oriented fighting philosophy.

Northern Shaolin (bei Shaolin, pei Shaolin)   A Northern branch of the Shaolin external martial arts systems known for its long and extended body movements, high kicks, and long-distance fighting. Also, a specific martial art within the entire family of Northern Shaolin.

O

Okinawan karate   *See* Karate.

Old Yang style   Tai chi methods taught by the first and second generations of the Yang family, which clearly emphasized fighting applications.

Open/close (kai/he)   The Chinese yin/yang paired opposites concept of growing/shrinking, expanding/contracting, and lengthening/shortening, etc. This universal pulsing occurs at the subatomic level, cellular level, and cosmological level.

Outer-dissolving process   A basic Taoist chi (nei gung) practice for releasing blocked internal energy within the body and projecting it externally. Used primarily to heal and strengthen the energies related to the physical body.

P

Pai da (pai ta)   A Shaolin method of developing the ability to take blows with impunity. The method involves hitting the body with progressively harder objects, such as cloth sacks full of beans, stones, marbles, iron pellets or filings, and rods made of bamboo, wood, or iron.

Pao chuan (pao quan)   Pounding Fist. One of the five basic techniques of hsing-i chuan.

Penchat/Silat   Indonesian martial arts that have a wide variety of specific styles, mostly external and external/internal.

Peng (p'eng)   Ward Off or rising energy of internal martial arts.

Peng jin (peng jing, peng chin)   Expansive energy. The rising, pushing outwards internal power that forms the basis of the yang chi aspect of internal martial arts.

Pi chuan (pi quan)   Chopping or Splitting Fist. One of the five basic techniques of hsing-i chuan.

Posture   The last static position that ends a martial art technique or chi gung movement. Also, a whole movement for which a specific martial art or chi gung technique is named.

Post-birth (hou tien)   That which happens to a person after leaving the womb. Talents, skills, or accomplishments not inherent but acquired after birth.

Post-birth ba gua   The linear as opposed to Circle-Walking practice of ba gua chang.

Post-birth chi   The chi a human gets by eating, drinking, sleeping, breathing, and exercising.

Pre-birth (hsien tien)   Whatever has happened to a human between conception and the time of birth.

Pre-birth ba gua   The Circle-Walking practice of ba gua whose purpose is to develop pre-birth chi in the same manner as it was done in Taoist monasteries.

Pre-birth chi   The energy an individual absorbs from its mother and the cosmos while in the womb. The quantity and quality of this energy basically determines the genetic strength or weakness an individual has for life. Normally, the amount of this chi is fixed for life at birth. However, through certain pre-birth chi cultivation practices, an adult is again able to store this chi, thus potentially overcoming genetic limitations.

Push Hands (tui shou)   The continuous two-person hand-touching practice of the internal martial art of tai chi chuan, which forms the bridge between the form movements of tai chi and its self-defense techniques.

Q

Qi *see* Chi.

R

Randori Japanese term for the free sparring used in judo, jujitsu, and aikido.

Reversal A martial technique wherein the practitioner goes in one direction and then does a complete 180-degree turn to the opposite direction in order to complete a fighting application. Used equally in strikes, throws, and joint-locks.

Right channel One of the three primary energy lines of the body. *See* Left channel.

Rooting The technique of sinking body energy and rooting it into the earth. It is difficult to physically move a martial artist who has mastered rooting. In the internal martial arts, rooting gives a practitioner tremendous power.

Rou Shou Soft Hands; also known as San Shou or Free Hands in Taiwan. A two-person fighting preparation technique practiced in ba gua (and some hsing-i schools) in which the arms of the partners are in continuous spiraling contact. Rou Shou can be likened to a combination of tai chi Push Hands, judo, and Wing Chun sticky hands.

S

Samadhi A meditative experience that is indicative of a specific stage of "enlightenment."

Samurai The warrior knights of ancient Japan who became the classic role models of the Japanese martial arts. Their most distinguishing characteristics were the top-knot hair style, and the wearing of two swords, which they were expert at using.

Savate A French martial art that combines kicking and Western boxing.

San chin A martial art stance where one foot is in front of and the other behind the torso, with both feet curved inward to some degree and facing each other. A commonly used stance to develop power breathing in several styles of karate and Southern Shaolin schools.

San Ti The primary internal power development technique of hsing-i. San Ti is done standing still and holding a specific static arm posture.

Seventy-two leg techniques A series of ba gua martial art techniques concerned with kicks, leg-locks, and footwork procedures.

Sha chi (sha qi) Chi that kills upon contact.

Shang pan gung fu Martial art techniques that derive their skill and development from the power of the upper body rather than from the legs.

Shao Twei (shao tui) A Northern Praying Mantis leg cut, ankle sweep, or kick aimed at the calf or Achilles tendon.

Shansi hsing-i Original form of hsing-i that came from the northwestern Chinese province of Shansi.

Shaolin gung fu (*sil lum* in Cantonese) The Shaolin monastery is the legendary (but not the historic) birthplace of the martial arts in China. Shaolin is synonymous with the external martial arts. The higher levels of Shaolin have chi gung practices but as a general rule, the development of physical strength and aggression is emphasized over cultivation of chi.

Shiatsu A Japanese massage method based on the principles of traditional Chinese medicine. Shiatsu uses the fingers to press acupuncture points for therapeutic effect.

Shorin Ryu *See* Karate.

Shotokan *See* Karate.

Shuai jiao (shwei jiao, shuai chiao) Chinese wrestling.

Shun shr jang (shun shi zhang, shun shi chang) Smooth palm changes. A palm change in ba gua that involves a mixing of yin and yang energies as opposed to being purely yang or yin. The generic phrase for any palm change in ba gua besides the Single and Double Palm Changes.

Silat *See* Penchat.

Single Palm Change (dan huan zhang, tan huan chang) The most fundamental technique in ba gua. The Single Palm Change is a microcosm of the whole system based on the first (heaven) trigram of the *I Ching*.

Sixty-four hexagrams Sixty-four basic energetic changes of the *I Ching*.

Snake   A Southern Shaolin style.

Soft martial arts   Those fighting arts whose defensive techniques are based upon not opposing force with force but rather upon yielding and redirecting an opponent's force. Soft martial art strikes have no outward appearance of force but are devastatingly powerful, being based on chi and subtle body mechanics. Soft martial arts can be external or internal. Even the most ardent "hard" martial art system will have some soft techniques.

Southern Praying Mantis   The external/internal Southern branch of Praying Mantis that uses arm-touching practices extensively and has more internal chi work than the Northern branch.

Southern Shaolin (nan Shaolin, nan quan/chuan)   A style of fighting known for movements that can be done in a small space, the classical example being on a boat. Southern Shaolin styles are characterized by short, close-in, tight arm movements, low kicks, and short, tight footwork.

Staff (or pole)   A primary non-cutting weapon of Chinese martial arts that is usually made of wood, but can be made of metal. Its length varies from four to nine feet, with a length of five to six feet being the most commonly used.

Standing chi gung (jan chuang, zhan zhuang)   Chi gung that is done standing still, either with the practioner's arms resting at the sides of the body or else held in the air in a static arm posture. Standing chi gung is one of the most basic techniques for developing internal power.

Static arm postures   The practice in which an individual holds his or her arms motionless in space, whether or not the feet are moving. The practice is done in order to bring the chi from the belly and spine to the fingertips and stabilize the internal alignments of the upper body.

Sticking power (nien, nian)   The martial skill of sticking to either your opponent's skin or weapon with your own hands, arms, body, or weapon in order to control a combat situation defensively or offensively.

Straight double-edged sword   The basic sword used for single one-on-one combat in the Chinese martial arts. This sword cuts equally with both edges and the sharp pointed tip can pierce flesh.

Straight step   One of the three basic steps in ba gua where the practitioner steps forward.

Suei   Magnetizing. A technical term for one of the four stages of sticking energy in tai chi chuan.

Sun style tai chi   A combination style of tai chi created by Sun Lu Tang that amalgamates the Hao style with hsing-i and ba gua.

Swari waza   The ground-fighting technique of aikido where the practitioner is upright with one or both knees touching the ground, either still or moving across the mat.

Synovial fluid   A bodily fluid that is present in the space between the joints of the body.

T

Tae kwon do   A Korean external martial art that emphasizes kicking techniques; also known as Korean karate.

Tai chi chuan (tai ji quan, taijiquan, tai chi ch'uan)   Supreme ultimate martial arts fist. One of the three internal martial arts of China, most known for its emphasis on softness, slow-motion movement, and its sophisticated chi gung methodology based on whole-body physical coordination. Done by the majority of its practitioners primarily for health, not combat. As a martial art, tai chi emphasizes softness, yielding techniques and counterattack strategies, and a blending of soft and hard internal power.

Tai Chi Classics   A nineteenth-century treatise on the foundational principles of tai chi chuan, said to be written by Wang Tsung Yueh. Contains short, cryptic phrases having multilayered meanings.

Tai chi men   A tai chi chuan school that has the complete martial tradition of tai chi chuan intact, usually from a lineage source.

Tang ni bu (t'ang ni pu)   Mud-walking. The basic chi and physical mechanics principles upon which the circle-walking steps of ba gua are based.

Tantien (tant'ien, dantian)   The three primary centers in the human body where chi collects, disperses, and recirculates. They govern the energetic anatomy of a person. The practices of the three tantiens are at the operational root of all Chinese chi practices.

Tao/Taoism (dao)   The Way. The practical mystical religion of China that forms the original underpinnings of classical Chinese culture, including the yin-yang play of opposites, Chinese medicine, and the art of strategy and war.

Tao jia (dao jia, tao chia)   The mystical inner esoteric practices of Taoism. Includes the beginning stage of Taoist meditation that involves methods for completely stilling the mind and an advanced stage, which involves internal alchemy, or transformation of inner energies for realizing and becoming one with the Tao, the nature of the universe itself.

Tao jiao (dao jiao, tao chiao)   The outer aspects of Taoism, including mediums, idol worship, and fortune telling.

Taoist master   An accomplished or "enlightened" adept of Taoist meditation, who has reached and completed the highest practices in Taoism. These individuls are exceeedingly rare.

Thai boxing (muay thai)   The traditional external martial art of Thailand. Originally practiced with gloves studded with ground glass, Thai boxing is now done with regular boxing gloves in a boxing ring. Known for its kicks, knee butts, and elbow strikes, this style of boxing is the original input for the full contact karate/kickboxing circuit that has become a major venue in the world of commercial martial arts tournaments.

Three burners (san jiao)   A Chinese medicine tenet concerning how the chi of the body is separated into three parts that need to be integrated to achieve optimum health and balanced chi circulation. The *upper burner* refers to the part of the body that includes the chest, arms, upper spine, neck, and head. The *middle burner* begins at the the solar plexus and ends at the lower tantien. It includes the middle spine, liver, kidneys, and spleen. The *lower burner* includes the lower belly, lower spine, sexual organs, hips, and legs.

Ti tang earth boxing (di tang)   Various systems of Chinese martial arts concerned with ground (earth) fighting.

Ting jin (t'ing chin, ting jing)   The ability to listen to and interpret the energy of another person in the internal martial arts.

Toe-out/toe-in (bai bu/kou bu)   Basic step performed in ba gua Circle-Walking.

Tomeki style   *See* Aikido.

Traditional Chinese martial arts   The martial arts that traditionally existed in China before the Communist revolution. Traditional martial arts are based on pragmatic fighting skills with the religious and philosophical underpinnings of Confucian, Buddhist, and Taoist precepts.

Tsa jr chuei   One of the forms of hsing-i based on the Twelve Animal forms.

Tsai (cai)   Pull Down energy in tai chi chuan.

Tsuan chuan (zuan quan, juan chuan)   Drilling Fist. One of the five basic techniques of hsing-i chuan.

Tui na (twei na)   The therapeutic bodywork system of China, which is considered to be of a higher level than ordinary Chinese massage (known as *ammo*). Included within its therapeutic interventions are acupressure, bone setting, and joint and vertebral manipulations, along with deep tissue myofascial, craniosacral, tendon and ligament work, and internal organ/gland realignment and rebalancing. When combined therapeutically with chi gung, it is called *chi gung tui na*.

Tui Shou   *See* Push Hands.

Tun tu   The Shaolin martial art term for sucking in and spitting out, which is not the same as, but which on the gross level bears similarities to, the internal arts practice of open/close.

U

Universal Consciousness   The underlying something, which cannot be defined, of which the whole universe is composed. Called the Tao in ancient China.

Upper tantien (dantian)   Located in the brain, this tantien controls human perceptual mechanisms and psychic functions.

W

Wai ba jang (wai ba zhang, wai pa chang)   Outer eight palms. Basic pre-birth ba gua chang practice of secondary circle-walking techniques that function as fighting applications only.

Wai jia (wai chia)   External practices. Practices that do not appreciably cultivate the inner part of a person's being, but are primarily concerned with accomplishing goals in the external world.

Water element   In Chinese cosmology, one of the basic energies or elements from which all manifested phenomena are created.

Water method   A meditation or energetic technique that emphasizes using full effort without strain or force.

Wei chi   The layer of energy between a person's skin and muscle that protects against disease entering the body from the external environment.

White Crane   An external/internal Chinese martial art that mimics the actions of the bird called the white crane. There are three branches to this style: Cantonese, Fukien, and Northern, each having different specialities.

White Eyebrow (*pak mei* in Cantonese, *bai mei* in Mandarin)   An external/internal, short-hand Southern Shaolin fighting style from Canton province.

Wing Chun   A southern Chinese external martial art based primarily on hand strikes. Its primary fighting development methodology is called "sticky hands" or *chi sau*, a practice in which both opponents keep arm/hand contact as they try to hit and defend against each other's attacks.

Wood element   In Chinese cosmology, one of the basic energies or elements from which all manifested phenomena are created.

Wu mei   An external/internal Southern Shaolin martial art.

Wu style tai chi   A style of tai chi chuan especially known for its healing and meditation components. A small-frame fighting style that developed from the Yang style. Wu style is the second most popular form of tai chi in China and is becoming more available in the West.

Wu wei   Doing without doing. The fundamental Taoist concept of having action arise from an empty mind without preconception or agenda, action that operates by simply following the natural course of universal energy as it manifests itself without strain or ego involvement.

Wushu   A generic term that refers to martial arts used at various times in Chinese history. Sometimes called "modern martial arts." Contemporary Wushu is now based on sport or stage performance value rather than fighting. It is philosophically different from traditional martial arts.

Y

Yang style tai chi   The most popular form of tai chi today.

Yin and yang meridans   The twelve major vertical subtle energy channels of the body.

Yin fu style of ba gua   Second most popular form of ba gua today; uses the Willow Leaf Palm.

Yin yang   The classic Taoist concept that the universe is composed of opposites (sun/moon, active/passive, work/rest, happiness/sadness, etc.) that are not antagonistic, but complementary and necessary to ful-fill each other. It is through the yin-yang play of opposites that all manifestation, obvious or subtle, occurs.

Yung fa (yong fa)   The fighting applications of a Chinese martial art move.

Z

Zen (*Zen* is Japanese; in Chinese: *Chan*)   A spiritual discipline created by a fusion of Taoist and Buddhist methods. Zen practices are sometimes adapted to the martial arts. *See* Buddhism.

THE B. K. FRANTZIS ENERGY ARTS® PROGRAM

Trainings Available

Mr. Frantzis and/or his trained instructors teach various aspects of Taoist Energy Arts in seminars, retreats, and classes at locations in North America and Europe. For information concerning instruction schedules, books, videos, and audiotapes, contact:

> B. K. Frantzis Energy Arts®
> P. O. Box 99
> Fairfax, CA 94978-0099
> USA

Phone: (415) 454-5243   Fax: (415) 454-0907
Web site: www.4taichi.com

THE SIX-PART CHI GUNG PROGRAM

This program teaches the internal energy work of the 16 Taoist nei gung components (see p. 62). Together, these courses provide a complete chi gung regimen, combining the energy work of Oriental medicine, Taoist meditation, and physical movement. The courses are:

Dragon and Tiger Chi Gung   This 1500-year-old traditional chi gung practice is a seven-movement exercise, ideal for any age or fitness level. Easy to learn, it quickly allows you to recognize the chi in your body and project/absorb energy from your hands. These techniques have been applied since antiquity to heal by clearing the blockages in human energy auras.

Opening the Energy Gates of Your Body   Learn to focus your awareness to consciously coordinate and control your body's flow of chi. *Energy Gates* teaches basic Taoist breathing, how to do standing chi gung, dissolve energy blockages, and feel your energy gates and their functions. You are taught to energize your internal organs and adjust internal biomechanical alignments to promote healing and begin to control the movements of your individual spinal vertebrae.

The Marriage of Heaven and Earth   This simple, one-movement exercise is widely used in China to relieve back, neck, joint, and neuromuscular problems. It is effective for increasing elasticity of the joints, overall strength, and upper-body flexibility. The openings and closings of the muscles (to induce the movement of energy through your acupuncture meridians) and the joints taught here are important internal techniques of Taoist martial arts for controlling chi.

Spinal Chi Gung: Bend the Bow and Shoot the Arrow
Learn the deepest level of Taoist breathing in which the spinal vertebrae, joints, cavities, glands and muscles physically and energetically link by expanding or contracting together with each breath. Learn how to fully control the multidirectional movement of all your vertebrae, correct back problems, and amplify your strength.

Spiraling Energy Body   Here, you learn to direct the upward flow of energy in your body, project your chi along spiraling pathways, open the right, left, and central energy channels, neutralize and transform negative energy, and direct energy at will to any point in your body.

Gods Playing in the Clouds   The six movements of *Gods* encompass all the internal techniques of chi gung. This powerful Taoist rejuvenation method amplifies all the material in the earlier chi gung courses. You also learn to make your bones harder, cleanse your emotional body of negative energy, and open and stabilize your heart center and central energy channel.

MARTIAL ARTS AND OTHER PROGRAMS

Instruction in the internal martial arts of ba gua, tai chi, and hsing-i, as well as Taoist meditation, chi gung tui na courses, and instructor training programs are available at various times. Write, call, fax, or visit our website for more information.

Please note: Mr Frantzis does not generally undertake one-on-one healings for specific problems. His time is currently devoted to instructing groups, training teachers, writing, and public health education.

B. K. Frantzis Energy Arts®
Post Office Box 99
Fairfax, CA
94978-0099
USA

B. K. Frantzis Energy Arts®
Post Office Box 99
Fairfax, CA
94978-0099
USA

Please tell me
more about
**B. K. Frantzis
Energy Arts®.**

I'm interested in:

☐ Retreats
☐ Seminars
☐ Videos
☐ Books
☐ Audiotapes

☐ Martial Arts
☐ Health
☐ Healing
☐ Meditation
☐ Tai Chi
☐ Hsing-I
☐ Ba Gua
☐ Chi Gung
☐ Tui Na

Name

Street Address

City

State

Zip

Country

Phone
(day)   (evening)
Fax

Comments

Please tell me
more about
**B. K. Frantzis
Energy Arts®.**

I'm interested in:

☐ Retreats
☐ Seminars
☐ Videos
☐ Books
☐ Audiotapes

☐ Martial Arts
☐ Health
☐ Healing
☐ Meditation
☐ Tai Chi
☐ Hsing-I
☐ Ba Gua
☐ Chi Gung
☐ Tui Na

Name

Street Address

City

State

Zip

Country

Phone
(day)   (evening)
Fax

Comments